D1125300

THE CLARITY *OF* SCRIPTURE

HISTORY, THEOLOGY & CONTEMPORARY LITERARY STUDIES

JAMES CALLAHAN

InterVarsity Press
Downers Grove, Illinois

InterVarsity Press
P.O. Box 1400, Downers Grove, IL 60515-1426
World Wide Web: www.ivpress.com
E-mail: mail@ivpress.com

InterVarsity Press® is the book-publishing division of InterVarsity Christian Fellowship/USA®, a student movement active on campus at hundreds of universities, colleges and schools of nursing in the United States of America, and a member movement of the International Fellowship of Evangelical Students. For information about local and regional activities, write Public Relations Dept., InterVarsity Christian Fellowship/USA, 6400 Schroeder Rd., P.O. Box 7895, Madison, WI 53707-7895.

Cover photograph: Michael Goss

ISBN 0-8308-1584-8

Printed in the United States of America ∞

Library of Congress Cataloging-in-Publication Data

Callahan, James Patrick, 1960-
The clarity of Scripture : history, theology & contemporary literary studies / James Callahan.
p. cm.
Includes bibliographical references.
ISBN 0-8308-1584-8 (alk. paper)
1. Bible—Hermeneutics. I. Title.
BS476 .C35 2001
220.6'01—dc21

00-067346

---

23 22 21 20 19 18 17 16 15 14 13 12 11 10 9 8 7 6 5 4 3 2 1
20 19 18 17 16 15 14 13 12 11 10 09 08 07 06 05 04 03 02 01

Harold Sturdy Smith (1898-1987)
Helen Julie Smith (1905-)

CONTENTS

Introduction

You diligently study the Scriptures because you think that by them you possess eternal life. These are the Scriptures that testify about me.

JOHN 5:39

In the struggle of the church, it becomes increasingly clear that the confessed perspicuity is not a mere notation of a "quality" of Scripture in the manner in which we attribute certain qualities to other things, after which we can relax. This confession of the church will only be meaningful if it includes an insight into the power of the Spirit's way through the Word (divine and human) in its historical form. This occurs with such strong and prevailing force that it is not possible for man to relax. We are being challenged by ever-increasing responsibility in the face of new questions and tasks. . . . No confession concerning Scripture is more disturbing to the church than the confession of its perspicuity.

G. C. BERKOUWER, *HOLY SCRIPTURE*

SCRIPTURE CAN BE AND IS READ WITH PROFIT, WITH APPRECIATION AND WITH TRANSformative results. It is open and transparent to earnest readers; it is intelligible and comprehensible to attentive readers. Scripture itself is coherent and obvious. It is direct and unambiguous as written; what is written is sufficient. Scripture's concern or focal point is readily presented as the redemptive story of God. It displays a progressively more specific identification of that story, culminating in the gospel of Jesus Christ. All this is to say: Scripture is clear about what it is about.

Scripture's clarity is a straightforward, unambiguous and heartening conviction about how Christians read and regard the Bible. It is a routinely assumed, often asserted, occasionally defended but rarely explored belief for Christians.

There exists an almost casual assumption that when used Christianly, Scripture's clarity is precisely what characterizes our relationship with the Bible. That is, Scripture is available (and makes its message available) to those who humbly approach, read carefully and obediently respond to God's Word.

It should also be noted that Scripture's clarity is an equally incredible tenet for many others. How can anyone be naive enough to believe that the Bible is clear without significant qualification or severe limitation, especially in light of almost three centuries of critical historical study, five centuries of serious division among Christians over the message of Scripture, and two millennia of often curious and colorful embellishments in intricate allegory and innumerable commentaries? It seems obvious that belief in Scripture's clarity is severely compromised by the real history of Christian disagreements about what the Bible says.[1]

It is important to recognize that even the most positive defenders of Scripture's clarity do not ignore the complexities of the subject. The Westminster Confession (1647) offers this well-known and often-repeated assertion, with interesting qualifications:

> All things in Scripture are not alike plain in themselves, nor alike clear unto all; yet those things which are necessary to be known, believed, and observed, for salvation, are so clearly propounded and opened in some place of Scripture or other, that not only the learned, but the unlearned, in a due use of ordinary means, may attain unto a sufficient understanding of them.[2]

Phrases such as "not alike plain," "not alike clear," "due use of ordinary means" and "sufficient understanding" help temper what otherwise might appear to be a simplistic and unsuspecting affirmation of clarity from certain Christians (evangelical Protestants, that is). The Westminster Confession also helps focus our attention on what Scripture is about, its message—salvation—to be known, believed and observed. Scripture is filled with details of great variety. Some are admittedly simple and others consciously mysterious, yet not all are clear, even to the learned. And even though "ordinary means" are employed, this is no guarantee: "nevertheless we acknowledge the inward illumination of the Spirit of God to be necessary for the saving understanding of such things as are revealed in the Word."[3]

Statements of Scripture's clarity, like that offered by the Westminster Confes-

---

[1]James Callahan, "The Bible Says: Evangelical and Postliberal Biblicism," *Theology Today* 53, no. 4 (1997): 449-63.

[2]The Westminster Confession of Faith 1.7, in Philip Schaff, ed., *The Evangelical and Protestant Creeds*, vol. 3 of *The Creeds of Christendom: With a History and Critical Notes,* ed. David S. Schaff (Grand Rapids, Mich.: Baker, 1983), p. 604.

[3]Ibid.

sion, therefore lead to healthy and serious questions. In what way is Scripture clear? In its language, its translation, its every word, its expression of the authors' intent, its reference to historical matters, its narration of its story? And what do these matters have to do with Scripture's purpose? And further, what makes one text so easily understood and others so obscure? Isn't all writing intended to be clear, and all communication meant to be understood? And if so, what is special, if anything, about the Bible's clarity? And another important question follows: To whom is Scripture clear? To Christians only, to the critically educated, to church authorities like pastors or bishops, or to anyone at all? Interestingly, even the more explicit accounts of Scripture's clarity lack a suitable explanation of the complexities of its simple assertion.

An Overview

It is the contention of what follows, especially so in the first part from a historical-theological perspective, that the belief and practices associated with Scripture's clarity have been persistent elements in the history of Christianity's identity, although the actual assertion and demonstration of clarity have not always been as noticeable. It is very much a systemic axiom within Christian history, particularly when we attempt to account for how Christians read and regarded Scripture. How confidently and conspicuously Scripture was used in theological commentary, in preaching, in liturgy and in educating Christians amply demonstrates how important its accessibility and perspicuity were in historic Christianity. Simply put, Christians have believed that Scripture works—Scripture accomplishes its purpose when read as Scripture, as Christians should read Scripture. And that is what we have come to refer to as Scripture's clarity.

In the second part in particular, with a literary-theological focus, an account will be offered of how Scripture's clarity might be understood at the present time. This will take on a threefold focus: the expression *clarity of Scripture* refers to how Christians account for the union of Scripture that is read, an appropriate reading of Scripture and Scripture's readers. Scripture, when read in a Christian manner, can be said to be clear in itself but not by itself (it has never been isolated from its readings or readers, historically or theologically). The relationship of this threefold focus is usually explained by means of the two-dimensional notions such as letter and spirit, or the outer and inner clarity of Scripture. Explaining Scripture's character in terms of outer and inner dimensions summarized the routine manner in which Christians accounted for the differing but unitive ways Christians actually use Scripture. Inner clarity of Scripture, according to Luther, "is internal, whereby through the Holy Spirit or a special gift of God, anyone who is enlightened concerning himself and his own salvation, judges and discerns with the greatest certainty the dogmas and opinions of all men." The outer clarity of Scripture "belongs to the public ministry of the Word . . . and is chiefly the concern of leaders and preachers of the Word. We make use of it when we seek to strengthen those who are weak in faith and confute opponents."[4]

The threefold focus, explained by means of a two-dimensional explanation, is characteristically offered as a single assertion of Scripture's clarity. It is our common confession as Christians. As G. C. Berkouwer has said, it is "a confession of faith that praised the Word in its clarity and power."[5] Christians make use of the text in a way that both presumes and asserts the attitude toward how one reads and regards the sacred text; it summarizes the intrinsic union of theological commitments concerning the illumination of the Spirit, divine rather than simply conventional authority of the text, and the characterization of Scripture as realistically perspicuous (and many more and equally important topics).

The notion of clarity has served the Christian tradition well inasmuch as it represents the widespread working premise that the Bible aims (by God) to be understood after a certain fashion and is understandable (by Christian readers) when read as a Christian should read Scripture. Scripture's clarity helpfully addresses these basic assertions. And in this manner the subject of Scripture's clarity is a barometer of the continuing struggle with the interpretation of Scripture within Christianity.

The Way Forward

Some will ask whether the effort is worthwhile—whether historical- and literary-theological deliberations of Scripture's clarity will revive what has become a subject of disdain in certain circles. I hope that this volume will contribute to an ongoing retrieval of historical-theological interests within a climate of literary-theological deliberation known by the label *postcritical.* It will take some effort to explain and unpack the significance of postcritical approaches, but suffice it to say at this point that the cues for this investigation of Scripture's clarity are taken in part from the effort to retrieve dominant themes from the Christian interpretative tradition and in part from the burgeoning interest in the Bible as literature (thus this volume divides along the lines of historical-theological and literary-theological topics).

---

[4]Martin Luther, "On the Bondage of the Will," in *Luther and Erasmus: Free Will and Salvation,* ed. and trans. Gordon Rupp and Philip Watson (Philadelphia: Westminster Press, 1969), p. 159.

[5]G. C. Berkouwer, *Holy Scripture,* trans. Jack Rogers (Grand Rapids, Mich.: Eerdmans, 1975), p. 273.

One goal is to take advantage of this greater attention to the texture of Scripture as an opportunity to retrieve the interests of the Christian interpretative tradition; as George Lindbeck offered: "Modern literary approaches with their emphasis on textuality increase the possibility of a retrieval of the classic hermeneutics."[6] Appreciating the relationship of these historical and literary themes in a manner similar to a social scientist's approach to culture sets the stage for a renewed interest in Scripture's clarity in the Christian community. But this also presents a tempting opportunity to retell the story of perspicuity in a way that conforms to our sensibilities, justifying our interests in a subject that many believe to be an idea that has seen its best days.

While it will take the bulk of what follows to recommend Scripture's clarity, several provisions that orient what follows can be addressed in brief. Most important, it is not my goal to champion a retreat to the good ol' days when people did not question Scripture's authority, sufficiency and clarity. The struggle is as much with self-critical awareness wherein what is clearest from one perspective is indistinct from another, and I do not wish to retreat from this encounter. The assertion of Scripture's clarity does concern the character of Scripture itself but not without immediate attention to Scripture's readers and the readers' communities. As John Goldingay notes, "Behind the argument about the clarity of scripture is an argument about whom scripture belongs to and whether it is a means of control."[7]

Another Caution

It is not wise to rely on a strictly modern attempt to justify the confession of Scripture's clarity, a literary-critical model of Scripture without the influence of the Christian theological tradition. Reading the Bible as one would read any other book, for example, is simply another way of saying that the Bible should not be afforded any special privilege but should exert its influence as the equal of all texts. (Optimists believed that this would vindicate the uniqueness of Christian Scripture in the modern world. No longer artificially supported by church tradition or authority, it would be free to accomplish its true purposes. Antagonists were convinced that treating the Bible as one would any literature would display the artificiality of its authority and bring about an end to Scripture's despotism.) There is another objectifying effort, fondly adopted by some Christians in their struggle for certain and authoritative interpretation of the Bible, to fix meaning in the intent of

---

[6]George Lindbeck, "Scripture, Consensus, and Community," in *Biblical Interpretation in Crisis*, ed. Richard John Neuhaus (Grand Rapids, Mich.: Eerdmans, 1989), p. 96.

[7]John Goldingay, *Models for Scripture* (Grand Rapids, Mich.: Eerdmans, 1994), p. 345.

the authors of the biblical text. Authorship was and remains a significant topic in the interpretation of Scripture. However, there has been a dramatic shift from the general neglect or dismissal of this topic in early Christian circles, to the medieval contention that authorial intent was significant precisely because Scripture's author was God, to the rather routine presumption of historical and philosophical interest in a text as an expression of its human author's will in the author's historical setting, to the current literary discussion of the author's death (usually at the hands of the reader). These are not insignificant matters for our topic precisely because they raise the question of how it is that Scripture is clear and in what respects.

Within modern models the shift of authority is away from a privileged text, within a privileged community, understood by a privileged mode of interpretation, to the justification of Scripture's nature and message by matters formally external to the norming influence of Scripture, community and self-critical interpretation. It would be a great dereliction of Christian particularity to renounce claims to privilege, precisely when these contentious matters occupy our concern. Likewise, to fix matters of authority in extrinsic fields of understanding (such as authorial intent, history, writing or reading) misses the (almost) universal Christian confidence in Scripture read by Christians in a Christian manner. The assertion of Scripture's clarity both illustrates the substance of such debates and might offer Christians a way to survive these conflicts without losing Scripture in the battle.

The way of retrieval is historical precisely because discerning wisely our tradition of biblical *and* theological interpretative interests requires self-critical interest, not detachment. The main features of Scripture's clarity form a sometimes complicated network of themes: matters of Scripture's authority, history and literary quality (its realistic texture), origin, inspiration and message, and the subject of its meaning; as well as how Scripture is best considered—discerning meaning, sufficiency, the manner of reading we employ and how one form of attentiveness is preferred to another. It appears that the actual use made of Scripture (how it functions within the Christian community), Scripture's idiosyncratic nature (how Scripture itself is represented within the Christian community) and Scripture's relationship with the Christian reader (how to judge our understanding of Scripture) converge in the subject of Scripture's clarity. In one sense this consideration involves all facets of biblical interpretation and hermeneutics but only inasmuch as it deals with the particular, focused subject of Scripture's clarity.

A word of explanation regarding the dedication seems in order before beginning the first chapter. Harold and Helen Smith, my wife's paternal grandparents, were longtime Gideons. The Gideons International, founded in 1899, is dedicated to placing and distributing Bibles and New Testaments.[8] Interestingly, Grandpa Smith spent his adult life without sight, but this did not dissuade his love for God's word; his fifty years with the Gideons serves as ample testimony to his confidence in the accessibility of Scripture's message when Scripture is accessible. And Grandma Smith, at ninety-five years of age, continues to begin each day by reading Scripture—something she has done for many, many years. She has modeled a devotion to Scripture—to reading and appreciating her Bible—that has greatly influenced her family. This volume is written in loving memory of Grandpa Smith and dedicated to the Christian example of a devoted reader of Scripture, Grandma Smith.

[8]<www.gideons.org/about.html>.

PART I

HISTORY & THEOLOGY OF SCRIPTURE'S CLARITY

THE BELIEF AND PRACTICES ASSOCIATED WITH SCRIPTURE'S CLARITY HAVE BEEN PERSISTENT elements in the history of Christianity's identity, although the actual assertion of Scripture's clarity has not always been as noticeable. It would be an overstatement, on the one hand, to argue that Scripture's clarity was a topic of principal concern (something akin to christological focuses in the first millennium of Christian history), and it would be an understatement, on the other hand, to dismiss the significance of Scripture's clarity as simply a later (that is, Protestant and early modern) sentiment. The first five chapters trace the story of the fledgling efforts of Christians to interpret Scripture appropriately—appropriate to Christian interests—enabling us to see thereby how the assertion of Scripture's clarity serves to demonstrate a Christian reading of Christian Scripture.

Within the first fifteen hundred years of Christian history our topic is not discussed without a corresponding contention regarding the proper interpretation of the meaning of Christian Scripture, nor is it discussed explicitly apart from a contrasting admission regarding Scripture's obscurity (perceived or real). It is much more of an assumption than a conscientious assertion, at least until the modern era. When clarity is separated from Christian interpretative interests, it tends to suffer distortion and carry with it an obvious artificiality, but when subsumed within a pattern of Christian interpretative interests, it surfaces alongside the most essential elements of the interpretation of Scripture. The presence of the notion of Scripture's clarity within early Christianity is demonstrable but somewhat anonymous (chapter two); it is more explicit within early

Christian and early medieval theologians, but only inasmuch as Scripture's obscurity is also asserted (chapter three). We must wait until late medieval and Protestant theology to delineate the potential of emphasizing Scripture's clarity against other Christian interpretative premises—including the church and the tradition of Scripture interpretation (chapters four and five).

Prior to entertaining this history, a description of the present circumstances is in order, paying particular attention to how Christians have characterized the subject of Scripture's clarity. In more recent times it has become routine to associate historical concerns with the interpretation of Scripture, with serious consequences for the subject of clarity and the character of Christian faith itself. Christians of great variety share the assumption that Scripture clearly justifies their understanding of the nature and purpose of the Christian faith, but the tendency to distort such awareness is the most immediate problem we face (chapter one). Can Scripture be understood by anyone and by any means, or are there necessary conditions whereby one must understand Scripture if one is to understand it properly? And how might one use the appeal to Scripture's clarity at the present time? These questions are addressed by considering what it means for Christians to be readers of Scripture, particularly in light of so-called postcritical models of interpretation.

Illustrations and instances of Scripture's clarity—a survey of sorts—from Christian history are selected. It is an uneven treatment of the topic because the topic itself appears unevenly in Christianity's theological story. But the misshapen history of the topic should not force us to dismiss its significance. Scripture's clarity describes how Christians read and regard their Scripture. How that surmise is established, how it is practiced and how it is justified (when it is dealt with explicitly, which rarely occurs) is the concern of the first section of this book.

1

CLARIFYING CLARITY

Now what I am commanding you today is not too difficult for you or beyond your reach. It is not up in heaven, so that you have to ask, "Who will ascend into heaven to get it and proclaim it to us so we may obey it?" Nor is it beyond the sea, so that you have to ask,"Who will cross the sea to get it and proclaim it to us so we may obey it?" No, the word is very near you, it is in your mouth and in your heart so you may obey it.

DEUTERONOMY 30:11-14

Suppose it was said in the New Testament—we can surely suppose it—that it is God's will that every man should have 100,000 dollars: do you think that there would be any question of a commentary? Or would not everyone rather say, "It's easy enough to understand, there's no need of a commentary, let us for heaven's sake keep clear of commentaries—they could perhaps make it doubtful whether it is really as it is written. (And with their help we even run the risk that it may become doubtful). But we prefer it to be as it stands written there, so away with all commentaries!"

But what is found in the New Testament (about the narrow way, dying to the world, and so on) is not at all more difficult to understand than this matter of the 100,000 dollars. The difficulty lies elsewhere, in that it does not please us—and so we must have commentaries and professors and commentaries; for it is not a case of "risking" that it may become doubtful to us, for we really wish it to be doubtful, and we have a tiny hope that the commentaries may make it so.

SØREN KIERKEGAARD, "THE 100,000 DOLLAR GIFT"

THE EXPRESSION "THE CLARITY OF SCRIPTURE" IS BOTH HELPFUL AND MISLEADING. Scripture's clarity is, simply put, how Christians account for the union of text, reader and reading. It is not simply that the text is clear by itself, but that the (Christian) reader makes use of the text in a way that both presumes and argues that Scripture is clear itself. When used in this manner, the clarity of Scripture describes a Christian attitude toward how one reads and regards the sacred text. As such it summarizes the intrinsic union of theological commitments concerning the illumination of reader by the Spirit, divine rather than simply conventional authority of the text, and characterization of Scripture as realistically self-evidenced or perspicuous.

The notion has served the Christian tradition well inasmuch as it represents the widespread working premise that the Bible aims (by God) to be understood after a certain fashion and that it is understandable (by Christian readers) when read as a Christian should read Scripture. Scripture's clarity is a helpful way of addressing these basic assertions. One goal of this book will be to explain how the subject of Scripture's clarity is a barometer of the continuing struggle with the interpretation of Scripture. That is, one story can be told alongside the other, with both being better understood thereby. My procedure will be to rehearse how a Christian can read Scripture as Scripture; my goal is to indicate what Christians mean by Scripture's clarity.

With this said, we are faced with an irony: the assertion of Scripture's clarity—that the Bible can be read and understood plainly—is a complex and enigmatic subject. Why? Well, as a start, we assert that Scripture itself is clear, but Scripture is never by itself—never without historical settings, language grammar(s), never without readers both ancient and contemporary and everyone in between; nor is Scripture without academic scholarship, professional associations and publishing markets, the power structures of institutional academic accreditation; nor is Scripture without, for Christian theology, the Spirit; nor is it without Christians with their wide variety of interests or Christian authorities such as bishops, preachers and so many others.

In addition, the recent history of Christian interpretation of Scripture shows us that the notion of Scripture's clarity has been thought of as exhausted by history, personality, language, doctrine or a varied combination of these. That is, Scripture is said to be clear in a qualified sense in most Christian traditions: clear in essential matters, things having to do with saving faith, clear in articulating the identity of Jesus Christ, the nature of indispensable matters such as the church or God's grace or election or the return of Christ (depending on the Christian tradition). But other matters (the list of which could be interminably multiplied) are obscurities, mysteries, superfluous or ancillary matters; background information, sources or references external to the text itself.

In an attempt to overcome the seemingly inconclusive or unfounded trust in Scripture's clarity, Christian interpreters in recent years have misdirected our attention in an effort to ground clarity in other, discrete domains of knowledge instead of exploring how it is that Scripture's clarity might itself be understood. That is, the story of Scripture's clarity and the interpretation of Scripture cannot be told without rehearsing the (often negative) lessons that accompany what it means to assert that the Bible should and can be understood. This chapter focuses on recent examples of the employment of historical, authorial and methodological interests to demonstrate how Scripture can be regarded as clear. These areas of concern demonstrate the ongoing struggle to understand Scripture's significance in recent interpretative efforts.

Rehearsing the Threefold Concern

If Scripture's clarity were understood historically (usually described in terms of what it *meant,* which then generates what is important or significant for us to understand—what Scripture *means*), then this would effectively nullify Scripture's relevance. The resulting historical discontinuity would distance us from what Scripture is about. Such a view "sacrifices relevance, and it perpetuates concepts, forms, laws, and beliefs that belong squarely in the ancient world: it confers eternal sanctity on fossils."[1] In the split between *meant* and *means* the critical category of historical has become the dominant methodology by which understanding and meaning are established. Scripture's *meaning* would then be its original meaning, and its original meaning is its plain meaning, and its plain meaning is clear to us inasmuch as we have historically proximate knowledge of what was originally meant. One effect is that understanding Scripture becomes a technician's responsibility or an activity that is only professionally performed (as if Scripture is held captive to intellectually or academically professional criterion, and what is clear is what this class of professionals tells us is clear *according to them*). Theologically, this would mean that access to something other than, outside and apart from the text of Scripture itself (or its keeper, the Christian community) would be necessary to assert clarity. Another result is that a strictly historical understanding of the Bible's meaning is an attempt to interpret without commentary; for some this is sufficient (allowing God's Word to speak for itself or literalistically letting God speak for Godself), while for others this is corrective (avoiding the imposition of Christianity's doctrine on the real, historical nature of biblical literature). In each instance historical concerns govern our understanding of Scripture and effectively undercut assertions of Scripture's clarity.

Regarding our second area of concern: if read in terms of authorial intent (intrinsic in or through the text, or generated by collateral information about the author[s] of texts), then Scripture's clarity has to do with the objectivity of purpose and is based in a confidence in authors' abilities to express themselves clearly. Authorial intent takes two general forms: historical and literary, but each tends toward a similar emphasis upon authorial objectivism. The simplest form emphasizes the union of author and historical circumstances where the

---

[1]The phrase is from another setting—about plain or applied meanings regarding Jewish interpretation of the biblical text—with specific attention toward historical views of the Bible (Baruch J. Schwartz, "On *Peshat* and *Derash:* Bible Criticism, and Theology," *Prooftexts* 14 [January 1994]: 81).

meaning of a text is limited to what the author could have intended in the circumstances of the text's composition. Thus, historical circumstances joined with authors' consciousness yield the possible object of the authors' meaning. Historical authorial intent stresses that reference is essential to meaning. Understood in this light, Scripture is a work product of the mechanism of writing, and the "meaning of a word sequence depends on our ability to relate it to a historical author."[2] A second form of intentionalism allows for an extension of meaning beyond (but consistent with) the authors' original intended meaning. A text's meaning is not only fixed by its intended reference but also involves the sense and significance of what was said. This allows for extensions and applications of the authors' intent based upon the capacity of authors to intend a sense that was provisionally more than what was said (there is much more to this second form of intentionalism, which we will return to in chapter six).

Historical authorial intent is often emphasized to the extent that we are told to resist treating a text's meaning simply in light of its reception or reading. The argument runs something like this: the *cause* of a text, any text, is author of the text; the text is only properly considered an *effect* of the author. In this manner *realism* is a synonym for *reference,* and reference is only validated by reliable appeal to the chronologically objective and prior event, saying, instance or activity depicted by means of the text. The appeal of this model of reference is the historical assertion that unless an event really happened, exactly as an author recorded it, then there is no reason to affirm the truthfulness of what was written. In this form of referentiality the text perspicuously refers to a previous, historical, extrinsic reality of authorial intent realized in text. Scripture's clarity is a matter of clarity of reference, a perspicuous mediator or a sign of the true reality—the reality of the author. This undercuts both a theological and historical understanding that Scripture itself is clear.

This raises a third concern regarding methodology: an exclusive (and unhealthy) focus upon personality dictates that the exertion of an author's will must control and manipulate the text itself, the reader of the text and any justifiable reading of the text. The necessary and important observation that biblical texts are authored texts is often developed into a methodological criterion of authentic interpretation. Noting the characterizations of Kevin Vanhoozer helps us understand how the appeal to authorial intent fixes the effort to interpret texts: "The author's will . . . imposes itself on language and literature. Precisely because they have authors, texts don't mean just anything. The author's will acts as a control on interpretation. Thanks to the author's willing *this* rather

[2]Kevin J. Vanhoozer, *Is There a Meaning in This Text? The Bible, the Reader, and the Morality of Literary Knowledge* (Grand Rapids, Mich.: Zondervan, 1998), p. 109.

than *that,* we can say that there is a definite meaning in texts prior to reading and interpretation."[3] This union of author and words and meaning and reference can be linked with a concern for a rather straightforward understanding of language (that words simply mean by referring to what is real). This is articulated by Gleason Archer, who contends, "Remember, no interpretation of Scripture is valid that is not based on careful exegesis, that is, on wholehearted commitment to determining what the ancient author meant by the words he used."[4] Meaning is what the author accomplished or hoped to accomplish in using certain words in a certain way in a certain setting, nothing less. Meaning is treated as a commodity, with the reader treated as a passive receiver of merchandise.[5] This is a more nuanced, but still troubling, characterization of meaning that fixes, authorizes or controls meaning by means of a theory that is not necessarily generated by and remains extrinsic to Scripture itself (such as the author's will or historic grammar). One result is that Scripture's clarity is understood in terms of readability or the accessibility of Scripture's language (the letters, put together this way or that, are of a meaning fixed by the author of the words themselves). Then anyone should be able to follow the text clearly simply by virtue of learned grammar or lexical sense, or at least acquiescence to the premise that meaning is something to be owned and vended.[6] In each of the three areas of concern Scripture's clarity is unfortunately about something other than Scripture itself.

Our dilemma is whether the texts of Scripture are ever independent of their generation (historically or authorially), reception (originally or presently), or

---

[3]Ibid., p. 47. Vanhoozer's own account is much closer to the second type of authorial intent, appealing to that which lies in front of the text as well as the production of the text itself by the author (with the notion of a speech act accounting for the union of authored texts and intended meaning among the readers).

[4]Archer continues: "This is accomplished by painstaking study of the key words, as defined in the dictionaries (Hebrew and Greek) and as used in parallel passages." And referring to how a word can be used in various ways he noted, "Presumably each of these completely different uses of the same word go back to the same parent and have the same etymology" (Gleason Archer, *Encyclopedia of Bible Difficulties* [Grand Rapids, Mich.: Zondervan, 1982], pp. 15-16).

[5]The ideological premise is a type of "capitalist psychosis," the performance of which takes particularly practical and conservative forms; see David S. Cunningham, *Faithful Persuasion: In Aid of a Rhetoric of Christian Theology* (Notre Dame, Ind.: University of Notre Dame Press, 1990), pp. 108-9.

[6]Note the following as an example of the notion of simplicity and lexical sense: "The clarity of Scripture lies in the fact that what we need to know from the Bible can, in fact, be known simply by reading it. The Bible is not a book of mysteries; it is not impossible to understand. What it has to say, it says clearly to all who read and study it. True, some parts are more difficult than others, and Bible teachers and scholars are needed to sound its depths. But what they teach about the necessary truths of the Bible should be clear to any reader of the Bible" (John Sailhamer, *Christian Theology* [Grand Rapids, Mich.: Zondervan, 1998], p. 16).

reputation (fame or ascribed authority). At this point I would offer a qualified yes. The texts of Scripture are dependent regarding generation, reception and reputation for the purpose of orientation but not in the sense of limitation. Matters such as linguistic, literary, historical and cultural contexts of biblical texts are not incidental, especially when the concern is to offer historical demonstration in a historically privileged setting (contemporary academic and cultural settings, in particular). If we are attempting to study the Bible historically, then historical matters must dominate. But studying the Bible historically or authorially is not necessarily the same as studying the Bible Christianly. The role of the author as character is an important aspect of biblical texts themselves but often in a manner dissimilar from current assertions.

The authority of authorial matters is not and has not always been obvious, especially in the actual presentation of Scripture within Christian churches. Gregory the Great (540-604) insisted that it is "very superfluous" to inquire about the author of Job, for instance, because it is sufficient to regard the Spirit as Scripture's author. He offers: "If we were reading the words of some great man with his epistle in our hand, yet were to inquire by what pen they were written, it would be an absurdity."[7] The greater part of the history of Christian interpretation of Scripture treated that task as primarily theological, even at the expense of historical authorship. Thus, "traditional commentators admitted that they were less concerned about what an author intended than about how the text could be applied to particular circumstances."[8] Such a characterization is justified, only so, in such explicitly Christian terms.

After this fashion, the texts of Scripture are independent regarding generation, reception and reputation for the purpose of meaning but not in the sense of emancipation. One should not advocate the death of historical or authorial constraints in favor of readerly freedom but instead *contend* for the threefold, mutually dependent, practice of Scripture's texture, its reading and its readers.

What this has to do with Scripture's clarity is to point in a direction that might help us identify how sincere Christian people might proceed—people who wish to read the Bible for themselves, with some sense of confidence that God desires to communicate with them, with the corresponding confidence that God's communication is understandable. But what are we left with then inasmuch as affirming Scripture's clarity appears to be simplistic, misplaced or futile? (In the next section we will see illustrations of appeals to Scripture's clarity that should concern us, in part because they demonstrate that the ways

---

[7]Cited in Beryl Smalley, *The Study of the Bible in the Middle Ages* (Notre Dame, Ind.: University of Notre Dame Press, 1964), p. 33.

[8]Cunningham, *Faithful Persuasion*, p. 221.

recent biblical interpreters appeal to clarity have little to do with anything uniquely Christian, historically or theologically. As unfortunate as it is, we have many lessons to learn from negative examples.) In addition, not only do these contentions challenge a notion that Scripture is clear in any simplistic sense, but so many more challenges are raised in contemporary literary and philosophical circles (to be discussed in the second half of this book) that it is hardly possible to speak of Scripture's clarity without seriously qualifying and even restraining what is meant thereby.

Not Simply Clear, Not Simply Obscure

As a positive assertion the clarity of Scripture seeks to capture a distinctly Christian confession regarding the text's accessibility and use by Christian readers. But when severed from actual attention to the text itself, perspicuity tends to foster misleading ideas about Scripture, interpretation and Christian identity. Perspicuity is not properly a theory about texts or human language in general, it is not a code that treats Scripture as a cryptogram, and it is not an appeal to additional information supplied from outside an actual reading of Scripture. It is, as G. C. Berkouwer reminds us, a *confession* (made in faith—concerning its own means of understanding). Rather than simply an "objective," predetermined quality of Scripture *prior to* any actual investigation, or simply a "subjective" *result* of the "process of disclosure" known as interpretation, perspicuity concerns accessibility without necessarily a theoretical construction of how this is possible. Thus, it "evidently does not in any way have the character of simplicity."[9]

A consistent check on grandiose estimates of perspicuity has been the simultaneous emphasis that Scripture is not simply clear, and similarly, not simply obscure. Instead, Scripture is both clear and obscure, not merely clear or obscure—a tension not simply attributable to the imbalance of objective or subjective. Either in the celebration of obscurity to the detriment of clarity, or vice versa, the confession of the clarity of Scripture resists an easy resolution.

It is very tempting, and also pious in certain circles, to take a seeming shortcut to justify the assertion that Scripture is clear by asserting the self-evidentiary nature of Scripture's clarity. But this is rarely, if ever, a self-evident matter. What we are referring to is the hermeneutical policy of interpreting unclear or obscure texts by means of clear or obvious texts—a procedure with a profitable as well as perverted history (which we will only illustrate here). Augustine, bishop of Hippo, offered one of the most interesting and influential char-

[9]G. C. Berkouwer, *Holy Scripture,* trans. Jack B. Rogers (Grand Rapids, Mich.: Eerdmans, 1975), pp. 269-70.

acterizations of this procedure. He remarked:

> Among those things which are said openly in Scripture are to be found all those teachings which involve faith, the mores of living, and that hope and charity. . . . Then, having become familiar with the language of the Divine Scriptures, we should turn to those obscure things which must be opened up and explained so that we may take examples from those things that are manifest to illuminate those things which are obscure, bringing principles which are certain to bear on our doubts concerning those which are uncertain.[10]

Sound counsel, which unfortunately has been adhered to by every dominating tradition within the history of Christianity; used to oppose all variants of Christian practice: the persecution of Jews, Christian dissenters or so-called Anabaptists; the rejection of alternative views of communion and sacrament; one experience of God's grace as opposed to another; the presence or absence of spiritual gifts such as tongues and prophecy; the affirmation or rejection of the women preaching or ordination; even the sanctioning of slavery throughout the greater history of Christianity.[11] We are forced to ask, how is this possible?

The self-evident assertion that Scripture is clear dictates that any problems produced by *supposedly* obscure texts will be resolved upon further historical examination (texts really don't disagree, it is said, when understood in their original setting) or through harmonization (the Bible can be rearranged, it is said, so as to fit one simple history of what really happened). Interpretative practices derived from mathematical or scientific sources resolve otherwise obscure or difficult practices. For example, were there two angels at Jesus' tomb (as in Jn 20:12) or just one (as in Mt 28:5)? A well-liked and conservative harmonizing solution reads like this: "These are not contradictory reports. In fact, there is an infallible mathematical rule that easily explains this problem: wherever there are two, there is always one—it never fails! Matthew did not say there was *only* one angel."[12]

Historical harmonization is also employed to explain that contemporary readers find discrepancies in the Bible because we do not understand what really happened. In part this is because our world is so different from the

---

[10]Augustine, *On Christian Doctrine,* trans. D. W. Robertson Jr. (Indianapolis: Bobbs-Merrill, 1958), p. 40.

[11]For example, Norman Geisler and Thomas Howe argue that "some passages of Scripture are hard to understand. Sometimes the difficulty is due to their obscurity. At other times, the difficulty is because passages appear to be teaching something contrary to what some other part of Scripture is clearly teaching. For example, James appears to be saying salvation is by works (James 2:14-26), whereas Paul taught clearly that it was by grace (Rom 4:5; Titus 3:5-7; Eph 2:8-9)" (*When Critics Ask: A Popular Handbook on Bible Difficulties* [Grand Rapids, Mich.: Baker, 1999], pp. 17-18).

[12]Ibid., pp. 21-22.

world in which the Bible was produced, or the manner of representing what really happened is at variance with how it is presented in Scripture. The undergirding conviction is that chronological accuracy is what justifies saying the Bible is clear because clarity is about whether the Bible clearly depicts what really happened—as in the simple, single event that logically stands behind different representation in this manner of understanding.[13] Ironically, the most conservative as well as typically liberal historical scholars (strange bedfellows, to be sure) share this orientation. While the former orientation defends confession on the basis of ancient justification of the present, the latter defends the ancient as a reform of confession. The obvious contrast stems from the use of historical justification, either from feigned historical objectivity (apologetic historical harmonization) or eschewing confessional prejudice (now traditional critical scholarship).[14] (All this is to say that the outline below of conservative apologetics for historical harmonization is similarly applicable to dominant forms of critical historical scholarship.) The practical effect of such harmonizations is, as one commentator observes, "damaging to the clarity of Scripture. They actually subvert scriptural authority by implicitly denying the plain meaning of the text."[15]

Harold Lindsell's argument in his famous *The Battle for the Bible* demonstrates how the rather straightforward assertion of Scripture's clarity is linked with historical harmonization in defense of his position on the subject of Scripture's inerrancy. "Those who advocate inerrancy," Lindsell writes, "take the Bible in its plain and obvious sense." That the argument is historical in nature is doubtless: "The spades of a thousand over the centuries have not discredited the truth of Scripture nor has the turned-over earth proven the Bible to be untrue."[16] So obvious is this historical argument Lindsell offers that he asserts, "One of the greatest Old Testament prophecies foretold the Diaspora of the Jews because of their sins, with the promise of the regathering of Israel in the latter days. Who can doubt that the return of the Jew to Palestine, even though

---

[13]Gleason Archer offers an example of historical harmonization based in chronological or representation of one simple, single event: "In the case of parallel passages, the only method that can be justified is harmonization. That is to say, all the testimonies of the various witnesses are to be taken as trustworthy reports of what was said and done in their presence, even though they may have viewed the transaction from a slightly different perspective. When we sort them out, line them up, and put them together, we gain a fuller understanding of the event that we would obtain from any one testimony taken individually" (*Bible Difficulties,* p. 16).

[14]James Callahan, "The Bible Says: Evangelical and Postliberal Biblicism," *Theology Today* 53, no. 4 (1997): 449-63.

[15]Robert H. Gundry, *Matthew: A Commentary on His Literary and Theological Art* (Grand Rapids, Mich.: Eerdmans, 1982), p. 626.

[16]Harold Lindsell, *The Battle for the Bible* (Grand Rapids, Mich.: Zondervan, 1976), p. 37.

in unbelief, is anything other than a fulfillment of biblical prophecy?"[17]

How many times did Peter actually deny Jesus in relation to the cock crowing, or how many times did Jesus "cleanse" the temple (the Synoptic Gospels have it at the culmination of Jesus' career, while the Gospel of John has it at the beginning of Jesus' career)? Lindsell's now infamous resolutions to these seeming discrepancies display a preoccupation with historical harmonization: "None of it is incompatible; the accounts only supplement each other . . . and make the seeming contradictions in the Synoptics understandable."[18] Numerical and measuring discrepancies are not errors, just misinterpretations of measuring procedures, ignorance of geometry or even accurate use of inaccurate statistical information; conflicting details in Jesus' statements are not contradictory, Jesus could have easily said both or many more similar things, or the Gospel writers could be quoting different parts of Jesus' conversation.[19] The idea that Scripture is in error here or there "appears only to those who read the account superficially and have not probed into the real possibilities. . . . Thus there is no error, no incongruence, no real problem of any kind, at least not in the words of Scripture."[20] Interestingly, one of the most significant causes for the troublesome circumstances of those who castigate Scripture's authority, according to Lindsell, is from biblical critics or practitioners of "hermeneutics" because under this guise "it is possible to destroy the idea of biblical infallibility neatly by providing interpretations of Scripture at variance with the plain reading of the texts." Unbelief, it turns out, is at the root of denials and reinterpretations of "what the Scriptures clearly teach."[21] There is more to the sound and viable defense of inerrancy than this idea of clarity, and there is more to clarity than this simplistic characterization.

In the effort to employ clarity in relationship to historical harmonization, Lindsell's argument is not unique. On the contrary, the sometimes-spoken and often-unspoken assumptions of many late modern apologetic works is precisely that "difficulties" or "hard sayings" of certain biblical texts can be resolved by means of accurate historical information about *what really happened*.[22] This indicates a uniquely historical commitment to a greater notion of

---

[17]Ibid., p. 35.
[18]Ibid., p. 176.
[19]Ibid., pp. 164-66.
[20]Ibid., pp. 164, 169.
[21]Ibid., pp. 39, 40.
[22]An illustration of this assumption in evangelical scholarship is the following: "Thanks to [archaeology's] skilled and scientific application it is possible today to understand the Bible in its setting of time and place as never before. To grasp with clarity the writer's first meaning and original purpose is manifestly the first step towards the elucidation of that which is permanent and universally significant in his theme" (Bernard Ramm, "The Use of Archaeology in Interpretation," in *Hermeneutics* [Grand Rapids, Mich.: Baker, 1971], p. 55).

chronological authority—literally a spirit of historical objectivism. The biblical text is a species of historical understanding and functions within another, dominant framework instead of creating its own sense of authority.

We might pause to ask why these sayings are hard or difficult to accept at face value (but would require a rehearsal of cultural and religious factors such as issues of politics, economics, philosophy, sociology and gender). That not all expressions, sentences, or even stories or narratives within the larger biblical text are clear or self-evident to readers is a weighty admission itself and offers one of the best apologies for why we should be concerned with any affirmation of Scripture's clarity. The premise, then, is that the reason we affirm Scripture's clarity is due to Scripture's obscurity. Augustine put the matter in Christian terms when he advised that God was the author of this obscurity, not in order to confuse the pious but "provided by God to conquer pride by work and to combat disdain in our minds, to which those things which are easily discovered seem frequently to become worthless." Thus, he concludes, "the Holy Spirit has magnificently and wholesomely modulated the Holy Scriptures so that the more open places present themselves to hunger and the more obscure places may deter a disdainful attitude. Hardly anything may be found in these obscure places which is not found plainly said elsewhere."[23]

The question this raises is whether all obscurities can or should be resolved through historical, interpretative or spiritual discernment. Does obscurity rest in the readers' lack of information at the present time, something akin to a scientific pursuit of information? Note how this argument is presented in a popular guide addressing the Bible's difficulties: "*Mistake 1: Assuming that the Unexplained is Not Explainable.* No informed person would claim to be able to explain fully all Bible difficulties. However, it is a mistake for the critic to assume, therefore, that what has not yet been explained never will be explained."[24] Is clarity a matter of acquiring better interpretative skills? Again,

---

[23]Augustine, *Christian Doctrine,* pp. 37-38.

[24]The authors continue by comparing the natural scientist to the Christian activity of interpreting the Bible: "When a scientist comes upon an anomaly in nature, he does not give up further scientific exploration. Rather, he uses the unexplained as a motivation to find an explanation. No real scientist throws up her hands in despair simply because she cannot explain a given phenomenon. She continues to do research with the confident expectation that an answer will be found. And, the history of science reveals that her faith has been rewarded over and over again. . . . Likewise, the Christian scholar approaches the Bible with the same presumption that what is thus far unexplained is not therefore unexplainable. He or she does not assume that discrepancies are contradictions. And, when he encounters something for which he has no explanation, he simply continues to do research, believing that one will eventually be found. In fact, if he assumed the opposite, he would stop studying. Why pursue an answer when one assumes there is none. Like his scientific counterpart, the Bible student has been rewarded for his faith and research. For, many difficulties for which scholars once

from another popular guide: "In dealing with Bible problems of any kind, whether in factual or in doctrinal matters, it is well to follow appropriate guidelines in determining the solution."[25]

Then we come to our third type of query: Is obscurity a spiritual problem that, like better historical information and interpretative skills solve historical and interpretative obscurities, is a problem to be solved by better spirituality? This account of clarity and obscurity reads something like this: "The mistakes are not in the revelation of God, but are in the misinterpretations of man. . . . The Bible is without mistake, but the critics are not. All their allegations of error in the Bible are based on some error of their own."[26] And of Christians who struggle with obscurities this advice is offered: "It is well to follow appropriate guidelines in determining the solution [to] Bible problems of any kind, whether in factual or in doctrinal matters."[27] But there is much more to the question of clarity and obscurity than historical characterizations (this is evident for the greater part of Christian history). But this baptism of historical justifications in the rhetoric of Christian spirituality provides a strong explanation why contemporary biblical studies have been so closely associated with a cul-

---

had no answer have yielded to the relentless pursuit of truth through history, archaeology, linguistics, and other disciplines" (Geisler and Howe, *When Critics Ask,* pp. 15-16). Also note: "Be fully persuaded in your own mind that an adequate explanation exists, even though you have not yet found it. The aerodynamic engineer may not understand how a bumble bee can fly; yet he trusts that there must be an adequate explanation for its fine performance since, as a matter of fact, it does fly! Even so we may have complete confidence that the divine Author preserved the human author of each book of the Bible from error or mistake as he wrote down the original manuscript of the sacred text" (Archer, *Bible Difficulties,* p. 15).

[25]Archer, *Bible Difficulties,* p. 15. Also note: "When we are not sure, then several things should be kept in mind. First, we should not build a doctrine on an obscure passage. The rule of thumb in Bible interpretation is 'the main things are the plain things, and the plain things are the main things.' This is called the perspicuity (clearness) of Scripture. If something is important, it will be clearly taught in Scripture and probably in more than one place. Second, when a given passage is not clear, we should never conclude that it means something that is opposed to another plain teaching of Scripture. God does not make mistakes in His Word; we make mistakes in trying to understand it" (Geisler and Howe, *When Critics Ask,* pp. 18-19).

[26]Geisler and Howe, *When Critics Ask,* p. 15. Also note: "I am well aware that one class of people will call the Bible a hopelessly obscure volume, namely, all those who wish to understand what finite minds simply cannot grasp," with the result that "this makes many sections of the Bible unacceptable to those haughty minds whose motto is to reject as untrue whatever they cannot comprehend." In contrast, "the simple Bible Christian, however, who trusts in God's power and truthfulness, will not experience much difficulty when he reads the Scriptures" (W. Arndt, *Bible Difficulties: An Examination of Passages of the Bible Alleged to Be Irreconcilable with Its Inspiration* [St. Louis: Concordia, 1971], p. 15).

[27]Archer, *Bible Difficulties,* p. 15. To continue, Archer recommends paying attention to those who have "carefully and prayerfully studied the Bible," which he later associates with those able to employ historical, archaeological and etymological resources to clarifying both factual and doctrinal difficulties.

tural project of certainty, historical objectivity and a perspicuous notion of truth (this subject will be explored in chapter five).

Interestingly, the story of Scripture's clarity has most often been told in contrast to the employment of critical reason, historicity and singleness or simplicity of meaning. A theological account of clarity and obscurity is a fair bit dissimilar from the clarifying of difficult sayings through better historical information that characterizes more recent accounts of Scripture's supposed obscurity. But the spirit of objectivism, probably the dominant account of perspicuity of late, renders any concrete discussion of Scripture that acknowledges a genuine tension of clarity and obscurity moot, impious or uninformed.[28] For example, in Kevin Vanhoozer's development of a Christian theology of interpretation he seeks to ground obscurity in human depravity (sin) and clarity in the objectivist character of language: "In a fallen world language no longer infallibly does what it was designed for." Thus, "we humans know in part, through the glass of language, darkly—not because of some defect in language but because of our unseeing eyes and unclean lips." Language itself is not at fault; it is of God—a gift that remains trustworthy as an "institution." He concludes, "It is therefore no little part of our Christian vocation to bear witness to the trustworthiness of the institution of language by being responsible authors and responsible readers."[29] Scripture, because it is part of the historical objectivity of language (a fixed and closed notion), renders the Bible closed to readers (i.e., not open, clear or accessible).

This does not demonstrate that the type of argument we have just encountered—that clarity is a principle of historical argument—is completely inappropriate or has nothing to do with Scripture's clarity, but it does offer a strong encouragement to look for more. What stimulates a concern for Scripture's clarity is an admission of its genuine or seeming obscurity. And any defense of clarity must acknowledge that the need to interpret after one fashion or another is premised upon the lack of clarity on Scripture's pages. It also explains, in part, why the subject of Scripture's clarity is a topic routinely ignored by Christian interpreters so intimately involved in the cultural project of modernity with its quest for reasonable certainty, simplicity and objectivity, by means of objective (as in simply historical rather than sensual) knowledge.[30] In the historically privileged

---

[28]Note Lindsell's counsel regarding historical ignorance (which he must depend on by his own admission): "For the problem areas for which we have no clear answer at the moment, we are to be content to wait until all the evidence is in. Apparent discrepancies are no more than that. Additional information in a thousand instances has proved that the Bible's critics were wrong" *(Battle for the Bible,* p. 39).

[29]Vanhoozer, *Is There a Meaning?* p. 207.

[30]The phrase is adapted from Merold Westphal, "Post-Kantian Reflections on the Importance of

framework of early modernity, itself an effort to overcome suspicions of subjectivity encroaching upon the text, historical critics stress the cognitive aspects of meaning in terms of reference—the text is taken to be clear inasmuch as it serves as an accurate representation of history and objective event. Correspondingly, by accepting the historically privileged form of understanding, experientially oriented religionists take Scripture as symbolic representation of the possibility and realization of the human experience of God in Christ—the text is taken to clearly represent or correspond with this orientation regarding God.[31] In between and revolving around these models of conceiving of clarity are the Reformed and evangelical tendencies to appeal to an objectivist historical characterization of cognitive knowledge and the experiential justifications for spirituality.[32]

Here is the crux of the argument thus far: we must resist the temptation to retreat under the carapace of early modernity's simple historicity and rhetoric of objectivity as a suitable explanation of what Scripture's clarity means. The retreat is inadvisable for several reasons. First, it ignores the actual textures of clarity and obscurity depicted in Scripture (the play, give-and-take between what the text identifies as clear [and might not be clear to the reader] and what the text asserts to be obscure [and correspondingly might be thought of as clear to the reader]). Second, it assumes a historical gap between text and reader that is overcome by locating a perspicuous union in the common human experience or understanding (either historical, authorial, psychological, cultural or a combination thereof). And third, it ignores the dynamic relationship between the text's clarity and the reader of the text, otherwise known as the social construct of the reader. We now turn to these three subjects in this order—this is our threefold contention.[33]

Hermeneutics," in *Disciplining Hermeneutics: Interpretation in Christian Perspective,* ed. Roger Lundin (Grand Rapids, Mich.: Eerdmans, 1997), pp. 62-63. He recalls, "I shall never forget the lecture I heard at an evangelical seminary on the perspicuity of Scripture. A distinguished theologian argued that since the Bible interprets itself, there is no need for us to interpret it. He saw clearly that interpretation was at odds with the objectivism that was as basic to his credo as was his theism."

[31]This term, *religionists,* directs our attention to the type of theological hermeneutic associated with the legacy of Schleiermacher and the greater liberal tradition, usually concerned with how Scripture represents human existence. George Lindbeck referred to this as disposition toward theology as "experiential-expressivist" in his *The Nature of Doctrine: Religion and Theology in a Postliberal Age* (Philadelphia: Westminster Press, 1984), p. 16.

[32]The association of Reformed and evangelical characterizations of Scripture and its interpretation in the nineteenth and twentieth centuries is argued by James Barr, *Holy Scripture: Canon, Authority, Criticism* (Oxford: Clarendon, 1983). We will return to this subject in chapter five.

[33]This threefold linguistic model of clarity will reoccur throughout this work, in contrast to a

The Texture of Clarity

There is no direct statement in Christian Scripture that says that it is clear and not obscure—at least not without reference to the effects of this awareness. As close as we come is the employment of metaphors and symbols such as light and radiance, guidance and surveillance, nearness and presence. There are occasions when the writings are made plain to a certain audience by overcoming linguistic and perspectival shortcomings. There is also the ever-present demonstration—through allusion, self-reference and self-criticism—that in its actual use of itself, Scripture is properly regarded as clear and not obscure to its readers.

The vocabulary that leads us to speak of Scripture's clarity includes: Scripture's character as light, lamp and enlightenment (Ps 19:8; 119:18, 105, 130; Prov 6:23; Rom 2:17-20; 2 Cor 4:2-4; 2 Pet 1:19); how it reveals, makes known, and we know thereby (Deut 4:35; 8:2-3; 29:29; Ps 78:3; 119:125; Mk 4:11-13; Rom 1:16-17; 16:25-26; 1 Cor 2:6-10; Eph 3:3-5; 2 Tim 3:15; 1 Pet 1:10-12; [cp. Is 6:9-10 and Mt 11:25]); and the openness and accessibility of what is written (Deut 4:9-10; 30:10-14 [cp. Rom 10:6-8]; Ps 78:1-8; 147:19; Acts 17:2-3, 11; 2 Cor 2:17). The awareness of God's word, confirmed through its enactment, offers the essential description of Scripture's accessibility. In its intelligible demonstration (in the Exodus and at Sinai, and, in Christian teaching, the death and resurrection of Jesus) and the corresponding acknowledgement and response among God's people, the expectations of the text presumes the openness of what is written.

What one does with this representation is crucial. The tendency of late, especially within historical and authorial interpretative models, has been to take the textual assertions as simply referring to a given meaning without necessarily considering whether such texts refer to something outside themselves or even if reference itself is a useful characterization of such materials. In this manner, mention of Scripture's clarity by Scripture itself are taken as indicators that Scripture refers to something external to the text *clearly*—fairly or truthfully representing what really happened as an accurate historical witness. Scripture then serves as a perspicuous mediator of something

---

unitary historical framework in which Scripture is one instance of what a text is historically, and in contrast to a strictly binary framework of breaching the distance between what a text meant and what it means. Among the sources for this threefold model please see Charles Sanders Peirce, *Collected Papers of Charles Sanders Peirce,* ed. Charles Harteshorne, Paul Weiss and Arthur W. Burks (Cambridge, Mass.: Belknap, 1934-1958); and the development of Peirce's triadic distinction of *sign, meaning* and *interpretant* by Peter Ochs, "An Introduction to Postcritical Scriptural Interpretation," in *The Return to Scripture in Judaism and Christianity: Essays in Postcritical Scriptural Interpretation,* ed. Peter Ochs (New York: Paulist, 1993), pp. 12-13.

more important or other than the text itself.

Our alternative is that the text's clarity may be regarded as truly a representation (a symbol) instead of taking claims to textual clarity as referring to that which is not the text itself.[34] Scripture's clarity, after this fashion, does not refer to historical referent, actual event behind, beneath or outside of the representation of the text itself. Clarity does not necessarily concern historical reference, nor is meaning simply established or singular in orientation. The meaning of a biblical text is not necessarily the single historical reference that might have generated it (as if the text were simply an effect of something more important that could or should be harmonized to that referent), and clarity is not historical in reference. Texts do refer, and they do mean something, but the subject matter of reference is that of the text itself and involves the reader along with this awareness of textuality. That the Bible addresses clarity, and its own clarity, is an indication that understanding what Scripture's clarity involves cannot be divorced from understanding how modes of interpretation and interpreters interact with the text itself. In this manner Scripture is genuinely indispensable; it cannot be reduced to something more basic or fundamental nor can it simply function as a mediator of cognitive knowledge in historical form.

We can offer several observations about the explicit reports of recording writing within the writings themselves that indicate that while the text has a reference and meaning(s), these are not exhausted by external reference. For example: "Moses wrote down all the words of the LORD" (Ex 24:4 NRSV); this theme is also developed in Isaiah 8:1, Amos 7:14-15, and Revelation 1:10-11. But why? Descriptions of the phenomenon of inscripturation concentrate on the efficacy and proficiency of "what is written" (Ex 17:14; Jer 30:2-3; 36:2-3, 6-7; Jn 20:30-31; 21:25; 1 Cor 14:37), and the aim of similar observations seems to focus on what is to be done with what is written (Deut 6:6-12; Josh 1:8; 23:6; Ps 102:18; Rom 15:4; 1 Cor 10:11; 1 Tim 4:13). In each instance there is a presumption of clarity and accessibility that corresponds to moral responsibility. To interpret a text does not simply have an ethical dimension (as it were the fair application of general or universal rules of interpretation or historical criticism), but interpretation is itself ethic.

This correspondence between clarity and responsibility can be illustrated by appealing to the book of Ezekiel. The charge to Ezekiel is characteristic of this reflexive attitude toward prophetic inscripturation. The yielding, receptive posture of the prophet ("He said to me, Mortal, eat this scroll that I give you and

[34]Again, by appealing to Peirce, Ochs argues that this understanding of textuality in interpretation is an offering found among postcritical practitioners wherein "a symbol is a *sign* (1), that displays its *meaning* (2), with respect to some particular *interpretant* (3)" (Ochs, "Introduction to Postcritical Scriptural Interpretation," p. 13).

fill your stomach with it. Then I ate it; and in my mouth it was as sweet as honey" [Ezek 3:3 NRSV]) is starkly contrasted with the stubborn rejection of God's words.[35]

> He said to me: Mortal, go to the house of Israel and speak my very words to them. For you are not sent to a people of obscure speech and difficult language, but to the house of Israel—not to many peoples of obscure speech and difficult language, whose words you cannot understand. Surely, if I sent you to them, they would listen to you. But the house of Israel will not listen to you, for they are not willing to listen to me; because all the house of Israel have a hard forehead and a stubborn heart. (Ezek 3:4-7 NRSV)

The house of Israel is not open to a conversation with God, not because of unfamiliarity or obscurity of speech, but because they have refused to be addressed by God and understand their circumstances in terms of God's form of discourse (Ezek 3:10-11, 27; 24:27). In God's taunt of Israel's exiles in the foreign land of Babylon, there is a contrast between verbal intelligibility (speech and language) and indecipherable speech (obscurity and difficulty). The willingness to listen is the true barrier, not simply the obscurity of speech or difficulty of language (which might offer an excuse for unresponsiveness). The rebuke is bound up in the rhetorical play: if the prophet had been sent to those of "obscure speech and difficult language," they would have listened!

Prophetic discourse, we learn from Ezekiel, is reflexive and indicates that clarity is immanent to the employment of a socially common language. It is within their common language or shared linguistic medium that intelligibility is realized.[36] The language of this conversation concerned Israel's failed attention to God's laws (Ezek 20:5-26) and their hope of restoration is a renewed spirit to follow God's decrees and keep God's laws and thus live as God's people (Ezek 11:18-20 [cp. 36:27]; 44:23-24). Their discourse, that to which God holds them accountable, is bound up with fidelity to the scriptural anthology (that which the prophet and the people should share as much as they do share a

---

[35]"The prophet has no prophetic training because none is necessary, and none is available. He is not a sorcerer, because he deals not so much with 'secrets' or hidden things as with that which has been revealed (cf. Deut. 29:28—30:3)" (David Lyle Jeffrey, *People of the Book: Christian Identity and Literary Culture* [Grand Rapids, Mich.: Eerdmans, 1996], p. 23); within Judaism see Samuel C. Heilman, *People of the Book: Drama, Fellowship and Religion* (Chicago: University of Chicago Press, 1983).

[36]See Northrop Frye, *Words with Power: Being a Second Study of "The Bible and Literature"* (New York: Harcourt Brace Jovanovich, 1990); Paul Ricoeur, "The Model of the Text: Meaningful Action Considered as a Text," in *Interpretative Social Science: A Reader,* ed. Paul Rabinow and William M. Sullivan (Berkeley: University of California Press, 1979), pp. 73-101; George Steiner, *After Babel: Aspects of Language and Translation* (New York: Oxford University Press, 1975).

dialect of speech and language).[37] Such statements represent the constitution and identity of the community in relation to the text. They are not simply accidental clues or curiosities, nor glimpses into the authors' motives, nor demonstrations for attention to the formation of the text rather than its final form. They are, instead, instructive about the use of the text itself. The text is self-reflective; that is its texture.

Rather than simply stating its clarity as a concluded matter without regard for its influence, Scripture seems to engage its audience and thereby render its efficacy.[38] There is, at a level wherein the text advises the reader of the appropriate use of itself, instruction by demonstration of attentiveness to the text as Scripture. This is evident, for example, in the Pauline use of the Torah: "Now the words 'it was reckoned to him,' were written not for his sake alone, but for ours also" (Rom 4:23-24 NRSV); "For whatever was written in former days was written for our instruction, so that by steadfastness and by the encouragement of the scriptures we might have hope" (Rom 15:4 NRSV); "Or does he not speak entirely for our sake? It was indeed written for our sake" (1 Cor 9:10 NRSV); and "these things . . . were written down to instruct us" (1 Cor 10:11 NRSV). It seems that this advice about how to use Scripture is not ancillary to the nature of Scripture as text—Scripture's clarity and obscurity are realistic *character*-izations of the text itself.

Examples of why we speak of Scripture's clarity are focused on the interplay of text, reading and reader. This is not an argument for a concept of clarity unrelated to the actual shape of the biblical texts themselves (abstract, or a priori conditions for understanding), but descriptive of texts, the interplay of which causes us to apply to a defense of proper reading as clear. Not that this proves our assertions, but instead it offers sufficient demonstration of a necessary dialogue concerning the relational nature of text, reading and reader as intrinsic to the interpretation of Scripture.

What the Bible *Says*

A second area of concern has to do with the relationship between the (historical) text of Scripture and the contemporary reader. Occasionally we will avail ourselves of sincere historical excuse: if only we had *more* information about

---

[37]For the varied use of phrases such as "scriptural anthology," "rhetorical coherence," "implicit metaphor" and similar literary observations, see Robert Alter and Frank Kermode, eds., *The Literary Guide to the Bible* (Cambridge, Mass.: Harvard University Press, 1987); Northrop Frye, *The Great Code: The Bible and Literature* (New York: Harcourt Brace Jovanovich, 1982); Regina M. Schwartz, ed., *The Book and the Text: The Bible and Literary Theory* (Oxford: Basil Blackwell, 1989).

[38]Berkouwer, *Holy Scripture,* p. 273.

ancient customs, word usage, the problems or occasion that prompted a particular writing, the background of the author, the author's personality or the author's world, the readers' circumstances and background, and the biographies of the readers, *then* we could understand this text more clearly. Very often this excuse is justified by a distinction between what a text *meant* and what a text means; and in our modern setting the former usually determines the latter (or at least we argue that it should). This "gap" is historical and chronological; for some it is also philosophical and metaphysical. And it appears to be naive, to say the least, to ignore this gap, either with pious platitudes about what the Bible "says to us" (as if it were our contemporary) or speculation about what it "can mean for us" (as if meaning for the original audience can easily be acquired today and be equivalent to its original significance).

Contemporary Christian scholarship has built itself a hermeneutical model founded upon historical characterizations of gap: contextual and contemporary, meant and means, knowledge and use, exposition and application. As Charles Woods noted:

> It is commonly assumed that the interpreter's first major task is somehow to isolate and identify the subject matter of the text—its *raison d'être*, its point, the central phenomenon from which it takes its life—so that the various elements of the text can be related to that center and understood in its light. The interpreter can thus give proper emphasis to those features of the text that illuminate and are illuminated by the subject matter and can properly dispose of the less illuminating residue.[39]

Note how the metaphors concern clarity and clarification and indicate a necessary privileging of historical *rather than* contemporary orientation to guarantee that this goal is accomplished. Indeed it is this use of the rhetoric of either/or that grounds the characterization of Scripture's clarity in historical authority or authorization, and leads to the chronological compartmentalization of how Christians might understand Scripture's significance. The extent to which the binary models of exposition and application, description and use, dominate the concern for interpreting Scripture is almost overwhelming, especially in the areas of biblical studies and homiletics (areas desperately concerned with displaying their practical contribution to Christian existence, their necessity). The *Life Application Bible,* with its explicit focus on bridging "the gap between the past and present, the conceptual and practical," is typical of this emphasis,[40] and this practice is especially evident in marketing popular

---

[39]Charles M. Wood, *An Invitation to Theological Study* (Valley Forge, Penn.: Trinity Press International, 1994), p. 48.

[40]*Life Application Bible: King James Version* (Wheaton, Ill.: Tyndale House, 1986), pp. xiv-xvi. In the course of *Life Application Bible's* practice, "each application note has three parts:

biblical commentary in recent publishing. Repeated phrases such as *practical* and *application* indicate how these characterizations authorize what the interpreter sees as significant for readers.

The constitution of this temporal and intellectual *gap* is, according to Nicholas Lash, founded in the common use of a metaphor of *translation* that we implement in order to *bridge the gap*. Lash observes, "The assumption that the task of the systematic theologian is that of transposing meaning recovered by the New Testament scholar into contemporary idiom presupposes what we might call the 'relay-race' model of the relationship between the two enterprises." The premise of this translation metaphor is "the mistaken belief that texts 'have meaning' in somewhat the same way that material objects 'have mass.' "[41] In practice, the metaphor looks something like this according to Lash:

> When the New Testament scholar has done his job, produced his completed package of "original meanings," he hands this over to the systematic theologian, whose responsibility it is to transpose the meanings received into forms intelligible within the conditions of our contemporary culture. Systematic theologians who subscribe to this model are sometimes irritated by the fact that, because the work of the New Testament interpretation is never finished, the baton never reaches them. The New Testament scholar appears to be "running on the spot"; he never arrives at the point at which the baton could be handed over. The New Testament scholar, for his part, either ignores what the systematic theologian is doing (it is not his business: he is only running the *first* leg of the race) or disapproves of the fact that the baton is continually being wrenched prematurely from his hands.[42]

This means, "Christian hermeneutics is principally concerned with negotiating the 'gap' between what was once said and what might appropriately be said today." And, for example, "Christian living is conceived as the practical application or implementation of meanings thus recovered and transposed."[43] Christian faithfulness, in this orientation, is both historical and analytical in nature; even to the extent that (historical or scholarly) ignorance is one's best excuse in response to the challenge of Christian faithfulness regarding weighty matters of discipleship, martyrdom, sacrifice or relationships of differently religious peoples. But as illustrated by Kierkegaard's parable of the $100,000 gift

(1) an *explanation* that ties the note directly to the Scripture passage and sets up the truth that is being taught, (2) the *bridge* which shows you how to take the timeless truth and make it relevant for today, (3) the *application* which shows you how to take the timeless truth and apply it to your personal situation."

[41]Nicholas Lash, "What Might Martyrdom Mean?" in *Theology on the Way to Emmaus* (London: SCM Press, 1986), p. 85.

[42]Ibid., p. 79.

[43]Ibid., p. 75.

cited at the beginning of this chapter, the divide between *meant* and *means* tends to be moral in orientation and not simply historical.

Lash's response to the gap is dialectical: "We do not *first* understand the past and *then* proceed to understand the present. The relationship between these two dimensions of our quest for meaning and truth is dialectical: they mutually inform, enable, correct and enlighten each other."[44] His characterization is satisfying in that it maintains the form of a genuine tension between then and now—an element inherent in the moral use of historical matters for scriptural interpreters in that implicit in seemingly descriptive accounts of what a text meant is the assertion that what it meant should function authoritatively in the present in some fashion. The distortion of the mutually informing relationship of descriptive and historical versus normative and contemporary is Lash's problematic.

There is no pardon given Scripture's readers because of a historical gap, as real and as intimidating as it may be. This is because there is another type of gap, oriented to usage, explained in terms of presence and governed by the presumption of accessibility; this is the gap associated with clarity. Thinking in this way directs our attention to biblical literature such as Deuteronomy, in part because of its unique, governing role within the identity of Judaism and Christianity, and in part because of its explicit focus on overcoming gaps and its focus on the present (i.e., today). It is here that we learn not how to know God via Moses but how "the LORD knew [Moses] face to face" (Deut 34:10 NRSV; i.e., spoke to him as one human speaks to another; Ex 33:11; Num 12:8), as well as how "the LORD spoke with you [Israel] face to face" (Deut 5:4; 5:23—6:3 NRSV).

The gaps within the structure of Deuteronomy itself display a *tension* between the wilderness and the Transjordan land (looking backwards and Moses' leadership related to looking forwards and Joshua's leadership), especially in the two outer frames of the book (Deut 1—3 and 31—34).[45] There exists a tension between God's laws and desires and the people's responses (obedience vs. disobedience), especially evident in the institution of God's law and its ratification by the people in the inner frames of the book (Deut 4—11

---

[44]Ibid., p. 80, citing Lash, "Interpretation and Imagination," in *Incarnation and Myth: The Debate Continued,* ed. M. Goulder (London: SCM Press, 1979), p. 25.

[45]For a structural appraisal of the book of Deuteronomy we will observe the work done by Duane Christensen, *Word Biblical Commentary: Deuteronomy 1—11* (Dallas: Word, 1991):

A Outer Frame: A Look Backward (1—3)
  B Inner Frame: The Great Peroration (4—11)
    C The Central Core: Covenant Stipulations (12—26)
  B´ Inner Frame: The Covenant Ceremony (27—30)
A´ Outer Frame: A Look Forward (31—34)

and 27—30), which sandwiches the central core of the book's covenant stipulations (Deut 12—26). More synthetic and stylistic gaps exist in the relationship of God's words and Moses' words (Deut 1:1-6, where they are brought together or just confused; and thus to hear Moses is to hear God); while Moses' leadership fades and Joshua's ascends, God's word remains constant, present and pressing for the nation (Deut 3:21-29); there is an offering of guidance about (re-)hearing the commands of God *today* (Deut 10—11) and a renewed opportunity for keeping, observing, hearing, listening, and obeying today (Deut 4).

These matters are historical in the sense that the reader must offer a response as a reading of the text, in the present, as the reader seeks to stand within the same story (not simply the same setting, framework or time space; matters we will address in chapters eight and nine). But there is no temporal lag offered to either excuse a failure to comply with God's desires articulated by Moses (as the text portrays the instructions it offers) or encourage an archaeological retrieval for the genuine relic of Deuteronomy's prehistory (which the text obviously implies to historically concerned readers). Instead of attempting to bridge such gaps, Deuteronomy offers a (historically) indeterminate interplay of tensions that frustrates historical purists and biblicists alike, as it is not simply a repetition of the law first given at Sinai.[46]

Articulating the Torah in the setting of Deuteronomy is not simply an application of the past (as a historical construct or repeating the past lest it be lost) but an instituting via enactment for those who name the Lord as their God (Deut 5:2-5; 6:1-25). It is the present, "today," and what will result that concerns Deuteronomy.[47] Thus the saying common in rabbinic circles—that the Torah is new every time it is read—offers a different than historical signifi-

[46]Robert Polzin, "Deuteronomy," in *The Literary Guide to the Bible,* ed. Robert Alter and Frank Kermode (Cambridge, Mass.: Harvard University Press, 1987), pp. 92-101; and Robert Polzin, *Moses and the Deuteronomist: A Literary Study of the Deuteronomic History* (New York: Seabury, 1980).

[47]This pedagogical theme is developed extensively by source critics who see lapses, gaps, stylistic shifts as flags of editorial or authorial work subsequent to the historical-literary orientation of the Tetrateuch (Genesis through Numbers) and indicative of post-Mosaic Deuteronomistic history (Deuteronomy, Joshua, Judges, 1-2 Samuel and 1-2 Kings—all productions of the Deuteronomist redactor[s]). Deuteronomy is forward looking and offers accessibility inasmuch as the "redactors did not passively collect and reproduce the old traditions that came down to them, but often recast them substantially by inserting editorial comments and organizing them according to a schematic plan" (Douglas A. Knight, "Deuteronomy and the Deuteronomists," in *Old Testament Interpretation: Past, Present, and Future,* ed. James Luther Mays, David L. Petersen and Kent Harold Richards [Nashville: Abingdon, 1995], pp. 61-62). Also consult Martin Noth, *The Deuteronomistic History,* trans. J. Doull, 2d ed., JSOTSup 15 (Sheffield: JSOT, 1991); and Robert Polzin, *Moses and the Deuteronomist: A Literary Study of the Deuteronomic History, Part I: Deuteronomy, Joshua, Judges* (New York: Seabury, 1980).

cance. In Deuteronomy, where obedience is described in terms of memory and disobedience in terms of forgetfulness (Deut 7—8), the pedagogical purpose of the work is explicit and explicitly linked with the structure of the narrative itself, and that narrative structure is asserted to be clear, accessible: "The word is very near you, it is in your mouth and in your heart so you may obey it" (Deut 30:14). Deuteronomy is literally a pattern of instruction or form of address ("these are the words" Deut 1:1) by some thought to extend to and form the substance of Israel's historiography itself; it is not simply a second telling of the same law (as is often said of Deut 17:18 LXX), and it does not "suggest distance from God's original speech" as historical objectivists would have it.[48] The shaping of this scriptural anthology or rhetorical coherence of the sacred text itself is found in the shaping influence of the Deuteronomist model—even to the point of exaggeration. "Deuteronomy was the gem out of which the whole canon eventually developed."[49] This instructional orientation is evident throughout the structure of the work, for example:

> When your children ask you in time to come, "What is the meaning of the decrees and the statutes and the ordinances that the LORD our God has commanded you?" then you shall say to your children, "We were Pharaoh's slaves in Egypt, but the LORD brought us out of Egypt with a mighty hand. (Deut 6:20-21 NRSV)

And

> When all Israel comes to appear before the Lord your God at the place that he will choose, you shall read this law before all Israel in their hearing. Assemble the people—men, women, and children, as well as the aliens residing in your towns—so that they may hear and learn to fear the Lord your God and to observe diligently all the words of this law, and so that their children, who have not known it, may hear and learn to fear the Lord your God. (Deut 31:11-13 NRSV)

Thus, instead of orienting us to the text as an artifact clear only within the historical framework of its initial composition, the narrative literally commands attention to its form, and that form is accessible in that it is possible to keep, observe, hear, listen and obey today.

A faithful interpretation of Deuteronomy, then, would not be exhausted by a plausible historical account of its compositional structure, authorial circumstances or even function within the historiography of Joshua, Judges, 1-2 Kings and 1-2 Samuel. While including historical and obvious tensions between the original settings of the text and its function within its own history and our settings, the meaning of Deuteronomy involves the varying ways in

---

[48]Vanhoozer, *Is There a Meaning,* p. 176.
[49]Frye, *Great Code,* p. 201.

which it has and can be performed faithfully or justifiably executed. The contention is that this operative interest is represented by the text itself. So instead of moving from validating one's interpretation historically or authorially to possible applications of that interpretation, we suggest the movement is one of a parallel pilgrimage in that a genuinely historical text is also our contemporary.

Here is our suggestion to this point: the *clarity* of Deuteronomy does not reside *in* the text as something to be unearthed apart from this pilgrimage. Its clarity is historical, not in that one renders historical events in contemporary understanding, but historical in the sense that one's enactment or embodiment of the text's display of what was once offered and instructed is necessarily rooted in contemporary circumstances. (As Lash put it: "the gap [is] between what was once achieved, intended, or 'shown', and what might be achieved, intended, or 'shown' today)."[50]

People of the Book

A third feature of concern has to do with the social construct of the reader. Simply put, how does the reader relate to reading or what constitutes a reading of the text itself? Various characterizations of this relation include: social dimensions of knowledge related to the various function of texts within a community; readers' contextual and historical orientation toward reading or the constructs that form the background to any reader/reading; and theories of reader response or reader reception, subjectivity or relativity of all knowledge and representations of knowledge. (The latter grouping of themes will be taken up in chapter eight, while the social nature of textuality will be our concern in this section.)

Instead of conceiving of the reader as a consumer of a text's substance or raw material, or reading as a secondary exercise responsive only to the intentions of the author behind or hidden within a text, the sociality of reading orients us to the conversational nature of text, reading and readers. Historically this *conversation* has discriminately limited itself to author's intent and intended readers with the text as the evidentiary bridge or the antecedent probable literary development of this bridge from its final state as product back to its sources of origin(s). The notion of Scripture's clarity has been shaped by this historical orientation to indicate historically perspicuous information or evidence of intent, setting and subject matter—a matter essentially closed to the reader. But by admitting the working presumption of the historicity of the *interpreter* as a reader within various social constructs, we are led in a new direction—we are led to consider how the assertion of Scrip-

[50]Lash, "What Might Martyrdom Mean?" pp. 90-91.

ture's clarity is immediately related to how a reader reads.

The practice of attending to Scripture in light of an appeal to its clarity (i.e., how a reader reads) is itself justified by an appropriation of the text by readers that is purposefully realistic—a derivation of what is involved with affirming Scripture as text. As J. Wentzel van Huyssteen notes, "Reading is not merely a reproductive but also a productive activity" that leads us to consider "the world of the reader as presupposed by the text." That is, not simply the historical setting of the original text composition but the "world of the text"—the realistically depicted world the text continually points toward, creates—"and this continuous reference is the essence of what we have come to call the realism of the text."[51] Instead of realism acting as a synonym for objectivism (sometimes known as naive realism, often practiced by those who import pseudoscientific claims of certainty into religious domains[52]) critical realism practices the objectification of texts only as a means to read after a certain fashion, purposefully rejecting any appeal to prior meaning to justify interpretative claims. Thus, critical realism is necessarily explained in terms of the social construct of interpretation (readings) and interpreters (readers). The validation of this assertion of critical realism—texts, maybe especially religious texts, refer but refer for the reader—is necessarily established within the social exercise of reading itself.

This can be described through reference to the common characterization that Christians share an orientation with so-called similar religions, namely, Judaism and Islam, because, as the Qur'an asserts, they are "people of the book." This is particularly interesting when we pay attention to and emphasize what it means to be this *people* in relation to *the book*.

Because of an encompassing monotheism—al-Lah is "the God"—the Islamic faith guards and grants religious freedom to Jews and Christians as recognized minority groups *(dhimmis)*.[53] Instead of a simple rejection of Judaism or Christianity as incomplete in themselves, the Qur'an teaches that God sent prophets to every people, with messages for each people, but this is guided by the Islamic premise that "our God and your God is one and the same, and it is unto him that we surrender ourselves."[54] On this basis Islam accounts for the existence of Jews and Christians by means of an Islamic account of al-Lah (simply the one God, and thus the common thrust of monotheism serves as a char-

[51]J. Wentzel van Huyssteen, "The Realism of the Text: A Perspective on Biblical Authority," in *Essays in Postfoundationalist Theology* (Grand Rapids, Mich.: Eerdmans, 1997), pp. 152-53.

[52]Ibid., pp. 42-52, 129-30.

[53]Karen Armstrong, *A History of God: The 4000-Year Quest of Judaism, Christianity and Islam* (New York: Knopf, 1993), pp. 132-69.

[54]Qur'an 29.46, from *The Message of the Qur'an,* trans. Muhammad Asad (London: Dar al-Andalus, 1980).

acteristic of these peoples),[55] the prophets (e.g., Jewish and Christian prophets such as Noah, Abraham, Moses, David and Jesus, along with uniquely Arabian prophets such as Hud, Salih, Shu'ayb and Luqman),[56] the true religion of Abraham (*hanifiyyah,* which existed before the divisive perversions of the message of the prophet Moses [for the Jews] and the prophet Jesus [for the Christians] introduced impious teachings),[57] and the Qur'an (which accounts for Jews and Christians as "people of earlier revelation," not all of which are corrupt).

The charitable attitude toward "people of the book" is tempered with a plea for "true faith" in contrast to some "people of the book," who are unfaithful and hypocritical (Jews who name al-Lah with other names, or polytheists like Christian trinitarians). The warning of the Qur'an is that such people must adhere to the precepts of "the book" according to its true (i.e., Islamic) meaning: "People of the book, go not beyond the bounds in your religion, other than the truth"—that truth being belief in "God and the Prophet and what has been sent down to him."[58] So the Muslim addresses Jews and Christians in this manner: "Be courteous when you argue with the People of the Book, except with those among them who do evil, and say: 'We believe in that which has been revealed to us and which was revealed to you; our Lord and yours is one, to Him we surrender ourselves.' "[59]

On this basis a unified characterization of "people of the book" emphasizes both the unique completeness of the Qur'an as the "whole of the book" (the book or *katib* is the foundation of all Revelation, and it is known as "the Mother of the Book") and the partial notion of revelation ascribed to the Hebrew Scriptures and the New Testament known in the Qur'an as "portions of the Book, being called to the Book of God"[60] (and so "people of the book" in this sense refers to peoples who are attentive to the writings of their religion, especially Jews and Christians).[61] While the Islamic faith emphasizes the

---

[55]"Say: 'People of the Book! Come now to a word common between us and you, that we serve none but God' " (Qur'an 3.57).

[56]For example, of Moses: "The People of the Book will ask thee to bring down upon them a Book from heaven; and they asked Moses for greater than that, for they said, 'Show us God openly.' And the thunderbolt took them for their evildoing. Then they took to themselves the Calf, after the clear signs had come to them; yet We pardoned them that, and We bestowed upon Moses a clear authority" (Qur'an 4.152-53).

[57]"People of the Book! Why do you dispute concerning Abraham? The Torah was not sent down, neither the Gospel, but after him. . . . No; Abraham in truth was not a Jew, neither a Christian; but he was a Muslim and one pure of faith; certainly he was never of the idolaters. Surely the people standing closest to Abraham are those who followed him, and this Prophet, and those who believe; and God is the Protector of the believers" (Qur'an 3.56-62).

[58]Qur'an 5.81, 84.

[59]Qur'an 29.45.

[60]Qur'an 3.22.

[61]Faruq Sherif, *A Guide to the Contents of the Qur'an* (London: Ithaca Press, 1985), pp. 89-90.

former, those characterized by the Qur'an as "people of the book" attend to the later depiction.

Inasmuch as Hebrew writings and the New Testament reflect the One God in principle (al-Lah), they are regarded as true to the "Mother of the Book"; however, the reverse is excluded: "O believers, if you obey a sect of those who have been given the Book, they will turn you, after you have believed, into unbelievers," but "you are the best nation ever brought forth to men . . . believing in God. Had the People of the Book believed, it were better for them; some of them are believers, but the most of them are ungodly."[62] True believers among "people of the book" are those who acknowledge all divine revelations (culminating in the Prophet of Islam).[63] Accounting for the difficulty of seeing or understanding this matter, the Qur'an offers:

> From God nothing whatever is hidden in heaven and earth. It is He who forms you in the womb as He will. There is not god but He, the All-mighty, the All-wise. It is He who sent down upon thee the Book, wherein are verses clear that are the Essence of the Book, and others ambiguous. As for those in whose hearts is swerving, they follow the ambiguous part, desiring dissension, and desiring its interpretation; and none knows its interpretation, save only God. And those firmly rooted in knowledge say, "We believe in it; all is from our Lord"; yet none remembers, but men possessed of minds.[64]

By explicitly addressing the matter of clarity and obscurity and linking such matters with how one faithfully understands as a Muslim (i.e., one who submits to God), the Qur'an asserts that it is "the *people* of the Book" who know, read and hear this message as clear *(mubeen)*. It should not surprise us that the Qur'an teaches its own clarity, nor that such clarity is linked with faithfulness to al-Lah, for Hebrew and Christian texts do the same. Indeed, the Qur'an is itself addressed "for people who understand."[65] We take note that the *book*

---

[62]Qur'an 3.95, 106.

[63]See Sherif, *Guide to the Contents,* p. 90.

[64]Qur'an 3.4-7. On the subject of the Qur'an as a text among Muslims, see Kenneth Cragg, *The Event of the Qur'an: Islam and Its Scripture* (London: Allen & Unwin, 1971); Helmut Gatje, *The Qur'an and Its Exegesis: Selected Texts with Classical and Modern Muslim Interpretations* (Berkeley: University of California Press, 1976); Mahmoud M. Ayoub, *The Qur'an and Its Interpreters,* vol. 1 (Albany: State University of New York Press, 1984); Morris S. Seale, *The Qur'an and Bible: Studies in Interpretation and Dialogue* (London: Croom Helm, 1978).

[65]These matters are addressed along with the increasing interest in interpretative difficulties associated with a (historically critical) study of the Qur'an by Toby Lester, "What Is the Koran?" *The Atlantic Monthly,* January 1999, pp. 43-56. Lester concludes his observations with a telling comparison: "Increasingly diverse interpretations of the Koran and Islamic history will inevitably be proposed in the coming decades, as traditional cultural distinctions East, West, North, and South continue to dissolve, as the population of the Muslim world continues to grow, as early historical sources continue to be scrutinized, and as feminism meets the

and the *people* thereof are inseparable so that according to the Qur'an Jews and Christians who persist in unbelief fail to perceive "the Essence of the Book" and appeal to ambiguous parts relying upon "interpretation" that twists what is clear.

The Qur'an, then, uses the title "people of the book" in both a seemingly neutral as well as negative fashion; negatively to refer to a blasphemous tendency within Judaism to think of Torah as a book descended from heaven, and similarly within Christianity to attend to "the book" instead of Jesus who was "but a messenger of God."[66] In other settings the phrase comes to be associated, in a positive fashion, with rabbinic appreciation of the Torah, and in modern evangelical Protestantism with the appeal to Scripture alone as the sure and certain authority for saving faith and practice. In its development the phrase "people of the book" comes to represent, within Judaism and Christianity, distinct social networks of appealing to and justifying claims from within those social networks.

Interestingly, the Islamic faith describes Jews and Christians in a manner that is not embraced by Jews or Christians because to do so would mean that Jews and Christians would be identified not in their own terms but by means of the Islamic faith. To read Hebrew Scriptures or the New Testament through the Qur'an's phrase "people of the book" is to be read by Islam (to do so, in effect, is to read their Hebrew and Christian writings as Muslims and not as Jews or Christians). So it is observed, "The Qur'anic designation of Jews and Christians as People of the book epitomizes . . . a model which reflects the Muslims' paradigm of reality and their own self-understanding."[67] And while many Christians take the title "people of the book" with pride, even though its origin and use are obviously contrary to any uniquely Christian readership, the appropriation transforms the meaning of that phrase into something so self-evi-

---

Koran. With the diversity of interpretations will surely come increased factiousness, perhaps intensified by the fact that Islam now exists in such a great variety of social and intellectual settings. . . . More than ever before, anybody wishing to understand global affairs will need to understand Islamic civilization, in all its permutations. Surely the best way to start is with the study of the Koran—which promises in the years ahead to be at least as contentious, fascinating, and important as the study of the Bible has been in this century." Study and reflection on the immutable and perspicuous Qur'an, Lester observes, must account for and interact with the shifting cultural settings of Islamic faith, just as assertions of the Christian's immutable and perspicuous Bible have to be understood within the shifting cultural settings of historical and cultural social existence.

[66]Qur'an 4.165-69.

[67]A. H. Mathias Zahniser, "People of the Book or People of the Person? A Christian Model for Witness to Muslims in a Pluralistic World," in *Proceedings of the Wheaton Theology Conference,* vol. 1, *The Challenges of Religious Pluralism: An Evangelical Analysis and Response,* ed. David K. Clark (Wheaton, Ill.: Wheaton College, 1992), pp. 137-38.

dent, so obvious within the Christian use of the Christian texts of Scripture, that one would hardly doubt its appropriateness.

Within the appropriation of the "older" writings as Christian (by blending, co-opting, capturing or inheriting the Hebrew writings) Christians assert purposeful historical as well as theological claims about interpreting these Hebrew writings (we will look further at the use of phrases such as Hebrew Scriptures and Old Testament in chapter two). Likewise, the Qur'an capitalizes on a similar appropriation of the textual traditions as it interprets the significance of Hebrew and Christian writings for the readerly community of the Muslim. The prophets of al-Lah (Moses and Jesus in this case) have faithfully revealed the mother book to Jews and Christians, but its corruption by these peoples explains why the one God is named by names other than al-Lah. For example, Jesus the prophet was sent (only) to the people of Israel with a revelation of God's words, the Gospel *(Injil),* but the revelation of God was distorted by the "Nazarenes" (an expression used in the Qur'an to identify Christians).[68] This is in contrast to Muhammad, who was sent to the entire creation, whose message alone is adequate for all humans and the sole source of reliable revelation. So, "Say: 'People of the Book! Come now to a word common between us and you, that we serve none but God, and that we associate not aught with Him, and do not some of us take others as Lords; apart from God.' And if they turn their backs, say: 'Bear witness that we are Muslims.' "[69] The failure to present the partial revelation is explained in this manner: "And when God took compact with those who had been given the book: 'You shall make it clear unto the people, and not conceal it.' But they rejected it behind their backs and sold it for a small price—how evil was their selling!"[70]

In a more generous sense a commitment to the legacy of "the book"—a term that can be used in a sense much broader than the Qur'an's identification of Jews and Christians—is often noted of religious peoples constituted immediately in relation to their writings. This way of referring to writings can include a literary emphasis (the Bible as literature), an emphasis on original language(s) or even an emphasis on literacy itself. In each of these broader uses of "the book" there is attention given to an explicit framework within which we learn (i.e., are instructed) not only in how we came to associate our identity with the

---

[68]Zahniser, "People," p. 140. "Nazarenes" is used fourteen times, while the phrase "people of the book" is used more than thirty times (the later phrase often refers to both Jews and Christians). The seeming imprecision of the Qur'an's reference to Christians is actually a subject of considerable interest in light of its apparent divine praise of Christians; see Jane Dammen McAuliffe, *Qur'anic Christians: An Analysis of Classical and Modern Exegesis* (New York: Cambridge University Press, 1991).

[69]Qur'an 3.57.

[70]Qur'an 3.184.

book but that our identity is founded in a unitive fashion in the book.[71] It literally explains how things can appear clear to a community of readers while the same "book" is obscure, closed or of another meaning to other communities of readers. Therefore, instead of uniting Jews, Christians and Muslims (as the Qur'an supposes in its essentially supercessionist representation of Judaism and Christianity), to be a "people of the book" points to our essential and irreconcilable divide. What is clear to the Muslim is predicated upon the Islamic reading of the texts of Jews and the texts of Christians; just as what is clear to Christian or Jewish readers is the Christian or Jewish resistance to being read by Islam.

Conclusion

The path we have traversed thus far begins to unfold an involved story of struggle and confidence—the confidence sometimes misplaced, often simplified, but nonetheless a part of what it has meant for Christians in recent years to speak of Scripture's clarity. We have just begun to see how we might utter, with a confidence corresponding to its words, the text of Deuteronomy 30:14: "The word is very near you, it is in your mouth and in your heart so you may obey it." Anything less is to miss what God has for us as readers of Scripture. So while dissatisfied with being led astray by turning to historical, authorial and methodological characterizations of how Scripture might be thought of as clear (the threefold concern), we turned to a threefold contention for Scripture's realistic sociality. It matters how we see text, reading and reader united—this union being described by means of Scripture's clarity. So we are concerned with Scripture's generation, reception and reputation as a matter of orientation, and we are constructively interested in how these matters represent the particular Christian interest in text, reading and readers.

To begin the examination of what it means for Christians to assert Scripture's clarity with this tangled and often-pessimistic rehearsal of how the idea has been promoted in recent years might lead us to reject the plausibility of affirming the clarity of Scripture altogether. Many observers of Christian interpretative practices have done just that—rejecting the idea as pure fantasy, simplistic and unrealistic. But a rehearsal of the story of Christian interpretative practices as they influence, address or depend upon the thought that Scripture is clear yields another lesson for us. We join dissenters in rejecting an idea of simplicity (historical, objectivistic or scientific) in favor of a threefold contention regarding an interplay of Scripture's texture, its reading and its readers.

In the next four chapters I turn to the Christian practices of interpretation

---

[71]Barr, *Holy Scripture,* pp. 1-2.

used to advance the notion of Scripture's clarity. This will yield a much more positive portrait of what it means to be Christians who are a people of the book, so to speak. How and why Christians have appealed to Scripture's clarity to describe what Christians see when they read the Bible is to be discovered in the emergence of the Christian interpretative tradition, in its sometimes contentious articulation as well as in its unique formation as a distinctly Christian practice for regarding the text called God's Word.

2

CHRISTIANLY CLEAR

"Oh, how foolish you are, and how slow of heart to believe all that the prophets have declared!" . . . Then beginning with Moses and all the prophets, he interpreted to them the things about himself in all the scriptures.

LUKE 24:25, 27 (NRSV)

And when the Bridegroom comes, he who has his lamp untrimmed, and not burning with the brightness of a steady light, is classed among those who obscure the interpretations of the parables, forsaking him who by his plain announcements freely imparts gifts to all who come to him, and is excluded from his marriage-chamber.

IRENAEUS OF LYONS, *AGAINST HERESIES*

WHERE DOES THE BELIEF THAT SCRIPTURE IS CLEAR COME FROM? IT comes from the union of Scripture read by Christians after a certain (that is, Christian) fashion; this seems to be the most common explanation within earliest Christianity. The focus moves from Scripture to Christian reading because the text is said to be clear, not from something separable or beyond Scripture back toward the text in order to clarify. In large part this movement is defended inasmuch as Christians wish to say that Scripture's clarity is not forced upon or used as an excuse to disguise obscurity. And this type of response certainly seems to fit the subject matter. That is, if Scripture is clear, it would be appropriate to demonstrate as much from Scripture (and as such it is characteristically argumentative in nature). This approach also tends to be pragmatic and deliberate: Scripture gives every indication that it is to be taken *as* clear.

The clarity of the text's meaning is not simply "in" the text apart from how the Scripture is treated but has to do with how we read Scripture as Christians. This is particularly evident within the earliest Christian readings of Scripture in that the reading of Scripture (that is, the Jewish writings) is arguably so closely associated with the text that it is often indistinguishable from the text of Scripture itself. Therefore, while functioning objectively within uniquely Christian frameworks and experiences, the textual assertion is also open to change or development, verification and falsification (it can never be demonstrated on a basis acceptable beyond uniquely Christian frameworks and experiences, but we can be made to see how it is a reasonable, justifiable judgment for Christians to make). Irenaeus serves as fitting example of this emphasis, as does Tertullian, especially in the effort to interpret Scripture textually in order to understand it spiritually.

Another type of response to the question of where belief in Scripture's clarity comes from is concerned with larger suppositions, taking a step back and offering the grounds to believe. This response is philosophical in nature, emphasizing ontological and metaphysical grounds (how it is possible to say something like Scripture is clear). On occasion this type of response tends to emphasize the nature of language itself. The primary characteristic of this response is positional (the premises cannot be tested), and the primary declaration is that Scripture *is* clear (at least the part of it Christians take as primary, namely the New Testament, and secondarily through this perspective, the Old Testament). The assertion follows the reasoning that ultimately, because Scripture is taken as God's word, and God would not deceive (i.e., God would not intentionally obscure his own message because this would be contrary to God's nature), we must say Scripture is clear. Clement and Origen are good examples of this type of position—interpreting Scripture spiritually in order to understand it truthfully—and their influence is felt well into the medieval church. Interestingly, this assertion grows in popularity as the formal nature of Christian theology grows in prominence.

In either type of response (though I prefer the former to the latter), the affirmation of Scripture's clarity is a matter of justifying that confession. The claim that Scripture is clear should be testable; it should be verifiable. What we seek is to offer a responsible judgment of clarity's significance by means of its history (the experience of Scripture as clear) as well as its historical significance (the experiential utility of Scripture's clarity). Supporting such claims requires that we recognize what may be called the context of justification—the setting and frameworks of knowing and experiencing that delineate the privileged Christian reading of Scripture. The text of Scripture and the reading community (Christians) are thus united by this context of justification.

Describing the context of justification begins by addressing the question of where confidence in Scripture's clarity comes from and leads us to consider how we might maintain such a claim in our circumstances. But it is not merely a matter of sources—historical or traditional, textual or authorial, theological or ecclesiastical. Instead, this is a matter of identity: Christians are those who affirm that Scripture is sufficiently clear so as to be understood (by *understood* we mean sufficiently clear for us to be *Christians*). Thus, the formation of Christian interpretative frameworks is the justification for Christian readings of Scripture as clear. In this chapter I offer an example of the type of textual argumentation, alongside a religious history of Christian readings of Scripture, that seeks to offer a justification for the working premise that Scripture can be taken as clear within the Christian faith. To say Scripture is clear is to say, in part, what it means for a Christian to read Scripture Christianly.

The Formation of Christian Interpretative Frameworks

To be Christian is to affirm that *our* readings of *our* writings are appropriate, that they elicit perception and faith, and that they are clear. This is demonstrated within our understanding of Christian writings themselves. The struggle to represent our reading as the appropriate, that is, the obvious reading is a reoccurring theme within the formation of Christian Scriptures (the New Testament), from "you have heard that it was said . . . but I tell you" (Mt 5:21-22), to "these things happened so that the scriptures would be fulfilled" (Jn 19:36); from "this is what was spoken" (Acts 2:16), to "as it is written" (Rom 11:26). How one advances this demonstration to Christian perception and faith is our present concern—its formation, comparison and contrast with other ways of reading and regarding what Christians call their Scripture.[1] Of particular interest is the nature of the (developing) relationship between what some refer to as the first and second or older and newer testaments.[2]

The story of Christianity's origins and sources is actually quite strange when told through the eyes of historical scholarship—strange to those who think of Christianity as atypical, pure and simple. However, this is not just a description of how it was or how it happened. This is an instance of argumentation in the form of a historical characterization of how Christians brought together Scripture and Christian identity. The formation and consequential union of Christian identity and Christian interpretative practices takes place within a concrete (that is, historical) setting that greatly contributes to its character. We can look to one of the most respected classical historical scholars of primitive Christian literature for this story or Christianity and its relationships to its setting in antiquity.[3]

In his Society of Biblical Literature presidential address Hans Dieter Betz

---

[1]For a good summary and argument of these matters, consult John Goldingay, *Models for Scripture* (Grand Rapids, Mich.: Eerdmans, 1994), pp. 85-116, 151-67.

[2]Ibid.

[3]The address by Betz is essentially a rehearsal of his own work on the subject of antiquity and Christianity, with two dozen footnotes referring to his works on supporting subjects (Hans Dieter Betz, "Antiquity and Christianity," *Journal of Biblical Literature* 117, no. 1 [1998]: 3-22).

reminds us that the concepts of "antiquity and Christianity" are heuristic in nature: each "designates the contentious relationship between the culture of antiquity and the emerging Christianity." He contends Christianity arose within the conflicting relationship of Judaism, although the "actual circumstances [of such conflicts] are mostly inaccessible to the historian."[4] From extant sources (i.e., later Christian writings) we are able to affirm that Christianity began with two Jews—John the Baptist and Jesus of Nazareth. And it concerned the "integrity of obedience toward the will of God as revealed in the Torah," which was a challenge to the continuing influence of Hellenistic culture and the question of how God's kingdom might be exhibited while under Roman occupation. This, as Betz acknowledges, was a Jewish problem, both chronologically and theoretically because "Christianity as an identifiable entity did not yet exist."[5] John the Baptist and Jesus of Nazareth offered an alternative characterization of Jewish Scripture to confront their circumstances and to justify their claims to authority, each man's life ending with a violent death directly attributable to his confrontational message.

Christianity comes into existence with Jesus Christ, who carries on the message of John the Baptist, who had carried on dissension from Hellenism and its influences upon Judaism.[6] And the troubling status of Jesus' identity after his death (i.e., resurrection and appearances to disciples in bodily form) directly confront both "Hellenistic-Jewish and Greco-Roman religious concepts regarding postmortem existence."[7] How should these subjects be interpreted, and by what means? Ironically, the uniquely Christian depiction of Jesus as resurrected is a reinterpretation of an older Jewish eschatology of bodily resurrection, a foretaste of a general resurrection in which Jesus is enthroned in heaven as "son of God" and Lord.[8]

What transpires next is the sometimes-conflicting missions of Paul and his

---

[4]Ibid., p. 6. Antiquity is taken as the larger cultural setting, including Hellenism with its various potential influences upon the formation of the unique entity called Christianity. The confrontation between these mutually influencing and influenced forces lead to phases of cultural renewal and transformation, according to Betz.

[5]Ibid., pp. 7-8.

[6]Jesus' disputes with his circumstances, while clearly concerned with the influence of Hellenism, are portrayed in Christian literature as disputes with the Jewish leadership (creating the impression that Jesus was opposed to Judaism and implicitly fond of Hellenism). Jesus' direct and unambiguous denunciations of Jewish leadership are regarded as a denial of Judaism's claim to its own Scriptures; the failure to understand their clarity by means of Christian Scripture is regarded as a signal of spiritual disobedience. One unfortunate result is the growing tendency among Christian theologians to engage in an anti-Semitic polemic, in part, to help sustain their claims to privilege.

[7]Betz, "Antiquity and Christianity," pp. 8-9.

[8]Ibid., p. 9.

company (often in contrast to those surrounding Peter [Gal 1—2], the Jewish parties reforming the missionary-evangelistic work of both Paul and Peter [Gal 3—4], and the growing opposition to Christianity as a sect of Judaism of which Saul was once a prominent member [Acts 4—12]). What results are various forms of Christianity (i.e., Jewish Christianity and probably a Jewish-Christian reform Judaism [the "Israel of God"? Gal 6:16], Gentile Christianity, as well as geographic, ethnically and socially differentiated forms of Christianity). There is no return to Judaism, even the Judaism of Jesus, available to Christianity. There is only the reinterpretation of present and diverse religious and cultural circumstances in the name of Jesus. For example, Gentile Christians "remained culturally Greco-Roman, but ceased religiously being pagan polytheists." This required "the development of a new religious and cultural identity, including theological doctrines, rituals, and codes of behavior and ethics, which would establish and maintain their special place in the ancient world as a corporate entity."[9]

Missions, whether predominantly Jewish or Greco-Roman, were both "culture-specific" and operating under the perspective that they were each part of the one salvation of the world, according to Betz. A prime example of this is evidenced in the varied, sometimes conflicting, writings known as the Gospels.[10] The biographical rendering of Jesus' identity in each Gospel directly confronts the ongoing struggle to realize a uniquely Christian identity, without glossing over or converting diverse religious and cultural struggles that differentiate the emphases of each Gospel.

Betz makes two important points in the course of his survey of antiquity and Christianity that concern our interest in the formation of Christian interpretative frameworks. First, even though Jesus was definitely (and only) a Jew (by birth, character and message), what comes to be known as Christianity is inseparable from his identity: "The *Ursprung* was Jesus himself, his *persona*, not anything detachable from him."[11] Christianity is Jesus; nothing else, less or more important than the identity of Jesus. Interpreted otherwise, Christianity is not Christian (thus while there can be a Jesus without Christianity, there cannot be a Christianity without Jesus).

Second, stemming from the Jewish-Christian council in Jerusalem (according to Acts 15 and Gal 2:1-10), Gentile Christianity as a unique social, religious entity was recognized as both a continuation of Jewish-Christian mission and yet not a part of Judaism: "The decision of the majority was that the Christian

[9]Ibid., p. 10.
[10]Hans Dieter Betz, "Jesus and the Purity of the Temple (Mark 11:15-18): A Comparative Religion Approach," *Journal of Biblical Literature* 116, no. 3 (1997): 455-72.
[11]Betz, "Antiquity and Christianity," p. 8.

converts of the Pauline mission would constitute a new entity that was on the one hand a secondary extension of the Jewish-Christian mission to the Jews, while on the other hand not a part of the Jewish religion."[12] Christianity is not Judaism, not a successor to Judaism; yet the identity of Christianity cannot be told without telling the story of Judaism (both in regard to Jesus' Judaism as well as the Judaism confronting and relating to the fledgling movement known as Christian [Acts 11:19-30]).

The formation of *Christian* texts, like the formation of uniquely *Christian* attitudes toward dominant culture and religions, is a much larger story, and admittedly we are jumping into the story of Christian interpretative interests midstream.[13] However, I offer the summary of Betz for this reason: a uniquely Christian interpretative framework is difficult to establish apart from a textual argument inasmuch as there is no independent access to the origins, events and settings portrayed by the Christian writings. For Betz this is a historical problem, for us it prompts a positive response, maybe even a beneficial theological assertion.[14] What we do have are the (Christian) writings that are explicit in articulating the two themes noted: Jesus' identity in relation to Christianity, and Christianity's identity in relation to Jewish and Greco-Roman religion. Each "phase," to use Betz's term, in Christianity's subsequent development, from the company of Jesus' followers, to its formative writings, to its response to persecution and (mis-)understanding, is explicitly concerned with interpretative legitimacy or justifications for holding to the Christian faith as unique.

Christianity's identity is articulated as an alternative interpretation of Jewish religious writings, an interaction with, appraisal and adaptation of Greco-Roman religion, and a fledgling new movement justified by its claims to be a witness to the eschatologically justified revelation of God to the world. That leads us to question how one can characterize the relationship of Christian identity and its Scriptures with phrases such as clarity and ostensiveness. This is complicated

---

[12]Ibid., p. 10.

[13]Matters that contribute to the argument about the formation of a Christian interpretative framework, such as the Christian canon, are as theologically important as they are historically vague. For an introduction to the discussion concerning the significance of canon for the interpretation of Scripture, consult F. F. Bruce, *The Canon of Scripture* (Downers Grove, Ill.: InterVarsity Press, 1988); Moshe Halbertal, *People of the Book: Canon, Meaning, and Authority* (Cambridge, Mass.: Harvard University Press, 1997); Joseph T. Lienhard, *The Bible, the Church, and Authority: The Canon of the Christian Bible in History and Theology* (Wilmington, Del.: Michael Glazier, 1995); K. Lawson Younger, William W. Hallo and Bernard F. Batto, eds., *The Biblical Canon in Comparative Perspective* (New York: Edwin Mellen, 1991).

[14]So Betz offers, "How matters developed after Jesus' death is to a large degree obscured by the lack of unbiased source material" (Betz, "Antiquity and Christianity," pp. 8-9).

by one of the most common theological fallacies in the history of Christianity that has to do with the supposition that primitive Christianity was a simple unity, with all forms of dissension and differentiation receiving severe criticism and censure (e.g., how many understand the "party spirit" in 1 Cor 1:10-17 to exclude all forms of diversity rather than censuring the exclusivity of one party above others). This characterization might be termed a fallacy of primitive simplicity (with one, single Christianity existing ideally in and after the first generation of Jesus' followers and correspondingly one simple interpretative formula that regulates thought and practice).[15] A religious history of primitive Christianity yields a different portrait: its writings are argumentative, the movement itself is struggling with its identity (along with its personalities) both within and without, and Christian identity is comprised of rather diverse, sociocultural existence operating with an assumption of a conventional religious experience.

Thus, instead of appealing to a uniformly defined and simple formula of Christian identity (which would authorize how Christians regard their own efforts to interpret Christian texts), we are left with a diverse and developing, loosely defined movement with a correspondingly diverse gathering of texts. Affirming a simple notion of the clarity of its own writings and its own interpretation of its writings is historically complicated and theoretically doubtful, especially as Christians routinely affirm that it is the Jewish Scriptures that give credence and orientation to their own writings. All of this is to say that a notion of Scripture's clarity does not depend on—indeed it cannot depend on—a strictly historical justification for perspicuity. Nor does it depend on a simplistic characterization of primitive Christianity. Instead, it must be justified by observing a textually oriented awareness of a *Christian* interpretative framework.

Christian Interpretative Interests

Three factors contribute to what we may term an interpretative framework operative within primitive Christianity. They function as ingredients that help us understand how Christian identity is linked with Christian reading of Scripture. They do not ignore the complicated and genuinely diverse character of primitive Christianity and yet make room for a notion of clarity associated with

---

[15]Religious primitivism appears in various forms within Christian traditions (historical, cultural, social and even economic), and in the hands of some it is the chief characteristics of a movement identity. See Michael Bell, *Primitivism* (London: Methuen, 1972); Mircea Eliade, *Myths, Dreams, and Mysteries: The Encounter Between Contemporary Faiths and Archaic Realities*, trans. Philip Mariet (New York: Harper, 1960); and Arthur O. Lovejoy and George Boas, *Primitivism and Related Ideas in Antiquity* (Baltimore: Johns Hopkins Press, 1935).

a Christian interpretative premise. The three factors are a developing authority of Christian writings identified with Jesus' continuing authority, a recognition of a distinct Christian interpretive understanding used to reinterpret Jewish Scriptures and (the result) a reinterpretation of Jesus' Scriptures.

First, within the developing and diverse setting of primitive Christianity there is a growing association of Christianity's source (Jesus Christ and the message inseparable from Jesus' identity known as the gospel) and Christianity's sources (Christian writings, Gospels, letters). The progression of authorizing teaching, from "the Lord Jesus said" to "the Lord in his Gospel" to simply "the Gospel" or "the writings" or "Scripture says," depicts a positive association of Jesus' authorizing identity and the Christian writings (both about Jesus as well as about Christian identity). That such statements within Christian Scriptures are contemporaneous one with another effectively eliminates chronological or literalistic characterizations of historicity and brings together under the umbrella of the common writings a conventional manner of representing Christian identity. This is evident in appeals to the sayings or teachings of Jesus in other Christian Scripture (e.g., Acts 20:35; 1 Thess 4:15; 1 Cor 7:10, 12, 25; 9:14; 1 Tim 5:18 [combining Deut 25:4 with Lk 10:7]; cp. 2 Cor 11:17). This pattern is also very much evident in earliest Christian writings with appeals to "remember the words of the Lord Jesus" (1 Clement 13:1-2; 46:7-8), "pray as the Lord commanded in his gospel" (Didache 8:2; 15:4; cp. 9:5; Polycarp, *To the Philippians* 2:3; 2 Clement 5:2; 8:5), combined with appeals simply to "the gospel" (Didache 11:3; 15:3). That is, the pattern of associating Jesus' authorization with Christian writings continues well into the second century of Christian existence.

Because of the authorizing agency of Jesus' identity, not accessible apart from the means of Christian biographical and apostolic texts (i.e., authorizing and authorized assertions of Christian identification), we are lead to affirm that congruity with Christ is congruity with Christian writings (how this is the case, we will see shortly). The relationship between Jesus' identity and orienting disposition within Christian writings is portrayed in terms of both authority and clarification: authorizing characterizations of Christian instruction by constituting them as Jesus' teaching and clarifying the function of Christian instruction in association with Jesus' identity. The relevance of Jesus Christ for Christian existence is supported by an admission of compatibility (the concrete identity of Jesus Christ) and continuity (a textually justified assertion of coherence between Jesus Christ and our existence as Christians).[16]

[16]On the subject of Christian identity and the imitation of Christ, see Richard B. Hays, *The Moral Vision of the New Testament* (San Francisco: HarperCollins, 1996), pp. 159-61; R. E. O. White, *Christian Ethics* (Atlanta: John Knox Press, 1981); and James M. Gustafson, *Christ and the Moral Life* (New York: Harper & Row, 1968).

Second, Christian texts display a recognition of a distinct Christian interpretive understanding used to reinterpret Jewish writings. The book of Acts offers a persistent argument that this reinterpretation of Jewish writings justifies what is transpiring within the fledgling movement known as Christianity. Peter's sermon on Pentecost argues, "Fellow Jews and all of you who live in Jerusalem, let me explain this to you; listen carefully to what I say. . . . This is what was spoken by the prophet Joel" (Acts 2:14, 16). The eschatological judgment articulated in Joel is understood to justify what had occurred to Jesus' disciples (the presence of tongues of fire and speech in other tongues by means of the Spirit [Acts 2:1-2]). In addition, Davidic psalms (Psalm 16:8-11; 110:1) are interpreted not to reference David but Jesus of Nazareth (Acts 2:24-36).[17]

This reinterpretation of the Jewish writings, as if they depicted with utter clarity Christian claims about Jesus of Nazareth, is difficult to justify on historical grounds. Think of the episode of Philip's Spirit-led confrontation with the traveling Ethiopian official, a God fearer (thus open to instruction from Philip, a Jew). This episode undoubtedly concerns the interpretative interests of reading the writings with an interest in understanding the identity of Jesus:

> This man had gone to Jerusalem to worship, and on his way home was sitting in his chariot reading the book of Isaiah the prophet. The Spirit told Philip, "Go to that chariot and stay near it." Then Philip ran up to the chariot and heard the man reading Isaiah the prophet. "Do you understand what you are reading?" Philip asked. "How can I," he said, "unless someone explains it to me?" So he invited Philip to come up and sit with him. The eunuch was reading this passage of Scripture: "He was led like a sheep to the slaughter, and as a lamb before the shearer is silent, so he did not open his mouth. In his humiliation he was deprived of justice. Who can speak of his descendants? For his life was taken from the earth." The eunuch asked Philip, "Tell me, please, who is the prophet talking about, himself or someone else?" Then Philip began with that very passage of Scripture and told him the good news about Jesus. (Acts 8:27-35)

Attention to what is not obviously there, in Isaiah, in Scripture, is precisely

[17]Stephen's speech before the Sanhedrin, in response to the charges that he uttered "blasphemy against Moses and against God" (Acts 6:11) argued "that this Jesus of Nazareth will destroy this place and change the customs of Moses handed down to us" (Acts 6:11, 14), offers a christological reinterpretation of the land, the law and the temple (Acts 7:1-50), which incriminated "you stiff-necked people, with uncircumcised hearts and ears" (Acts 7:51). They failed to understand the significance of the "Righteous One" because of their failure to interpret (read) the writings' characterization of land, law and temple in relation to this prophet, Jesus of Nazareth (Acts 7:52-53). Richard Longenecker's comments on this section of Acts are particularly helpful; see his "Acts of the Apostles," in *The Expositor's Bible Commentary,* ed. Frank E. Gaebelein (Grand Rapids, Mich.: Zondervan, 1981), pp. 333-54; and consult Richard N. Longnecker, *Biblical Exegesis in the Apostolic Period* (Grand Rapids, Mich.: Eerdmans, 1975).

Philip's purpose in confronting the official's desire to understand whom this text is about. There is simply no evidence of a suffering Messiah in pre-Christian Judaism, nor is there evidence in "the whole Jewish Messianic literature."[18] So when Philip suggests the convergence of this figure in Isaiah with the crucified Jesus, he displays not only an interpretative twist completely unacceptable within Judaism but also one that Christians (universally) accept as obvious. As Christians of succeeding generations read similar texts (the book of Isaiah like the Ethiopian, or Davidic psalms as Peter did) and believe that such texts are clearly and directly speaking about Jesus Christ, they are reading in continuity with the primitive Christian practice and regard their readings as the ostensive (Christian) meaning attributed to such texts.[19]

Third, authorizing this display of a distinct, Christian, interpretive understanding, when united with the agency of Jesus' identity, leads us to examine the reinterpretation of Jesus' Scripture. As has been said, primitive Christianity regarded Jesus as both the exegete and the exegesis of Scripture.[20] By this we point to the practices of the Gospels in their representation of Jesus' narrated identity in relation to the appeal to "Scripture" and "the writings." The life of Christ itself can be termed "a fulfillment" (e.g., Mt 1:22; Lk 4:16-21; with Is 61:1-2). But a fulfillment of what, and how does one see that clearly and as clear? The life Jesus lived, as represented in the Gospels, would be meaningless, lack reference and motivation without the fulfilling orientation of his life. This is Jesus' assertion in the final chapter of Luke. To the two traveling disciples informed but confused about the events surrounding Jesus' death and reportedly empty tomb, Jesus berated them:

> He said to them, "How foolish you are, and how slow of heart to believe all that the prophets have spoken! Did not the Christ have to suffer these things and then enter his glory?" And beginning with Moses and all the prophets, he explained to

---

[18]Joseph Klausner, *The Messianic Idea in Israel,* trans. W. F. Stinespring (New York: Macmillan, 1955), p. 405; also see W. D. Davies, *Paul and Rabbinic Judaism* (London: SPCK, 1955).

[19]Interestingly, each of these episodes explains how initial Christian interests are misrepresented or obscured: "They have had too much wine," and "members from the Synagogue of the Freedmen (as it was called) . . . produced false witnesses"; even the Ethiopian's question to Stephen supposes some initial obscurity: "How can I [understand] unless someone explains it to me?" In the case of Stephen, while his accusers argue that he is speaking against Moses and God, the accusers are represented as "false witnesses." But Stephen certainly was speaking against Moses and God according to the group assembled against him, for they understood and read texts that spoke about the land, the law and the temple as justifying their defense of Judaism against the followers of Jesus of Nazareth.

[20]Attributable to Henri de Lubac; for support consult his *Medieval Exegesis,* vol. 1, *The Four Senses of Scripture,* trans. Mark Sebanc (Grand Rapids, Mich.: Eerdmans, 1998), pp. 234-41. His source for the dual notions of instructor and instruction are most directly discussed by Clement of Alexandria in *The Instructor* (see the following section for Clement's argument).

them what was said in all the Scriptures concerning himself. (Lk 24:25-27)

This explanation is offered in a pejorative tone, not because the disciples necessarily lacked information about Jesus but because they did not perceive the convergence of Jesus' affirmations regarding his identity (prior to the crucifixion) predicated upon the Scriptures.[21] This pejorative tone extends well into the history of Christian interpretation with Scripture's supposed obscurity regarded both as a spiritual problem of religious and moral dimensions and as a problem of studious attentiveness and comprehension of textual significance. The representation "all the Scriptures," coupled with the emphatic pronoun "himself," leaves little room for doubt that this reinterpretation in the hands of Jesus is itself offered as simply the interpretation of the Jewish writings. As in the confrontation of Philip and the traveling Ethiopian, Jesus confronts the traveling disciples with what is, for these Christian representations, the clear, obvious interpretation of "all the Scriptures."

Primitive Christians revered and read the Jewish writings in light of their commitments to Jesus—to the extent that they represented what the Jewish writings said with what it would mean to understand the identity of Jesus of Nazareth. Indeed, there was no discernable difference between the writings and the Christian interpretation in primitive Christian literature. And it was this argument that was used to justify Christian interpretative practices, even though Christians were very aware that there were other, multiple ways of understanding the same texts. Thus, the composition of literature known specifically as Christian permanently assembled and transformed the manner in which Jesus' followers regarded their own and Jesus' own Scripture. This transformation is the decisive factor in our ability to articulate what it is that constitutes Christian identity (as distinct from the varieties of religious experience found in Judaism and Greco-Roman religions). And it is this literature's representation of interpretation that prompts us to offer a textual justification of Scripture's clarity, especially as we observe the development of these themes in the first centuries of Christian interpretation.

Rereading Scripture

When Christians read texts as Scripture that were not written to, for or about Christians as Christian texts, they simultaneously perform a subversive and constitutive activity. Any reading, translation or rewriting tends to subvert the

---

[21]Particularly helpful on the topic of the interpretation of Scripture in the Gospel of Luke are the works of R. J. Dillon, *From Eyewitnesses to Ministers of the Word* (Rome: Biblical Institute Press, 1978); and Charles H. Talbert, *Literary Patterns, Theological Themes, and the Genre of Luke-Acts* (Missoula, Mont.: Scholars, 1977).

privilege those writings afford the people constituted by those writings; in this case, Jewish writings written to, for and about Jews, while *re*-reading the texts of Judaism with a concerted effort and expectation to ascertain the identity of Jesus and their own identity functions as the primary constituting activity of Christian identity. This eventually led to the routine distinctions of Old and New Testaments—a development not without its troubles.

The phrases and concepts of two discernable books or canons, the Old and New Testaments, is of later Christian reckoning (in what we refer to as the New Testament the Jewish writings are simply and specifically referred to as "the Scriptures," "Moses and the prophets," "it is written" or designated by the names of the books, "Isaiah the prophet," but not as a dissimilar collection [dissimilar from Christian writings]). I agree with the summary of James McEvoy:

> The Christian writers who followed those first generations would gradually be placed in a position where two series of sacred, canonical books could be compared with one another, as the Old Testament and the New Testament, but this opposition of strict correlatives had no meaning in that earliest time, when the spiritual sense of Scripture could not possibly mean an older text interpreted in the light of a newer one.[22]

The convergence of the apostolic witness to Jesus' life, death and resurrection and the sacred writings was, instead, read as a unitive spiritual promise: "Read in that way, the Apostles and evangelists found that the Bible made complete sense, as it never had done to them beforehand." McEvoy continues:

> Christian use of the Bible . . . is neither a reactualization of the sacred texts nor an extension of the unvarying, original meaning identically into the present circumstances; it rather takes the form of a constant reference to the authoritative text in order to deepen understanding of the recent events surrounding Jesus. Christian use of the Bible was led by what had then so recently happened, the events which filled the minds of believers to the point of excluding all else,—save, indeed, the Sacred books that could, and did, offer altogether indispensable help towards building the edifice of that understanding. The specifically Christian use of Bible did not aim at extending the Torah to circumstances unforeseen or acts not already explicitly covered by it; it did not aim to recall past events in order to grasp their present importance for life under God and in hope.[23]

How that happens with Justin (110-165), as for many early theologians, is that "what the prophets said and did they veiled by parables and types . . . so

[22]James McEvoy, "The Patristic Hermeneutics of Spiritual Freedom and Its Biblical Origins," in *Scriptural Interpretation in the Fathers: Letter and Spirit,* ed. Thomas Finan and Vincent Twomey (Cambridge: Four Courts, 1995), p. 5.
[23]Ibid., p. 6.

that it was not easy for all to understand the most since they concealed the truth by these means, that those who are eager to find out and learn it might do so with much labor."[24] Christian interpretation read the books of Judaism but intended Jesus Christ; the text is unaltered as text but read as Christian and read as fulfillment of God's promise written therein. One might say, to Christians the reading is differentiated but not disparate regarding (Jewish) Scripture.

The development of assertions of *old* and *new* are linked with the primitive Christian practices regarding the unity of interpretation and identity, both Christ's and Christians'. So Tertullian submits Christ "casting light, as he always did, upon ancient prophecies," while Justin offers that Jesus is "the interpreter of prophecies that are not understood."[25] Clarity is found in christology; that is to say, by means of the Christian assertions about the identity of Jesus Christ, established by means of the relationship of old (Jewish) and new (Christian) writings. Clement of Alexandria maintained that Christ is the Instructor, "With the greatest clearness, accordingly, the Word has spoken respecting himself by Hosea, 'I am your Instructor.' "[26] The forceful assertions within the new (i.e., Christian) writings regarding the reinterpretation of the established (i.e., Jewish) writings are carried on in Christian interpretation as a practical necessity.

There is probably no theme within Christian interpretation that draws us so directly into the discussion of Scripture's clarity than this concept of two discernibly differentiated anthologies, testaments, covenants or dispensations. Yet it is the assertion of unity, that there is really (spiritually) only one book, which explains how Christians argue for a sense of Scripture's clarity. The New is considered to be new not due to time but timeliness; it is second in time but new in the sense that it is definitive, always new and properly always enlightening our understanding of past and future.[27] The Old is renewed, made relevant and applicable, made spiritual and clarified by the New; so Origen: "The shadows came first and the truth followed."[28]

There is also a swift movement from fulfillment to harmony in Christian

---

[24]Justin Martyr, *Dialogue with Trypho,* The Ante-Nicene Fathers, ed. Alexander Roberts and James Donaldson (Grand Rapids, Mich.: Eerdmans, 1988), 1:244-45.

[25]Tertullian, *The Five Books Against Marcion,* The Ante-Nicene Fathers, ed. Alexander Roberts and James Donaldson (Grand Rapids, Mich.: Eerdmans, 1988), 3:418; Justin Martyr, *The First Apology of Justin,* Ante-Nicene Fathers, 1:173; Jesus "interpreted the prophecies which were not yet understood."

[26]Clement of Alexandria, *The Instructor,* The Ante-Nicene Fathers, ed. Alexander Roberts and James Donaldson (Grand Rapids, Mich.: Eerdmans, 1988), 2:222-23.

[27]So de Lubac characterizes second-century concern with the construct of the two successive testaments; see *Medieval Exegesis,* pp. 226-28.

[28]Cited in ibid., p. 429 n. 92.

interpretation of Jewish Scripture, a move that is disturbing in its argument but understandable in its focus in that Christians wish to assert the continuity of the testaments. Almost every Christian interpreter argues forcefully that Christian identity supplants Israel's spiritual identity: the church is the new or spiritual Israel and is the true meaning of Israel's Scripture, God's chosen people. Justin's dialogue with the rabbi Trypho (d. 134?) undertakes a strenuous denunciation of the Jews' privilege to their own Scriptures: "For the true spiritual Israel, and descendants of Judah, Jacob, Isaac, and Abraham . . . are we who have been led to God through this crucified Christ."[29] The extent to which this argument is carried illustrates the forcefulness of argumentation regarding meaning and clarity. The promise of Christ is "contained in your scriptures, or rather not yours but ours. For we believe them; but you, though you read them, do not catch the spirit that is in them."[30] As one historian put Justin's argument, the church supplanted the synagogue in its relationship to Scripture and the Synagogue, "which has become blind and sterile, is merely her librarian."[31]

Justin often goes beyond the specific instances of fulfilled prophecy found within New Testament itself in his discussion of Jesus as the historical fulfillment of Old Testament prophecies (indeed, even Justin's notion of what constitutes a prophecy seems to expand proportionately with his ability to locate veiled instances that he sees as applicable to the gospel's depiction of Jesus' identity). According to Justin, Isaiah 33:16 is applied to Jesus' birth ("their refuge will be the fortresses of rocks" [NRSV], taken as an allusion to Jesus' birthplace). Such identifications of Jesus with Jewish Scriptures, for Justin, demonstrate the clarity and clarifying of the Christian position.[32]

This kind of appropriation is specifically characterized as a transformation, a conversion within the second and third centuries. Although the names (Moses, David, etc.) do not change, Origen maintains "there is a transformation of the way in which these things are understood."[33] This conversion takes up the author's original writing, the text's historical reference and reception, and gives it a new intent, a new use—events become types with new significance: the exodus, travel from Egypt to crossing the Jordan river, the conquest of the Promised Land, the Passover and feast days, even the regulations regarding diet, hygiene and clothing are useful. Israel's scriptural history serves as a key by which the

---

[29]Justin, *Dialogue with Trypho,* p. 200.

[30]Ibid., p. 209.

[31]de Lubac, *Medieval Exegesis,* p. 242.

[32]Justin, *Dialogue with Trypho,* pp. 237-38: "Moreover, these Scriptures are equally explicit in saying, that those who are reputed to know the writings of the Scriptures, and who hear the prophecies, have no understanding."

[33]Cited in de Lubac, *Medieval Exegesis,* p. 229.

present can be understood: "By re-reading and meditating on the ancient texts in the light of recent events or new situations and then re-using them and reworking them, they were led to come to a clearer and deeper understanding of the theological content of these texts and thus to promote the progress of the revealed message."[34] Instead of completely abrogating the Old it is given an additional meaning by this rereading; not a different meaning but a new meaning: "For Christ did not change their names . . . but the way in which they were understood."[35]

The question of original meaning (history) and original authorship (intent) are for the most part left intact (especially for the historically minded in Justin). But the concrete is theologically transformed by the "inner" meaning not exhausted by historicity, authorial intent or reception (knowing such matters, which most Christian interpreters thought they did know, did not exhaust the clear meaning of the texts, in fact such historical knowledge was thought to mitigate against the true, spiritual meaning of texts only clarified in the Christian dispensation).

The motivation behind this discussion in patristic circles is in large part the need to justify how the diametrically opposed notions of clarity and obscurity can be encapsulated or brought together in one mode of understanding. So this union of writings (Old and New) is justified by means of a charitable Christian assumption that Jewish and Christian writings share the same story (the one true God of the Jewish writings is the same God and Father of Jesus Christ, who is himself identified in union and equality with this God)[36] and an indulgent expectation that when considered from a Christian perspective previously hidden, instruction is now manifestly clear. The argument concerns continuity: essential (that is, explicitly theological) or textual (as in the actual use and appropriation of the Old in the New), but a continuity that is not simplistic in

---

[34]Ibid., p. 230.

[35]Cited in ibid., p. 230 (Origen *In Gen.* h.13, n. 3).

[36]So says Irenaeus: "As with the Father there is nothing inconsistent, so with the Son nothing is incomplete or out of time. For all things were foreknown by the Father but they are fulfilled by the Son in consistent and orderly sequence and at the proper time." Irenaeus, *Against Heresies,* The Ante-Nicene Fathers, ed. Alexander Roberts and James Donaldson (Grand Rapids, Mich.: Eerdmans, 1988), 1:443. With Irenaeus there are a variety of historic economic dispensations, multiple covenants, two testaments, but one economy or dispensation of God's plan of salvation, from creation to the return of Jesus Christ (p. 458). While there is one divine covenant, it has an old and a new form (pp. 472-73). And Clement of Alexandria contends that the testaments "are two as to name and date of composition, having been dispensed according to a wise ordering that followed growth and progress of humanity, but they are nevertheless virtually one, deriving as they do from the same God through the mediation of the Son." Clement of Alexandria, *The Stromata, or Miscellanies,* The Ante-Nicene Fathers, ed. Alexander Roberts and James Donaldson (Grand Rapids, Mich.: Eerdmans, 1988), 2:354.

nature. Justin distinguishes between Old and New, between historical Israel of the old covenant and those who, enlightened by Jesus Christ, are constituted according to the new covenant, in order to argue for a distinction between Christ's first advent in humiliation and obscurity and his second advent to judge and renew the world. Discerning the proper reference—first or second advent—is the necessary means to render the meaning of Scripture clearly.[37]

In part, the failure to perceive predictions about the nature of the coming Messiah (according to Christian conceptions) has to do with the hardness of the Jews' hearts, especially for Justin. But the relationship of before and after dominates explanations of why something appears entirely absent in itself but appears clearly upon Christian reflection, As Irenaeus asserts:

> Every prophecy before its fulfillment is enigma and ambiguities, but when the time has arrived, and what was prophesied comes to pass, then the prophecies have a clear and certain exposition. And for this reason when at this present time the law is read to the Jews, it is like a fable; for they do not possess the explanation of all things pertaining to the advent of the Son of God, which took place in human nature; but when it is read by Christians, it is a treasure, hid indeed in a field, but brought to light by the cross of Christ, and explained, both enriching the understanding of men, and showing forthe the wisdom of God.[38]

Both essentially and textually all Scripture, when interpreted Christianly, properly and clearly depicts the identity of Christ and Christian identity.[39] This is not simply a matter of chronology, although previously the hidden nature of predictions did influence the ability to clearly perceive the true affirmation of

---

[37]So argues Thomas F. Torrance, *Divine Meaning: Studies in Patristic Hermeneutics* (Edinburgh: T & T Clark, 1995), pp. 99-100. He concludes, regarding Justin: "The fact that the old covenant carries within it already the promise of the new and points ahead to it, implies that many Old Testament statements have a double meaning, for in addition to their obvious sense they may have a hidden or predictive sense, which is revealed only in the light of the new covenant. But within the new covenant, and in our present existence in the time between the advents, we have to discern the immediate reference or statements in the economy of Christ's Passion, and look out also for a possible reference to the future advent in glory."

[38]Irenaeus, *Against Heresies*, pp. 496-97; cf. pp. 330-31.

[39]Justin stated what he believed the Jewish writings clearly depicted about Jesus Christ: "In the books of the prophets we find it announced in the writing that Jesus, our Christ, is to come, that he will be born of a Virgin, that he will grow to mature manhood, that he will heal all maladies and all infirmities, that he will raise the dead; we read that he will be misunderstood and persecuted, that he will be crucified, that he will die, that he will rise and ascend to Heaven; we read that he is and is called Son of God, that he will send men to announce these things in the whole world and that it will be the Gentiles above all who will believe in him. The prophecies were made five thousand, three thousand, two thousand, one thousand, eight hundred years before his coming, for the prophets followed one another from generation to generation" (Justin, *First Apology*, p. 173).

Jesus' human nature. Just how this assertion is defended is where we turn next.

Obscurely Clear

Within Christian theology the intertwined themes of Scripture's clarity and obscurity give rise to a genuine difference concerning the manner in which clarity is affirmed without neglecting genuine obscurities. Addressing the nature of that relationship becomes a very important topic within the second and early third centuries; in part, according to Thomas Torrance, "it became increasingly evident that *interpreting* the Scriptures and faithful *understanding* of their material content could not be held apart—they had to go together if interpretation was not to operate from an alien centre of reference."[40] Matters of great concern within Christianity focus upon how (and why) Christians should avoid such an alien center and on what basis Christians argue from Scripture, when it is the interpretation of Scripture that is itself so hotly debated. Interestingly, the answers are routinely linked with the subject of Scripture's clarity and obscurity.

A significant example of the theological effort to unite Scripture and its reading is found in Tertullian's (145-220) writings against heretics:

> What indeed has Athens to do with Jerusalem? What concord is there between the Academy and the Church? What between heretics and Christians? Our instruction comes from "the porch of Solomon," who had himself taught that "the Lord should be sought in simplicity of heart." Away with all attempts to produce a mottled Christianity of Stoic, Platonic, and dialectic composition! We want no curious disputation after possessing Christ Jesus, no inquisition after enjoying the gospel! With our faith, we desire no further belief. For this is our palmary faith, that there is nothing which we ought to believe besides.[41]

Instead of simply calling for intellectual retreat or an incipient fundamentalism, Tertullian's claim is founded upon his conviction that Christ's word in Scripture is sufficient for belief, clear in its expression. Contradicting the heretics' abuse of Scripture in looking to something before, after, greater or more sublime than that which Christ has said, Tertullian comments on Jesus' words in Matthew 7:7, "Seek and you will find":

> You must "seek" until you "find," and believe when you have found; nor have

---

[40]Torrance, *Divine Meaning,* p. 106. He continued: "Or to bring to the Scriptures a preconceived system. The proper framework for their interpretation must be built up from out of the Scriptures themselves, for only then could it proceed in accordance with the rule of faith." Torrance argues that in accord with Patristic arguments, the "rule of faith" was itself justified as a summation of the truth of the gospel taught in the Scriptures.

[41]Tertullian, *On Prescription Against Heretics,* The Ante-Nicene Fathers, ed. Alexander Roberts and James Donaldson (Grand Rapids, Mich.: Eerdmans, 1988), 3:246.

> you anything further to do but to keep what you have believed, provided you believe this besides, that nothing else is to be believed, and therefore nothing else is to be sought, after you have found and believed what has been taught by Him who charges you to seek no other thing than that which He has taught.

This proper seeking has what Christ taught as its matter; it yields to belief when it finds what it seeks as to its timing and ceases to seek when it has found what sought as to its limit. So, Tertullian concludes:

> For you would not have believed if you had not found; as neither would you have sought except with a view to find. Your object, therefore, in seeking was to find; and your object in finding was to believe. All further delay for seeking and finding you have prevented by believing. The very fruit of your seeking was determined for you this limit. This boundary has He set for you Himself, who is unwilling that you should believe anything else than what He has taught.[42]

To abuse the command "seek" is the occasion for heretics for "importing the scrupulosity (of their unbelief)."[43] In contrast to such flights of fancy Tertullian argues that "no divine saying is so unconnected and diffuse, that its words only are to be insisted on, and their connection left undetermined."[44] It is a rule of reason, says Tertullian, that we seek in the connection of the sense of the words the divine saying. And it is the rule of faith, in similar fashion, to seek after divine knowledge in that which is Christian rather than "foreign" or extraneous: "As for us, although we must still seek, and that always, yet where ought our search to be made? Amongst the heretics, where all things are foreign and opposed to our own verity, and to whom we are forbidden to draw near?" Tertullian concludes:

> No man gets instruction from that which tends to destruction. No man receives illumination from a quarter where all is darkness. Let our "seeking," therefore be in that which is our own, and from those who are our own, and concerning that which is our own,—that, and only that, which can become an object of inquiry without impairing the rule of faith.[45]

Thus, when Christ addressed Jews (as Tertullian believes he is doing primarily in Mt 7:7), Christians are to read in this manner: "All the Lord's sayings, indeed, are set forth for all men; through the ears of the Jews have they passed on to us. Still most of them were addressed to Jewish persons; they therefore did not constitute instruction properly designed for ourselves, but rather an example."[46] This we discover from within the Christian writings

---

[42]Ibid., p. 248.
[43]Ibid., p. 247.
[44]Ibid., pp. 247-48.
[45]Ibid., p. 249.
[46]Ibid., p. 247.

wherein Christ speaks "plainly" and "clearly."[47]

What is particularly instructive is Tertullian's insistence upon the unity of Scripture, its readings and its readers or, to use Tertullian's phrases, "wherever it shall be manifest that the true Christian rule and faith shall be, there will likewise be the true Scriptures and expositions thereof, and all the Christian traditions."[48] This means that one may not argue or discuss with heretics what constitutes the rule of faith from Scripture because Scripture and its understanding does not belong to heretics.[49] According to Tertullian heretics "have acquired no right to the Christian Scriptures."[50] In contrast, what it means to be Christian is inseparable from what it means to understand Scripture.

> Now, what is there in our Scriptures which is contrary to us? What of our own have we introduced, that we should have to take it away again, or else add to it, or alter it, in order to restore to its natural soundness anything which is contrary to it, and contained in the Scriptures? What we are ourselves, that also the Scriptures are, (and have been) from the beginning.[51]

For Tertullian the union of Scripture, its readings (the rule of faith) and its readers (Christian people) is amply and (we quickly add) correctly demonstrated in such assertions. Scripture clearly identifies its own reading and readers, nothing less is to be expected, and nothing more is to be sought (contrary to the heretics).

Likewise, Irenaeus of Lyons (120-202) offers a compelling example of one type of justification for Scripture's clarity, all the while defending Christianity's larger claims regarding the identity of Jesus Christ and Scripture's identification of him. Knowledge of God is disclosed within Scripture, such knowledge of

---

[47]Ibid.

[48]Ibid., pp. 251-52.

[49]So Tertullian argues, "If in [Scriptures] lie their resources, before they can use them, it ought to be clearly seen to whom belongs the possession of the Scriptures, that none may be admitted to the use thereof who has no title at all to the privilege" (ibid., pp. 250-51). Speaking to heretics, he adds, "Now this heresy of yours does not receive certain Scriptures; and whichever of them it does receive, it perverts by means of additions and diminutions, for the accomplishment of its own purpose; and such as it does not receive, it receives not in their entirety; but even when it does receive any up to a certain point as entire, it nevertheless perverts even these by the contrivance of diverse interpretations" (p. 251).

[50]Ibid., p. 261. The paragraph also includes this argument: "Since this is the case, in order that the truth may be adjudged to belong to us, 'as many as walk according to the rule,' which the church has handed down from the apostles, the apostles from Christ, and Christ from God, the reason of our position is clear, when it determines that heretics ought not to be allowed to challenge an appeal to the Scriptures. For as they are heretics, they cannot be true Christians, because it is not from Christ that they get that which they pursue of their own mere choice, and from the pursuit incur and admit the name of heretics."

[51]Ibid., pp. 262-63.

the gospel is open and can be known through careful (Christian) study, so Irenaeus submits:

> What is required is the healthy mind . . . that concentrates upon what God has placed in the authority of men and has subjected to our knowledge and will advance his learning easily through daily study. These are the things that fall under our direct observation, and are manifestly and unambiguously declared in plain terms in the divine Scriptures.[52]

Thus, with great confidence Irenaeus believes, "If anyone, therefore, reads the Scriptures attentively he will find in them the word about Christ and a prefiguring of the new calling."[53] Finding Christ in the Jewish writings unites the faith of biblical patriarchs and Christian faith, having united the God of the Torah with the Father of Jesus Christ, and this, he maintains, is clear enough to those studiously and properly motivated.[54] Dedicated study observing this "rule of clarity" safeguards against erroneous explanations of Scripture and the truth of the Christian gospel.[55]

This rule of clarity is predicated upon the practice of moving from texts and ideas of an already established meaning to more obscure or contradictory texts and ideas. Irenaeus's *Against Heresies* is particularly interesting in that it argues that the misrepresentation of Scripture must be met with an assertion of its clarity (albeit with the dual interpretative interest of defending the truth of the Christian gospel and rejecting the false assumptions of the heretics). He argues, "No question can be solved by another which itself awaits solution. Nor among those who have sense, can one ambiguity be explained by another ambiguity, or enigmas by another greater enigma. Rather do things of this kind receive their solution from those that are manifest and consistent and clear."[56] This assertion that one must interpret the unclear or ambiguous by means of the clear is presented as a working premise by Irenaeus; so he offers, "Those who shut their eyes to what is so clearly disclosed, only put fetters on themselves."

---

[52]Irenaeus, *Against Heresies,* p. 398.

[53]Ibid., p. 397.

[54]"Certain facts had to be announced beforehand by the fathers in a paternal manner, and others prefigured by the prophets in a legal manner, but others delineated according to the pattern of Christ by those who perceived the adoption, for in one God are all things shown forth." Irenaeus, *Against Heresies,* pp. 396-97. Compare this with Clement of Alexandria: "The God of the two Testaments is one only, for the same promises have been made to us that were made to the Patriarchs" (*Stromata,* pp. 353-54).

[55]The expression "rule of clarity" is from Bertrand de Margerie, *An Introduction to the History of Exegesis,* vol. 1, *The Greek Fathers* (Petersham, Mass.: Saint Bede's Publications, 1993), p. 82.

[56]Irenaeus, *Against Heresies,* pp. 369-70.

> And when the Bridegroom comes, he who has his lamp untrimmed, and not burning with the brightness of a steady light, is classed among those who obscure the interpretations of the parables, forsaking him who by his plain announcements freely imparts gifts to all who come to him, and is excluded from his marriage-chamber.[57]

Irenaeus, then, rejects the interpretative demands of the heretics in that their assertions depend on obscurity, disguise and allegory rather than clarity and a simplicity that encourages belief among children. The revelation of God as Father is disclosed to Christians "not by parables, but by expressions taken in their obvious meaning."[58]

According to Irenaeus his opponents appealed to a secret tradition of interpretation supposedly traced back to Jesus' private instructions to his disciples, a tradition that concerned "arguments, enigmas and parables." Such appeals were offered to counter and question what Irenaeus maintains is perfectly clear: "Parables do, of course, admit of many interpretations, but what lover of the truth will not acknowledge that to claim that inquiry about God must start from enigmas and parables to the neglect of what is certain, indubitable and true, is the part of men who throw themselves into danger and are destitute of reason?"[59]

Irenaeus justifies his claims to interpretative privilege by appealing to the privileged community of the church that bears "the certain gift of the truth."[60] Specific Christian doctrines form the body of truth, uniquely drawn together within the Scriptures and apart from which they are indiscernible. When heretics withdraw "terms, expressions, and parables taken from the Scriptures," the subject that they treat is not recognized. If one "will restore each of the texts to its respective place and fit them all to the body of the truth," then one will discern their harmony or consonance within Scripture.[61] Not all uncertainties and obscurities will necessarily become clear, but all that is clear is harmonious and all regarded as harmonious will become clear thereby.

> If, therefore, according to the rule which I have stated, we leave some questions in the hands of God, we shall both preserve our faith uninjured, and shall continue without danger; and all Scripture, which has been given to us by God, shall

---

[57]Ibid., p. 398. He continues: "And then everyone who thinks through dark interpretations of the parables he has found out a God of his own."

[58]Irenaeus, *Against Heresies,* p. 525.

[59]Ibid., p. 399.

[60]Ibid., p. 496.

[61]Irenaeus uses the phrase *consonare* when referring to the interpretative task; so one interprets a text well when it expresses the harmony of the whole of Scripture. De Margerie offers examples of how the idea of harmony functions as in a technical fashion in Irenaeus (*Introduction*, pp. 55-56).

> be found by us perfectly consistent; and the parables shall harmonize with those passages which are perfectly plain; and those statements the meaning of which is clear, shall serve to explain the parables; and through the many diverse utterances there shall be heard one harmonious melody in us, praising in hymns that God who created all things.[62]

This interplay between clarity and obscurity is justified, primarily textually (one interprets texts by means of and as one text—in symphony) and essentially (the text identifies Scripture's subject as singular—God's Word).[63] Scripture's interpretative unity is offered in terms of Scripture's subject:

> The entire Scriptures, the prophets, and the gospels, can be clearly, unambiguously, and harmoniously understood by all, although all do not believe them; and since they proclaim that one only God, to the exclusion of all others, formed all things by his word . . . as I have shown from the very words of Scripture.[64]

Scripture itself is to be regarded as clear, according to Irenaeus, and it is to be employed to defend the faith against heretics' claims to the contrary.

Defending Scripture when the meaning of Scripture itself is being contested is a particularly difficult task. Tertullian, like Irenaeus, contends that heretics' readings of Scripture are objectionable because they disregard both the truth of Jesus Christ and distort the text itself: "Truth is just as much opposed by an adulteration of its meaning as by corruption of the text."[65] Interpretive justification presumes a coherence within Scripture and moves toward understanding with a corresponding assumption of its clarity: "So long as its form exists in its proper order, you may investigate and discuss, and indulge all your passion for curiosity into what appears doubtful and obscure."[66]

As Torrance observes, the rejection of heretical interpretations of Scripture by Irenaeus and Tertullian rest upon their common rejection of "allegorizing in reverse." That is, interpreting what Irenaeus and Tertullian regard as clear (the Gospels and epistles of the New Testament) as allegories of another, previous and more important interpretative framework. Instead, Scripture is to be regarded as clear, certain, indubitable and true, even while describing myster-

---

[62]Irenaeus, *Against Heresies,* pp. 399-400.

[63]Irenaeus's argument is uniquely Christian: "Wherefore also John does appropriately relate that the Lord said to the Jews: 'You search the Scriptures, in which you think you have eternal life; these are they which testify of me. . . .' How therefore did the Scripture testify of him, unless they were from one and the same Father, instructing men beforehand as to the advent of his son, and foretelling the salvation brought in by him?" (ibid., p. 473).

[64]Ibid., p. 398.

[65]Tertullian, *Prescription Against Heretics,* p. 251.

[66]Ibid., p. 250.

ies or employing enigmatic descriptions that lack cogent understanding. They did not abandon the *practice of clarity* when faced with conflicting assertions of Scripture's meaning; suggesting that the unwillingness to proceed on the basis of Scripture's clarity itself was one major downfall of heretics.

Clearly Obscure

By means of contrast, Origen's defense of the Old Testament depends upon a distinction between the spiritual and the corporeal sense: "The Holy Spirit wished to enclose and to conceal secret mysteries in ordinary words behind the screen of a story and an account of visible things." His explanation reads as follows:

> The chief object of the Holy Spirit is to preserve the coherence of the spiritual meaning, either in those things which ought to be done or which have been already performed, if He anywhere finds that those events, which, according to the history took place, can be adapted to a spiritual meaning, He composed a texture of both kinds in one style of narration, always concealing the hidden meaning more deeply; but where the historical narrative could not be made appropriate to the spiritual coherence of the occurrences, He inserted sometimes certain things which either did not take place or could not take place; sometimes also what might happen, but what did not: and He does this at one time in a few words, which, taken in their "bodily" meaning, seem incapable of containing truth, and at another by the insertion of many. . . . Now all this, as we have remarked, was done by the Holy Spirit in order that, seeing those events which lie on the surface can be neither true nor useful, we may be led to the investigation of that truth which is more deeply concealed, and to the ascertaining of a meaning worthy of God in those Scriptures which we believe to be inspired by Him.[67]

Scripture as a divine book is composed by God, crafted by God's wisdom so as to cover the spiritual sense with a woven veil. This encourages inquiry because of its outward obscurity and discourages simplicity because of its inner clarity.

> The exact reader will hesitate in regard to some passages, finding himself unable to decide without considerable investigation whether a particular incident, believed to be history, actually happened or not, and whether the literal meaning of a particular law is to be observed or not. Accordingly he who reads in an exact manner must, in obedience to the Savior's precept which says, "search the Scriptures," carefully investigate how far the literal meaning is true and how far it is impossible.[68]

---

[67]Origen, *De Principiis,* The Ante-Nicene Fathers, ed. Alexander Roberts and James Donaldson (Grand Rapids, Mich.: Eerdmans, 1988), 4:364.

[68]Origen, cited in Gerard Watson, "Origen and the Literal Interpretation of Scripture," in *Scriptural Interpretation in the Fathers: Letter and Spirit,* ed. Thomas Finan and Vincent Twomey (Portland, Ore.: Four Courts, 1995), p. 83.

Origen's assertion is that all of Scripture has a hidden spiritual sense, there by means of Scripture's author, the Spirit, and open to those who read the Scriptures (literally, pray the Scriptures, which Origen says one may do with the whole of the writings "in the Spirit").[69] For Origen the whole of Scripture reads as a parable but not without reason or purpose.

He also advances the notion of three senses to Scripture, corresponding to the tripartite model of body, soul and spirit, not to suggest three disagreeing senses but to encourage understanding appropriate to one's Christian development: "For as man is said to consist of body, and soul, and spirit, so also does sacred Scripture."[70] The ordinary interpretation that follows the narrative (or body) is instructive for the simplest reader, the broadening connections (both comparisons and contrasts) those more advanced see within Scripture correspond to its soul, and the spiritually wise who perceive God's wisdom understand Scripture's spirit.[71] The simple can grasp just the body, the advanced understand both Scripture's body and soul, while the perfect comprehend all of Scripture's senses.[72] What prompts Origen's desire to look for Scripture's soul and spirit is his doubt that the literal, historical or body sense is always fitting to God whose book Scripture is: "The literal sense designates not only illogical things, but even impossible things."[73] Thus the soul and spirit must be hidden and are often obscured by the ordinary sense. Origen, it appears, learned this from Clement's influence (an influence that extends through Ambrose and Gregory of Nyssa).[74]

Clement's and Origen's intellectual and philosophical backgrounds (Alexan-

---

[69]Origen, *On First Principles* (Washington, D.C.: Translation of the Fathers), pp. 184-85; McEvoy, "Patristic Hermeneutic," pp. 13-14.

[70]Origen, *De Principiis,* p. 359.

[71]Origen also argues that the third, spiritual sense of Scripture itself has three senses: allegorical, tropological and anagogical. See de Lubac, *Medieval Exegesis,* pp. 161-224.

[72]"Each one, then, ought to describe in his own mind, in a threefold manner, the understanding of the divine letters—that is, in order that all the more simple individuals may be edified, so to speak, by the very body of Scripture; for such we term that common and historical sense: while, if some have commenced to make considerable progress, and are able to see something more (than that), they may be edified by the very soul of Scripture. Those, again, who are perfect . . . all such as these may be edified by the spiritual law itself (which has a shadow of good things to come), as if by the Spirit" (Origen, *First Principles,* p. 359).

[73]Ibid., p. 367. Also, "The object of all these statements on our part, is to show that it was the design of the Holy Spirit, who deigned to bestow upon us the sacred Scriptures, to show that we were not to be edified by the letter alone, or by everything in it,—a thing which we see to be frequently impossible and inconsistent; for in that way not only absurdities, but impossibilities, would be the result; but that we are to understand that certain occurrences were interwoven in this 'visible' history, which, when considered and understood in their inner meaning, give forth a law which is advantageous to men and worthy of God."

[74]R. P. C. Hanson, *Allegory and Event: A Study of the Sources and Significance of Origen's Interpretation of Scripture* (London: SCM Press, 1959), pp. 239-50.

drian Platonism, and in particular the influence of Philo in biblical interpretation) are quite evident in their characterizations of the spiritual hidden within and discernable by means of the corporeal; visible nature is symbolic of the invisible world, and all that is visible has a corresponding type represented in the ideal world.[75] One important effect is that their ideas of obscurity and clarity (and in that order) are philosophically positional (their defense is truly a defense of a Christian Platonism instead).[76] For example, both make use of Philo's allegorical rendering of the biblical story of Abraham's "buried cakes" (i.e., unleavened cakes of Gen 18:6, following Philo's reading of *unleavened* as "hidden, mysterious"). Clement writes, "He ordered 'unleavened cakes' to be made so that the truly sacred mystic word . . . ought to be concealed."[77] Clement's justification for "concealment" lies not simply in Jewish writings but in the writings of the Egyptians and the philosophical writings of the Greeks as well: "Those taught in theology by those prophets, the [Greek] poets, philosophize much by way of a hidden sense.[78]

Scripture conceals and veils, and spiritual meaning is embedded in enigmas, symbols and parables, "expressly then respecting all our Scripture, as if spoken in a parable."[79] Also, "it were tedious to go over all the Prophets and the Law, specifying what is spoken in enigmas; for almost the whole of Scripture gives its utterance in this way."[80] Spiritual meaning is concealed for many reasons, among them, interestingly, to add dignity to the hidden truth: "All things that

[75]Note the summary of Origen's philosophical interests in de Margerie, *Introduction,* pp. 96-116; Jean Daniélou, *Origen,* trans. Walter Mitchell (New York: Sheed & Ward, 1955); and the interesting comments of John Henry Newman, *The Arians of the Fourth Century* (New York: Longmans, Green, 1888), pp. 46-64.

[76]Unlike Philo, who offers that allegory has dual senses of physical or cosmology and ethical, Clement has a seemingly Christian argument about what the differing senses of Scripture are mystical (or physical), moral (ethical), and prophetic. Fearghus Ó. Fearghail, "Philo and the Fathers: The Letter and the Spirit," in *Scriptural Interpretation in the Fathers: Letter and Spirit,* ed. Thomas Finan and Vincent Twomey (Cambridge: Four Courts, 1995), p. 55.

[77]Clement, *Stromata,* p. 463.

[78]"Wherefore, in accordance with the method of concealment, the truly sacred word, truly divine and most necessary for us, deposited in the shrine of truth, was by the Egyptians indicated by what were called among them *adyta,* and by the Hebrews by the veil. Only the consecrated—that is, those devoted to God, circumcised in the desire of the passions for the sake of love to that which is alone divine—were allowed access to them. For Plato also thought it not lawful for 'the impure to touch the pure.'" And, "I mean Orpheus, Linus, Musaeus, Homer, and Hesiod, and those in this fashion wise. The persuasive style of poetry is for them a veil for the many. Dreams and signs are all more or less obscure to men, not from jealousy (for it were wrong to conceive of God as subject to passions), but in order that research, introducing to the understanding the enigmas, may haste to the discovery of truth" (Clement, *Stromata,* pp. 450-51).

[79]Ibid., p. 450.

[80]Ibid., p. 452.

shine through a veil show the truth grander and more imposing."[81] Ignorance of this interpretative premise—that truth must be spoken by means of obscurity and enigmas—demonstrates impiety. Thus Clement maintains that nearly all Scripture speaks the truth by means of enigmas, just as Egyptian symbols and enigmas represent sacred truth, and Greek poets and philosophers employ symbol, and Roman civic allegiance is measured in terms of coins and observances that represent justice. He even recounts the story of Hipparchus the Pythagorean who was found guilty of "writing the tenants of Pythagoras in plain language [and] was expelled from the school, and a pillar raised for him as if he had been dead." Clement concludes, "Further, those who instituted the mysteries, being philosophers, buried their doctrines in myths, so as not to be obvious to all. Did they then, by veiling human opinions, prevent the ignorant from handling them; and was it not more beneficial for the holy and blessed contemplation of realities to be concealed?"[82]

Interestingly, Clement observes that this idea of concealment is "clearly written" of in Christian writings but accessible only through contemplation of that which is hidden; he appeals to what he claims are "clear" statements (from Christian Scriptures) when he asserts Scripture supports his position regarding ambiguity and obscurity (usually regarding the Jewish Scriptures). His argument is not that meaning is finally indeterminate but that knowledge of God is not to be equated with knowledge of what is plainly written. Clement's understanding of writing is a mirror image of his conception of God's existence:

> Rightly then, Plato, in the Epistles, treating of God, says: "We must speak in enigmas; that should the tablet come by any mischance on its leaves either by sea or land, he who reads may remain ignorant." For the God of the universe, who is above all speech, all conception, all thought, can never be committed to writing, being inexpressible even by his own power. And this too Plato showed, by saying: "Considering, then, these things, take care lest some time or other you repent on account of the present things, departing in a manner unworthy. The greatest safeguard is not to write, but learn; for it is utterly impossible that what is written will not vanish."[83]

The "milk" of Christian teaching is actually a form of concealing truth from abuse, guarding it from profane use, and "meat is the mystic contemplation." His conclusion: "It is but for few to comprehend these things."[84]

Clement claims the apostle Paul as his source for depicting the truth of God in mysteries (citing the representation of "mystery" in 1 Cor 2; 2 Cor 4; Eph 3;

---

[81]Ibid., p. 457.
[82]Ibid., p. 458.
[83]Ibid., p. 460.
[84]Ibid., p. 459.

and Col 1—2). The revelation of God's mystery continues within Christian circles, according to Clement, distinguishing between the simple (through plain language) and the mature (through enigmas and knowledge of mysteries) "for that the knowledge does not appertain to all."[85] There are two ways in which mysteries are described in Christian teaching: the first, hidden until the time of the apostles but revealed openly in the appearance of Jesus Christ and spoken of through the gospel; and the second, disclosed only by means of illumination and having to do with plumbing the depths of the riches of Christian knowledge itself. One's goal is to receive the illumination of teaching about Christian mysteries, through devoted study of Scripture under the tutelage of mature instruction. It seems appropriate to characterize the Christian fathers as "united in their insistence that the text of Scripture opens itself to those who approach it reverently and receptively."[86]

Conclusion

We have some significant contrast between Irenaeus's characterization of Scripture's clarity and Clement's rendering of Scripture's obscurity, and this contrast is carried on as well as contested through the medieval church. While Irenaeus moves from clarity to address obscurity, Clement genuinely celebrates Scripture's obscurity both as a virtue of Scripture as well as the correspondingly virtuous interpretative regard for this obscurity. Both share an explicitly Christian affirmation regarding the identity of Jesus Christ and Christian identity, linked differently but equally with a Christian reading of Scripture (both Jewish Scripture and primitive Christian writings). Scripture's clarity is asserted within primitive Christian writings and Christian theologians (an observation that itself is important) but never as an isolated notion—never isolated from the ecclesial claims after the manner of Irenaeus, nor from the affirmation of *Christian* knowledge in Alexandrians such as Clement and Origen.

The belief that Scripture is clear arises from a growing consensus, a distinctly Christian sense, that Jewish Scripture reread in terms of Christian convictions regarding the identity of Jesus are justifiable in two respects: first, that when read in this manner Jewish Scripture identified Jesus for Christians; and second, these writings are clear enough to render their current Christian identity. Such affirmations are bold in that they are distinctly Christian readings of Jewish Scripture, and they are exacting in the manner in which the themes of

---

[85]Ibid.

[86]Christopher A. Hall, *Reading Scripture with the Church Fathers* (Downers Grove, Ill.: InterVarsity Press, 1998), p. 9. Hall continues: "In short, the fathers consistently treat the Bible as a holy book whose riches can be mined adequately only by those prepared to honor and obey the message the Scripture contains."

clarity or obscurity are employed to justify these readings. As John Goldingay observes, one effect of this "process is to obscure its historical nature in such a way as to make it easier for readers in other historical contexts to identify with the text."[87] Taking their cue from the identity of Jesus as both the interpreter as well as subject of Jewish Scripture, primitive Christian representations progress understandably in an effort to justify how what is not there, not obviously or historically the case with many prophetic and poetic texts, is justifiable for Christians to affirm as clear, or at least obscurely presented but interpretatively perspicuous.

As we turn our attention toward the solidification of Christian interpretation in the early Middle Ages, the traditions associated with Irenaeus and Clement are evident as well as enlarged. This is especially apparent in the convention of employing the notion of multiple senses when interpreting Scripture, a corresponding debate regarding the nature of Scripture's literal sense (which all Christian theologians *tend* to affirm), and the formulation of what we shall refer to as Christian testamental interpretative obscurity (the Old Testament) and clarity (the New Testament).

[87]Goldingay, *Models for Scripture,* p. 106.

3

SPIRITUAL CLARITY & LETTERAL OBSCURITY

Your word is a lamp to my feet and a light to my path.

PSALM 119:105

I rejoiced also that the old Scriptures of the law and the prophets were laid before me, to be perused, not now with that eye to which they seemed most absurd before, when I criticized your holy ones for thinking this or that which in plain fact they did not think. And with delight I heard Ambrose, in his sermons to the people, oftentimes most diligently recommended this text as a rule, "The letter kills, but the Spirit gives life." And he would go on to draw aside the veil of mystery and lay open the spiritual meaning of things which, accepted according to the letter seemed to teach perverse doctrines. Nothing of what he said struck me as false, although I did not as yet know whether what he said was true.

AUGUSTINE OF HIPPO, *CONFESSIONS*

WITHIN EARLY CHRISTIANITY (C. 300-600) THE THEME OF SCRIPTURE'S clarity was used to buoy confidence in distinctly Christian interpretative practices as much as Scripture's obscurity was used to implore serious Christian study of Scripture. A proper (that is, Christian) understanding of Scripture held multiple senses, plural meanings, but not without or apart from the observation that Scripture is also genuinely obscure in many respects. The discussion of clarity was never without the admission of obscurity. One can even say that an emphasis upon obscurity dominates early portrayals of clarity. Priority (obscure to clear or clear with obscure), degree (clear as in simple or obscure as in profound) and prospect (hopelessly obscure or able to be clarified) are key factors in approaching Scripture's interpretation within the first millennium of Christian history.

The actual experience of Scripture's obscurity and clarity within this setting is akin to conversion to the Christian message itself; to perceive the sense of

Christian faith is to perceive that Scripture clearly depicts as much.[1] Why would Christians affirm anything less than this? John Cassian's (c. 360-432) instructions to his monks suggested a mode of contemplation by which the spiritual meaning of Scripture becomes clearer, not through accumulating information but from the experience of reading Scripture itself "for those who liked, and who were eager to gain by constant study a mind well stored with Holy Scripture" and "whose concern is the reading and the recollection of the Scriptures.[2] To be a Christian is to be a reader of Scripture. The infamous example of Augustine of Hippo is both characteristic and an explanation of this experience. He once perceived Scripture as absurd and foolish and obscure but was transformed inasmuch as his manner of regarding the Christian faith was transformed. That is, Augustine became a different kind of reader.[3] And although Augustine's experience is interestingly common, it does not explain how Christians understood *how* Scripture was to be regarded as clear, how the otherwise obscure message could possibly be regarded as clear and by whom.

While the manner in which affirmations of obscurity and clarity were maintained differed within early Christianity, the subjects addressed in contemplations of clarity and obscurity were uniform, even among the divergent interpretative schools of Alexandria and Antioch. These include the formulation of what we shall refer to as Christian testamental interpretative obscurity (concerning the Old Testament) and clarity (concerning the New Testament), Scripture's supposed multiple senses, and the relation of multiple senses to Scripture's literal sense. *How* Scripture is a lamp to our feet and a light for our path is defended and established by means of developing interpretative interests, reflecting upon the study of language and eventually grammar, and even wrestling with the very basic and necessary but tangled question of what it means to confess that Scripture is God's Word. There is an intricate and engag-

---

[1]On the background to this discussion—the relation between the personal narratives of Christian theologians and the development of Christian doctrine—consult Hans von Campenhausen, *Men Who Shaped the Western Church,* trans. Manfred Hoffmann (New York: Harper & Row, 1964); Jean Daniélou, *The Development of Christian Doctrine Before the Council of Nicaea,* ed. and trans. John A. Baker (London: Darton, Longman & Todd, 1964); George L. Prestige, *Fathers and Heretics: Six Studies in Dogmatic Faith with Prologue and Epilogue* (London: SPCK, 1948); and Robert V. Sellers, *Two Ancient Christologies: A Study in the Christological Thought of the Schools of Alexandria and Antioch in the Early History of Christian Doctrine* (London: SPCK, 1940).

[2]John Cassian, *The Twelve Books of John Cassian on the Institutes of the Coenobia, and the Remedies for the Eight Principal Faults,* A Select Library of Nicene and Post-Nicene Fathers of the Christian Church, ed. Philip Schaff and Henry Wace, 2nd series (Grand Rapids, Mich.: Eerdmans, 1986), 11:207.

[3]Brian Stock, *Augustine the Reader: Meditation, Self-Knowledge, and the Ethics of Interpretation* (Cambridge, Mass.: Harvard University Press, 1996).

ing story to be told about the development of Christian notions of obscurity and clarity—a story that captures the significant limitations and potential of affirming Scripture's clarity.

Antioch Against Alexandria

In terms of developing interpretative interests it is routine within the summary of early biblical interpretation to distinguish between two different approaches, the so-called Antiochene and Alexandrian, and more specifically to describe how the latter dominated and the former was a reaction to the extremes of the latter.[4] Alexandrian influences encouraged medieval exegetes to look through all of Scripture for hidden mysteries—all was parable, all was allegory, all was prophecy of Jesus Christ.[5] This is to say that when one refers to Alexandrian influences one refers to Origen's legacy; as Beryl Smalley notes, "To write a history of Origenist influence on the west would be tantamount to writing a history of western exegesis."[6] We tell the story of Antioch not to reject Alexandrian practices (the results of each approach were not significantly different in Christian doctrine) but to better understand the significant interplay of Scripture's obscurity and clarity within these distinguishable perspectives.

Antiochene interests were corrective, calling for restraint in the use of allegory (actually, they just rejected allegory altogether) and a much more modest attitude toward prophecies (stressing typological significance). While instances of metaphorical expression in Scripture were regarded as an open invitation for allegorical musings for Alexandrians, they were regarded as hyperboles, historically interpreted as clear for Antiochenes.[7] And unless a metaphorical expression in the Old was addressed by the New Testament, the clear meaning

---

[4]Robert M. Grant and David Tracy, *A Short History of Biblical Interpretation* (Philadelphia: Fortress, 1984); G. R. Evans, *The Language and Logic of the Bible: The Early Middle Ages* (Cambridge: Cambridge University Press, 1984); Maurice F. Wiles, *The Spiritual Gospel: The Interpretation of the Fourth Gospel in the Early Church* (Cambridge: Cambridge University Press, 1960).

[5]"In allegorical exegesis the sacred text is treated as a mere symbol, or allegory, of spiritual truths. The literal, historical sense, if it is regarded at all, plays a relatively minor role, and the aim of the exegete is to elicit the moral, theological or mystical meaning which each passage, indeed each verse and even each word, is presumed to contain" (J. N. D. Kelly, *Early Christian Doctrine* [New York: Harper & Row, 1976], p. 70).

[6]Beryl Smalley, *The Study of the Bible in the Middle Ages* (Notre Dame, Ind.: University of Notre Dame Press, 1964), p. 14.

[7]So David's words: "For you do not give me up to Sheol, / or let your faithful one see the Pit" (Ps 16:10 NRSV), is metaphorically and maybe hyperbolically realized in David's experience and literally true of Jesus Christ (as Acts 2:27-31; 13:35-37). Thus, the psalm is interpreted in a hyperbolic sense. See the discussion in Bertrand de Margerie, *An Introduction to the History of Exegesis,* vol. 1, *The Greek Fathers* (Petersham, Mass.: Saint Bede's Publications, 1993), pp. 178-79.

of a text was expressed in the words themselves. So Chrysostom: "Nowhere does Scripture depart from this rule. It always supplies the key for the allegories it employs, wishing in this way to prevent minds that are keen on such figures from straying off at random and without purpose, from letting their imaginations go wild."[8] Such matters became more focused in the fourth and fifth centuries in light of the continual pressure from heretical Christian groups regarding the reading and relationship of the Old and New Testaments.[9] Differences arose in how this affirmation would be defended and practiced. Antiochenes affirmed the literal nature of both of the testaments, while Alexandrians insisted that it was necessary to defend the accuracy and divine nature of Scripture by distinguishing between allegorical manner of the Old by means of the literal nature of the New.

The persistent suspicion of Alexandrian interpreters is that such literal reading of the Old led to error (to the same extent that allegorical reading of the New was the characteristic move of heretics).[10] It was suspected that the Antiochene emphasis upon the literal (factual, historical) sense obscured the clear Christian teaching (hidden or symbolized) in all Scripture, while Antiochenes contended that the extremes of Alexandrian interests essentially disconnected what Christians said Scripture taught from Scripture itself. Antiochenes generally regarded Scripture's literal sense as clear enough; the text means what it says and not necessarily more than what it actually says.

John Chrysostom (347-407) is a good example of Antiochene interests (as much because of his colorful story as his numerous extant sermons).[11] His early monastic life included continual Bible reading and a period of two years without lying down "apparently in the belief that a Christian must stand in order to obey the injunction: 'be ye watchful.'"[12] Interesting, even if odd, but it

---

[8]Cited in ibid., p. 170.

[9]Christianity in Antioch endured a controversial existence in the late fourth century as four Christian bishops (one Arian, one Apollinarian, one old Nicene and one new Nicene) contended for power. Yet, "in the midst of this turmoil there seems to have been a more or less constant theological and exegetical tradition." Add to this the list of names connected in one way or another with the Antiochene location—Nestorius, Theodoret and Ibas—and the controversial circumstances of the Antiochene approach to Scripture interpretation become more obvious (Rowan A. Greer, *Theodore of Mopsuestia: Exegete and Theologian* [London: Faith Press, 1961], p. 93). Also consult Dimitri Z. Zaharopoules, *Theodore of Mopsuestia of the Bible: A Study of His Old Testament Exegesis* (New York: Paulist, 1989).

[10]See Jaroslav Pelikan, *The Christian Tradition: A History of the Development of Doctrine,* vol. 1, *The Emergence of the Catholic Tradition (100-600)* (Chicago: University of Chicago Press, 1971), pp. 55-67.

[11]Jaroslav Pelikan, ed., *The Preaching of John Chrysostom: Homilies on the Sermon on the Mount* (Philadelphia: Fortress, 1967).

[12]Robert Payne, *Fathers of the Eastern Church* (Crestwood, N.Y.: St. Vladimir's Seminary Press, 1989), p. 197.

indicates the degree to which Chrysostom's life was dominated by the perceived tension between such literal interpretation and allegory. The rationale of the Bible's teaching, Chrysostom offered, was instruction in thinking and living like a Christian. As a preacher who is said to have mined the literal (i.e., realistic) sense of the text for spiritual meaning, Chrysostom offers a characteristically straightforward rendering of Scripture's message as clear in itself.

Chrysostom addresses the troublesome realization that Scripture, even though clear, still needs to be preached: "Wherefore any necessity for a sermon? All things are clear and open that are in the divine Scriptures; the necessary things are plain." The trouble rests not in Scripture's character but in the lack of character among those who listen to Scripture proclaimed. Chrysostom plays up what he understands to be the straightforward quality of Scripture's address and downplays the charges of obscurity: "For tell me, with what pomp of words did Paul speak? and yet he converted the world. Or with what the unlettered Peter?" Then why do we not understand (more of) Scripture?

> Why? For are they spoken in Hebrew? Are they in Latin, or in foreign tongues? Are they not in Greek? But they are expressed obscurely, you say: What is it that is obscure? Tell me. Are there not histories? For (of course) you know the plain parts, in that you enquire about the obscure.[13]

The appeal to obscurity is an excuse for inattentiveness and laziness; while the charge that the subjects of Scripture are commonplace and simple is an excuse for ignorance. Chrysostom does not retreat into an argument that equates clarity with simplicity.

This is not to say that all Scripture is alike, clear and plain, but instead one should be cautious about what he or she expects from the study of Scripture. As summarized by Margerie, for Chrysostom all statements of Scripture are of three categories: "Some reveal, beyond their letter, a more profound sense, the object of *theoria;* others can be understood only according to their literal affirmation; . . . still others can be understood only according to a sense different from that suggested by the sound of the words."[14] *Theoria* does not preclude the admission of genuine prophecy, but it works literally and thus in a backwards direction: if a New Testament writer refers to or even implicitly shows an awareness of a messianic significance of a text, it may properly be regarded as an instance of *theoria* (but not therefore an invitation to go

---

[13]John Chrysostom, *Homilies on Thessalonians*, A Select Library of the Nicene and Post-Nicene Fathers of the Christian Church, ed. Philip Schaff, 1st series (Grand Rapids, Mich.: Eerdmans, 1988), 13:388.
[14]De Maegerie, *Greek Fathers,* p. 169.

further).[15] By *theoria,* it will shortly become evident, Antiochenes meant a narrowly understood, pragmatic manner of accounting for infrequent matters disproportionate to the Old Testament writers' personages or events.

In contrast to the Alexandrians' commonplace emphasis upon Scripture's explorable depth, its oblique but discoverable letter, Chrysostom offers this caution: "Since it is a great sign of knowledge not to be curious about everything, nor to wish to know all things. And if you will allow me, I will explain myself by an example."

> Let us suppose a river, or rather rivers . . . all are not of the same depth. Some have a shallow bed, others one deep enough to drown one unacquainted with it. In one part there are whirlpools; and not in another. It is good therefore to forbear to make trial of all, and it is not small proof of knowledge not to which to sound all the depths: whereas he that would venture on every part of the river, is really most ignorant of the peculiar nature of rivers, and will often be in danger of perishing, from venturing into the deeper parts with the same boldness with which he crossed the shallows. So it is in the things of God. He who will know all things, and ventures to intrude into everything, he it is that is most ignorant what God is. And of rivers indeed, the greater part is safe, and the depths and whirlpools few, but with respect to the things of God, the greater part is hidden, and it is not possible to trace out His works. Why then art thou bent on drowning thyself in those depths?[16]

Chrysostom's employment of images (rivers with shallow and deep beds [Scripture as variegated] and whirlpools [Scripture as dangerous]) focuses our attention toward the necessity of careful and cautious inquiry. *Inquiry* may be an appropriate characterization for the concerns of interpretation by Antiochenes like Chrysostom.

As a preacher Chrysostom is not afraid to advise us that it takes intention, skill and practice to unearth Scripture's meaning; that is, inquiry. Commenting upon John 5:31-32, Chrysostom observes:

> If any one unpracticed in the art undertake to work a mine, he will get no gold,

---

[15]De Margerie observes, "*Theoria* is the rule to follow when an apostle of the New Testament, by citing an oracle as having been verified in Jesus of Nazareth, guarantees at least implicitly that the prophet was aware of the messianic signification of his words, even if the context makes it clear that these same words do refer to another, more proximate, historical object (compare, for example, Ps 16 with Acts 2:30; Zec 9 with Mt 21:4 and Jn 12:16); and when, even in the absence of such an apostolic witness, one finds in the same prophetic context hyperbolic traits which could only apply to the Messiah together with other features that better describe a historical personage who prefigures the Messiah" (ibid., p. 171).

[16]John Chrysostom, *Homilies on Timothy,* A Select Library of the Nicene and Post-Nicene Fathers of the Christian Church, ed. Philip Schaff, 1st series (Grand Rapids, Mich.: Eerdmans, 1988), 13:507.

> but confounding all aimlessly and together, will undergo a labor unprofitable and pernicious: so also they who understand not the consequence of Holy Scripture, nor search out its peculiarities and laws, but go over all its points carelessly and in one manner, will mix the gold with earth, and never discover the treasure which is laid up in it. I say this now because the passage before us contains much gold, not indeed manifest to view, but covered over with much obscurity, and therefore by digging and purifying we must arrive at the legitimate sense.[17]

Attention to textual (i.e., historical, particular) detail displays the call for careful study emphasized in Chrysostom's preaching. The meaning is "in" the text, as it displays its true meaning in itself, by means of its own understanding (contrary to the extratextual emphasis upon detail and circumstances Antiochenes were accused of by Alexandrians and contrary to the extratextual emphasis upon surplus meaning Antiochenes often suspected Alexandrians were guilty of).

Antiochene interests did not reject *Christian* interpretation of historical (i.e., Old Testament) texts but insisted that Christian interpretation must build upon historical revelation as text; so Diodore of Tarsus (d. 390) argues:

> We do not forbid the higher interpretation and *theoria,* for the historical narrative does not exclude it, but is on the contrary the basis and substructure of loftier insights. . . . We must, however, be on our guard against letting the *theoria* do away with the historical basis, for the result would be, not *theoria,* but allegory.[18]

The exclusion of allegory is understandable when read as the Antiochenes read allegory (as disregard for or antithetical to letter or narrative itself). Allegory, of course, was not absent from Scripture itself, and to Antiochene practices the recognition of instances of allegory was based in attention to the text itself (e.g., the story of Hagar in Gal 4) and therefore tolerable only because it was historical. So Diodore contends, "Holy Scripture knows the term 'allegory' but not its application."[19] Diodore goes so far as to contend that in the instance of Galatians 4:24 *allegory* actually is to be understood as *theoria*—the analogy of two covenants is historical in orientation, the reference to the Genesis text is concrete in substance. Speaking of his approach to Scripture:

> This method neither sets aside history nor repudiates *theoria*. Rather, as a realistic, middle-of-the-road approach which takes into account both . . . it frees us, on the

[17]John Chrysostom, *Homilies on St. John*, A Select Library of the Nicene and Post-Nicene Fathers of the Christian Church, ed. Philip Schaff, 1st series (Grand Rapids, Mich.: Eerdmans, 1988), 14:143.

[18]Diodore's statements are cited in Kelly, *Early Christian Doctrine,* pp. 76-77.

[19]Diodore of Tarsus, *Preface to the Commentary on Psalm 118,* in *Biblical Interpretation in the Early Church,* ed. Karlfried Fooelich (Philadelphia: Fortress, 1984), p. 87; it is also quoted and addressed in Hall, *Reading Scripture,* p. 161.

> one hand from a Hellenism which says one thing for another and introduces foreign subject matter; on the other hand, it does not yield to Judaism and choke us by forcing us to treat the literal reading of the text as the only one worthy of attention and honor, while not allowing the exploration of a higher sense beyond the letter also.[20]

Understanding Scripture realistically entails the admission that a given text is simply not written about or to contemporary (Christian) readers but is appropriate to the circumstances of "those who first uttered it as well as those who come after them." Instead of rendering Scripture irrelevant to its readers, Diodore contends that a given statement of Scripture is "adaptable to many situations according to the grace of him who gives it power." This, Diodore reminds his reader, "is not a case of allegory."[21]

Theodore of Mopsuestia[22] (c. 350-428), likewise, negatively assessed the Alexandrian emphasis upon allegory, arguing that the appeal to "allegory" from Galatians 4:24 should not be used to justify the actual allegorization of any text; some "use the apostle's term as a blank authorization to abolish all meanings of divine Scripture." To be exact, Theodore says that Paul does not even allegorize the narrative of Hagar and Sarah but instead *compares* them within Galatians: "For the apostle neither does away with history nor elaborates on events that happened long ago. Rather, he states the events just as they happened and then applies the historical account of what occurred there to his own understanding."[23] The comparison ("just as" in Galatians 4:24) cannot be sustained unless the elements of the narrative have genuinely historical meaning (independent of another appeal to their meaning). And the trouble with Alexandrian emphasis on allegory is that "they will have no history left."[24] Theodore's approach to historical and comparative (figural) understanding, in contrast to allegorical, will continue to surface in the history of Christian inter-

---

[20]Diodore of Tarsus, *Commentary on the Psalms: Prologue,* in *Biblical Interpretation in the Early Church,* ed. Karlfried Fooelich (Philadelphia: Fortress, 1984), p. 86; quoted in Hall, *Reading Scripture,* p. 161.

[21]Diodore of Tarsus, cited in Hall, *Reading Scripture,* p. 162.

[22]On Theodore consult Joanne M. Dewart, *The Theology of Grace of Theodore of Mopsuestia* (Washington, D.C.: Catholic University of America, 1971); L. Patterson, *Theodore of Mopsuestia and Modern Thought* (London: SPCK, 1926); Francis A. Sullivan, *The Christology of Theodore of Mopsuestia* (Rome: U. Gregorianae, 1956); and D. S. Wallace-Hadrill, *Christian Antioch* (Cambridge: Cambridge University Press, 1982).

[23]Theodore of Mopsuestia, *Commentary on Galatians 4:22-31* in *Biblical Interpretation in the Early Church,* ed. Karlfried Fooelich (Philadelphia: Fortress, 1984), p. 95, quoted in Hall, *Reading Scripture,* p. 165. Theodore compares allegorical understanding to dreams: "as if the entire historical account of divine Scripture differed in no way from dreams in the night."

[24]"Theodore of Mopsuestia: Commentary on Galatians 4:22-31," in *Biblical Interpretation in the Early Church,* ed. and trans. Karlfried Froelich (Philadelphia: Fortress, 1984), p. 97.

pretation (as we will see when considering letter and spirit below). Because the historical understanding of the text is understood to be clear, it resists (forcefully) simple assimilation or transformation by means of allegory. So Theodore:

> The same God, who alone is Lord of both Testaments, master and author of all things, ordered the content of the two covenants to a single goal. He had decided already at the beginning to reveal the future state whose principle he displayed in the economy of Christ. He judged it necessary, however, to set us first in the present condition and only then to transfer us to the other through the resurrection of the dead. His purpose here was to help us to come, through the comparison of the one state with the other, to appreciate the grandeur of the good things that await us. But he had also to make clear how his plan was twofold so that we would not be lead to imaging that we might someday be the object of a new scheme or of a subsequent resolution. This is why we find him at work in the history of humanity leaving numerous hints regarding the coming of the Lord Christ. And it is why the Jews were awaiting him for so long before he came.[25]

The complaint of Theodore and company is that allegory is not, in fact, interpretation—it does not interpret the Bible historically (realistically/literally), directly or textually. Rowan Greer comments that Origen and Alexandrian allegory "was unable to understand inspiration in any way but that which involved direct revelation in the Bible itself, and because [they were] unable to take seriously the narrative, historical character of Scripture, [their] method fails to interpret the Bible."[26] Theodore, contrary to the almost universal reading of Song of Solomon as an allegory of Christ's love for the church or the soul's love of Christ, was quite happy to regard it in predominantly literal (historical and realistic) terms as composed by Solomon for the Egyptian princess. Song of Solomon could have a greater significance than simply the actual historical significance of the occasion, but that would be typically (i.e., figuratively and historically) understood.[27] But to hold that Song of Solomon concerned love and sex seemed profane, and the literal reading of the text demanded allegorical understanding to the great majority of early Christian interpreters. This would be necessarily contrary to historical and realistic understanding to Theodore.

---

[25]Cited by de Margerie, *Greek Fathers,* pp. 183-84, as an example of the theological orientation of Antiochene interpretative practices (confirming their general orthodoxy).

[26]Greer, *Theodore of Mopsuestia,* pp. 92, 94-95. The repeated complaint among Antiochenes was that allegory was essentially nonhistorical in order to function theologically; denying the historical (realism) of the relationship between prophecy and fulfillment by transcending (and thereby ignoring) the literal meaning of texts and substituting a true meaning that is not directly justified by the text itself.

[27]Kelly, *Early Christian Doctrine,* p. 78.

All of Scripture was literal and to be understood as such in order to be understood clearly according to Antiochene practices. Christian meaning was found by means of explicit types, not (implicit) allegories; types represented the spiritual sense that was proper to Scripture's Christian reading. Thus, a realistic tension between prophecy and fulfillment was to be maintained (whether thought of as two poles, two or more events or themes). Consider the instance of Jesus speaking the words "My God, my God, why have you forsaken me" while on his cross (Mt 27:46). What are we to make of this "quote" of Psalm 22? Was Jesus' quote a fulfillment of a prophecy with the psalm taken as primarily messianic in nature (with David as prophet of Jesus' words)? Are the words understood as allegorical for both David and Jesus (significant in terms of Jesus' and David's experiences but not to be literally understood as estrangement from God)? Antiochene emphases lead us to consider how Psalm 22 is to be understood as realistically (historically) appropriate for David's experience and typologically quoted by Jesus on his cross. As one commentator put it, Psalm 22 "lent [itself] to this use, not because [it was] predictive, but because His spiritual predicament has been analogous to the Psalmist's."[28] Jesus is forcing the reader to understand his experience on the cross by means of David's experience rendered in Psalm 22. So, the meaning of such texts is understood by means of "juxtaposing events of the past and present."[29] In contrast, the effect of allegory in contrast to historical (i.e., literal) typology is the practical dismissal or dissolving of David's life and circumstances (or Moses' or Joseph's, etc.). Typology played upon the "correspondence between the two Testaments" (with the Old read as anticipating the New), and is the closest we have to a "characteristically Christian" approach.[30] Figures of Old Testament narrative no longer stand with any sense of integrity (i.e., are not taken as clear in themselves) when subsumed by means of allegory.[31]

Antioch and Alexandria: Affluence and Poverty

Detractors from the influence of Alexandria complained that allegory effectively undercut the strenuous nature of Christian practice. Theodore of Mop-

---

[28]Ibid., p. 77.

[29]Theodore of Mopsuestia, quoted in Hall, *Reading Scripture,* p. 167.

[30]On the distinction between allegory and typology in the Alexandrians and Antiochenes, see Kelly, *Early Christian Doctrines,* pp. 69-71.

[31]Here following the suggestions offered by John David Dawson, "Figural Reading and the Fashioning of Christian Identity in Boyarin, Auerbach and Frei," *Modern Theology* 14, no. 2 (1998): 181-96.

suestia argued against the influence of Origen and the practices of allegory (his work entitled *On Allegory and History* was unfortunately lost), particularly when addressing the moral teaching of both Old and New Testaments. John Chrysostom's sermons argue that Scripture's literary-historical representation offers sufficient basis for moral exhortation without recourse to allegory. This was accomplished by linking Scripture's sense with its moral force (both Alexandria and Antioch did this but in differing ways). While Alexandrian influence emphasized obscurity of text and clarity of interpretative resolutions, Antiochene influence emphasized a form of textual clarity and invoked an obscurity of conclusiveness.

However, such Antiochene advocacy and practices have little or no influence in early and medieval Christianity; again, as Smalley notes, "Antiochene exegesis as a distinct method had been forgotten by the time it would have been useful, forgotten beyond hope of recovery." And so, even though "the allegorical method captivated the Latin world," the Antiochene emphasis that the literal sense encompassed the whole meaning of Scripture failed to survive, except maybe in insignificant or incipient ways.[32]

In practice the appeal to *theoria* instead of allegory is sustained by the Christian premise that there is to be a unified reading of Old and New Testaments in terms of the christological rule of faith or the church's instruction regarding the purpose of Scripture (typology proper). Kelly summarizes this Antiochene emphasis: it is necessary "(a) that the literal sense of the sacred narrative should not be abolished, (b) that there should be a real correspondence between the historical fact and the further spiritual object discerned, and (c) that these two objects should be apprehended together, though of course in different ways."[33] After this fashion Antiochene appeal to *theoria* is a rival to Alexandrian insistence on the encompassing notion of allegory. But what substantive and practical differences are there between the Antiochene and Alexandrian approaches? In one sense there is little practical difference in that both approaches appeal to typological orientation (interpreters of both schools of thought tend in the same or similar directions when interpreting a specific biblical text).[34]

This is best exemplified by focusing attention on a persistent concern within

---

[32]Ibid., pp. 20 and 19.

[33]Kelly, *Early Christian Doctrine,* p. 76.

[34]"It has been fashionable to distinguish different schools of patristic exegesis, notably the Alexandrian with its bias towards allegory, and the Antiochene with its passion for literalism. Valid though this contrast is, it should not be pressed to the extent of overlooking the underlying unity, at the deeper level of typology, of the fathers' approach to the Scriptural revelation" (ibid., p. 72).

early Christianity having to do with riches and Christian faith, especially in light of the reoccurring discussion of wealth and poverty in the Gospels. Thanks to a helpful summary of these themes by Christopher Hall, we have access to a diverse body of Christian interpretative literature addressing this topic.[35] What is one to do with Jesus' statements in Matthew 19 such as his conversation with a rich young man: "Sell your possessions and give to the poor," and "It is hard for a rich man to enter the kingdom of heaven" (Mt 19:21, 23)?

The commands seem impossible, or at least impractical, if taken literally; so Clement of Alexandria cautions that the text should not be hastily interpreted (i.e., taken literally), but according to its more important meaning (spiritual meaning). Thus, "What [the rich young man] is told to banish from his soul are his notions about wealth, his attachment to it, his excessive desire for it, his morbid excitement over it, and his anxieties."[36] And in contrast Clement dismisses any virtue being attached to poverty (again, taken as another spiritual implication of the text); the condition of poverty would preoccupy the poor person so that spiritual things will be neglected.

> If there is something extraordinary that the new creation, the Son of God, reveals and teaches, then it cannot be the outward action that he is commanding; others have done that. It must be something else that is being indicated through it—something greater, more divine and more perfect. It is the stripping off of the passions from the soul itself and from its disposition; all that is alien must be uprooted and expelled form the mind.[37]

The clear meaning of the text must not be taken as the literal reading, not because that is unlikely according to the text itself but because it would restrict the meaning of the text to what is plainly read and (seemingly) violate Christian teaching on the subject of riches and poverty according to Clement (the rich can and are encouraged to seek redemption, the poor are not necessarily privileged before God, and the actual, physical riches can be spiritually employed). Following Origen's emphasis upon the body, soul and spirit dimensions of meaning, Alexandrians tend to dismiss actual riches and poverty as conclusively significant in themselves (the body), looking further toward the moral and spiritual implications *in* all texts.

The so-called Latin synthesis of Alexandrian emphases (in the fourth and fifth centuries) follows Origen as well. Jerome (c. 340-420) reads Jesus' commands as a call to "careful stewardship" but not necessarily a command; it is an invitation to the soul to seek perfection (Mt 19:21). So also Augustine contends

---

[35]Hall, *Reading Scripture,* pp. 170-76.
[36]Cited in ibid., p. 171.
[37]Ibid., pp. 171-72.

that it is not the actual riches that hinder a rich person from heaven but "pride" or a lack of God's grace that makes the impossible possible (Mt 19:26). Ambrose of Milan, likewise, understands the text in terms of proportion (the rich lack a good sense thereof) and morality (the rich ignore the poor to their own peril); his exhortation (or better, his effort to induce a sense of guilt) is to moral sensibilities.[38] The literal meaning of the text, which is clear enough to disqualify it as the true, only or conclusive sense, must be understood in light of spiritual meaning(s).

By means of contrast, John Chrysostom understands the text by means of its literal meaning, building upon the tangible to articulate the spiritual. Jesus' play between earthly riches and heavenly treasure highlights contrast: "He called it a treasure, showing the plenteousness of the recompense, its permanency, its security, so far as it was possible similitudes to intimate it to the hearer."[39] Fittingly for Antiochene emphases, the actual riches of the young man do indicate spiritual disposition—silver, riches, possessions, houses, servants and celebrity—are for this world.

> If you consider how these things affect your soul, how dark, and desolate, and foul they render it, and how ugly; if you consider how many evils were committed to obtain these things, and how much work it takes to keep them, with how many dangers; indeed, can they be kept at all? . . . When you see any resplendent outwardly with fine clothes and people in attendance, lay open his conscience. You will find many cobwebs within, and much dust.[40]

For both Alexandria and Antioch the text is about riches, about the contrast between devotion to earthly riches and Jesus' call to the kingdom of heaven. For Antiochene interests the rich young man's experience is the rich young man's experience from which we may learn (indirectly, by means of a specific text), while in Alexandrian thought the emphasis seems to rest not in riches but in the deeper and larger soulish trouble that the rich young man only seems to depict (indirectly, by means of the abstruse concept of riches). The Antiochene example may be concrete and direct with the text but more indirect when depicting the moral compunction requisite of Christian readers, while the Alexandrian route to a similar conclusion is more indirect with the actual text and more direct with its moral force. We are hard pressed to say less than that the practical differences are insignificant in this respect.

Where does this take us with regard to the subject of Scripture's clarity? As

---

[38]Ibid., pp. 173-74.
[39]Ibid., p. 175.
[40]Ibid., p. 176.

we will see in the life of Augustine of Hippo, the Latin synthesis of Alexandrian emphases serves to provide a Christian interpretative legacy that lasts a millennium. The letter and figural emphasis of the Antiochenes is subsumed and thereby lost (maybe until the mid-twentieth century). What is also lost is a practically dominant sense of Scripture's clarity in Christian interpretation of Scripture—the Old Testament in particular. What precisely is clear (What is the sense of Scripture?), what is obscure (What must be understood for Scripture's message to be made clear?), and how one discerns the significance of these questions is addressed by means of discerning Scripture's senses in early Christianity.

Making Senses of Scripture

The history of Christian biblical interpretation is sometimes tortuous by virtue of the creativity and imagination of the particular interpreters sustained by a commitment to Scripture's fecundity. It is fair to say that all interpreters were "fishermen" and prone to "flights of contemplation"; for all good interpretation, "to meander like a river is the ideal."[41] To read Scripture in a Christian manner entails rejecting any reading that is content with and limited to simplicity or mere factuality (i.e., without interest in a whole and Christian meaning).[42] Instead, moving from the simplicity of the letter to the heights (and depths) of spiritual meaning represents the manner in which interpreters are responsible for their representation of Scripture as Christians. Scripture's fecundity encourages "diverse ways of understanding that are accommodated to the diverse dispositions and necessities of souls."[43] Gregory the Great (540-604) offers that Scripture is "a river in which the lamb may ford and the elephant must swim." Augustine notes, "We feed upon the plain parts, we are exercised by the obscure."[44] Godfrey of Saint Victor (twelfth century) writes:

---

[41]Smalley, *Study of the Bible,* pp. 32-33. Quoting Gregory the Great, Smalley observes, "He that treats of sacred writ should follow the way of a river, for if a river, as it flows along its channel, meets with open valleys on its side, into these it immediately turns the course of its current, and when they are copiously supplied, presently it pours itself back into its bed. Thus unquestionably, thus should it be with everyone that treats of the Divine Word, that if, in discussing any subject, he chance to find at hand any occasion of seasonable edification, he should, as it were, force the streams of discourse towards the adjacent valley, and when he has poured forth enough upon its level of instruction, fall back into the channel of discourse which he had prepared for himself."

[42]The extremes early Christian interpreters avoided were antisymbolic literalism, on the one hand, and antiliteralistic symbolism, on the other hand. See de Margerie, *Greek Fathers,* p. 153.

[43]Saint Bernard, cited in Henri de Lubac, *Medieval Exegesis,* vol. 1, *The Four Senses of Scripture,* trans. Mark Sebanc (Grand Rapids, Mich.: Eerdmans, 1998), p. 77.

[44]Gregory, quoted in Frederick W. Farrar, *History of Interpretation* (Grand Rapids, Mich.: Baker, 1961), p. 329; Augustine, "Sermons on Selected Lessons of the New Testament," A Select Library of the Nicene and Post-Nicene Fathers of the Christian Church, ed. Philip Schaff, 1st series (Grand Rapids, Mich.: Eerdmans, 1986), 6:321.

> This stream has four different features:
> In some parts it can be crossed, in other parts it is deep.
> Here it is more pleasing to the taste, sweet and delightful,
> Nor does it flow back to the heights from which it has sprung.
> When it is more clearly history, it is easy to cross,
> Whereas it is hard to swim the deep waters of allegory,
> It is easy to drink the savory waters of morality,
> While anagogy is regurgitated and does not stay down.[45]

Scripture, to employ John Cassian's imagery, is a fruitful field yielding a banquet of distinct foods for all variety of readers due to the involved relationship between its clarity and obscurity: "Holy Scripture is fitly compared to a rich and fertile field."[46]

> And we can clearly see that the same system holds good in that most fruitful garden of the Scriptures of the Spirit, in which some things shine forth clear and bright in their literal sense, in such a way that while they have no need of any higher interpretation, they furnish abundant food and nourishment in the simple sound of the words, to the hearers.[47]

This is as God designed Scripture:

> The authority of holy Scripture says on those points on which it would inform us

---

[45]Cited in de Lubac, *Medieval Exegesis,* p. 2; along with the teaching of Giles of Paris concerning the way Scripture should be read:

> This well is deep, it plumbs the abyss . . . ,
> This simple outward shell contains a great variety of food:
> The letter is to be thought of as the outward shell, the senses as three varieties of food.
> Investigate the historical, typical, and moral senses . . .
> When you read the historical text, a kind of milky sweetness is imbibed, or rather a draught of simple water . . . ,
> In the typical sense the keen tang of wine can be felt . . .
> Whoever drinks this wine of Scripture hunts for Jesus and finds him, reaching him on the wooded heights.
> Then it is as if your mouth were sucking on a honeycomb.

[46]John Cassian, *The Second Conference of Abbot Serenus: On Principalities*, A Select Library of Nicene and Post-Nicene Fathers of the Christian Church, ed. Philip Schaff and Henry Wace, 2nd series (Grand Rapids, Mich.: Eerdmans, 1986), 11:376. Cassian continued, "While bearing and producing much which is good for man's food without being cooked by fire, produces some things which are found to be unsuitable for man's use or even harmful unless they have lost all the roughness of their raw condition by being tempered and softened down by the heat of fire. But some are naturally fit for use in both states, so that even when uncooked they are not unpleasant from their raw condition, but still are rendered more palatable by being cooked and heated by fire. Many more things too are produced only fit for the food of irrational creatures, and cattle, and wild animals and birds, but utterly useless as food for men, which while still in their rough state without being in any way touched by fire, conduce to the health and life of cattle."

[47]Ibid.

> some things so plainly and clearly even to those who are utterly void of understanding, that not only are they not veiled in the obscurity of any hidden meaning, but do not even require the help of any explanation, but carry their meaning and sense on the surface of the words and letters: but some things are so concealed and involved in mysteries as to offer us an immense field for skill and care in the discussion and explanation of them. And it is clear that God has so ordered it for many reasons.

Those reasons include the differentiation of "the profane as well as the faithful" and "between the lazy and the earnest." Another reason involves "the household of faith" and "immense differences of intellectual power," which offers "the opportunity of reproving the slothfulness of the idle, and proving the keenness and diligence of the earnest."[48] When Scripture is difficult to understand, when its meaning is veiled, the Holy Spirit has reserved this for "our meditation and exercise," but when Scripture is clear, Cassian recommends boldness: "Wherefore on those passages which are brought forward with a clear explanation we also can constantly lay down the meaning and boldly state our own opinions."[49] All of Scripture's meaning is regarded as unified—what is clear with what veiled—in order to appeal to all.

In a similar fashion Gregory the Great comments on the imagery of the rolled-up scroll of Ezekiel 2:9-10, unrolled by a (divine?) hand to reveal writing inside and out: "And so the rolled up scroll is unrolled when that which had been obscurely stated is opened, through the opening-out of interpretation."[50] He envisioned his work as a preacher as the work of an interpreter, purposefully choosing difficult, obscure biblical books to preach through and thereby clarify (e.g., Job, Ezekiel and Kings). This opening-up, this interpretation of obscurity, is to be accorded a primary importance according to Gregory. Dissatisfied with the unthinkable prospect of simply representing a text's original (historical) intent, meaning or reception, and utterly convinced that Scripture's relevance required moving beyond a literal (as in historical) sense, all varieties of Christian interpretative strategies advanced strong and Christian arguments for Scripture's spiritual senses.

The ingenuity of the interpreter is supported by the routine assertion that "the interpretation of Scripture is indefinite" in large part due to the infinity of Scripture's genuine author—God's Spirit.[51] Scripture *itself* is regarded as "undecipherable in its fullness," "a deep forest with innumerable branches," a "true

---

[48]Ibid.

[49]Ibid., p. 377. Also consult Owen Chadwick, *John Cassian: A Study in Primitive Monasticism* (Cambridge: Cambridge University Press, 1950).

[50]Cited in de Lubac, *Medieval Exegesis,* pp. 76-77.

[51]Ibid., p. 77.

labyrinth," an "unfathomable abyss," a "vast sea" or an "ocean of mystery."[52] Hidden behind the letter is spiritual meaning; Origen and company established the precedent, now western Christian theology refined the practice. For example, when Scripture's letter is simple and plain, obvious and clear, then its (hidden or secret) meanings are regarded as more consequential. Instead of relying upon what appears as plain and clear as itself significant, they indicate depth and majesty, Scripture that "seems as simple and easy in the way it is worded as it is deep in the majesty of its meanings."[53]

The modern defense of Scripture's multiple senses is well represented in the work of Henri de Lubac (he provides the best summary of a vast amount of early and medieval theological material). While de Lubac's work is seemingly a historical study of interpreting Scripture in medieval Christianity, it is really more of an apology—for theology of an ancient sense, an Origenist sense. Commentary *is* theology (and the more one appreciates the creativity of spiritual senses, the easier this is to affirm). In principle there is no possible division between theology and comment upon Scripture, and thus the justification for multiple meanings is also a justification for the theology of early and medieval Christianity. After this manner de Lubac's argument is direct: through faith in Scripture's divine nature we must also confess Scripture's duality, a twofold sense that is literal and spiritual. It is the literal sense itself that suggests the spiritual.

As threatening as these ideas of indefinite interpretation and Scripture's fecundity appear to modern sensibilities, they are conventional, systematic and pious within the developing faculty of Christian biblical interpretation. Origen contends that "one form of knowledge is not hindered by another," as does Gregory:

> To achieve an understanding of Sacred Scripture, one does not have to reject anything that does not oppose a sound faith. For just as it happens that from one lump of gold there are some who fashion necklaces, others rings, and still others ornamental bracelets, so from one science of Sacred Scriptures all of its interpreters gather up various ornamental embellishments, as it were, by way of innumerable understandings of the text. All of these ornamental embellishments add to the beauty of the celestial bride.[54]

Instead of canceling other assertions of meaning, the many sided or multifaceted shapes of God's truth—Scripture—encourage indefinite readings, with the one caveat that a uniform understanding of the one (Christian) faith must be

---

[52]The summary is found in ibid., pp. 75-76.
[53]Jerome, cited in ibid., p. 325 n. 14.
[54]Origen and Gregory, cited in de Lubac, *Medieval Exegesis*, pp. 80, 330 n. 84.

affirmed thereby. All suspected obscurity of Scripture is clarified by not one but three, four or even seven means.

Literal (historical or letter), allegorical, moral (tropological) and anagogical—these four, traditional and contrasting senses are offered often and insistently in early and medieval Christianity. There is no real difference between the quadruple senses made famous by Augustine of Hippo and Cassian, and Origen's triple senses (similar to Jerome's three senses); from the fourth century on theologians appeal to three or four senses without discrimination within a single work. Our question is whether a certain sense is regarded as clear while others are obscure? And if no particular sense is taken to be clear then is clarity a realistic assertion? It appears that the literal sense is regarded as obscure in that taken alone it will obscure multiple additional senses. However, the literal sense is clear in that properly interpreted it does not disagree with Scripture's true sense, which is Christ Jesus. By reading Scripture through the identity of Jesus Christ and orienting Christian readings around the biographically narrated first advent and the confessed second coming, interpreters were able to articulate Scripture's clarity *and* obscurity; even while uttering complete confidence in their readings they were liable to be enlightened by means of the further and future influence of the Spirit. Thus, Scripture, even in its different senses or modes of understanding, is regarded as both obscure and clear. As de Lubac summarizes:

> Thus there is a twofold fullness of time, a twofold coming of Christ. the first coming had revealed the hidden meaning of the ancient Scripture. The second coming would cause this meaning to become manifest in the full light of day. In both cases, it was even a matter of the same mystery, of that unique mystery, that was to remain veiled, albeit in a different way, until the time established by the Lord. Whether it be the mystery of Scripture, the mystery of the history of salvation, or the mystery of Christ, it was always likewise the mystery bestowed and then revealed by the sevenfold Spirit.[55]

Sevenfold? Yes, even more interesting than the assertions of quadruple meaning is the ninth century avowal of Scripture's sevenfold significance, based in part upon the significance of the number seven, especially its place in the book of Revelation. Superimposed upon the entirety of Scripture as seven historical economies, the number is linked with the seven signs of Jesus in the Gospel of John, the seven great patriarchs, some believe with the seven rules of Tyconius (which we will consider below when discussing Augustine), but most often with the seven signs seals of Revelation 5 and 6.

---

[55]Ibid., p. 86.

> Then I saw in the right hand of the one seated on the throne a scroll written on the inside and on the back, sealed with seven seals; and I saw a mighty angel proclaiming with a loud voice, "Who is worthy to open the scroll and break its seals?" And no one in heaven or on earth or under the earth was able to open the scroll or look into it. And I began to weep bitterly because no one was found worthy to open the scroll or look into it. Then one of the elders said to me, "Do not weep. See, the Lion of the tribe of Judah, the root of David, has conquered, so that he can open the scroll and its seven seals. (Rev 5:1-5 NRSV)

Encompassing both the interpreters' consternation over inaccessibility and unworthiness as interpreter of the "scroll" (taken to represent the whole of Scripture itself), it is opened, seal by seal, by the Lamb. The first level is historical, the second is allegorical and the third encompasses both historical and allegorical. The fourth regards the nature of the trinity, the fifth is parable and the sixth is about the two advents of Jesus. The seventh is concerned with moral or spiritual formation and requires the most care. These are seven modes (possibly rules) different from one another with respect to subject and therefore meaning.[56] It is not that all senses are found in all texts but that all Scripture is treated as yielding the fullness of what Christians require to live faithfully. Interestingly, since the effect of Scripture's focus is charity (actually for Augustine "there are three things for which all knowledge and prophecy struggle: faith, hope, and charity")[57] Scripture is practically dispensable: "Thus a man supported by faith, hope, and charity, with an unshaken hold upon them, does not need the Scriptures except for the instruction of others."[58]

Even as multiple sense is highlighted by such commentary (much to the chagrin of modern critics, both explicitly Christian and otherwise), simultaneously the plainness and clarity of Scripture is enunciated with reference to literal, historical or ostensive details of the text and its significance. Multiple senses constitute a "reasoning process," "styles of discourse" or "modi" with regard to the interpretation of Scripture.[59] Scripture's multiple senses are not

---

[56]De Lubac offers, "Whether it be the mystery of Scripture, the mystery of the history of salvation, or the mystery of Christ, it was always likewise the mystery bestowed and then revealed by the sevenfold Spirit. It was precisely about the Spirit that the Book of Revelation had spoken in a symbolic way by alluding to the 'seven spirits of God,' symbolized themselves by the seven torches of fire and by the seven eyes of the Lamb" (ibid., pp. 86, 88-89).

[57]Augustine, *On Christian Doctrine,* trans. D. W. Robertson Jr. (Indianapolis: Bobbs-Merrill, 1977), p. 32.

[58]Ibid. In turn, "when anyone knows the end of the commandments to be charity 'from a pure heart, and a good conscience, and an unfeigned faith,' [1 Cor 13:13] and has related all of his understanding of the Divine Scriptures to these three, he may approach the treatment of these books with security."

[59]De Lubac, *Medieval Exegesis,* p. 127.

differing applications of Scripture's simple, one meaning (or differing contemporary significance in relation to historical meaning), but charitably unified pluirform meanings, harmonious with Scripture's Author but not contradictory.

Letter *and* Spirit

In theological parlance there are not three, four or even seven ways to understand Scripture in early Christianity but really two larger and more inclusive alignments: the literal, which is also the history, the Old Testament; and the allegorical, moral and anagogical, which are also the spiritual, the New Testament. Christian theologians' defense of this distinction depends upon the authority of the New Testament rather than the Old, with a corresponding twofold perception of meaning. So de Lubac summarizes:

> The Christian tradition understands that Scripture has two meanings. The most general name for these two meanings is the literal meaning and the spiritual ("pneumatic") meaning, and these two meanings have the same kind of relationship to each other as do the Old and New Testaments to each other. More exactly, and in all strictness, they constitute, they are the Old and New Testaments.[60]

It is this relationship (not divide)—between the letter and spirit, between Old and New Testaments—that permeates the greater history of interpretation, in particular regarding the treatment of how Christians are to understand, and correspondingly what is regarded as clear and obscure.

Origen's antithetical characterization of "letter" versus "spirit" was carried on within Christian theology as an explanation of obscurities and a direction for perspicuous (i.e., Christian) interpretation. The spiritual sense was not only more important than the literal sense, but some followers of Origen's lead even claimed that certain passages had no literal sense.[61] When dealing with the occasional "deeds and utterances considered to be shameful" offered by Scripture's authors, Augustine leans in this direction also when he comments that "they are entirely figurative." Ordinary, historical expressions and actions that would usually be taken as shameful actually have a "secret meaning" that stands in contrast to the profane meaning but depends upon it to instruct.[62]

---

[60]Ibid.

[61]Beryl Smalley, "Peter Comestor on the Gospels and his Sources," *Recherches de Théologie ancienne et médiévale* 46 (1979): 84-129.

[62]Augustine, *On Christian Doctrine,* p. 90. The quote reads in full: "Those things which seem almost shameful to the inexperienced, whether simply spoken or actually performed either by the person of God or by men whose sanctity is commended to us, are all figurative, and their secrets are to be removed as kernels from the husk as nourishment for charity. . . . Thus no reasonable person would believe under any circumstances that the feet of the Lord were anointed with precious ointment by the woman in the manner of lecherous and dissolute men whose banquets we despise."

Augustine offers an interesting suggestion that the possibility exists of multiple literal meanings of some sections of the biblical text exists. As one reader of Augustine offers, there is a polysemy of the literal sense even within an essential monosemy that leads one to speak of "the meanings of the meaning."[63]

Early Christian interpreters couch the oblique and seemingly contradictory character of the Old Testament with a fittingly Christian reading in his preaching, a practice that helped convince a young Augustine to look for the spirit instead of simply at the letter. The practice is easily stated: it is the New Testament that is "spirit," that is taken literally and interpreted figuratively only when figures are obvious (e.g., the parables of the Gospels), and it is the Old Testament that is "letter," which if taken only or primarily as historical is insufficient (and obscure) but when taken as historical and also spiritual is regarded as clear.

One of the several questions that tormented Augustine while he was a student at Carthage was his concern with the troublesome understanding of the Old Testament, which was relieved only when he learned to read it by means of allegory. Hearing portions of the Old Testament explained as mysteries enabled the young Augustine to take Scripture seriously:

> I resolved, therefore, to direct my mind to the Holy Scriptures, that I might see what they were. And behold, I perceive something not comprehended by the proud, not disclosed to children, but lowly as you approach, sublime as you advance, and veiled in mysteries; and I was not of the number of those who could enter into it, or bend my neck to follow its steps.[64]

At first Augustine viewed Scripture as embarrassingly simple, obscure and absurd: "They appeared to me to be unworthy to be compared with the dignity" of philosophers. His "inflated pride shunned their style, nor could the sharpness of my wit pierce their inner meaning."[65]

What cured Augustine's embarrassment, he relates, had to do with a newfound interest: "I find Christ everywhere in those books."[66] Christ is the "total

---

[63]Bertrand de Margerie, *An Introduction to the History of Exegesis,* vol. 3, *Saint Augustine* (Petersham, Mass.: Saint Bede's Publications, 1991), p. 37.

[64]Augustine, *Confessions,* A Select Library of the Nicene and Post-Nicene Fathers of the Christian Church, ed. Philip Schaff, 1st series (Grand Rapids, Mich.: Eerdmans, 1988), 1:62 (3.5.9).

[65]Ibid.

[66]Augustine, *Contra Faustum,* A Select Library of the Nicene and Post-Nicene Fathers of the Christian Church, ed. Philip Schaff, 1st series (Grand Rapids, Mich.: Eerdmans, 1989), 4:192; cf. Philo's interpreting without Christ: "What a difference it makes whether you refer everything to Christ, with reference to whom everything was truly said in this way, or ignoring him, you hunt after no-matter-what conjecture ingenuity of mind" (Augustine *Contra Faustum* 12.39).

meaning" of Scripture to Augustine, thus the text is not limiting itself for its sense—Jesus Christ the wisdom of God—is without limit. Correspondingly, Augustine speaks of Scripture's inexhaustible meaning: it involves the single and simple commitment to Christ as the total meaning of Scripture. He sees the relationship between Scripture and Christ in light of the incarnation itself (obviously a *Christian* characterization); so "charity, the end of scripture, is directed toward a Being who knows no end, and charity hopes to possess that Being endlessly."[67] Since the goal of Scripture is singular, what is clearly taught in Scripture is correspondingly singular: "Whatever appears in the divine Words that does not literally pertain to virtuous behavior or to the truth of faith, you must take to be figurative."[68] One may say that for Augustine charity is clarity.

For Augustine the concern for Scripture itself as the display of charity (as the Bible's normative theological content) is best exemplified in the concern for Scripture's clarity: "Among those things which are said openly in Scripture are to be found all those teachings which involve faith, the mores of living, and . . . hope and charity."[69] What Scripture says openly is the same thing as what the Christian faith teaches about the normativeness of faith, hope and charity; the result is that "whatever appears in the divine Word that does not properly pertain to virtuous behavior or to the truth of faith, you must take to be figurative."[70] James Preus observes that this prioritized reading of Scripture is best understood by means of a "two-value literal sense":

> The outcome is that the clear sense of Scripture comprises in itself two distinct levels of value: some of it is edifying (teaching faith, hope, and love) in itself *(proprie),* and some of it is not. And what is not edifying is to be interpreted as having "said one thing, but meant another." It is to be "allegorized."

Preus understands Augustine's appeal to the clear and obscure portions of the Bible to be an exercise in distinguishing the "normative literal" (which is the goal of interpretation for the Christian theologian, affirming faith, hope and love), from the (oft-times) "unedifying literal" (which is equal to the obscure or portions of the text which on the level of the simple literal sense are contrary to the teaching of faith, hope, and love). In this distinction, Preus argues, the stage is set for the growing emphasis upon Scripture's literal sense in the Middle Ages, without the loss of the necessary distinction between the clear and obscure of Scripture (which we will examine in the next chapter).[71] But how,

---

[67]De Margerie, *Saint Augustine,* p. 24.
[68]Augustine, *Christian Doctrine,* p. 88.
[69]Ibid., pp. 42-43.
[70]Ibid., pp. 87-88.
[71]James Samuel Preus, *From Shadow to Promise: Old Testament Interpretation from Augustine to the Young Luther* (Cambridge, Mass.: Belknap, 1969), pp. 13-16.

in practice, did Augustine accomplish such interpretative distinctions?

Clarifying Obscurity

When confronted with the difficult work of interpreting the biblical text, Augustine referred students to the work of a Donatist named Tyconius who wrote *Of Rules,*[72] in which "he explained seven rules with which, as if with keys, the obscurities of the Divine Scriptures might be opened."[73] Tyconius addressed the basic problem of how the Old Testament was to be understood in terms of the New: the meaning of the Old was not immediately apparent, yet it is a "vast forest of prophecy."[74] The rules themselves are characterized as explicitly Christian (christological and derived from the biblical narration of creation and recapitulation, evil [the Devil], promise and law). When applied they "are of no little assistance in penetrating what is covert in the Holy Scriptures," and yet "not all the things which are so written that they are difficult to understand may be cleared up by means of these rules."[75] Tyconius himself referred to the composition of the rules as "keys and windows for the secrets of the Law."

> For there are certain mystic rules which reveal what is hidden in the whole Law and make visible the treasures of truth which are invisible to some. If the sense of these rules is accepted without envy as we have explained it, whatever is closed will be opened, and whatever is obscure will be illuminated, so that he who walks through the immense forest of prophecy led by these rules as if by pathways of light will be defended from error.[76]

Augustine objects to the optimistic tone of Tyconius because the rules are only a partial help, addressing "some of the Law"; and instead of the "whole Law" being clarified, Augustine says "much that is closed will be opened."[77] There are two problems for Augustine: Tyconius's rules are helpful but only partially so, and portions of Scripture remain genuinely obscure (and no rules or study will resolve that obscurity).

---

[72]Tyconius, *The Book of Rules of Tyconius,* ed. F. C. Burkitt (Neudeln, Liechtenstein: Kraus, 1967).

[73]Augustine, *Christian Doctrine,* p. 104. The rules of Tyconius are (1) "Of the Lord and His Body"; (2) "Of the bipartite Body of the Lord"; (3) "Of Promises and the Law"; (4) "Of Species and Genus"; (5) "Of Times"; (6) "Of Recapitulation"; and (7) "Of the Devil and his Body."

[74]Burkitt, *Rules of Tyconius,* p. xiii.

[75]Augustine, *Christian Doctrine,* pp. 104-5. Augustine cites the inadequacy of the seven rules by appealing to Tyconius's own struggle with Scripture's obscurity and concludes, "To collect all the examples of places in the Scriptures which are obscure in such a way that no one of these seven rules applies would be too laborious and tedious."

[76]Augustine's citation of Tyconius in *Christian Doctrine,* p. 105.

[77]Ibid.

Augustine, of course, has a constructive twist to address Scripture's persistent obscurity. The "many and varied obscurities and ambiguities" in Scripture tend to deceive casual readers, but this is of divine design: "I do not doubt that this situation was provided by God to conquer pride by work and to combat disdain in our minds, to which those things which are easily discovered seem frequently to become worthless." Scripture's great message is, thus, obscured because of its value and significance. In this type of setting, to affirm Scripture's clarity would be tantamount to asserting its irrelevance or insignificance. But one does not need to assert Scripture's obscurity (that much is obvious to Augustine and the greater Alexandrian tradition); the challenge is to account for this obscurity without losing faith; so Augustine: "The Holy Spirit has magnificently and wholesomely modulated the Holy Scriptures so that the more open places present themselves to hunger and the more obscure places may deter a disdainful attitude."[78]

What is clear in Scripture, according to Augustine? Charity is clear (because that is the Christian message itself); understand and appreciate that and we have understood the purpose (intent) of Scripture. "The sum of all we have said," Augustine notes, "comes to this: it is to be understood that the plenitude and the end of the Law and of all the sacred Scriptures is the love of a Being which is to be enjoyed and of a being that can share that enjoyment with us." Any use of Scripture that does not encourage the double love (of God and neighbor) "does not understand it at all."[79] But, he quickly adds, if one finds in Scripture a lesson that usefully forges charity, "even though he has not said what the author may be shown to have intended in that place," is not being deceived." What is clear in Scripture is what Scripture intends; what is intended is instruction in charity. Even in the extreme situation where one misunderstands or is deceived, this intended meaning of charity within Scripture is the ruling principle of Scripture's clarity (i.e., purpose).

> But anyone who understands in the Scriptures something other than that intended by them is deceived, although they do not lie. However, as I began to explain, if he is deceived in an interpretation that builds up charity, which is the end of the commandments, he is deceived in the same way as a man who leaves a road by mistake but passes through a field to the same place toward which the road itself leads. But he is to be corrected and shown that it is more useful not to leave the road, lest the habit of deviating force him to take a crossroad or a perverse way.[80]

Even while instruction in interpretative precepts is a necessity, the understanding of Scripture is to be regarded as (ultimately) from God. Augustine

[78]Augustine, *Christian Doctrine,* p. 38.
[79]Ibid., p. 30.
[80]Ibid., pp. 30-31.

notes coyly that those who claim immediate divine assistance in understanding Scripture's obscurities do not practice what they preach:

> Whoever, instructed by no precepts, glories in his understanding of whatever is obscure in the Scriptures through a divine gift, believes correctly in thinking that his ability does not come from himself but is divinely given, so that he seeks the glory of God and not his own. But when he reads and understands without the explanations of men, why does he presume to explain to others? Why does he not rather send them to God that they also may be inwardly instructed, not by men but by Him?[81]

Augustine accepts that interpretative precepts are essential, as essential as understanding letters, words and discourse is to the notion of reading itself. What Augustine offers is that all who wish to understand must read, and reading itself includes grammar (knowing how to read) as well as communicating this as understanding: "In the same way, he who explains to listeners what he understands in the Scriptures is like a reader who pronounces the words he knows, but he who teaches how the Scriptures are to be understood is like a teacher who advises how the words are to be read."[82] Addressing Scripture's obscurities is, up to and after Augustine, to address the manner in which God wishes to be understood by means of Scripture, and this concerns the practice of discerning the killing letter and the life-giving spirit.

Paying attention to details of the Bible's grammar, however, is not an end in itself, and especially not to be confused with the meaning of the text for the likes of Augustine. The language of the Bible is instrumental, words are signs, and idolatry is to be found in identifying meaning with the letter. As G. R. Evans observes, "The consensus of interest in the West had tended to lie in the investigation of the 'higher' or 'deeper' interpretations which make use of the power of 'things' to act figuratively, that is, as signs. That was where the kernel of the meaning was thought to lie."[83] Relish for the literal sense would recast this Western tendency as a development of Augustine's influential grammar of signs (words that alone mean nothing) and things (all realities, all encompassing). So, "there are two reasons why things written are not understood: they are obscured either by unknown or by ambiguous signs."[84] And if "no one uses

---

[81]Ibid., p. 6.

[82]Ibid. Augustine continues: "Just as a man who knows how to read will not need another reader from whom he may hear what is written when he finds a book, he who receives the precepts we wish to teach will not need another to reveal those things which need explaining when he finds any obscurity in books, since he has certain rules like those used in reading in his understanding."

[83]G. R. Evans, *The Language and Logic of the Bible: The Earlier Middle Ages* (New York: Cambridge University Press, 1984), p. 53.

[84]Ibid., p. 43.

words except as signs of something else," then the understanding of signs is valued because they "signify something else. A sign is a thing that causes us to think of something beyond the impression the thing itself makes upon the senses."[85] This investigation, Augustine offers, is intended to consider whether one can "make the meanings of words clear."[86]

The actual experience of Scripture as God's word depends upon this consideration of grammar, and it is compounded by the admission that it is subject to translation. Augustine expresses the problem that confronts Christian readers in the fifth century (and beyond):

> Thus it happened that even the Sacred Scripture, by which so many maladies of the human will are cured, was set forth in one language, but so that it could be spread conveniently through all the world it was scattered far and wide in the various languages of translators that it might be known for the salvation of peoples who desire to find in it nothing more than the thoughts and desires of those who wrote it and through these the will of God, according to which we believe those writers spoke. But many and varied obscurities and ambiguities deceive those who read casually, understanding one thing instead of another; indeed, in certain places they do not find anything to interpret erroneously, so obscurely are certain sayings covered with a most dense mist.[87]

There is much to be concerned with when considering Scripture in translation according to Augustine, not the least of which is the tendency to obscure what would otherwise be plain and perspicuous expression among its primitive readers. The "sovereign remedy" for misunderstood literal signs is "a knowledge of languages,"[88] and often the remedy for clarifying an obscure translation is simply another translation ("for an inspection of various translations frequently makes obscure passages clear").[89] Poor translation is another explanation for misunderstanding and obscurity.[90]

---

[85]Augustine, *On Christian Doctrine*, p. 34. "Thus if we see a track, we think of the animal that made the track; if we see smoke, we know that there is a fire which causes it; if we hear the voice of a living being, we attend to the emotion it expresses; and when a trumpet sounds, a soldier should know whether it is necessary to advance or to retreat, or whether the battle demands some other response." To alter Augustine's analogy, what he is considering is how one understands the message conveyed by means of signs or what is clearly understood thereby.

[86]Ibid., p. 36.

[87]Ibid., pp. 36-37.

[88]Ibid., p. 43. Augustine maintains that "signs are either literal or figurative," with literal signs being understood by means of languages, history, or simply when they are used to "designate those things on account of which they were instituted, and figurative signs being understood to depict something else."

[89]Ibid., p. 44.

[90]Ibid., pp. 44-48.

Conclusion

If the history of early biblical interpretation is the history of Origen's influence, then the theologian of the convention of allegory is Augustine of Hippo—in no small part because his experience of Scripture is linked with his experience of the Christian gospel, his conversion and *Confessions.* Augustine's admission of Scripture's obscurity (understood as simply the letter sense, following Origen and Alexandrian influences) in relationship with its clarity (the spirit-sense, the Christian sense) came to dominate so much of what is now simply called the early and medieval tradition. This emphasis is also a significant part of what concerned reformers of both Catholic and Protestant churches, as we will see in the next chapter.

What kind of interpretative models accompany early Christian assertions of Scripture's clarity and obscurity, and by what means do Christians actually practice the distinction between clarity and obscurity? The dominant account of these questions is found by tracing the influence of the interpretative methods associated with Alexandria, linked with Scripture's multiple senses (especially when compared to discussions of Scripture's literal sense). The most concise description of this tradition is found in employment of allegory. Early Christian interests are further illustrated by observing the disputes raised by Antiochene interpreters such as Theodore and Chrysostom, especially when they go so far as to deny the validity of allegory itself!

What unites early Christian interpretation is the consistent and Christian appeal to typology—a dominant (and sufficient) theme for Antioch, but less so for Alexandria. The historical figure is trumped by the search for spiritual significance (meaning). Alexandrian emphases are further developed theologically by the like of Augustine of Hippo, with an emphasis upon discerning Scripture's message in dialogue with its obscurity and clarity. Clarity is a theological assertion for Augustine, having to do with the indispensable message of charity. The effort to represent the Christian faith itself came to be associated with the use of allegory as an antidote to Scripture's obscurity.

While Christian interpretative obscurity (regarding the Old Testament) dominates through early Christianity, it is consistently united with a corresponding sense of interpretative clarity (respecting the New Testament). The proper message of Scripture (i.e., the Christian message) is regarded as clearly depicted within the whole, but there is an unevenness to this clarity that is both illustrated by and explained by means of Scripture's multiple senses, especially as it is expressed by means of Alexandrian interpretative interests. When Scripture's obscurity is presumed, then the practice of allegory seems to be a practical necessity, while the assumption of textual realism seems to entail the necessity of clarity.

4

LITERALLY CLEAR

They read from the Book of the Law of God, making it clear and giving the meaning so that the people could understand what was being read.

NEHEMIAH 8:8

One should not want to force Scripture to have a single sense in such a way that other senses which have truth in them and can be adapted to Scripture by agreeing with the way the words go are completely excluded. . . . Every truth which can be adapted to divine Scripture, while agreeing with the way the words go, is the sense of Scripture.

THOMAS AQUINAS, *QUAESTIONES DISPUTATAE DE POTENTIA*

THE NOTION THAT SCRIPTURE CARRIES WITH IT ITS OWN CONVENTION OF reading—its own clarity—is beguilingly simple. There is an intense and yet dual concern in the Middle Ages to stress both the divine (i.e., theological) nature of Scripture properly understood and Scripture's literal sense. That one is seen and fulfilled in the other (with no particular priority to be observed between them) is what is so beguiling and at the same time simple about the way Christians read Scripture in the Middle Ages. It is not simply that the theological nature of Scripture cancelled grammatical and historical concerns, nor is it that historical and grammatical demands rendered what is theologically plausible about Scripture. Instead, the subject of Scripture's literal sense is the point of convergence between theological, grammatical and historical concerns. And Scripture's literal sense is found by reading and understanding, as Thomas Aquinas put it, "the way the words go."

Notwithstanding Protestant insistence (addressed in chapter five), we do not need to wait until early sixteenth-century Protestantism to discover our theme of perspicuity. It is evident in the cultivation of biblical interpretation of Scripture's literal sense in the Middle Ages (and the compromise of medieval interpretative interests in the early Protestant tradition). Linked with a conserving approach to Scripture's necessity and a commitment to Scripture's own grammar (theologically understood), we see an interesting display of the affirmation of Scripture's clarity—not exhausted but illustrated thereby. These two themes—Scripture's necessity and unique grammar—are united by a medieval effort to discern and defend Scripture's literal sense. "The medieval hermeneutical tradition," as James Preus expressed, "can be characterized as an authentic attempt to establish the *sensus litteralis* of Scripture as its principal meaning, and to give it a theologically normative role in the formation of Christian theology."[1] A quote from Paul of Burgos (c. 1351-1435) gives ample evidence of these sentiments: "It holds good therefore that all things that are handed down as necessary for salvation, to be believed or done, are found in Holy Scripture in its literal sense."[2]

Biblical interpretation in the Middle Ages genuinely struggled to realize the developing sense of an alliance of literal and spiritual senses, often seeking to overcome the antithesis of letter versus spirit characteristic of early Christian interpretative interests. The comparisons and contrasts between the letter (in contrast to spirit) and the literal (which encompasses spiritual) sense are amply explained by recognizing how the Bible functioned practically as God's word. As David Lyle Jeffrey observes: "For most Christians, at least until the time of the Reformation, the Bible was not so much itself the *locus* as the recording *witness* to God's authority. Its purpose as text was thought to assist in the reestablishment of right relationship between God, the ultimate Author, and his fallen alienated readers."[3] The relationship of Scripture as *witness* and Scripture as the *locus* of God's authority is significant in the story of Christian regard for the text and its interpretation, particularly in that the stronger the emphasis upon Scripture itself the stronger the insistence upon Scripture's clarity.

This chapter will provide a survey and summary of an expansive timeframe—from the fifth to the early sixteenth century—but not because of the insignificance of these times for our subject. In part this précis of the Middle Ages is to be explained by the more implicit (and sometimes sparse) nature of reflection on the subject. The unifying theme throughout this chapter is the matter of Scripture's literal sense in conversation with the persistent contrast of letter and spirit.

Positively Medieval

A developing appreciation of the literal sense of Scripture is what makes bibli-

---

[1]James Samuel Preus, *From Shadow to Promise: Old Testament Interpretation from Augustine to the Young Luther* (Cambridge, Mass.: Belknap, 1969), p. 3.

[2]Cited in ibid., p. 91.

[3]The result, in part, was that the distinctly Christian life was not as immediately or necessarily related to awareness of Scripture (or literacy) before the Reformation as it became after the Protestant (re-)turn to the text of Scripture (David Lyle Jeffrey, *People of the Book: Christian Identity and Literary Culture* [Grand Rapids, Mich.: Eerdmans, 1996], p. xv).

cal interpretation in the Middle Ages medieval.[4] In the growing concern for Scripture's literal sense—an interest usually associated with a theologically grammatical reading of Scripture—we observe a wonderfully attentive approach to interpreting Scripture with a renewed appreciation for its historical and theological significance.[5] That is, instead of limiting or dismissing the sustained significance of Scripture (especially Old Testament), the link between historical and theological heightened medieval appreciation for the divine meaning (and unity) of the text. Thus David Steinmetz observes, "Medieval theologians defended the proposition, so alien to modern biblical studies, that the meaning of Scripture in the mind of the prophet who first uttered it is only one of its possible meanings and may not, in certain circumstances, even be its primary or most important meaning."[6] This is manifest in three interrelated ways: the divine intent of Scripture's sense(s), the shifting landscape of the letter and spirit antithesis, which contributed to (as we will see here and in the next section) the developing appreciation for the literal sense of Scripture itself.

The almost routine association or conflation of the (human and historical) author of Scripture with Scripture's real author (God, the Spirit) is theologically justified by understanding the intersection of Scripture's primary theological character. While the subject of Scripture's literal sense is a vast (and diverse) field of study, in the Middle Ages it is best described as "the divine-literal sense," which "comprehends all the senses of Scripture—literal and spiritual, plain and hidden, present and future."[7] The literal sense is not simply the matter of human grammar but theologically understood as the primary sense intended by the principal Author. Because of this it is routine to suggest, as Ernald of Bonneval (c. 1351-1435) does, that it is a necessity to say that Scripture employs similitudes to express divine things in human signs (words). In turn, one must recognize similitudes in order to explain the obscurities of

---

[4]For helpful discussion and summary of biblical interpretation and the Middle Ages consult Jesse J. Gellrich, *The Idea of the Book in the Middle Ages: Language Theory, Mythology, and Fiction* (Ithaca, N.Y.: Cornell University Press, 1985); Jeffrey, *People of the Book,* pp. 139-66.

[5]Contemporary interpreters of Scripture routinely bemoan the flights of fancy attributed to allegorizing and nonhistorical (spiritual) readings of Scripture and suspect that the assumption of multiple senses is simply an excuse to find any meaning whatsoever in Scripture. Surprisingly, the turn to emphasize the literal sense in the Middle Ages engendered a similar suspicion: "the letter" [i.e., literal sense] is compared to "a harlot, open to any sense whatsoever" (anonymous commentator in the late twelfth century, cited in Beryl Smalley, *Studies in Medieval Thought and Learning: From Abelard to Wyclif* [London: Hembledon, 1981], p. 127).

[6]David C. Steinmetz, "The Superiority of Pre-Critical Exegesis," *Theology Today* 37, no. 1 (1980): 28.

[7]Preus, *Shadow to Promise,* p. 54.

Scripture. Likenesses are drawn thereby, either for ornament, to make something difficult easier to understand, or out of necessity "because there is no other way of making something clear."[8]

From the Christian fathers to late medieval theologians there exists an intense exertion to address, account for and effectively overcome the obscurities of the Bible, not just to point out the obscurities but provide a discretely Christian explanation of their place in Scripture. The most common account is after this fashion: In the garden of Eden God spoke directly and clearly to Adam, and Adam understood God perfectly (Gen 2). However Adam's willful disregard for the perspicuous direction of God consigned the progeny to a perpetual inability to hear God's clear commands clearly (Genesis 3 to the present). But in God's mercy Scripture still addresses the human in sin, indulging corrupted understanding, by purposefully employing oblique speech, allegories and human figures (particularly anthropomorphisms to represent divine identity). Shifting the culpability for Scripture's obscurities from God to humans in sin not only vindicated God but also effectively provided an explanation for Scripture's direct, plenary, verbal and errorless inspiration in spite of its apparent obscurities and inconsistencies. "Each obscure passage or tortuous narrative, each ambiguity or contradiction, meets an obscurity or twist or confusion in human thinking and in thus more, not less, intelligible to man's clouded sinful mind."[9]

How then to address the obscure is a significant part of serious attention to biblical interpretation in the Middle Ages, regarded as essential to *The Language and Logic of the Bible* (the title of G. R. Evans's work). In the eleventh century the study of the Bible in Latin necessitated the study of grammar (once Latin ceased as the vernacular) and the admission that the Bible "failed to conform to the rules of syntax, or to use words in the usual way." The attempt to

---

[8]So the summary of G. R. Evans, *The Language and Logic of the Bible: The Earlier Middle Ages* (Cambridge: Cambridge University Press, 1984), p. 102. Similitude (and correspondingly, analogy) serve to account for difficulties and even contradictions in Scripture. Abelard employs the image of the wax seal to explain how "the wax and the image made by the seal are both identical and different." Thus, "Abelard suggests that if we take the relation of the word and what it signifies in one way *(absolute),* a statement may be read in one sense, whereas if we take it another way *(relative),* the relation between word and thing signified yields another meaning. In this way irreconcilables may be present in a single statement and both be true" (p. 105).

[9]Ibid., pp. 2-3. Evans also offers, "These are ideas which would have been familiar to every Western reader of the Bible from the early Christian centuries to the Reformation and beyond. They are no longer a common heritage, and they require explanation if we are to understand the force they had for educated people for more than a thousand years. Their great attraction lay in the key they provided to everything which is obscure and apparently contradictory in the pages of the Bible."

resolve these difficulties was concerned with explaining the "obscurities in the Bible" by means of the principles of logic and laws of grammarians.[10] Grammar and logic were employed to resolve seeming contradictions in Scripture, focusing on smaller units such as figures, words and syntax in a manner that rivals and expands upon the early Christian assertion that clear texts are to be employed to understand obscure texts.[11] This attention to the details of the biblical text contributed to concern for how each text figured in the practice of theology. More precisely, and more theologically, Christians were concerned with how to stipulate the uniqueness of Scripture's meaning (understanding) without ignoring the letter (its ordinariness).[12]

From Augustine of Hippo's *On Christian Doctrine*[13] through John Wyclif's (1320-1384) *The Truth of Sacred Scripture,* the theological significance of grammar was essential to theological commentary and scriptural explanation—God's grammar as opposed to simply human and common grammar.[14] Scripture shows "a new grammar and new logic" according to Wyclif and should therefore be explained by a "new sense of the terms in Scripture, whose usage is not to be gotten out of grammar texts."[15] Wyclif recalls his early reluctance to

---

[10]Ibid., p. viii.

[11]G. R. Evans, "Wyclif's *Logic* and Wyclif's Exegesis: The Context," in *The Bible in the Medieval World,* ed. Katherine Walsh and Diana Wood (Oxford: Basil Blackwell, 1985), pp. 297-300.

[12]The study of the unique (theological) grammar associated with Scripture is one of the primary themes from Christian theology in the Middle Ages that contributes to the manner in which the themes of obscurity and clarity are understood. If one turns from letter to literal sense, as medieval theologians in the West tended to do, then the study of the manner of expression, specifically Scripture's grammar, becomes essential. Fulfilling (and possibly Christianizing) the displacement of Greek in favor of Latin in the Roman Empire toward the beginning of the third century, the famous Latin translator Jerome followed a long line of anonymous Christian translators of the Old Testament (Jaroslav Pelikan, *The Christian Tradition: A History of the Development of Doctrine,* vol. 1, *The Emergence of the Catholic Tradition [100-600]* [Chicago: University of Chicago Press, 1971], pp. 20-21). Pelikan observes that even with the rise of Latin and the obscuring of Greek in the Western parts of the Empire, no Jew translated the Old Testament into Latin; that is, Latin translation was a Christian task. By Jerome's admission, translation and theological grammar were essentially one exercise inasmuch as Christian interpretative interests were linked with the most intricate features of the text: "In the divine Scriptures every word, syllable, accent and point is packed with meaning" (cited in J. N. D. Kelly, *Early Christian Doctrines* [New York: Harper & Row, 1976], p. 62). Translations prompted interpreters to pay even greater attention to Scripture's detail (so as not to miss what God provides thereby), which in turn reinforced the allegorical interest in Scripture's minute detail, which in turn was coupled with the affirmation of Scripture's inspiration.

[13]Augustine wrote the first three books of *On Christian Doctrine* in 397; he added the fourth book in 426. Augustine, *On Christian Doctrine,* trans. D. W. Robertson Jr. (Indianapolis: Bobbs-Merrill, 1977).

[14]For more detailed summaries of Wyclif as a biblical interpreter, see S. H. Thompson, "The Philosophical Basis of Wycliffe's Theology," *Journal of Religion* 11, no. 1 (1931): 86-116; and Evans, "Wyclif's *Logic* and Wyclif's Exegesis," pp. 287-300.

[15]Cited in Jeffrey, *People of the Book,* p. 178.

go beyond a simple, univocal sense of Scripture toward an appreciation for "the mystical expressions of Scripture," specifically: "When I spoke as a child, I tied myself up in my anxiety to understand and defend the Scriptures according to their way of speech. . . . At last God of his grace opened their sense to me to understand the equivocation of Scripture."[16] Instead of childish equivalence (this is only that), Wyclif taps into the well-established polysemeity and equivocation attributed to scriptural language. So, he can assert that while Scripture is "written according to the pattern of our speech," its understanding is assuredly proper when conjoined with the expectation that Scripture is God's speech according to God's grammar.[17]

Much like Augustine's experience of Scripture as obscure until his "conversion" through the preaching of Ambrose, Wyclif's comprehension of Scripture experienced a conversion when he came to appreciate freedom from simple (Latin) grammar: "Blessed be God, who has freed us from the superficial snares of words in order to direct our mind's eye to penetrate to their meaning."[18] This put at his disposal all the theological (and correspondingly adapted philosophical) resources of the Christian faith to clarify Scripture's obscurities by means of the union of Author and reader by means of the text. Intention was of utmost importance, as it is linked with the will of both Author and reader, but primarily because it is God's intention that is to be accomplished by means of Scripture. Thus, to understand Scripture requires the virtuous desire of the reader—what David Lyle Jeffrey names as Wyclif's *faithful reader*—to understand the intention of Scripture's author—God's Spirit.[19]

---

[16]Quoted in Smalley, *Studies in Medieval Thought,* p. 405. Also, "Assuming the truth of the faith of Scripture, we must examine one by one what the words of this Gospel [i.e., Jn 6:59] signify to the faithful. It should be noted that the first word ["bread"] can have a double sense in a perfectly orthodox way" (cited in Evans, "Wyclif's Logic," p. 290).

[17]Cited in Jeffrey, *People of the Book,* pp. 9-10. Jeffrey reinforces the notion we have been pursuing regarding the interrelatedness of text, interpretation and interpreter in his discussion of polysemeity: "Language is polysemous simply as the human imagination is various at the practical level—yet polysemeity functions in relation to an intermediate *totum integrum,* either to the constructs of a text as a whole, or to the known community of interpreters. . . . The reading of any text by such a community is not then univocal, but, as Wyclif is at pains to say, is true of Jesus' use of language in parable, it is 'equivocal,' alternatively spoken, even 'poly-vocal.' What gets voiced, always partially even when truly, presumably continues to deserve diverse voicing because it is repeatedly found, in multiplied encounters, to be incomplete in itself, yet in some proper sense of the term meaning-full" (p. 10).

[18]John Wyclif, *De domino divino,* translated in Jeffrey, *People of the Book,* p. 406.

[19]Wyclif is truly a late medieval biblical interpreter, although his fame as a reformer or even a forerunner of Protestantism is often stressed (to the detriment of understanding his firm place in medieval theology). See Beryl Smalley, "Wyclif's *Postilla* on the Old Testament and his *Principium,*" in *Oxford Studies Presented to Daniel Callus, O.P.* (Oxford: Oxford University Press, 1964), pp. 253-96; and Smalley, *Studies in Medieval Thought,* pp. 399-404.

What is ultimately clear about Scripture is that which is of principal importance which is nothing else than what God intends to accomplish thereby. So, particularly Thomas Aquinas (1227-1274): "Truly, the literal sense is that which the author intended; but the author of sacred Scripture is God, who comprehends in his *intellectus* all things at once. Therefore it is not inappropriate . . . if even according to the literal sense there are several meanings in one letter of Scripture."[20] In this manner the so-called literal sense is not set against spiritual sense, but the former is most often explained in light of the latter. That is, the "literal sense is the whole meaning of the inspired writer, and the spiritual the significance which God has given to sacred history."[21] Aquinas treats Scripture as a sign of the faith (not faith's symbol, for the symbol of all the teaching of Scripture is Jesus Christ),[22] to be understood thereby: "The truth of faith is contained in sacred Scripture, but diffusely, in divers ways and, sometimes, darkly." The presumption is that Scripture is be understood by means of "a principle of charity," as Bruce Marshall suggests of Thomas's scheme. Therefore, Marshall observes:

> Precisely in order to minimize the likelihood that their identifications of the plain sense ascribe falsity to Scripture, Christians ought to be prepared, wherever possible (that is, insofar as the words allow), to revise and expand what they take to be the plain sense in light of whatever well-supported claims are pertinent. In doing so they will uphold what I have called the principle of charity, which stipulates that alien claims ought to be interpreted in such a way which, without ceasing to be a plausible interpretation, maximizes the range of such claims which can be held true according to standards internal to the Christian web of belief, primarily coherence with the plain sense of Scripture. . . . Christians should seek the plain sense in ways which maximize the number of well-supported beliefs they can hold true without prejudice to the way the words go.[23]

Although it is necessary for all to know the truth of the Christian faith from Scripture, not all have the capacity for such labor. Thus, summaries of the faith become necessary: "This is why there was a need to draw succinctly together out of the Scriptural teachings some clear statement to be set before all for their belief."[24] Such statements not only help clarify what one must understand

---

[20]Thomas Aquinas, *Summa Theologiæ,* ed. Thomas Gilby, 61 vols. (New York: Blackfriars, McGraw-Hill, 1964-1981), 1:39.

[21]Cited in Beryl Smalley, *The Study of the Bible in the Middle Ages* (Notre Dame, Ind.: University of Notre Dame Press, 1964), p. 41.

[22]Jeffrey, *People of the Book,* p. 243.

[23]Bruce D. Marshall, "Absorbing the World: Christianity and the Universe of Truths," in *Theology and Dialogue,* ed. Bruce D. Marshall (Notre Dame, Ind.: University of Notre Dame Press, 1990), pp. 96-97.

[24]Aquinas, *Summa Theologiæ,* 31:51.

by means of Scripture, they also serve to indicate the divine relationship of literal and spiritual in Scripture itself. So Aquinas offers:

> God, who is the author of Holy Scripture, possesses the power not only to adapt words to meanings, which we can do, but also to adapt things to meanings. What is peculiar to Holy Scripture is this, the things there signified by words may also in their turn signify other things. The first signification, whereby words signify facts, is called the historical and literal sense; the second signification, whereby the facts signified by the words also signify other facts, is called the spiritual sense. Note that the spiritual sense is based on, and presupposes, the literal sense.[25]

According to Aquinas, Scripture was to be explained by means of its literal sense (and original intention) but not so as to preclude the divine intent of Scripture (and expectation of the reader) in which "their spiritual interpretation was an addition, not a substitute."[26] And the literal sense of Scripture is "that which is gotten through what the letter signifies, by which words signify things."[27]

How is it that the ideas of the literal sense and spiritual (allegorical) sense collide in the same interpretative framework? From Augustine into the Middle Ages, higher, spiritual or divine sense is founded upon the notion that one thing is understood through another (the divine/spiritual sense is understood through the literal sense). Paul of Burgos echoed these sentiments: "Nothing is contained under the spiritual sense necessary for faith and morals which Scripture does not plainly give elsewhere through the literal sense."[28] Allegorical sense is not employed as an alternative to the literal or historical sense, nor is it thought to be contrary to human or historical intent. To offer a summary (probably overstated but nonetheless necessary): human intention, while distinguished to account for human mutability and historical experience, is best understood as the occasional means to express what is literal to God—the real literal sense of Scripture.[29] Indeed, in order for a sense to be designated literal,

---

[25]Aquinas, *Summa Theologiæ,* 1:37.

[26]Smalley, *Studies in Medieval Thought,* p. 162. Smalley's summary in full reads, "St. Thomas needed to clear his mind when he turned to the literal and spiritual senses of Scripture: he had to fight a war on two fronts. On one front, he had to engage in a mopping up operation. Masters of the sacred page had widened the literal sense of Scripture so as to include verbal simile, metaphor, parable and symbolic action or gesture. Words and actions recorded in Scripture had to be explained according to their first intention; their spiritual interpretation was an addition, not a substitute."

[27]Cited in Preus, *Shadow to Promise,* p. 90.

[28]Cited in ibid., p. 92.

[29]As Preus summarizes the kinds of literal sense in Aquinas: "The grammatical and historical, corresponding to the intention of the human author; the divine-literal, corresponding to the intention of the divine author and unfolded piecemeal to human beings; and the traditional normative-literal, to which the spiritual senses apparently are to conform" (ibid., pp. 54-55).

Paul of Burgos asserted, "it is required that it is intended by the author of sacred Scripture, who is God."[30] And even though defended differently during the Middle Ages, one may confidently say that the literal sense of Scripture is that which *corresponds with* God's intended sense. Some emphasize and others reject the significance of the historical sense, but a consensus exists in that the literal is the sense that God intends, and it is this literal sense that is regarded as clear.

Letter *and* Spirit

To emphasize the literal sense in the Middle Ages is to de-emphasize the sharp but prevalent contrast of letter versus spirit. For early and medieval Christian interpreters the antithetical characterization of letter and spirit was used to buttress the mandate to interpret the Old Testament allegorically if one was to interpret it Christianly.[31] But without losing sight of the necessity of allegory, biblical interpreters increasingly sought (spiritual) allegory in union with (historical) letter. As Wai-Shing Chau makes obvious in his work *The Letter and the Spirit,* there is a discernable shift from regarding letter versus spirit strictly as law not gospel with an either-or stress in terms of historical discontinuity and spiritual continuity, to letter and spirit as a dynamic contrast literally understood to portray the spiritual reality of the letter (which will eventually bear significant fruit in the likes of Martin Luther, as we will see shortly). The question became more and more about the spiritual and real purpose of the (Old Testament) letter as law and its clarity as the will of God itself.

In the letter versus spirit dichotomy the gospel is not thought of as new but rather hidden or obscured by the letter (and uncovered and clarified by allegorically rendering the letter by means of the spirit). And since all (of the Old) is mystery, an allegory (of the New), it lacks reality in itself. It literally kills when it is interpreted literally (i.e., without Christ and Christian salvation). To say that the Old Testament is to be read as clear in itself is explicitly rejected; the letter only obscures that which is real (spiritual), which is Christ everywhere present (as in the legacy of Origen).[32] In the letter and spirit contrast developed in Augustine, the letter is both the literal meaning of the text itself and a figure of the spirit, but not every letter is about Christ and the

---

[30]Cited in ibid., p. 90.

[31]Especially evident in Ernst Käsemann, "The Spirit and the Letter," in *Perspectives on Paul,* trans. M. Kohl (Philadelphia: Fortress, 1971), pp. 139-55.

[32]So Origen argued: "If anyone wants to hear and understand these things strictly literally, he ought to address himself to the Jews rather than to the Christians, but if he wants to be a Christian and a disciple of Paul, let him hear him saying 'For the law is spiritual' " (cited in Evans, *Language and Logic,* p. 115).

spirit is not obscurely hidden in every letter, but prefigures Christ.[33] So Augustine's 412 C.E. treatise, *The Spirit and the Letter,* admits a negative-positive (fear-love) character to the letter-spirit contrast. The law of Moses (the letter of 2 Cor 3:6) makes clear human sin, but this is only accomplished in conjunction with the grace of the spirit: "This grace lay hidden in the Old Testament under a veil. It is revealed in the gospel of Christ, according to that perfectly ordered dispensation of history by which the wisdom of God disposes all things in their time."[34] For Augustine, obscurity kills and clarity saves.

After this fashion it is often the case that the letter is taken to be the law of Moses (according to its purpose) and spirit as the Holy Spirit. The letter literally is about the purpose of the law and this function is said to be about Christ; that is, pointing the reader to the law's fulfillment in Christ, which is supplied by the message of the New Testament. It is clarified and clear in relation to Christ. So the *Glossa Ordinaria* (a mid-twelfth century compilation of patristic glosses from the school of Loan, widely used and significant)[35]: interprets the "end of the law" (Rom 10:4) as fulfilled (not destroyed) in Christ: "Righteousness is from Christ; because if it is through the written or natural law and not faith in Christ, Christ died to no purpose."[36] The "letter which kills" is interpreted as "the law without the spirit, which is thus misunderstood due to the lack of faith, and becomes condemning."[37] So, popular maxims read: "Truth puts the shadows to flight! Light gives illumination to the night!"; "The actual thing abolishes the figurative representation and light gives illumination to the shadowy darkness" (Adam of Saint Victor, twelfth century); "Thus, after the very truth that had been signified came on the scene, the cloak of shadowy meaning went into abeyance" (Peter Damian, 1007-1072); "With a sudden burst of light our Lord Jesus Christ broke out of the thick forest of allegory, in the dark gloom of which he had been hidden up to that point" (Aelred, 1109-1166); "The actual appearance of truth means an end to the figurative" (Pseudo-Hugh); and "But when, at the coming of the Savior, the truth was revealed, everything that had preceded him in the realm of shadow passed away" (Isidore of Seville, 570-636).[38] Clarity, then, arises from the awareness of Christ,

---

[33]Wai-Shing Chau, *The Letter and the Spirit: A History of Interpretation from Origen to Luther* (New York: Peter Lang, 1995), pp. 114-15.

[34]Augustine, "The Spirit and the Letter," in *Augustine: Later Works*, ed. J. Burnaby (Philadelphia: Westminster Press, 1955), p. 216.

[35]Smalley, *Study of the Bible,* pp. 56-66.

[36]Cited in Chau, *Letter and the Spirit,* p. 116.

[37]Ibid., p. 118.

[38]Cited in Henri de Lubac, *Medieval Exegesis,* vol. 1, *The Four Senses of Scripture,* trans. Mark Sebanc (Grand Rapids, Mich.: Eerdmans, 1998), pp. 231-33, 429 n. 87, n. 88, n. 92. We may

and the contrast of letter and spirit is resolved, as it were, and when the letter has been fulfilled it is left behind.[39] The shift, a minimal one admittedly, is from letter (Old Testament as always and only obscure) versus spirit (New Testament as literal and solely clear, following Origen's influence), to letter (what is obscure in both Testaments inasmuch as it is a shadow of something else and must therefore be understood allegorically) in contrast to spirit (that which is directly concerned with love and the grace of Christ).

The troubling tension between law and gospel is readdressed in a variety of twelfth-century commentaries, especially evident in works concerned with Leviticus. Usually Christian apologetes thought it necessary to ridicule the absurdity of reading the law literally—as Beryl Smalley describes the experience of interpreters:

> Many precepts struck them as irrational, inconsistent, trivial and impossible to observe; their literal sense made nonsense. Such precepts "cried out as with voices," to quote Ralph of Flaix, calling to Christians to interpret them according to their spiritual senses only. They had no true literal meaning; they conveyed a spiritual message instead. [But a certain anonymous commentator in the twelfth-century], on the contrary, believed that all precepts had a true literal sense, even though he could find no reason for some of them. He handled the denial of a literal sense with a cautious firmness.[40]

Specific commands such as circumcision and sacrificial details were understood to point the person toward God's promise of forgiveness (with forgiveness genuinely conferred by the rite itself but not apart from the Christian explanation of efficacy fulfilled in Christ's sacrificial death); dietary regulations, stipulations regarding livestock, calendars and sabbaths were read as instructions testing obedience, conferring and increasing virtue for any and all who sought God's will. The precepts of the law had a moral function: irregularities and obscurities were explainable (i.e., one could offer a reasonable explanation of how obscurities could be obeyed), and a spiritual (and moral) evaluation of the function of the law was offered as clarifying.

It seems no accident that twelfth-century interpreters who held an acute concern for seeking Scripture's literal sense also held audiences, consulted or even lived with Jews at times and sought to comprehend the positive value of

---

add Adam of Saint Victor's hymn: "The law came first by way of figures, the penal law, the shadowy law, then the light of the Gospel. Let the spiritual understanding, covered by the leaves of the letter, come forth into public view!" (p. 243).

[39]So Augustine: "When he has been made righteous, he is to use [the law] no longer, even as the use of a vehicle ceases at the journey's end, or the use of a tutor when instruction is completed" ("Spirit and the Letter," p. 206).

[40]Smalley, *Studies in Medieval Thought,* p. 39.

observing the (Old Testament) law.[41] Twelfth-century rabbis continued to assert the immutability of the law in its entirety and against Christian interpreters who they contended had arbitrarily selected this or that text to be taken literally while they consigned so much more to spiritual allegory (i.e., Christian interpretation). Part of the response was to distinguish layers or levels within the whole of the Old Testament itself, arguing that there was necessary to recognize an intertextual discrimination. This involved an appeal to the text that was validated by citing Scripture itself (so Ralph of Flaix in his copious commentary on Leviticus).[42] Simple rituals were clear themselves and addressed to the simple among the Jews, but even the plainly said commands required instruction to prevent idolatry and superstition in place of true religion (e.g., the way Isaiah [Is 1:10-20] comments upon the misuse and misrepresentation of the signs of sacrifice) or were instituted to prevent the kinds of idolatry the Israelites would have been accustomed to in Egypt. But this did not mean that ceremonies and rituals lacked additional senses, even indications of grace that the further instructed would appreciate, or a prophetic sense evidenced by the internal and spiritual tone of sacrifice mentioned by Samuel (1 Sam 15:20-31), David (Ps 51), the prophet Ezekiel (Ezek 20:18-26) and especially Jeremiah (Jer 31:31-34).[43]

Such matters were aided by the comments of rabbi Moses Maimonides (1135-1204) in his *Guide to the Perplexed,* who suggested that God adapted his commands to the particular circumstances of his people and regarded ceremonial precepts as "God's gracious ruse," intended to elicit a worshiping response from a struggling people.[44] That Maimonides regarded common people as inferior was not objectionable to most; God merely provided what the vulgar needed to know clearly, while the elite, faithful and intelligent during the dispensation of the old law looked for more than the simple, clear command.[45]

---

[41]Ibid., pp. 46-47. "What motives drove scholars to study the literal sense of the Old Testament books? That is one of the darkest problems connected with the twelfth-century [Victorines] revival. Hugh of St. Victor explained at length why the 'literal foundation' ought not to be neglected. But a rather shallow foundation for the superstructure of the spiritual senses had satisfied most exegetes in the early middle ages. Whence came the sudden urge to dig wider and deeper, to study Hebrew and to question rabbis?"

[42]Smalley, *Studies in Medieval Thought,* pp. 49-96.

[43]This line of argument was surprisingly common in twelfth-century biblical commentary among Christian apologetes involved in rejecting the Catharist heretics of Italy (who rejected the Old Testament as devilish) and preaching missionaries during the Albigensian crusades. See Smalley, *Studies in Medieval Thought,* pp. 121-81.

[44]Ibid., p. 134.

[45]Smalley observes the correspondences between Maimonides and Christian interpreters: "His belief in a hierarchy of wisdom corresponded to the Christian teaching that the élite of the Old Testament already belonged to the New, in that they perceived the prefiguration of the

The *Guide* would thus serve as an influential contribution to the Christian taste for the literal sense of Scripture (without lapsing back toward Judaism), in large part because it was a genuinely discriminating commentary upon the unevenness and development within Scripture itself.

Into the thirteenth century commentators cited Scripture to interpret Scripture, not simplistically (as in using the clear to interpret the unclear or later to interpret earlier statements) but by uniting signs and words in a literal union. Actions were used to depict words and "prophetic gestures were intended to make the words of the prophets clearer and more impressive to all."[46] So the prophets are attributed a generous and perspicuous spirit by twelfth-century commentators. But Moses remained an obscuring figure with spiritual intentions; he hides, conceals and obscures in secret language the divine message meant for the spiritual minority, the mature who understood that God lisps to the child (a notion in Ralph of Flaix that readers of John Calvin will find familiar). The test was whether a text will "stand according to the letter" with a goal to "save the letter."[47] If a text did not pass this test, then obviously the text was meant to teach a mystery, literally.

From Shadow to Clarity

The important question is, how did we get to this association of clarity with the literal sense as in the intent of God's Spirit? The larger subject of this understanding of literal sense is addressed by James Preus in his 1969 work *From Shadow to Promise*. His modus is to trace the pedigree of biblical interpretation in the Middle Ages as a means of characterizing Martin Luther's significance in his late medieval setting. In particular he focuses upon the literature of Scripture that tends to dominate methodological discussions during these times—the book of Psalms. Preus notes a significant shift that explains, in part, what is unique about the early Protestant Reformation—a shift from interpreting Christ as the speaker in the Psalms (taken as the literal sense of the Psalms) to the (Old Testament) speaker himself or

---

Gospel in *legalia*. Hence the *Guide* accorded with Christian tradition in presenting the Law as wholesome for all, sufficient for the people, and a mine of deeper wisdom for the élite." And "A book catches on if it broaches problems which concern its readers and if its answers forestall or put more clearly what readers had in mind beforehand. The *Guide* had just this relevance in the early thirteenth-century" (Smalley, *Studies in Medieval Thought*, pp. 135-36).

[46]Ibid., pp. 72-73.

[47]Ibid., pp. 75, 78-79. In fairness, Smalley thinks that the emphasis upon the literal sense in the twelfth century is uneven in its application (subject to suspension routinely in the likes of Ralph of Flaix). Commentators' efforts to discover absurdities and in light of such instances to suspend one's concern for the literal sense, should temper the idea that the literal sense simply dominated biblical interpretation during this time period.

the historical text itself (as the literal sense).[48]

In the course of making his argument we observe in Preus three important features associated with the literal sense of Scripture that bear on our consideration of Scripture's clarity. First, developing the significance of sign from Augustine, we observe that clarity is associated with a sacramental focus. Second, theologians accepted and developed the Augustinian axiom that theological assertions were to be justified by means of the clear passages of Scripture. And third, late medieval theologians shifted (and played with) the focus of the literal sense in association with the church (and other authority). These three themes are necessarily interdependent in nature as they will be in their telling.

Henry Totting of Oyta helped redefine what is normative about the literal sense by assigning principal significance to its correspondence with both the form of Scripture and the spiritual/mystical sense. "The literal sense is the primary sense intended by the Holy Spirit, the principal author of Scripture, and this sense can appear quite clearly from the form itself of Scripture, and from its circumstances, or is more or less in conformity with the circumstances of Scripture, or can be proved from them." The mystical sense is also according to divine intent, although "intended by the Holy Spirit, it does not appear primarily from the form of Scripture and its circumstances, nor can it be proved from them except together with the authority of the one who expounds it."[49] And building on this type of reasoning, Paul of Burgos concludes that "the literal sense of Holy Scripture ought not to be called that sense which in any way opposes the authority or the decision of the church" (because if a sense was allowed to be regarded as literal that was contrary to the church's sense "it would be contrary to that which has been revealed by the Holy Spirit").[50] Preus rightly observes the significance of such formulations is that "theological proof can be adduced from some source other than clear passages of Scripture."[51]

While insisting upon a type of two-value literal sense learned from Augustine (chapter three), biblical interpretation in the Middle Ages turned to a simpler characterization of Scripture's literal meaning in terms of Scripture's signification of that which is to be believed and its signification for moral ends. For example, Hugh of Saint Victor (d. 1141) offered, "Toward these two things—the cognition of truth and the love of goodness—we are instructed." Part of this characterization is an attack on careless allegorization, based upon an

---

[48]Preus, *Shadow to Promise,* p. 233; in particular he offers that the subject of the historical text (the faithful synagogue and speaker) is a model for Christians: "Christ can become the object of faith rather than its exemplary subject."

[49]Cited in ibid., p. 73.

[50]Cited in ibid., pp. 90-91.

[51]Ibid.

appeal to common sense as well as theological appreciation for the literal sense of Scripture itself:

> They say, "We read the Scripture, but we do not read the letter. We don't care about the letter; we teach allegory." But how do you read the Scripture without reading the letter? For if you take away the letter, what is Scripture? "We," they reply, "read the letter, but not according to the letter. For we read allegory, and we expound the letter not according to the letter, but according to allegory." But what is it to expound the letter without pointing out what the letter signifies?[52]

The theological argument is built upon Augustine's emphasis upon sign but extended so as to include a heightened importance of the word (sign): "As long as you remain ignorant of the letter, do not go around boasting about your understanding of Scripture. For to be ignorant of the letter is to be unaware of what the letter signifies, and of what is signified by the letter." The sense of Scripture is greater than the letter alone—either an obvious meaning that is beyond the letter or a spiritual meaning that must be explained in order to appear clear, and the sense of Scripture is more than the literal—either holding a plain meaning congruent with the literal or a hidden meaning.[53] Hugh concludes then: "Do not therefore despise the humility of the word of God, for through humility you will be enlightened to divinity."[54] The letter gives rise to awareness of things signified and the relation among things signified.

Hugh's insistence upon the realistic association of signs and meaning is not without another motive; it sustains a sacramental assertion—a sacramental perspicuity and realism.[55] This is built upon the sign/thing distinction of Augustine wherein Hugh conceives of Scripture in a sacramental fashion: words are signs ("letter") and necessarily ambiguous and obscure unless conjoined with meaning ("spirit"). Thus, sacramental perspicuity is grounded upon Augustine's notion of scriptural obscurity. As Preus observes:

---

[52]Hugh of St. Victor, cited in ibid., p. 28.

[53]Evans, *Language and Logic,* p. 140. Consult Evans's entire chapter "A New Approach to Resolving Contradictions" (pp. 140-63) for a detailed account of the interrelationship of grammar, logic and biblical interpretation in the Middle Ages. Speaking of the use of grammar and dialectic for the study of the Bible, Evans observes these addressed "the study of the Bible at its most technically demanding. To the simpler reader they can have had little to offer. To the student of theology in the schools—always a very small minority of the Bible's readers—they were a satisfactory, and surely immensely satisfying, means of understanding the reasons why a number of the Bible's statements are puzzling and rendering them clear and straightforward" (p. 163).

[54]Hugh of St. Victor, cited in Preus, *Shadow to Promise,* p. 29. Preus refers to this as how the Bible leads "one through the letter to the spirit."

[55]Preus: "The . . . word, to be sure, can be called the instrument *(organum)* of the Spirit in this view—but *not* because what God says is given in the plain meaning" (ibid., p. 252).

> In this hermeneutical structure, words have the same function as they have in medieval sacraments. They authoritatively describe the significance of the historical events, just as the sacramental *verba* describe the significance of the cultic events. In both cases, words give events "form"; biblical history is revealed to be a sacramental history. Thus, Hugh can speak for a host of medieval theologians when he says, "These things literally done, which represent spiritual things of this kind [that is, of the kind designated in allegory and anagogy], are called *sacramenta.*"[56]

Having accepted the working assumption that the New Testament says clearly what is necessary for Christian faith, Hugh also accepted Augustine's affirmation that what the New Testament teaches clearly the Old Testament says obscurely, and also, following Augustine, offers advice about discerning between the obscure and the clear: when reading one finds "many things obscurely written, many clearly, many ambiguously. . . . Set upon its base whatever you find clear, if it fits; interpret what is ambiguous, so that it, too, fits. Put on one side what is truly obscure, if you can."[57] Because the historical sense (as in the story told) of Scripture was sometimes obscure, clear or ambiguous, Hugh distinguishes between what is simply said (the historical sense) and what the text literally says (the literal sense as in what Scripture signifies). The casual association of the historical with the literal (common in early medieval interpreters) was growing into a distinction having to do with the purpose of Scripture itself. Historical and literal were necessarily complementary but distinct senses; Hugh's emphasis is properly upon the (theological) significance of the literal sense so as to reinforce the fuller, other (i.e., Christian) sense of the historical (Old Testament).

The tension in late medieval biblical interpretation concerns how the letter and spirit, the historical and the spiritual meaning of the Old Testament, are explained, by what means, and by whom. Aquinas and Nicholas of Lyra (d. 1340) are offered as examples of a "normative-literal sense," wherein the New Testament reading of the Old Testament is the Old Testament's literal meaning (recalling that for Thomas the literal sense is not simply the historical sense but the meaning intended by God). The spiritual meaning of the Old is clearly provided in the letter of the New.[58] More specifically, Nicholas argues that Psalm 2 is "literally about Christ."[59] In this practice of the normative-literal sense, history is itself insignificant (or at least it is never genuinely allowed to differ from the theological sense of the New Testament).

---

[56]Ibid., p. 37.
[57]Hugh of St. Victor, cited in Evans, *Language and Logic,* pp. 67-68.
[58]Preus, *Shadow to Promise,* pp. 67-70.
[59]Cited in ibid., pp. 70-71.

The New Testament is a reading and extension of the Old, and typology (as we have seen) is how Christians make these connections. Many, including the likes of Martin Luther, argue that if the Old Testament can be understood without the New, then the New is simply not necessary (see comments below). From there theologians in the Middle Ages move toward the justifications of theological assertions that serve as reading and extensions of the Testaments. The normativity of clear and plain statements (statements usually bearing directly on the subjects at hand; i.e., the church, Jesus Christ, Mary, salvation and especially charity) is taken as axiomatic for theological demonstration. Or as Augustine asserted and Aquinas defended, the plain and clear sense of Scripture is normative for theology. But if the plain and clear meaning of the Old is (found in) the New Testament, what is the plain and clear meaning of the New?

The Old to the New to the Church

This is an interesting and important question in the fourteenth, fifteenth and sixteenth centuries: if the literal sense of the Old Testament is the New, what is the literal sense and fulfillment of the New Testament? The argument runs like this: "If the Old Testament can be understood without the New, then the New Testament was given in vain. And if the New Testament can be understood apart from the Church, sacraments, and Christian people, then it was given in vain."[60] The New Testament is not necessarily an end in itself; possibly the New is like the Old, signifying something beyond itself. This is built upon the contrast of the Old and the New: the Old elicits hope but the New provides charity. So Aquinas offered that the two Testaments are alike in species, but the New is the perfection of the imperfection of the Old.[61] The hope of the Old has passed and the realized promise of grace is found in the sacramental grace of the church.

The focus of the literal sense of Scripture shifts from the New in contrast to the Old (the New being the divinely intended meaning of the Old) to the fulfillment of the identification of Christ in his church (the church being the divinely intended fulfillment of the words and deeds of Christ). The meaning of the things signified in the New Testament is found in the church. Thus, the plain and clear meaning of Scripture is, as Preus avers, the "literal sense of the Church," found in either the oral tradition of apostolic faith or the contemporary church itself.[62] This is in contrast to hermeneutical perspectives that argue

[60]Preus, *Shadow to Promise*, p. 236.

[61]Aquinas, *Summa Theologiæ*, 30:25, 27.

[62]So the summary of Preus, *Shadow to Promise*, p. 58. "The promise of Christ to the Church can now emerge as the third dimension of a schema in which *doctrina, lex,* and *promissio* are

for a solitary source of God's disclosure (Scripture) and principally reject other sources as determinatively authoritative (including the tradition of the church); Scripture as understood within early Christian interpreters is sufficient and clearly articulates what is necessary for faith, and the church is supported by Scripture thus understood.[63]

Instead of emphasizing a normative-literal sense, we find more of a ecclesial-literal sense in the writings of Henry Totting of Oyta. Agreeing with biblical interpreters of the Middle Ages that the literal sense of Scripture is that intended by God the Spirit and can be understood by the form of Scripture itself (e.g., in its grammar), Totting adds that the spiritual or mystical sense of Scripture is not to be derived from Scripture's form but is understood by means of the authoritative interpreter. Just as the apostle Paul was an authoritative interpreter of the Old Testament's spiritual sense, so there exists a proper authority, the church, to justify spiritual interpretations of Scripture. Totting insists the promises of Christ to the church are founded upon Scripture, so "the authority of the church is sufficiently founded in it," and "it is held that Christ promised to the apostles that many catholic truths were to be revealed in the future."[64] It rests in the authority of the church to discern what the text *means* for Christian faith (i.e., assent to the judgment of the church). Scripture itself, in all its theological significance, is understood to point beyond itself to the church.

---

three kings of normative Biblical word that are not susceptible of further spiritual or figurative interpretation. The correlate of *promissio*—the response to it—is not so much hope and trust in the promise itself as faith (understood as assent) in the judgement of the Church. When the promise to the Church is made the primary one, the way is clear for the claim that all the other biblical promises (such as that of the Spirit or of eternal life) are subject to the Church's interpretation of them, since Christ has granted her the normative key to Scripture. As a consequence, the hermeneutical function of promise is transferred out of the sphere of biblical interpretation into ecclesiology. The question now is: who in the Church is authorized to expound the normative-literal sense of Scripture?" (pp. 59-60).

[63]These characterizations are offered by Oberman as traditions one, two and three to address the relative relationship of Scripture and tradition (or church) in the interpretation of God's revelation. See Heiko A. Oberman, *The Harvest of Medieval Theology* (Cambridge, Mass.: Harvard University Press, 1963), pp. 365-75. Tradition one describes positions that envision a single source of revelation (Scripture) and deny extra categories of revelatory authority, arguing for the "sufficiency of Holy Scripture as understood by the Fathers and doctors of the church. In the case of disagreement between these interpreters, Holy Scripture has the final authority" (p. 372). Tradition two allows for the existence (and authority) of an oral tradition that accompanies Scripture, and "refers to the written and unwritten part of the apostolic message as approved by the Church. . . . The hierarchy is seen to have its 'own' oral tradition, to a certain undefined extend independent, not of the Apostles, but of what is recorded in the canonical books" (p. 373). And tradition three maintains that the contemporary teaching of the church authoritatively norms both Scripture and tradition (a more radical position in relation to Scripture but the most conservative in terms of ecclesial fidelity).

[64]Cited in Preus, *Shadow to Promise,* p. 76.

The effect of such an argument is that the normative-literal sense of Scripture is conjoined with the authoritative spiritual interpretation of the church—the ecclesial-literal sense. This form of contention is carried to the next level by Jean Gerson (d. 1429) who, in his 1414 work entitled *The Literal Sense of Sacred Scripture,* offers that it belongs to the church (i.e., the ecclesial-literal meaning of Scripture) to discern the meaning of Scripture itself (in its normative-literal sense). While there is an accessible and public, plain and grammatical sense to Scripture, Scripture's intended meaning is from God, who has granted to the church a manner of understanding that differs from simple grammar and logic. Gerson offers that Scripture has "its own proper logic," and it is the church alone that determines the normative sense of Scripture. There is no possibility that an accessible and public, plain and grammatical understanding can oppose the teaching of the church (in part, because such understandings are termed carnal, Jewish or heretical by Gerson). The literal sense, for Gerson, is united with the identity of the church: "Once decided and determined in decrees and decretals and councillor books, must be regarded as *theologia* and as belonging to Holy Scripture no less than the Apostolic Symbol."[65] The normative-literal sense is succumbed by the ecclesial-literal sense.

The consensus is that "one could no longer assume (especially after Gerson) that a reference to the 'literal sense' meant the historical, grammatical meaning of the text."[66] And it should be readily apparent that early sixteenth-century Reformers' protestations would tackle the issues raised by Gerson's equation of Scripture's literal sense with the church. But they do so in a manner that develops out of, rather than simply rejects, the equation. For example, a young Augustinian hermit named Luther argued in 1513 that the Old is not to be understood apart from the New Testament. Nor is Scripture's true literal sense (which is really the spiritual sense of the Old Testament understood by means of the New) known apart from the Spirit's revelation to the apostles, kept in the church.[67] This leads Preus to comment, "There is no incentive to understand the Old Testament historically, since all matters of theological interests are found in the New. Consequently, what matters in Old Testament exegesis is not what the text clearly says or intends but how it is 'handled' by the

[65]Cited in ibid., pp. 82-83. A corollary for Gerson is his denial that the Old Testament, in itself, has a proper literal sense (apart from Christ and the apostles): "The literal sense . . . was first revealed through Christ and the apostles and elucidated by miracles, then confirmed by the blood of martyrs; afterwards holy doctors searched this literal sense out against heretics. . . . Then followed the determination of holy councils. . . . Finally, punishments were added . . . against those who with wanton rashness refused to subject themselves to the determination of the church" (p. 83).

[66]Ibid., p. 176.

[67]Ibid., pp. 153-56.

interpreter."[68] This, as several have observed, situates Luther firmly in the tradition of Gerson.[69]

The young Luther's point is that if the Law had been sufficient, Jesus Christ would have died without reason. His argument arises out his comments on Galatians 2:21: "I do not nullify the grace of God; for if justification comes through the law, then Christ dies for nothing." This reading is christologically focused and significantly tempers historical and temporal characterizations of the relationship of Old and New Testaments.[70] Interpreting the Old Testament, he argues, is to be addressed in terms of the historical and prophetic: all the senses of Scripture must arise out of the historical setting the text itself speaks of, but the prophetic voice of Scripture is to be understood christologically. Indeed, the young Luther held that the clear meaning of historical Scripture is presumed to be historical unless it is obviously intended otherwise, and prophetic speech is taken as christological testimony unless demonstrated otherwise: "Every prophecy and every prophet ought to be understood as referring to Christ the Lord, except where it is clear from plain words that someone else is spoken of."[71] Almost as a barometer of late medieval biblical interpretation, the young Luther's regard for the simple historical sense (i.e., the letter, carnal or Jewish reading) is relatively unimportant (except as the medium of the Spirit of God).

The law, spiritually understood, is the gospel (the New Testament), but the New is purged of the earthly and carnal. So, "the law of Moses, although written with human letters, is also a living language to those who read and understand it spiritually. But it is only a 'pen,' or literature, to those who read it carnally."[72] The potential that the letter actually provides, rather than simply hiding it to be unearthed allegorically, is beginning to surface in Luther's lectures on the book of Psalms (occupying him from 1513 to 1515). We can see how a dual understanding of the Old Testament is grounded in a theological notion of simultaneous ways of understanding Scripture (inside [spirit] and outside [letter], conjoined rather than opposed). Luther begins to consider the faithful Jew (or the faithful synagogue) as historically exemplary and thus understood literally when discussing Psalm 101:2, "When will you come to

[68]Ibid., pp. 163-64.

[69]So Preus, *Shadow to Promise*, pp. 146-49; Steven Ozment, *The Age of Reform (1250-1550): An Intellectual and Religious History of Late Medieval and Reformation Europe* (New Haven, Conn.: Yale University Press, 1980), pp. 63-78; and Oberman, *The Dawn of the Reformation* (Grand Rapids, Mich. Eerdmans, 1992), pp. 269-96.

[70]For the discussion of Luther's christological focus, see Preus, *Shadow to Promise,* p. 143.

[71]Luther, *Luther's Works,* ed. Jaroslav Pelikan, 56 vols. (St. Louis: Concordia, 1955-1976), 10:7. He continued: "Otherwise it is most certain that the searchers will not find what they are searching for."

[72]Translated by Preus, *Shadow to Promise,* p. 164.

me?" He compares this anxious prayer in the Psalm as a longing for the Messiah with the tropological sense of a Christian's prayer for Christ's spiritual advent and then with the anagogical anticipation of the Christian for Christ's confrontation of the future antichrist.[73] The shift is from the Old Testament as simply a mouthpiece for the New to the voice of the Old itself heard as a faithful witness to Christ (especially in reference to Jn 5:39). Gone is the letter-spirit antithesis as Luther struggles to overcome the historical-prophetic opposition of his early lectures. Tempered is the antithesis of Jew and Christian by means of Luther's spiritual and theological interpretation of the faithful synagogue—the voice of those longing for the Christ—within the letter of the Old Testament. Yet, the text by itself does not speak Christianly or truthfully according to Luther (nor any other Christian interpreter observed during the Middle Ages).

Relying upon James Preus's summation of this diverse material we have been able to see how the notions of clear and obscure are theologically charged and explained categories in the late Middle Ages. Never isolated from the discussion of clarity or obscurity, the struggle to interpret the Old and New Testaments as one book leads us in two directions leading up to the sixteenth century: one tendency is to envision the fulfillment of the Old in the New and the New in the church (following Gerson), the other is to envision the Old as a (literal, as in historical and grammatical) witness to the New. This latter course, for Luther, offers an opportunity to reassert the normative-literal sense of all of the Old Testament as testimony (as anticipation of the New). So Preus concludes that for Luther "the Old Testament gets theological value not so much from the Christ it hiddenly describes as from the salvation it promises, and from the faith and expectation of the faithful whom this word invites."[74]

Luther's turn away from late medieval emphases to (what will become known as) distinctly Protestant approaches to understanding Scripture can be described as a theological conversion, with a distinct emphasis upon how Scripture's words can be considered clear. In 1521 he was able to assert "Holy Scripture . . . is the clearest book in the world" because, in part, he had come to the conclusion that all of Scripture speaks directly to the reader.[75] Gone is the sacramental-sign notion of clarity and obscurity that had occupied theology in the Middle Ages; instead God through Scripture speaks, acts, directs, commands, threatens and promises so that to listen to Scripture is to listen to (and believe) God. The "naked words" themselves accomplish God's desires, and the "naked words" themselves are thus regarded as utterly clear.

---

[73]So the summary offered in ibid., pp. 169-71.
[74]Ibid., p. 186.
[75]Cited in ibid., p. 253.

Conclusion

We have traversed a great deal of territory in this chapter. To overstate and simplify, we have seen Christian interpreters turn from the allegorical assumption that the letter *hides* the spiritual sense, to Thomas Aquinas and the medieval assertion of the literal sense whereby the spiritual sense is hidden *in* the letter, to Luther's early struggle to assert the clarity of the letter, which was inseparable from the letter.

Biblical interpretation in the Middle Ages did operate under the assumption that God intended the Bible to be understood as clear, but clarity was not a homogeneous notion. Grammatical clarity was itself a justification for allegorical interpretation so that the clear meaning of the Bible was understood on two planes: those passages that already teach charity clearly (as in plainly) and those that must be interpreted allegorically in order to teach charity. This is to be understood in terms of a transformation of the early Christian notion of letter versus spirit—a progression to spirit understood by means of the letter. It is the theological nature of Scripture that is rendered thereby, which permeates consideration of grammatical and historical matters and is identified with Scripture's literal sense. The "way the words go," as Aquinas noted, is the literal sense, but the literal sense is not simply the historical or authorial sense. Scripture's grammar is, quite literally, primarily theological when considered in the Middle Ages. With these matters in hand the stage is set for an examination how such subjects are addressed, extended and occasionally rejected in the protestations of the Protestant tradition.

5

PROTESTANTLY CLEAR

And even if our gospel is veiled, it is veiled to those who are perishing.

2 CORINTHIANS 4:3

Micaiah recognized as the Word of God the vision which God gave him and the message which accompanied it. And the fact that he did not dismiss it as a phantasy was not of man but of God (I Kings 22). For when 400 prophets stood up against him and contradicted Micaiah, especially Zedekiah who smote him on the cheek and said: "Which way went the Spirit of the Lord from me to speak unto thee?" The opposition of so many prophets of repute and the power of the two kings Ahab and Jehoshaphat ought naturally to have made him think: You cannot possibly be right, you either did not see or understand rightly. And if he had had no other light but that of the understanding there can be little doubt that this is what would have happened. But the Word of God revealed itself to him and brought with it its own clarity, holding and assuring the understanding in such a way that he held fast by that which he had heard and seen.

ULRICH ZWINGLI, *THE CLARITY AND CERTAINTY OF THE WORD OF GOD*

QUITE OFTEN THE SUBJECT OF SCRIPTURE'S CLARITY IS SIMPLY REFERRED TO as a Protestant notion, Protestant principle or Reformation doctrine.[1] That it is Protestants who have argued the importance of Scripture's clarity, in large part due to conflicts with Catholicism's affirmation of a perspective akin to Gerson's, is beyond question. Specifically, Protestant Christianity is routinely credited with revolutionizing the practices of biblical interpretation, particularly the subject of the Bible's clarity (an insistence that is surely overstated in light of material we have looked into thus far). It is common to read statements such as "the main contribution of the Protestant

[1]A statement concerning *the* Protestant doctrine of perspicuity is from Bernard Ramm, *Protestant Biblical Interpretation: A Textbook of Hermeneutics*, 3rd ed. (Grand Rapids, Mich.: Baker, 1970), p. 98; the phrase "Reformation Doctrine" is from Moisés Silva, *Has the Church Misread the Bible? The History of Interpretation in the Light of Current Issues* (Grand Rapids, Mich.: Zondervan, 1987), p. 77.

Reforms to biblical hermeneutics is their insistence on *the plain meaning* of Scripture."[2] Yet, while Protestants did not invent the notion, Protestantism certainly linked its own identity with a reinvented version of Scripture's clarity, making the claim to Scripture's "plain meaning," a logically necessary article of the Protestant faith. There develops a uniquely Protestant association of Scripture and its interpretation (a development within the tradition of the normative-literal sense), alongside a polemical rejection of late medieval Catholic assertions of the Bible's interpretation (the ecclesial-literal sense). This has its origins in Zwingli and Luther, and is particularly evident in the Protestant scholastic tradition.

The source of uniquely Protestant assertions of Scripture's clarity can be traced to Zwingli and Luther. To say with Zwingli that God's word is understood assuredly because it is accompanied by *its own clarity* is to say that Scripture's interpretation is not disassociated from Scripture itself; specifically, it is not disassociated from Scripture's purpose. This is to be explained by means of a certain Christian understanding that intrinsic to the confession that Scripture is God's word is a confession regarding Scripture's own clarification. What Protestants did was to inextricably link Scripture with its own purpose and thus interpretative means. So, Richard Muller offers, "Perspicuity is a doctrinal assumption, resting on the declaration of the inspiration, authority, and soteriological sufficiency of the biblical revelation."[3] We see added to this Luther's departure from sacramental-sign notions of obscurity and clarity, and his employment of renewed interest in a normative-literal sense of Scripture as God's address to Christian readers (especially conjoined with his growing aversion to ecclesially [and sacramentally] mediated grace and appreciation of the direct promise of God's grace). This offers us the best glimpse of what will be known as a distinctly Protestant notion of perspicuity. But what is *normative* about the literal sense is primarily christological and evangelical to Luther, as it was to Zwingli. The likes of Luther and Zwingli (whom we will focus on immediately) turned the subject of clarity against the church (their church) as a means of expressing and justifying reforming assertions.[4]

---

[2]Silva, *Has the Church Misread the Bible?* pp. 77-78, emphasis his.

[3]Richard A. Muller, *Holy Scripture: The Cognitive Foundation of Theology* (Grand Rapids, Mich.: Baker, 1993), p. 341. He continued, "The difficulties of interpretation, including the genuine and freely acknowledged obscurity of certain texts, are encountered in the context of the presupposition that whatever is needful for the preaching of the church and the teaching of its fundamental doctrines is somewhere stated clearly and plainly."

[4]A. Skevington Wood, *Captive to the Word: Martin Luther, Doctor of Sacred Scripture* (Grand Rapids, Mich.: Eerdmans, 1969), p. 175. Wood offers, "For a thousand years the Church had buttressed its theological edifice by means of an authoritative exegesis which depended on allegory as its chief medium of interpretation. Luther struck a mortal blow at this vulnerable spot" (p. 164).

Emphasizing Scripture's (Protestant theological) clarity leads, not surprisingly, to a renewed focus upon readers, their disposition and spiritual state. Can anyone who can read understand the Bible clearly? Since it is obvious that not all literate people are also Protestants, the answer must be found in something more than the ability to read. Early Protestants emphasized the distinction between what the text says and those who read the text, particularly focused upon the evangelical purpose of Scripture. Protestant scholastics of the late sixteenth and seventeenth centuries emphasized the distinction between Protestants who read the text and other self-proclaimed Christian people (heretics, Catholics, etc.), stressing that inabilities to see Protestantism in Scripture arose from an ignorance of Scripture's clear (and anti-Catholic) message. Pietists and dissenting Christians distinguished those who practiced (i.e., read, obeyed and embodied) what the text says from those who dispassionately read and abused others in the name of the text. And early moderns (known to most as Protestant liberals and conservatives) emphasized the distinction between what the text said (in the differing circumstances of its reception) and what it might mean in the present setting (focusing upon socially relevant application of what the Bible was really about), with some disassociating the two (liberals) and others conflating them (conservatives).

Perspicuity and Protestantism

It was in the summer of 1522 that Ulrich Zwingli (1484-1531) preached a sermon at the Dominican convent at Oetenbach, Zurich, on the subject of the Virgin Mary and the clarity of Scripture (an interesting choice of topics but understandable inasmuch as these topics were publicly debated at Zurich in July 1522).[5] Charged with the work of instruction by the Council of Zurich, Zwingli wasted no time in seizing the opportunity to appeal to the nuns; that many came from prominent families in Zurich did encourage Zwingli. The early 1520s were momentous times for the reform party in Zurich, especially concerning the city council's decision to sanction preaching according to the Word of God (in contrast to the established ecclesial calendar). Zwingli came to refer to his sermon in its published form as *Of the Clarity and Certainty or Power of the Word of God,* first published in September 1522.[6]

---

[5]Zwingli continued to expand this sermon in successive publications in 1522 and 1524.

[6]This information, along with the size of the convent (over sixty nuns and a dozen lay-sisters), and the report of the public disputation concerning Mary and Scripture, are relayed by Zwingli in his prefaces to the publications of the sermon; in Ulrich Zwingli, "The Clarity and Certainty of the Word of God," in *Zwingli and Bullinger,* ed. and trans. G. W. Bromiley (Philadelphia: Westminster Press, 1953), pp. 49-50. Also, for a good estimate of Zwingli's theological setting, consult Gottfried W. Locker, *Zwingli's Thought* (Leiden: E. J. Brill, 1981); and W. Peter Stephens, *The Theology of Huldrych Zwingli* (Oxford: Clarendon, 1986).

Interestingly, the piece begins with an extended discussion of the image of God in the human, which Zwingli takes as an indication that "we have a particular longing after God" and "that the image is implanted in us in order that it may enjoy the closest possible relationship with its maker and creator." This image is spiritual and inward, so the appeal of Scripture is likewise "inward"; so "we may see that there is nothing which can give greater joy or assurance or comfort to the soul than the Word of its creator and maker."[7] Scripture's "certainty or power" refers to its capacity to accomplish whereof it speaks, an emphasis he shares with Luther:

> The Word of God is so sure and strong that if God wills all things are done the moment that he speaks his Word. For it is so living and powerful that even the things which are irrational immediately conform themselves to it, or to be more accurate, things both rational and irrational are fashioned and despatched and constrained in conformity with its purpose.[8]

God speaks (in the word) and it is done, in both Old and New Testaments.[9] This assertion Zwingli aligns with the will (and freedom) of God: "And if you think that he does not punish or save according to his Word you are quite wrong. For if it could, if God could not always fulfill it, if some other were stronger than he and could resist it, it would not be almighty. But it must always be fulfilled. If it is not fulfilled at the time when you desire, that is not due to any deficiency of power but to the freedom of his will."[10]

It is important for Zwingli to consolidate the certainty of God's word to accomplish its end with its clarity because he understands Scripture's clarity in a practical and realistic manner: "When the Word of God shines on the human understanding, it enlightens it in such a way that it understands and confesses the Word and knows the certainty of it."[11] Troubles with understanding Scripture rest not with the word that is God's but with the unappreciative or unsuspecting reader who fails to succumb to "the voice of God," however it is

---

[7]Zwingli, "Clarity and Certainty," pp. 65, 67 and 68.

[8]Ibid., p. 68.

[9]So Zwingli offers several dozen examples from the New Testament and adds, "These passages from the New Testament will be quite enough to show that the Word of God is so alive and strong and powerful that all things have necessarily to obey it, and that as often and at the time that God himself appoints" (ibid., p. 71).

[10]Ibid., p. 72.

[11]Ibid., p. 75. Thiselton observes that the idea of Scripture's clarity served as an opening for action; he speaks of this notion emerging in Luther's conflict with Erasmus. But Zwingli's insistence upon this theme suggests we expand Thiselton's observation to protesting reformers more broadly; see Anthony C. Thiselton, *New Horizons in Hermeneutics: The Theory and Practice of Transforming Biblical Reading* (Grand Rapids, Mich.: Zondervan, 1992), pp. 175-89.

expressed.[12] Even though God speaks in parables or riddles, it is still God who speaks.[13] And if one is to understand this word, we must have "a mind to learn from the Word of God, [and] that man already has something, that is, he is not looking to himself, but gives himself wholly to God and to the voice of God." Thus, the contrast between obscure and apparently clear texts (addressing a similar topic) is to be resolved in favor of the passage that ascribes glory to God.[14]

Zwingli follows with a series of examples from the Old and New Testaments, which demonstrate (according to Zwingli) that the word of God is clear and brings "with it its own enlightenment" without the aid of "any human enlightenment." Zwingli avoids a rigid or static notion of Scripture's clarity (the Word of God is clear but not because it is expressed in human language or spoken simply), citing examples where God's word seemingly contradicted common sense or even God's previous instruction. Speaking of Abraham (Gen 22), Zwingli argues:

> Looking at it from a human standpoint Abraham must inevitably have thought: The voice is wrong. It is not of God. For God gave you this son Isaac, by your beloved wife Sarah, as a special token of his friendship. And in so doing he promised that of his seed the Saviour of all men should be born. . . . No, the voice cannot be of God. It is rather of the devil, to tempt you, and to destroy your best-loved son. But Abraham did not allow himself to be deflected by such acute questioning and extremity, nor did he follow his own counsel. And that was all of God, who so enlightened him with the Word that he knew it to be the Word of God, even though he was commanded to do something quite contrary to God's former promise. . . . And faith fained the victory; note well that it did so by the light which the Word of God had itself brought with it.[15]

Zwingli takes the contrariness of God's commands to Abraham, Moses (Ex

[12]"It [the Word of God] is right in itself and its proclamation is always for good. If there are those who cannot bear or understand or receive it, it is because they are sick. So much by way of answer to those who rashly maintain that God does not want us to understand his words, as though it were his will to bring us into danger" (Zwingli, "Clarity and Certainty," p. 75).

[13]"The fact that in times past God taught by parables but in these last days has revealed himself fully by the Lord Jesus Christ indicates to us that God wished to give his message to man in a gentle and attractive way; for it is the nature of that which is presented in parables and proverbs and riddles that it appeals to the understanding of men and brings them to knowledge and indeed increases that knowledge. . . . For when the parable or proverb has provoked us to search out its hidden meaning, once we have found it we value it more highly than if it had been presented to us plainly" (ibid., pp. 72-73).

[14]Ibid., p. 74. For examples throughout Zwingli's writings, see Stephens, *Theology of Huldrych Zwingli,* p. 183.

[15]Zwingli, "Clarity and Certainty," p. 76.

14), Jacob (Gen 28), Micaiah (1 Kings 22), and Jeremiah (Jer 26) as an adequate demonstration that God's word not only appears (and is received) as clear, but this is often in contrast to expectations. He seems to relish this feature: these passages are "enough to show conclusively that God's Word can be understood by a man without any human direction: not that this is due to man's own understanding, but to the light and Spirit of God, illuminating and inspiring the words in such a way that the light of divine content is seen in his own light."[16]

The contrast between the clarity of the word of God itself and human direction or interpreters is important for Zwingli because it demonstrates the spiritual nature of Scripture's clarity.[17] It also offers him a polemical edge against "official interpreters," against "the church's theologians," against "the teacher's office," against "the ramble of carnal divines that you call fathers and bishops"; "note who the teacher is: not *doctores,* not *patres,* not pope, not *cathedra,* nor *concilia,* but the Father of Jesus Christ." Zwingli's conclusion:

> The words are clear; enlightenment, instruction and assurance are by divine teaching without any intervention on the part of that which is human. And if they are taught of God, they are well taught, with clarity and conviction; if they had first to be taught and assured by men, we should have to describe them as taught of men rather than of God.[18]

Scripture's clarity has become, in the fashion of Zwingli, a genuinely Protestant confession, intimately joined with evangelical preaching, which has as part of its identification a rejection of prevailing (late medieval) insistence upon Scripture's ecclesial-literal sense. Scripture as God's direct address, focused inwardly, so that the "soul can be instructed and enlightened—note the clarity—so that it perceives that its whole salvation and righteousness, or justification, is enclosed in Jesus Christ, and it has therefore the sure comfort that when he himself invites and calls you so graciously he will never cast you out."[19]

Clarity is a confession of faith according to Zwingli; the light of God's word

---

[16]Ibid., p. 78.

[17]"If we are to receive and understand anything it must come from above [referring to John 3]. But if that is so, then no other man can attain it for us. The comprehension and understanding of divine doctrine comes then from above and not from interpreters, who are just as liable to be led into temptation as Balaam was" (ibid., p. 79).

[18]Ibid., pp. 79-80.

[19]Ibid., p. 84. Zwingli's insistence that Jesus Christ is both the source and only mediator of salvation, "often accompanied by a polemic against other so-called mediators or intercessors," is a consistent theme in his writings. On this theme see John B. Payne, "Erasmus's Influence of Zwingli and Bullinger in the Exegesis of Matthew 11:28-30," in *Biblical Interpretation in the Era of the Reformation,* ed. Richard A. Muller and John L. Thompson (Grand Rapids, Mich.: Eerdmans, 1996), pp. 61-81.

"is clarity itself," for "all things that are clear are necessarily clear by virtue of clarity."[20] That is, the enlightenment of salvation, promised in Scripture to be found in the evangelical message of Jesus Christ, is itself synonymous with "the clarity and certainty of the Word of God." So Zwingli, like many before him with similar experiences of Scriptures obscurity, understands the awareness of its clarity by means of his own conversion:

> I know for certain that God teaches me, because I have experienced the fact of it: and to prevent misunderstanding this is what I mean when I say that I know for certain that God teaches me. When I was younger, I gave myself overmuch to human teaching, like others of my day, and when about seven or eight years ago I understood to devote myself entirely to the Scriptures I was always prevented by philosophy and theology. But eventually I came to the point where led by the Word and Spirit of God I saw the need to set aside all these things and to learn the doctrine of God direct from his own Word. Then I began to ask God for light and the Scriptures became far clearer to me—even though I read nothing else—than if I had studied many commentators and expositors.[21]

We should, then, from experience learn to afford Scripture every confidence:

> We should hold the Word of God in the highest possible esteem—meaning by the Word of God only that which comes from the Spirit of God—and we should give to it a trust which we cannot give to any other word. For the Word of God is certain and can never fail. It is clear, and will never leave us in darkness. It teaches its own truth. It arises and irradiates the soul of man with full salvation and grace.[22]

Zwingli's attention to Scripture's clarity is actually more direct than that of Luther (the most celebrated proponent of perspicuity in the Protestant tradition). Yet Luther's sustained confrontations provide a richer (and later well-developed) theological polemic than Zwingli's.[23] For example, consider the tone (and insults) of this paragraph from Luther:

---

[20]Zwingli, "Clarity and Certainty," pp. 78-79.

[21]Ibid., pp. 90-91. Zwingli's reforming tendencies were significantly influenced by his contact with Erasmus (meeting with him in 1516), his study of Augustine, as well as the controversies surrounding Christian faith in Zurich; he also began to read Luther's writings (George R. Potter, *Zwingli* [Cambridge: Cambridge University Press, 1976]).

[22]Zwingli, "Clarity and Certainty," pp. 92-93.

[23]See David V. N. Bagchi, *Luther's Earliest Opponents: Catholic Controversialists, 1518-1525* (Minneapolis: Fortress, 1991); Rupert E. Davies, *The Problem of Authority in the Continental Reformers: A Study in Luther, Zwingli and Calvin* (London: Epworth, 1946); and Kenneth Hagen, *Foundations of Theology in the Continental Reformation: Questions of Authority* (Milwaukee: Marquette University Press, 1974).

> We Christians have the meaning and import of the Bible because we have the New Testament, that is, Jesus Christ, who was promised in the Old Testament and who later appeared and brought with Him in light the true meaning of Scripture. . . . For it is the all-important point on which everything depends. Whoever does not have or want to have this Man properly and truly who is called Jesus Christ, God's Son, whom we Christians proclaim, must keep his hands off the Bible—that I advise. He will surely come to naught. The more he studies, the blinder and more stupid he will grow, be he Jew Tartar, Turk, Christian, or whatever he wants to call himself. Behold, what did the heretical Arians, Pelagians, Manichaeans, and innumerable others among us Christian lack? What has the pope lacked? Did they not have the sure, clear, and powerful Word of the New Testament?[24]

While Zwingli and Luther both appealed to Scripture's obvious clarity,[25] they were not able to resolve their own disagreements regarding the eucharist—a point not lost on Catholic observers.[26] They also characterized their opponents differently: Zwingli struggled with authoritative ecclesial figures in contrast to his appeal to Scripture's clarity, while Luther literally demonized his opponents in the midst of discussing Scripture's clarity. For example, Luther was convinced that Satan's mission depends upon hiddenness—quoting (that is, misquoting) Scripture "under the name and guise of Christ."[27] This forces Luther to significantly qualify appeals to Scripture's clarity, especially in his interactions with his so-called Christian opponents.[28]

In particular, it was Luther's encounter with Erasmus during the years 1524 and 1525 that brought the subject of perspicuity into focus for

---

[24]Luther, *Luther's Works,* ed. Jaroslav Pelikan, 56 vols. (St Louis: Concordia, 1955-1976), 15:268.

[25]Susan E. Schreiner, " 'The Spiritual Man Judges All Things': Calvin and the Exegetical Debates About Certainty," in *Biblical Interpretation in the Era of the Reformation,* ed. Richard A. Muller and John L. Thompson (Grand Rapids, Mich.: Eerdmans, 1996), pp. 199-200.

[26]As John Eck (1486-1543) observed, "By this example, taken from the modern heretics (who reject any other judge than Scripture) is shown how the Lutherans and Oecolampadians and Zwinglians fight over the sacrament of the Eucharist, as to whether here is truly and spiritually the body and blood of Christ, or only a figure and sign. Who among them will be judge? Who will ever bring them into harmony? Scripture or the Church? (Apart from these no other judge can be provided.) It is not indeed upon Scripture, which each contends to be the judge, that they lay their foundation—all the while in the self-same words of Scripture—and thus they do not admit Scripture as judge against their own doctrine but they make themselves judges over Scripture. Accordingly, the Church will necessarily judge" (*Enchiridion of Commonplaces,* trans. Ford Lewis Battles [Grand Rapids, Mich.: Baker, 1979], p. 48).

[27]Luther, *Luther's Works,* 24:46. Also Heiko A. Oberman, *Luther: Man Between God and the Devil,* trans. Eileen Walliser-Schwarzbart (New Haven, Conn.: Yale University Press, 1989); Mark U. Edwards, *Luther and the False Brethren* (Stanford, Calif.: Stanford University Press, 1975).

[28]Mark U. Edwards, *Luther's Last Battles, Politics and Polemics, 1531-1546* (Ithaca, N.Y.: Cornell University Press, 1983). Luther reasoned regarding the inability of his opponents to compre-

Luther.[29] The exchange itself concerned other matters (predestination and the will, both God's and humans' will), but we will happily concentrate upon the persistent sniping from each concerning how Scripture is employed to justify each man's assertions. Erasmus had offered that since Scripture is ultimately obscure concerning a great number of matters, especially the relationship of the divine and human will, it is necessary to plead ignorance as well as appeal to the judgment of the church (and its tradition in late medieval theology) to address the question of sovereignty and freedom. Luther's objection was that Erasmus projected the reader's inability to understand Scripture on Scripture itself rather than admitting that the darkness of sin obscures the reader's understanding. So Luther contends, "Let miserable men, therefore, stop imputing with blasphemous perversity the darkness and obscurity of their own hearts to the wholly clear Scriptures of God."[30] Erasmus attributed to Scripture a lack of clarity when Scripture "simply confesses" certain assertions but does not explain how such doctrines can be: "Scripture simply confesses the trinity of God and the humanity of Christ and the unforgivable sin, and there is nothing here of obscurity or ambiguity. But how these things can be, Scripture does not say (as you imagine), nor is it necessary to know." That is, Luther charged Erasmus with obscuring Scripture when clarity is precisely what Scripture is guilty of.[31]

The skepticism of Erasmus bothers Luther as he challenges Erasmus to approach Scripture piously. Luther cautions any who would "trifle even a little and cease to hold the sacred Scriptures in sufficient reverence."[32] Luther's confidence that God in Scripture addresses the reader unambiguously is really at the heart of his assertion of clarity: "If Scripture is obscure or equivocal, why need it have been brought down to us by act of God? Surely we have enough obscurity and uncertainty within ourselves, without our obscurity and uncertainty and darkness being augmented from heaven!" So Luther maintains a very

---

hend the truth because of the blinding work of Satan: "Nowadays [Satan] is showing his ability to do this in fanatics, the Anabaptists, and the Sacramentarians. With his tricks, he has so bewitched their minds that they are embracing lies, errors, and horrible darkness as the most certain truths and the clearest light" (*Luther's Works* 26:192).

[29]See Friedrich Beisser, *Claritas scripturae bei Martin Luther* (Gottingen: Vandenhoeck & Ruprecht, 1966); and Rudolf Herrmann, *Von der Klarheit der Heiligen Schrift: Untersuchungen und Erörterungen über Luthers Lehre von der Schrift in De servo arbitrio* (Berlin: Evang. Verlagsanstalt, 1958).

[30]Martin Luther, "On the Bondage of the Will," in *Luther and Erasmus: Free Will and Salvation,* ed. and trans. Gordon Rupp and Philip Watson (Philadelphia: Westminster Press, 1969), p. 111.

[31]Ibid., p. 112.

[32]Ibid., p. 85.

generous estimate of what God is able to accomplish by means of Scripture, and thus a generous estimate of how one should regard Scripture itself.[33]

While Luther chastised Erasmus for impiety, equivocation and parroting the skepticism of the Sophists, the greater threat from Erasmus was his assertion that Scripture's obscurity bolstered the authority of the papacy.[34] Luther believed that in the pope's "kingdom nothing is more commonly stated or more generally accepted than the idea that the Scriptures are obscure and ambiguous, so that the spirit to interpret them must be sought from the Apostolic See of Rome."[35] He suggested that the entire design of Erasmus's diatribe was bent on demonstrating the Scriptures were not "crystal clear" in order to frighten people away from reading Scripture and into reliance upon Rome: "You are drawn rather to believe that the Scriptures are not crystal clear (for that is what you are driving at throughout your book)."[36] The price for Erasmus's skepticism toward clarity was, to Luther, an affront to those Christians who had lived and died with confidence in Scripture's clarity. As Luther chided Erasmus, so many "have found the Scriptures crystal clear and have confirmed this both by their writing and their blood," but those who castigate the Scriptures as obscure "made this assertion neither by their life for their death, but only with their pen."[37]

The enthusiasm of Luther's pen assumed a decidedly polemical tone when he refused to allow even the slightest hint that the message of Scripture might be obscure in any fashion. It was the matters essential to faith that were clear, if not in one place then in another. If a topic is unclear or obscure it "does not belong to Christians or the Scriptures." So, "the Scriptures are perfectly clear [and] a spiritual light far brighter even then the sun, especially in what relates to salvation and all essential matters."[38] Luther's logic is straightforward: "Christ

[33]Ibid., pp. 127-29. On this theme of Luther's confidence in God's Word—Scripture—consult Beisser, *Claritas Scripturae bei Martin Luther,* pp. 75ff.

[34]Protestant history of the debate has tended to vilify Erasmus, overlooking his many contributions to biblical studies, his desire that the Scriptures be disseminated and read by Christians, and his own problems with the authority of Rome. For a corrective see E. Harris Harrison, *The Christian Scholar in the Age of Reformation* (Grand Rapids, Mich.: Eerdmans, 1983), pp. 69-102; Steven Ozment, *The Age of Reform 1250-1550: An Intellectual and Religious History of Late Medieval and Reformation Europe* (New Haven, Conn.: Yale University Press, 1980), pp. 290-320; and Jerry H. Bentley, *Humanists and Holy Writ: New Testament Scholarship in the Renaissance* (Princeton, N.J.: Princeton University Press, 1983).

[35]Luther, "Bondage of the Will," pp. 158-59. Luther continued: "Nothing more pernicious could be said than this, for it has led ungodly men to set themselves above the Scriptures and to fabricate whatever they pleased, until the Scriptures have been completely trampled down and we have been believing and teaching nothing but the dreams of madmen."

[36]Ibid., p. 168.

[37]Ibid., pp. 168-69.

[38]Ibid., p. 133.

would not have enlightened us as deliberately to leave some part of his Word obscure while commanding us to give heed to it" and "if [a doctrine] does belong to Christians and the Scriptures, it ought to be clear, open, and evident, exactly like all the other clear and evident articles of faith." Also note his comments: "If there are any who do not perceive this clarity, and are blind or blunder in this sunlight, then they only show . . . how great is the majesty and power of Satan over the sons of men, to make them neither hear nor take in the very clearest words of God," and "See, then, whether you or all the Sophists can produce any single mystery that is still abstruse in the Scriptures."[39] When Luther referred to the subject matter of Scripture he spoke in the plural, including the incarnation of Christ, his substitutionary suffering, his resurrection and his heavenly reign. Luther also said christological and trinitarian doctrines were clear.[40]

Luther cautioned that we should not be surprised at the difficulties encountered by even the most learned; it is the rule that all are blind and the surprise is that any understand and clearly see the message of Scripture: "No man perceives one iota of what is in the Scriptures unless he has the Spirit of God."[41] Luther's optimism toward the clarity of Scripture was only matched by his pessimism toward the obscurity of those without the Spirit; any blindness "is not the fault of the Bible, which is very clear, so that even boys understand it!"[42] It was at this point of tension that Luther suggested a distinction between the outer clarity of Scripture (whereby Scripture is presented with pastoral intentions) and the inner clarity of Scripture (by means of the Spirit's illumination). The outer clarity of Scripture "belongs to the public ministry of the Word . . . and is chiefly the concern of leaders and preachers of the Word. We make use of it when we seek to strengthen those who are weak in faith and confute opponents." The inner clarity of Scripture "is internal, whereby through the Holy Spirit or a special gift of God, anyone who is enlightened concerning himself and his own salvation, judges and discerns with the greatest certainty the dogmas and opinions of all men."[43] Outer clarity eliminates the need for another factor to understand Scripture's literal sense (such as tradition or the church) and as such establishes a hermeneutical convention. Inner clarity

[39]Ibid., pp. 163, 167, 111.

[40]Ibid., pp. 110, 112.

[41]Ibid., p. 112. Luther added, "In divine things the wonder is rather if there are one or two who are not blind, but it is no wonder if all without exception are blind" (p. 166).

[42]Luther, *Luther's Works,* 16:242. Also see the discussion of this distinction in Wolfhart Pannenberg, *Basis Questions in Theology,* trans. George H. Kehm (Philadelphia: Fortress, 1970), 1:60-66.

[43]Luther, "Bondage of the Will," p. 159.

corresponds to personal certitude and persuasion brought about by the quickening and enlightening of the Spirit. Yet, outer clarity is not objectifiable, it cannot be thought of as separable from inner clarity, and appeals to Scripture's inner clarity must be confirmed according to an appeal to Scripture's outer clarity.

This was all obvious to Luther; his rhetoric would allow nothing less than absolute certainty about Scripture's clarity. He feigned weariness due to the tedium of having to explain at such great length something so obvious: "But I fancy I have long since grown wearisome, even to dullards, by spending so much time and trouble on a matter that is so very clear."[44] And on another occasion he sarcastically remarked, "Now what is clear enough, if the plain Word of God, given for our enlightenment and instruction is called unclear, even though it shines directly into our faces? This is as if a willful person closed his eyes to the bright sun and covered doors and windows and then complained about not being able to see."[45] Yet, observe that Luther has not said, in so many words, that Scripture in an isolated (or objectified) sense is clear. It is the thing that Scripture is about, its meaning, that is clear, and the meaning is the gospel of Christ: "What kind of deep secret can still be hidden in Scripture, now that the seals have been opened, the stone rolled away from the grave, and the deepest secret of all revealed: that Christ, the only Son of God, has become man, that there is one eternal God in three persons, that Christ has died for us, and that he reigns for ever in heaven?"[46] God has made this plain and clear, and it is not the ecclesial institution or its teachers that provide this according to Luther.

The inner message (Scripture's *res*) was thought to be consistent with its grammatical form, and the two were not mutually exhaustive one of another. As Pannenberg reminds us, the development of the tension between these topics has maintained that "the outer clarity of Scripture must have some connection with the inner—a tendency toward the inner, toward the illumination of the heart."[47] Luther rejected the pneumatic appeals of the Zwickau prophets and Dr. Karlstadt, for example, because they spiritualized away the literal meaning and required an additional condition or means of heavenly illumination to understand Scripture. Similarly, Lutheran theologians confronted and rejected, in the Rahtmannian controversy, the disassociation of the inner and outer meanings of Scripture—an error that was thought to infect early

---

[44]Ibid., p. 162.
[45]Luther, *Luther's Works,* 24.92.
[46]Luther, "Bondage of the Will," p. 110.
[47]Pannenberg, *Basic Questions,* 1:190.

Pietism.[48] The unity of outer and inner clarity, the relationship of the objectivity and subjectivity of clarity, and the tension of the clarity and obscurity of Scripture and the hermeneutical task were never finally severed but held in affinity within Protestant hermeneutics.[49] There exists a realistic tension in such neat distinctions, but a tension that is addressed (not explained) by the confessional role of perspicuity in Protestant hermeneutics. Perspicuity remained an invitation to believe—the existential correlation between God's promises and faith.

What Protestantism Does with Perspicuity

What was particularly Protestant about Luther's concept of Scripture's clarity? The context provides the ready answer: Rome advocated Scripture's obscurity and the necessity of church hierarchy as interpreter. Trent charged that it was the role of "holy mother Church . . . to judge of the true sense and interpretation of the holy Scriptures."

> In order to restrain petulant spirits, [the Council] decrees, that no one, relying on his own skill, shall,—in matters of faith, and of morals pertaining to the edification of Christian doctrine,—wrestle the sacred Scripture to his own senses, presume to interpret the said sacred Scripture contrary to that sense which holy mother Church,—whose it is to judge of the true sense and interpretation of the holy Scriptures,—hath held and doth hold; or even contrary to the unanimous consent of the Fathers; even though such interpretations were never [intended] to be at any time published.[50]

This was, of course, another way of asserting the authority of the church over Scripture according to Protestants. Instead, they opted for fusion of hermeneutic authority and Scripture's authority. So Luther responds to Scripture's injunction to "test the spirits" (1 Jn 4:1) with an appeal to "Scripture's external clarity": "If I am to test a spirit, I must have the Word of God. The latter is to be the rule or touchstone . . . by which I can tell black from white and evil from good."[51]

---

[48]On Luther's rejection of the pneumatic claims of Karlstadt and the Zwickau prophets, see Luther, "Against the Heavenly Prophets," in *Luther's Works,* ed. Jaroslav Pelikan, 56 vols. (St. Louis: Concordia, 1955-1976), 40:73-223 (especially pp. 189-91). For a discussion of Hermann Rahtmann's confrontation with Lutheran orthodoxy over the subject of Scripture's clarity see Otto Weber, *Foundations of Dogmatics,* trans. Darrell L. Guder (Grand Rapids, Mich.: Eerdmans, 1981), 1:284-85.

[49]See the review of this work in Herrmann, *Klarheit der Heiligen Schrift,* pp. 44-78; and Pannenberg, *Basic Questions,* 1:187-91.

[50]Canons and Decrees of the Council of Trent, fourth session, April 8, 1546. Cited in Philip Schaff, *The Creeds of Christendom: With a History and Critical Notes* (Grand Rapids, Mich.: Baker, 1983), 2:83.

[51]Luther, *Luther's Works,* 23:174, 229-233.

Such characterizations led Protestants in the later sixteenth and seventeenth centuries to equate outer clarity with objectivity in polemical writings. Testing Christian claims by means of Scripture's outer clarity tended to mitigate the pneumatic appeals that characterized the distinct tension of inner and outer clarity (for Luther) or the emphasis upon inward and direct address (for Zwingli). For example, if objective clarity can be described as a quality of or inherent in the nature of Scripture itself, then Protestant polemicists might lessen the interpretative tangles addressed by Rome's claims against Protestantism (or so thought Protestant scholastic theologians).[52] While perspicuity was the Protestant counterclaim to the charge of Scripture's obscurity—an assertion with a connotation of objectivity—the subjectivity and limits of Scripture's clarity were projected upon the interpreter to explain various interpretative discrepancies.

From the start Protestants conceded that perspicuity was never intended to supplant the necessity of interpretation, but it nonetheless emerged as a hermeneutic principle with far-reaching consequences—what we might refer to as perspicuity as hermeneutic. So Luther recognized that the nature of his debate with Erasmus involved the toil of interpretative problems but added that it was not Scripture that was at issue but its interpretation: "The dispute is not so much about Scripture, which may not yet be sufficiently clear, as about the meaning of Scripture."[53] The need to project upon Scripture characteristics that sustain Protestant claims regarding the nature of hermeneutics was at the heart of their claims to Scripture's clarity.[54] In turn, the hermeneutical debate over perspicuity was not severed from the debate over the nature of Scripture itself.

To illustrate, Protestant scholastic theologians consistently maintained that perspicuity was an attribute—a property—of Scripture. The distinctions between the spiritual message of Scripture and its outward form persist (spirit manifest by means of letter), but there is a concerted effort to address the clarity of the outward form (the letter's necessary clarity). Francis Turretin (1623-1687) insisted that Scripture not only made things clear (understood) but that "it is clear in itself."[55] And as the papacy was immune from criticism (and interpretation) within Catholic circles, so Turretin emphasized in his *Institutio theo-*

[52]G. R. Evans, *Problems of Authority in the Reformation Debates* (Cambridge: Cambridge University Press, 1992), pp. 35-112.

[53]Luther, "Bondage of the Will," p. 158.

[54]Anthony C. Thiselton, *New Horizons in Hermeneutics* (Grand Rapids, Mich.: Zondervan, 1992), pp. 180-84; Beisser, *Claritas scripturae*, pp. 27-31.

[55]Francis Turretin, *The Doctrine of Scripture*, ed. and trans. John W. Beardslee III (Grand Rapids, Mich.: Baker, 1981), pp. 188-89.

logiae elencticae (1688) a constant polemic against Rome and in favor of Scripture's independence. Having casually granted the need for the Spirit's illumination to appreciate the gospel of Scripture, Turretin stressed that there is a need to defend the external (and objective) clarity of Scripture against Roman insistence: "The question is of the obscurity or perspicuity of the object, or Scripture; is it so obscure that a believing person cannot comprehend it for salvation without the authority and decision of the church? This we deny." He admits, "It is not a question of the perspicuity or obscurity of the subject, or of persons; no one denies that Scripture is obscure to unbelievers and unregenerate people, to whom the gospel is its own concealment, . . . and we acknowledge that the illumination of the Spirit is needed by believers for its understanding."[56]

Turretin's desire (as an academic as well as a pastor) was to encourage Christian lay-people to read the Bible with the same kind of enthusiasm and piety that faithful Catholics exercised toward church authorities; indeed, "Turretin's scholasticism can be read as an academic's program for accomplishing this."[57] After defending the reliability (and readability) of translations (Questions 13-15), Turretin stressed Scripture's perfection (Question 16) to contradict "Roman Catholics [who] argue the imperfection of Scripture to support the need for tradition," and asserted its perspicuity (Question 17) to counter Catholics who "in order to keep people from reading it, and to hide the light under a basket, the more easily to reign in the darkness, they have begun to argue for its obscurity, as if there can be no trustworthy knowledge of its meaning without the decision of the church." His goal is "to deny any obscurity that keeps the common people from reading Scripture."[58] This to lead to the heart of the matter, whether Scripture should be read (Question 18), how it should be read (i.e., whether it can and should be read profitably) contrary to prohibitions against vernacular versions. Turretin concludes that "the reading of Scripture . . . is required of all as a responsibility.[59]

He acknowledges there are "obscurities," "mysteries," "secrets" and "abstruse matters" in Scripture; he is willing to admit that Holy Scripture is not "clear in all its parts." But all that is necessary for salvation, the what of Christian faith, is found "almost everywhere" and "could be found out easily."[60] Obscurities test readers and require "earnest effort" to be understood, citing Augustine, but they may be understood, Turretin assumes.[61]

---

[56]Turretin, *Doctrine of Scripture,* p. 185.
[57]Beardslee, "Introduction," in Turretin, *Doctrine of Scripture,* p. 11.
[58]Turretin, *Doctrine of Scripture,* pp. 185, 188-89.
[59]Ibid., p. 198.
[60]Ibid., p. 186.
[61]Ibid., p. 187.

> For Scripture is called "clear" not only because it throws light upon the matters that are understood, but also because it is clear in itself and has been made suitable for throwing light on these matters, if used by people with eyes of faith, so that it is lucid both formally and effectively, since it throws out rays like the sun, and offers itself for the contemplation of the eye. Finally, nothing more stupid can be said; it is as if I should say that Scripture does not enlighten unless it enlightens, for it enlightens by the very thing by which it is understood.[62]

It appears that the distinction between clarity and obscurity is, for Turretin, a way of expressing the distinction between believers (to whom all Scripture can, with due effort, be actually clear) and unbelievers (from whom the gospel is hidden). This is amply illustrated by the obscurity of the Old Testament (when read through the New) to Jews, according to Turretin: "The gospel is said to be hidden only from unbelievers, and plain to believers, not only as preached, but also as written, both because the apostles did not preach one thing and write another, and also because here [2 Cor 4:3] the clarity of the gospel is opposed to the obscurity of the Old Testament, in reading which Jews were busied, as Paul explains in 2 Corinthians 3:14."[63] For believers all is clear: "It is one thing for there to be in Scripture difficult passages, whose difficulties can be mastered, but another for there to be insuperable difficulties, which cannot be understood no matter how painstakingly they are investigated." And, "Some difficulty, which we grant, is one thing; a total difficulty, which we deny, is another." His conclusion: "It is one thing to say that the difficulties are in the language of Paul's letters, which we deny; another to say that they are in the very substance of what is taught. . . . Difficulties for the ignorant and unstable, who because of unbelief and ill will distort for their own destruction [2 Pet 3:15-16], are not the same as difficulties for believers, who are guided by the work of the Holy Spirit in humbly investigating them." In this Turretin expresses a degree of confidence which rivals the claims of his Catholic opponents.[64]

A telling example of a transformation of Scripture's clarity in Protestant circles is the manner in which it is demonstrated: instead of occupying the place of a confession of necessity (to justify one's claims on the basis of the biblical text), Scripture's clarity serves to censure and expose Protestant opponents and challenge claims to Christian faith.[65] John Barton observes that within the early

---

[62]Ibid., pp. 188-89.

[63]Ibid., p. 189.

[64]Ibid., pp. 190-91.

[65]The exegetical warrant for clarity was also the theological warrant that was also the confessional warrant. This internal apologetic or circularity was consistent with opponents'

Reformation, Scripture "did not function as tradition had come to function," yet "in subsequent Protestant orthodoxy, the Bible began to function in exactly the same way as ecclesiastical tradition functions for Catholics."[66] A defense of Scripture's clarity surfaces as a primary component in the defense of Protestant Christianity itself. Because Protestant claims are directly related to appeals to Scripture (direct, unmediated, not dependent upon ecclesial sense making), it must be clear in its entirety. This is because if Scripture were genuinely obscure, Protestant faith would likewise be subject to the charge that it was obscure.

The significant theological themes attached to the advocacy of perspicuity include the beliefs: (1) Scripture is a clear and certain rule of faith since no necessary doctrine is obscure; (2) clarity is a necessity since Scripture alone is the means of saving faith; (3) Scripture functions as its own interpreter with the unclear being explained by the clear; (4) perspicuity is only limited by human sin and ignorance; and (5) Scripture must be clear because God, its author, can only speak clearly and understandably.[67] Each assertion is predicated upon a consensual perception of Scripture's authority within Protestant hermeneutics—Scripture is clear because it is read as clear.[68] For example, Turretin's list reads:

---

arguments as well and represents a common theological method found in Reformed and Post-Tridentine theology. Removing this circularity seems to be a necessary burden during the reappraisal of Scripture's authority and clarity in the eighteenth and nineteenth centuries, but this segregates the exegetical exercise from its theological rationale. The result is an affirmation of Scripture's clarity that has little to do with a confession of this matter. See Muller, *Holy Scripture,* pp. 340-41, 347.

[66]John Barton, *People of the Book: The Authority of the Bible in Christianity* (Louisville: Westminster John Knox, 1988), p. 84. Barton's quote reads in full: "The true character of the opposition between gospel or Scripture and subsequent tradition, which is a qualitative one, has come to be misunderstood as quantitative. For Luther, say, Scripture was different in kind from subsequent tradition, because it was to be seen as the primary witness to the gospel in its original form. It did not function as tradition had come to function, as the horizon within which all Christian thinking had to take place, but as something objective, set over against the Church and demanding that its hard edges be respected. But in subsequent Protestant orthodoxy, the Bible began to function in exactly the same way as ecclesiastical tradition functions for Catholics, except that it was a tradition that had been artificially truncated. Scripture, for most sorts of Protestantism, is simply Catholic tradition with all the bits that happen not to lie within the pages of the Bible artificially removed."

[67]Muller, *Holy Scripture*, pp. 313-18, 340-57; and Weber, *Foundations of Dogmatics,* 1:281-84.

[68]Hans Frei suggested that when the Reformers articulated a defense of Scripture's clarity, we are witnessing merely the codification of a consensual reading of the Bible as realistic and perspicuous as to its message. The Protestant's appeal to an orthodox and traditional understanding of the Christian gospel was merely an articulation of the obvious—that the Bible means what it says and it doesn't mean something else. Hans W. Frei, "The 'Literal Reading' of Biblical Narrative in the Christian Tradition: Does It Stretch or Will It Break?" in *The Bible and the Narrative Tradition,* ed. Frank McConnell (Oxford: Oxford University Press, 1986), pp. 36-41.

> The following of Scripture proves its perspicuity: (a) its cause, God "the Father of lights" (James 1:17), who cannot be said either to be ignorant or not to wish to speak clearly, unless his supreme goodness and wisdom are called into question; (b) its purpose, which is to serve as canon and rule of faith and morals, which would be impossible if it were not understandable (*perspicuus*); (c) its content, namely the Law and the gospel, which are to be understood easily by everyone; (d) its form, for it is to us as a will, a treaty of alliance, the edict of a ruler, all of which must be clear and not obscure.[69]

While there is no isolation of clarity from the assertion of Scripture's authority, each of the themes revolve around the belief that clarity is a quality of Scripture itself, rather than something brought to the text by the reader (whether ecclesial official or Spirit-illumined believer).[70]

The investment in perspicuity's significance was high. It corresponds to God's character (to claim Scripture's message is obscure is to insult God),[71] and the accessibility and certain knowledge of salvation rest upon the appreciable nature of faith (divine promises are moot unless intelligible).[72] Muller accurately suggested that these themes "are intelligible only in the context of the debate over authority and interpretation."[73] Perspicuity was a necessary article to sustain distinctively Protestant hermeneutics, a contention necessary to preserve the insistence upon the privilege of interpretation without exercising deference to ecclesiastical authority as hermeneutic.[74] Rome did, after all, have its own view of Scripture's clarity—rendered through the church and its tradition. This meant that the real concern of a Protestant concept of perspicuity had to do with the belief that Scripture was both clear in itself and clearly interpreted itself without the necessity of a preemptory appeal to ecclesiastical authority.[75] Post-Reformation theologians insisted that perspicuity, as a quality of Scripture, was implied by the nature of Scripture's author-

---

[69]Turretin, *Doctrine of Scripture,* p. 189.

[70]The same can be said with regard to Lutheran theologians' reference to perspicuity in the years immediately following Luther; see Beisser, *Claritas scripturae;* Herrmann, *Klarheit der Heiligen Schrift;* Pannenberg, *Basic Questions,* 1:188-89.

[71]Turretin suggested that Scripture's "cause" is "God 'the Father of lights,' who cannot be said either to be ignorant or not wish to speak clearly, unless his supreme goodness and wisdom are called into question" (*Doctrine of Scripture,* p. 189).

[72]This led Anthony Thiselton to suggest that at times Protestants used perspicuity as a christological, ecclesiological and critical principle (Thiselton, *New Horizons,* p. 180).

[73]Muller, *Holy Scripture,* p. 347.

[74]Pannenberg, *Basic Questions,* 1:188. He argued that the Reformation solution to the problem of Scripture and tradition "was stated in the thesis about the clarity of Scripture. Only if the essential content of Scripture follows clearly and distinctly from its words can Scripture really exercise the function of the supreme norm and guideline of all dogmatic statements."

[75]See G. C. Berkouwer, *Holy Scripture,* trans. Jack B. Rogers (Grand Rapids, Mich.: Eerdmans, 1975), pp. 268-70.

ity. As such it has the tendency to downplay the significance of subjective interests (interpretative and salvific) and place Scripture's clarity within an objectifiable framework.

Reformed theologians similarly emphasized the inseparable relationship between the grammatical meaning of Scripture (its literal sense) and its theological clarity.[76] But how closely Post-Reformation theologians followed the Reformers is disputed. A common complaint is that there was a shift away from the perspicuity of the message of Scripture and toward the clarity of the words. Berkouwer's comments capture this complaint:

> Since Scripture is in the form of language, it does contain a certain degree of accessibility. But the confession of perspicuity obviously cannot be described in terms of the general accessibility that it has in common with other literature. Accessibility of this kind, one might point out, is an attribute of all written words and need not become the subject of an emphatic confession. [T]he Reformation doctrine of perspicuity did not aim at the clarity of the words as such, but at the message, the content of Scripture. A religious clarity was confessed concerning the good news for sinners. It is not until post-Reformation theology that a shift occurred: for the idea of perspicuity is then applied to the *words* of Scripture, particularly in their semantic function. In this perspicuity is no longer religious clarity in the midst of our sinful darkness. It is a theoretical and verbal perspicuity that the natural mind can appreciate and perceive in a general framework of knowledge.[77]

The heart of the contention concerns the relationship between perspicuity as a confession of religious accessibility and the words in their semantic function; the supposed error arises when the words of Scripture are separated from the matter of Scripture (the message conveyed by the words).[78] If perspicuity is confined to the words of Scripture, the confession turns away from its evangelical significance and toward a semantic principle. Berkouwer

---

[76]"The grammatical and theological issues stand together in the context of the Protestant movement away from allegorical exegesis toward a literal-grammatical reading of the text" (Muller, *Holy Scripture,* pp. 340-41).

[77]Berkouwer, *Holy Scripture,* pp. 274-75. Also, building on Berkouwer's assessment, see Jack B. Rogers and Donald K. McKim, *The Authority and Interpretation of the Bible: An Historical Approach* (San Francisco: Harper & Row, 1979), pp. 182-83; and Thiselton, *New Horizons,* p. 185.

[78]The opposite error is to maintain that somehow the message of Scripture is available without a realistic maintenance of the literal sense of Scripture's form or words. On the history of the larger hermeneutical issues, Muller offers a genuine starting point when he reminds us that the background of Luther's idea that words *(verba)* point to things *(res),* the precise question of relationship addressed in the debate, is founded in the Augustinian tradition of interpretation *(signa and res significata),* a tradition that continued to influence Reformed theology into the eighteenth century (Muller, *Holy Scripture,* p. 344).

offers, "The Reformation was not dealing with the words by themselves, but with the message in Scripture of which the words spoke. This clarity of the message *presupposes* the accessibility of the words, but that accessibility was not the subject of the real purpose of the confession."[79] But if perspicuity is simply about the words, it is not a Christian (and certainly not a specifically *Protestant*) concept, and it certainly is not fodder for creedal affirmation. The surrender of theological hermeneutics to a general theory of any words employed in any setting for any purpose means that perspicuity as a matter of confession is sacrificed.[80]

Perspicuous Piety and Gospel

This raises again the important question of who may understand Scripture as clear. Luther's distinction between inner and outer clarity actually served to confirm as well as mitigate accessibility to Scripture; its salvific message is accessible and efficacious only to those enlightened by the Spirit, although it is assumed to be clear to any reader exercising ordinary means to understand Scripture's literal sense. But was there an objective function to reading Scripture's outward form—almost a magical or spiritual cause-and-effect relationship between reading and redemption?

> A consistent check on Protestant estimates of perspicuity has been the dual emphasis that Scripture is not simply clear and, similarly, not simply obscure. Instead, Scripture is clear and obscure, not merely clear or obscure—a tension associated with human ways of knowing, and ignorance and sin from which there is no complete extrication. The problem of Scripture seeming or appearing obscure to most people is not going to leave us; all Christians have offered is accounts of why this is the case.[81] Such distinctions are almost routine in early

---

[79]Berkouwer, *Holy Scripture,* p. 275.

[80]In particular, notice the application of Ludwig Wittgenstein's proposition that a necessary condition for meaningful discourse is based in a concept of clarity to the subject of Scripture's clarity (against the likes of Dilthey, Heidegger, Bultmann and Gadamer) in Robert T. Sandin, "The Clarity of Scripture," in *The Living and Active Word of God: Studies in Honor of Samuel J Schultz,* ed. Morris Inch and Ronald Youngblood (Winona Lake, Ind.: Eisenbrauns, 1983), pp. 237-53. Sandin also argued that "biblical hermeneutics is an application of general hermeneutical principles. . . . If we begin by assuming that every meaningful utterance is clear in itself, we must then understand the task of interpretation as limited to that of removing hindrances that prevent the verbal statement from functioning effectively as a vehicle of communication," and that "a similar view of the task of interpretation emerges from the Reformer's view of the Bible [as] clear in itself and interprets itself. Wittgenstein's view of the clarity of meaningful utterance therefore has its counterpart in the Reformers' doctrine of the clarity of Scripture" (pp. 241-42).

[81]For example, John Calvin reminded his readers, "There is sometimes obscurity, which the unlearned take as an occasion to wander off to their own destruction" (*The Epistles of Paul the Apostle to the Hebrews and the First and Second Epistles of St. Peter* [Grand Rapids, Mich.Eerdmans, 1963], p. 367).

Protestants; as routine as their fondness for Gregory's adage: Scripture is "a river in which the lamb may ford and the elephant must swim."[82]

Admitting the tension of Scripture's obscurity and clarity rendered early Protestant hermeneutics more realistic in nature. This admission also mitigates the role of perspicuity in Protestant hermeneutics in three ways: (1) it introduces a pastoral focus in which clarity is linked with obedience; (2) it accounts for the weakness of the reader beset by sin and finitude; and (3) it emphasizes the evangelical certainty of the message. These are subtleties that are necessary to realize the intent of perspicuity as hermeneutic; and they were united in pietistic appeals with Scripture's affective perspicuous appeal. It fell to the pietistic reactionaries to scholastic Protestantism to regain the significance of a realistic characterization of Scripture's perspicuity.

Philipp Jakob Spener (1635-1705) was certain that "the Scriptures in themselves are not obscure" and therefore directed his interest to encourage "the means of proper Bible reading."[83] One must always approach the task of reading Scripture with prayer, asking the enlightenment of the Spirit, in reverence toward the text and leading to the response of obedience. These matters are then combined with the practical and routine matters of reading. So Spener offers, "Indeed the Scripture is a light for our enlightenment but it is a word of the Spirit and if we could separate the Holy Spirit from the Word (which we cannot do), the Scripture would no longer work." And, "Every person reading the Scriptures must first pay attention how the verses fit together and then pay attention to each individual word."[84] "Simple pious readers" is the expression Spener used to describe Scripture's recipients—it is only appropriate that Scripture is simple because it is directed at the simple. "Question 31. Are not the Scriptures too difficult for the uneducated to understand? No, for already in the Old Testament the divine Word was given to instruct the simple [and] the New

---

[82]Quoted in Frederick W. Farrar, *History of Interpretation* (Grand Rapids, Mich.: Baker, 1961), p. 329. Luther said, "An elephant drowns in this sea [of Scripture]; a lamb that is looking for Christ and perseveres, stands on firm ground and reaches the other side" (cited in Oberman, *Luther,* p. 309). The Reformers were also fond of the common patristic theme: "We feed upon the plain parts, we are exercised by the obscure" (Augustine, "Sermons on Selected Lessons of the New Testament," A Select Library of the Nicene and Post-Nicene Fathers of the Christian Church, ed. Philip Schaff [Grand Rapids, Mich.: Eerdmans, 1988], 6:321).

[83]Philipp Spener, "The Spiritual Priesthood, Briefly Described According to the Word of God in Seventy Questions and Answers" (1677) and "The Necessary and Useful Reading of the Holy Scriptures" (1694), in *Pietists: Selected Writings,* ed. Peter C. Erb (New York: Paulist, 1983), pp. 55, 71.

[84]Spener, "Necessary and Useful Readings," pp. 72, 74-75.

Testament is still more clear."[85] But he insisted that Scripture was both simple and demanding, and thus a challenge to both the learned and uneducated alike. Spener continued: "Question 32. But are not many things in the Scriptures obscure and too high for the uneducated? The Scriptures in themselves are not obscure, for they are light and not darkness . . . . However, there are many things in them too high not only for the uneducated, but also for the learned, which, on account of our darkened eyes, appear obscure to us."[86]

The purpose of Scripture, and the point of its clarity, is to provide a basis for proper (obedient) response. We observe in the comments of Johann Albert Bengel (1687-1752) that interpreting Scripture is not simply a matter of education or learning because "Scripture teaches its own use, which consists in action. To act it, we must understand it, and this understanding is open to all the upright of heart."[87] Bengel's commitments are very direct:

> Myriads of annotations were not written in the Church of the Old Testament, although the measure of light vouchsafed was far more scanty then than now; nor did learned men think, that the Church of the New Testament required to be immediately laden with such helps. Every book, when first published by a prophet or an apostle, bore in itself its own interpretation, clear by its inherent light, being accommodated to the then existing state of things. The text, which must have been continually in the mouth of all, and read by all, maintained itself its own perspicuity and integrity.[88]

So-called pietistic concern for the pastoral implications of Scripture's clarity drew the accusations of ambiguity and subjectivism, primarily because they suggested that spiritual affection was the necessary prerequisite to understand-

---

[85]Spener, "Spiritual Priesthood," p. 55. Like Luther, Spener viewed the Scripture's simplicity as synonymous with its clarity. On the widespread appeal to a "pious reader," the "contemplating subject" and the limits on perspicuity in relationship to piety, see Weber, *Foundations of Dogmatics,* 1:282-84.

[86]Spener, "Spiritual Priesthood," p. 55.

[87]Johann Albert Bengel, *Gnomon of the New Testament,* ed. Andrew R. Fausset, 5 vols. (Edinburgh: T & T Clark, 1866), 1:6-8. Bengel also argued that annotations were not necessary when Scripture was first delivered, and should only serve to "preserve, restore, or defend the purity of the text." That is, matters of textual criticism, historical background, etc., rather than the theologians' annotations. Bengel wrote, "The text, which was continually in the mouths of all, and diligently read by all, kept itself pure and intelligible. The saints were not busy with selecting the berries, as if the other parts were to be pruned away; nor with accumulating cumbrous commentaries. They had the Scriptures." Spener and Francke similarly advocated the priority of exegesis in response to those who find in Scripture only what justifies the confession of faith; or when criticizing annotated Bibles; see Dale W. Brown, *Understanding Pietism* (Grand Rapids, Mich.: Eerdmans, 1978), pp. 67-69.

[88]Bengel, *Gnomon of the New Testament,* 1:6.

ing Scripture.[89] They argued that Scripture remains clear in itself, but readers must exercise themselves, spiritually, to understand (and obey). Historians of Pietism are correct that Spener, Francke and their followers emphasized the teleology of Scripture. But it is necessary to add "these practical interests were but an application of the demands inherent in the Scriptures."[90] Pietists opposed the idea that Scripture was obscure with a traditionally Protestant response that such an idea would be inconsistent with the very intent of Scripture, and they wrestled with the pastoral need to stimulate readers to overcome the obscurity of the reader with spiritual ardor.[91]

A theme closely related to Pietism's emphasis upon the goal of Scripture's clarity was enunciated by Chrysostom, repeated by Luther and echoed by Protestant confessions; it is that "all things are clear and open that are in the divine Scriptures; the necessary things are all plain."[92] Not content with Chrysostom's optimism one can ask, which is it? Are all things clear or only those things necessary? Frederick Farrar argued that Chrysostom overstated his first point: "It is belied by the whole history of exegesis, which in different ages has come to opposite conclusions about matters of much importance," but was worthy of praise for asserting his second point: "This rule is our chief source of consolation amid the endless perplexities of divergent interpretation. If a truth be essential to salvation, it must appeal clearly on the pages that contain a Divine Revelation: otherwise the Revelation would not be a Revelation."[93] Similarly, Heiko Oberman comments that application of Luther's principle of *sola Scriptura* did not bring about "the certainty [Luther] anticipated. It has in fact been

---

[89]It is an overstatement to argue, as many have against the Pietist tradition, that it used the Bible as a devotional tool rather than a source of doctrine. For example, August Hermann Francke reasoned that since the affections of the inspired writers contributed to Scripture, it was "a cogent argument in favour of the study of the [author's] Affections; for when we have acquired ability to develop them, the Scriptures will, of course, cease to be ambiguous" (cited in Brown, *Understanding Pietism,* pp. 80-81).

[90]Brown, *Understanding Pietism,* pp. 71-80; and F. Ernest Stoeffler, *The Rise of Evangelical Pietism* (Leiden: E. J. Brill, 1965).

[91]One could argue that Pietism's teleological emphasis regarding perspicuity is closer to various patristic comments on the subject than the emphasis on perspicuity as a property found in Protestant scholastics. Comments from Christianity's first centuries tend to confirm that the greatest obstacle to understanding what is clear (as opposed to demonstrating that it is clear, certainly a distinct subject) rests with the pastoral needs of the reader. For example, one could summarize Chrysostom's comments on clarity as follows: Scripture is clear, but we are lazy. Chrysostom's concern rests with the effort exercised by his flock to understand the essential matters of Scripture that are altogether clear (see chapter three).

[92]John Chrysostom, *Homilies on Thessalonians,* A Select Library of the Nicene and Post-Nicene Fathers of the Christian Church, ed. Philip Schaff, 1st series (Grand Rapids, Mich.: Eerdmans, 1988), 13:388.

[93]Farrar, *History of Interpretation,* p. 473.

responsible for a multiplicity of explanations and interpretations that seem to render absurd any dependence on the clarity of the Scriptures." Instead, Oberman argues that one should read Luther's appeal to perspicuity in evangelical terms: "The clarity of the Scriptures leads to the recognition of man and his indestructible dependence either on God the Redeemer or Satan the corrupter."[94] The either-or response to Chrysostom's "all things are clear and open" and "the necessary things are all plain" is a problem occasioned by a distortion that isolates perspicuity from Scripture's teleology and authority. It does raise an important caution: "It is necessary to limit clarity."[95]

Westminster Protestants, for instance, admitted the reality of both Scripture's obscurity and clarity, primarily in the distinction between matters necessary for salvation and other matters. In both the Irish Articles of Religion (1615) and the Westminster Confession of Faith (1647) the defense of Scripture's clarity was solely concerned with the accessibility of the evangelical message. The Irish Articles read:

> Although there be some hard things in the Scriptures (especially such as have proper relation to the times in which they were first uttered, and prophecies of things which were afterwards to be fulfilled), yet all things necessary to be known unto everlasting salvation are clearly delivered therein; and nothing of that kind is spoken under dark mysteries in one place which is not in other places spoken more familiarly and plainly, to the capacity both of learned and unlearned.[96]

Note that the reference to "dark mysteries" still concerns matters necessary for salvation, and historical proximity accounts for some "hard things," as does the nature of prophecy itself. Westminster reads:

> All things in Scripture are not alike plain in themselves, nor alike clear unto all; yet those things which are necessary to be known, believed, and observed, for salvation, are so clearly propounded and opened in some place of Scripture or other, that not only the learned, but the unlearned, in a due use of the ordinary means, may attain unto a sufficient understanding of them.[97]

---

[94]Oberman, *Luther,* pp. 220, 225.

[95]Farrar, *History of Interpretation,* p. 329. Farrar added, "The strife of perfectly honest interpreters cries aloud to heaven. . . . The Scripture is perfectly perspicuous in those few and simple truths which suffice for salvation, but as to many other subjects, and even as to subjects which have been deemed to be of consummate importance, it may almost be said *Quot viri, tot sententiae.*"

[96]Schaff, *Creeds of Christendom,* 3:527.

[97]Ibid., 3:604. See John G. Leith, *Assembly at Westminster: Reformed Theology in the Making* (Richmond, Va.: John Knox Press, 1973).

Similarly, in 1615 an Irish work had argued concerning the difficult things in Scripture: "If we never understand we shall be never the worse for the attaining of everlasting salvation."[98]

The admission that "all things in Scripture are not alike plain in themselves" should not come as a shock to Protestants. Beginning with Luther, Protestants argued that it was the subject matter of Scripture—its *res* (the law and the gospel)—that was clear. This was affirmed, again, by Turretin (albeit in a slightly different manner).[99] And it is found, also, in William Tyndale (1494-1536) who offered that the distinction between law and gospel (after Luther's fashion) unlocks the Bible for the reader:

> These things, I say, to know, is to have all the scripture unlocked and opened before thee; so that if thou wilt go in, and read, thou canst not but understand. And in these things to be ignorant, is to have all the scripture locked up; so that the more thou readest it, the blinder thou art, and the more contrariety thou findest in it, and the more tangled art thou therein, and canst nowhere through: for if thou had a gloss in one place, in another it will not serve.[100]

This perspective serves as a limiting notion in that it is employed to account

---

[98]*A Body of Divinity,* attributed to James Ussher; cited in Jack Rogers, *Scripture in the Westminster Confession: A Problem of Historical Interpretation for American Presbyterians* (Grand Rapids, Mich.: Eerdmans, 1967), p. 370.

[99]Turretin argued that "a believer who has enlightened eyes of the mind can comprehend [the] mysteries sufficiently for salvation if he reads carefully." Turretin also stated, "It is not a question of whether the Holy Scripture is clear in all its parts, so that it guides with no interpreter and no exposition of doubtful matters. . . . But the question deals only with the matters necessary for salvation, and with them only in reference to aspects which must be known." He continued, "It is not a question of whether matters necessary for salvation are presented clearly everywhere in Scripture. Indeed we grant that there are many passages that are difficult to understand, by which God wills to exercise our effort and the skill of the scholar. The question is whether [these necessary matters] are presented somewhere in such a manner that a believer can recognize their truth when he has given them serious consideration, because nothing is learned from the more obscure passages that is not found most plainly taught elsewhere" (*Doctrine of Scripture,* pp. 186-87).

[100]William Tyndale, "A Pathway into the Holy Scripture," in *Doctrinal Treatises and Introductions to Different Portions of the Holy Scriptures,* ed. Henry Walter (Cambridge: Cambridge University Press, 1848), pp. 27-28. Tyndale continues: "And therefore, because we be never taught the profession of our baptism, we remain always unlearned, as well the spiritually, for all their great clergy and high schools (as we say), as the lay people. And now, because the lay and unlearned people are taught these first principles of our profession, therefore they read the scripture, and understand and delight therein. And our great pillars of holy church, which have nailed a veil of false glosses on Moses' face, to corrupt the true understanding of his law, cannot come in. And therefore they bark, and say the scripture maketh heretics, and it is not possible for them to understand it in the English, because they themselves do not in Latin. And of pure malice, that they cannot have their will, they slay their brethren for their faith they have in our Saviour, and therewith utter bloody wolfish tyranny, and what they be within, and whose disciples." Also, in his comments on the book

for what is essentially the evangelical message, even though it is admitted that the Bible has more to it than that essential message.[101]

We may say at this point that a notion of plenary perspicuity—that the entirety of the Bible is clear in itself—is foreign to early Protestant hermeneutics, or at least an anomaly or a misrepresented objectifying of the responsive and pragmatic justification of the evangelical message.[102] Evangelical clarity is a positive affirmation and consistent with the intent of perspicuity for Protestant theologians. It accounts for the manner in which Scripture presents what is necessary for salvation, but not the how or why of a given doctrine or to deny the necessity of interpretation.

The practical need to encourage the use of necessary means to understand Scripture does not demonstrate that Protestants believed Scripture's clarity to be merely a matter of education or learning, though such things were presupposed. Otto Weber, reflecting upon the larger Protestant tradition, noted that perspicuity was not viewed "as something absolute but rather conditional. It did not apply to the geographical, historical, and other scientific statements of Scripture, for which scientific insights were necessary, and it did apply to Scripture only to the degree that someone could translate it from the original languages or was able to read such a translation. There are thus presuppositions of a purely factual nature which have to be fulfilled."[103] For example, after his

---

of Genesis, Tyndale advised, "Seek therefore in the scripture, as thou readest it, chiefly and above all, the covenants made between God and us; that is to say, the law and commandments which God commandeth us to do; and then the mercy promised unto all them that submit themselves unto the law" (p. 403).

[101]So observes David F. Wright, "Scripture and Evangelical Diversity with Special Reference to the Baptismal Divide," in *A Pathway into the Holy Scripture,* ed. Philip E. Salterthwaite and David F. Wright (Grand Rapids, Mich.: Eerdmans, 1994), pp. 257-75. "The clarity and certainty (of definiteness) of Scripture, as Zwingli termed it, was thought to function more in a responsive mode. It denoted the verifiability of the Reformation gospel in the pages of the Bible by literate citizens at last able, thanks to translation and printing, to check for themselves" (p. 259).

[102]See the arguments offered by Barton, *People of the Book,* pp. 84-86; Pannenberg, *Basic Questions,* 1:190-91; Farrar, *History of Interpretation,* p. 328; Beisser, *Claritas scripturae,* pp. 79-87; and Herrmann, *Klarheit der Heiligen Schrift,* pp. 19-23.

[103]Weber, *Foundations of Dogmatics,* 1:282. Similarly Charles Wood noted, "The idea that every believer should have direct access to the message of scripture along with the right of private judgement as to its content has come more and more to be seen, and rightly so, as a matter of principle rather than of fact. Properly qualified, it amounts to the claim that every believer with the requisite exegetical preparation may be a competent interpreter. Although this necessary proviso is sometimes decried as the surrender of a Reformation principle and a return to interpretation by authority (the new 'papacy' of scholars), this is surely a mistaken charge. There is a vast difference between a competence defined by demonstrable exegetical abilities and a competence bestowed by ecclesiastical status. That the responsible handling of scripture requires the former has been generally acknowledged in the Protestant tradition,

sustained argument regarding the sufficiency of Scripture's character, its superiority of content, antiquity, prophetic demonstration and transmission, even within the constraints of human judgment, Calvin offered this disclaimer:

> There are other reasons, neither few nor weak, for which the dignity and majesty of Scripture are not only affirmed in godly hearts, but brilliantly vindicated against the wiles of its disparagers; yet of themselves these are not strong enough to provide a firm faith, until our Heavenly Father, revealing his majesty there, lifts reverence for Scripture beyond the realm of controversy. Therefore Scripture will ultimately suffice for a saving knowledge of God only when its certainty is founded upon the inward persuasion of the Holy Spirit. Indeed, these human testimonies which exist to confirm it will not only be vain if, as secondary aids to our feebleness, they follow that chief and highest testimony. But those who wish to prove to unbelievers that Scripture is the Word of God are acting foolishly, for only by faith can this be known.[104]

Following such arguments the Westminster Confession affirmed that evangelical clarity is available "in a due use of ordinary means," which included the means of human learning and language, the means of preaching, as well as the illumination of the Spirit.[105] The subject of Scripture's clarity was not equated with a translation, nor with historical proximity—knowledge alone can never overcome one's blindness to Scripture's clear message. Nor does the affirmation of perspicuity mean that Scripture is simple as if it lacks obscurity in certain respects.

There is a healthy tendency within Protestant hermeneutics that assumes if obscurity exists, it exists for the reader—not simply because of sin but also because of a theologically historical perspective. As a theological assertion a primary concern for the text is demonstrated in the distinctive attention to the two testaments, two sources of knowledge. There is a unity concerning the knowledge of God, between that which is made available naturally or universally and that which is particularly revealed; however, the latter clarifies the former.[106] Calvin distinguished between the clarity of God's works and the obscuring of that knowledge: "The manifestation of God by which

---

however firmly the latter has been excluded" (*The Formation of Christian Understanding: An Essay in Theological Hermeneutics* [Philadelphia: Westminster Press, 1981], pp. 116-17).

[104]Calvin, *Institutes of the Christian Religion,* Library of Christian Classics, ed. John T. McNeill, trans. Ford Lewis Battles (Philadelphia: Westminster Press, 1960), p. 92.

[105]Schaff, *Creeds of Christendom,* 3:604.

[106]The relationship between natural and particular knowledge of God is usually understood to be a commentary on Calvin's thought; see Richard A. Muller, *Prolegomena to Theology* (Grand Rapids, Mich.: Baker, 1987); T. H. L. Parker, *Calvin's Doctrine of the Knowledge of God* (Grand Rapids, Mich.: Eerdmans, 1959); Susan E. Schreiner, *Theatre of His Glory: Nature and the Natural Order in the Thought of John Calvin* (Durham, N.C.: Labyrinth, 1991); and David Steinmetz, *Calvin in Context* (New York: Oxford University Press, 1995), pp. 23-39.

he makes his glory known among his creatures is sufficiently clear as far as its own light is concerned."[107] We see this theme developed in the Reformed tradition's distinction between God's revelation in nature (which makes humans culpable) and God's revelation in Scripture, which is more clear and more pointed to reveal God's salvation (which makes the gospel available, and which is otherwise unavailable to or by means of natural understanding). There is a clearer and a more obscure means of God's revelation. There are two books that reveal God: creation or nature and universal providence, which is sufficient to make humans accountable before God, and in Scripture that, as the Belgic Confession (1561) reads, "He makes himself more clearly and fully known to us by his holy and divine Word; that is to say, as far as is necessary for us to know in this life, to his glory and our salvation."[108] This argument is also found in the *Confessio Fidei Gallicana* (1559), "God reveals himself to men; firstly, in his works, in their creation, as well as in their preservation and control. Secondly, and more clearly, in his Word [the] Holy Scriptures."[109] Within the theological vision of Protestant thought clarity is employed at various junctures (knowledge of God, historical progress and circumstance of revelation, and the actual character of Scripture's message) but regularly represented as moral in character and significance.[110]

For Calvin, what is important is that Scripture provides what otherwise is unavailable to the reader. The problem he saw was for "those who, having forsaken Scripture, imagine some way or other of reaching God."[111] And in his comments on John 5:39, Calvin comments:

> We are taught by this passage, that if we wish to obtain the knowledge of Christ, we must seek it from *the Scriptures;* for they who imagine whatever they choose concerning Christ will ultimately have nothing instead of him but a shadowy phantom. First, then, we ought to believe that Christ cannot be properly known in any other way than from *the Scriptures;* and if it be so, it follows that we ought to read *the Scriptures* with the express design of finding Christ in them. Whoever

[107]John Calvin, *The Epistles of Paul the Apostle to the Romans and to the Thessalonians* (Grand Rapids, Mich.: Eerdmans, 1961), pp. 31-34.

[108]Schaff, *Creeds of Christendom,* 3:384.

[109]Ibid., 3:360. And from the "Brief Statement of the Reformed Faith" (1902): "We believe that God is revealed in nature, in history, and in the heart of man; that He has made gracious and clearer revelations of Himself [in Scripture]" (3:922).

[110]The theological relationship of the Testaments is also portrayed in terms of Scripture's clarity, the New clarifying the Old as much in terms of perspective as subject matter as textually oriented: "I consider this knowledge of the subject matter nothing other than a knowledge of the New Testament, for when this is well known it clarifies the entire scripture of the Old Testament" (Luther, *Luther's Works,* 3:73).

[111]Calvin, *Institutes,* p. 93.

> shall turn aside from this object, though he may weary himself throughout his whole life in learning, will never attain the knowledge of the truth; for what wisdom can we have without the wisdom of God?[112]

According to Calvin, perspicuity appears to be, in a rhetorical manner, the function of Scripture itself in dispelling the obscurity of the message: "Scripture, gathering up the otherwise confused knowledge of God in our minds, having dispersed our dullness, clearly shows us the true God."[113] And as we have seen, the Westminster Confession affirms that not only are "all things in Scripture not alike plain in themselves" but neither are all things "clear unto all." Both Scripture and the reader are, in some sense, obscure or obscured. One should not stray too far into an either/or choice between whether Scripture is clear or readers are obscured in their understanding; such a dichotomy does not account for the complex relationship between reader and text.[114] What the affirmation of perspicuity upholds is the priority of evangelical clarity. The aspiration of Protestant hermeneutics is to bring together Scripture with its clearly presented message of salvation and an enlightened reader.

The Bible as a Book and Beyond

This brings us to a brief final section that serves as both a capstone to our historical investigation of the place of clarity in the interpretation of Scripture as well as a preparation for the second section of this work concerned with contemporary interaction with the literary qualities of our subject. In particular we focus on the now-routine notion that the Bible should be treated as a book, as one would any other book, which grows out of the early modern suspicion that perspicuous readings of the Bible are artificially sustained by the prejudice of religious traditions (theology). Historical and critical understanding might help clarify in a more credible, rational manner the supposedly perspicuous and dubious traditions that had led Christianity to dominate the Western world and lead to so much violence. Thus, the tension between the form and the function of Scripture and between its clarity and obscurity was intensified as

---

[112]John Calvin, *The Gospel According to St John,* ed. David W. Torrance and Thomas F. Torrance, trans. T. H. L. Parker (Grand Rapids, Mich.: Eerdmans, 1961), p. 139. Calvin went on to explain, "By *the Scriptures,* of course, is here meant the Old Testament. For Christ did not first begin to be manifested in the Gospel; but the one to whom the Law and the Prophets bore witness was openly revealed in the Gospel."

[113]Calvin, *Institutes,* pp. 69-72. For Calvin's use of the terms *claritas* and *perspicuitas* see Ford Lewis Battles and Richard Wevers, *A Concordance to Calvin's Institutio* (Grand Rapids, Mich.: Calvin College and Seminary, 1980).

[114]On the relationship between the subject-object distinction in the Protestant development of perspicuity, see Weber, *Foundations of Dogmatics,* 1:283-84.

much by Protestantism's engagement with the early modern world (eighteenth and nineteenth centuries) as it was by the discussion of Scripture's multiple meaning in Scripture in early Christian circles.

Placing the Bible within the larger field of literature and admitting that it should be interpreted as any other book brought about the regression of perspicuity to a component of a general theory of language, criticism and history. As the Enlightenment took root among Christians, perspicuity was either banished to the prison reserved for arbitrary religious authorities or prostituted as another form of rational, empirical accessibility. A characteristic aspiration is offered by Benedict Spinoza: "I determined to examine the Bible afresh in a careful, impartial, and unfettered spirit, making no assumptions concerning it, and attributing to it no doctrines, which I do not find clearly set down therein."[115] Why is this sentiment so threatening in the modern era? Precisely because the appeal to what is clearly found in Scripture is coupled with the setting of rational, critical and historical influences purposefully distanced from Christian interpretative interests.

With such sentiments becoming more prevalent, the loss of a confession of Scripture's clarity is occasioned by a turn away from its uniquely Christian character to an implicit role in the isolation of the Bible's words, grammar and history. Critical knowledge would remove the "obscurities [and] apparent contradictions," according to Thomas Arnold.[116] In the name of empirical and historical and critical studies we are counseled to reread the Bible, not religiously, but as one would read any other book (which we will take up in the following chapter). This encouragement was based on the confidence that reason was a sufficient authority in religious inquiry and that the Bible was fully accessible, even to unbelieving study.[117]

Several important and differing emphases tended to collide with the tradi-

---

[115]Cited in Nigel M. de S. Cameron, *Biblical Higher Criticism and the Defense of Infallibilism in 19th Century Britain* (Lewiston: Edwin Mellen, 1987), p. 16. Cameron has convincingly shown these links as the proper background for the rise of critical studies in nineteenth century Britain; particularly Cameron cites Spinoza's significant role in the debate over Scripture's authority and interpretation that would blossom in late eighteenth and nineteenth Britain (pp. 7-114, 263-89).

[116]Thomas Arnold, *Essay on the Right Interpretation and Understanding of the Scriptures,* cited in Cameron, *Biblical Higher Criticism,* p. 34.

[117]The characteristics included under the theme of critical study and the Bible's perspicuity were: clarity's implicit role in an empirical method; an openness to examine Scripture in itself rather than from tradition or ecclesiastical authorities; and a sense of realism allied with a form of biblicism that would remain a strong tendency into the twentieth century among Protestants. See John Drury, ed., *Critics of the Bible 1724-1873* (New York: Cambridge University Press, 1989); Henning Graf Reventlow, *The Authority of the Bible and the Rise of the Modern World,* trans. John Bowden (Philadelphia: Fortress, 1985), pp. 289-410; Cameron, *Biblical Higher Criticism,* pp. 18-28; Nathan O. Hatch, *The Democratization of American Christianity* (New Haven, Conn.: Yale University Press, 1989), pp. 179-89.

tion of asserting a notion of Scripture's clarity in the early modern era. These three emphases genuinely set the stage for contemporary discussions of Scripture's clarity. First, the Protestant heritage of vernacular translations is often expressed in terms of accessibility to an understandable Bible.[118] The goal of translations was, of course, accessibility, and accessibility was premised upon the notion of clarity. "Tyndale, like all other Reformation translators, worked hard to keep as close as possible to his original, for . . . the Protestant emphasis on the centrality of the text required Bible translation to be as transparent as possible."[119] Thus, perspicuity was a precious and widespread assumption of nineteenth-century British evangelicalism.[120] The distribution of Protestant translations of the Bible literally disseminated Protestantism; it was a form of evangelism precisely because it assumed access to Protestant doctrines.[121] That is, there is a distinct but related understanding of clarity in the history of Protestant translations—a clear vernacular translation promotes fidelity to the gospel which is clear.[122]

Second, if British Protestants occasionally viewed perspicuity in generous terms and thereby capitalized on the religious sentiments of its culture, then in North America the sentiments of culture remade the religious spirit of ideas such as perspicuity. George Marsden, among others, reminds us that the per-

---

[118]We can only note the significance of this line of study within Protestant history; see F. F. Bruce, *History of the Bible in English,* 3rd ed. (New York: Oxford University Press, 1978); A. G. Dickens, *The English Reformation* (New York: Schocken, 1964); S. L. Greenslade, ed., *The Cambridge History of the Bible,* 3 vols. (Cambridge: Cambridge University Press, 1963); and Nathan O. Hatch and Mark A. Noll, *The Bible in America: Essays in Cultural History* (New York: Oxford University Press, 1982).

[119]Gerald Hammond, "English Translations of the Bible," in *The Literary Guide to the Bible,* ed. Robert Alter and Frank Kermode (Cambridge, Mass.: Harvard University Press, 1987), p. 648.

[120]Newman's comment is found in his *Apologia Pro Vita Sua* (reprint, Glasgow: Collins, 1977), p. 96. On the subject of the role of the Bible in early nineteenth-century Protestantism in Britain see James Patrick Callahan, *Primitivist Piety: The Ecclesiology of the Early Plymouth Brethren,* vol. 12 of *Studies in Evangelicalism,* ed. Donald W. Dayton and Kenneth E. Rowe (Lanham, Md.: Scarecrow, 1996). And the significant efforts of Bible societies in late eighteenth-century and nineteenth-century Britain demonstrate as much in their persistent efforts to distribute Bibles as a means of checking the tide of Catholicism and expanding the influence of Protestantism in British lands. See Desmond Bowen, *The Idea of the Victorian Church: A Study of the Church of England, 1833-1889* (Montreal: McGill University Press, 1968); Robert Currie, Alan D. Gilbert, and Lees Horsley, eds., *Churches and Churchgoers: Patterns of Church Growth in the British Isles Since 1700* (Oxford: Clarendon, 1977); George I. T. Machin, *The Catholic Question in English Politics, 1820 to 1830* (Oxford: Clarendon, 1964); *Politics and the Churches in Great Britain 1832-1868* (New York: Clarendon, 1977).

[121]See David W. Bebbington, *Evangelicalism in Modern Britain: A History from the 1730s to the 1980s* (London: Unwin Hyman, 1989), pp. 12-14, 75-77.

[122]On this theme, see Werner Schwarz, *Principles and Problems of Biblical Translation: Some Reformation Controversies and Their Background* (Cambridge: Cambridge University Press, 1955); Berkouwer, *Holy Scripture,* pp. 213-39; and Oberman, *Luther,* pp. 209-25.

spicuity of Scripture was subsumed under the "broader philosophical assumption of the perspicuity of truth generally."[123] A populist sentiment took root in the intellectual and religious climate of the eighteenth and nineteenth centuries to produce a distinctly American biblicism.[124] In nineteenth-century America perspicuity became a democratized affirmation of religious equality; lost was the responsibility of a spiritual priesthood and gained was the right of private judgment. It appears that Protestants viewed Scripture's clarity as a pedestrian opinion. Charles Hodge argued that the perspicuity of Scripture meant the "Bible is a plain book," that it "is intelligible by the people," and that Scripture was addressed to "the people." Therefore, according to Hodge, "To them are directed these profound discussions of Christian doctrine, and these comprehensive expositions of Christian duty. They are everywhere assumed to be competent to understand what is written." So he believed, "If Scripture is a plain book . . . it follows in inevitably that [the children of God] must agree in all essential matters in their interpretation in the Bible," and that "it is maintained that in all things necessary to salvation [the Scripture] are sufficiently plain to be understood even by the unlearned."[125] And Hodge went on to add, "It need hardly be remarked that this right of private judgment is the great safeguard of civil and religious liberty."[126]

And third, as a reaction to the enthusiastic association of clarity with accessibility, some Protestants offered a strenuous corrective. For example, in an effort to arrest the influence of the right of private judgment, coupled with and justified by an appeal to Scripture's clarity, John Nevin advocated "a lim-

---

[123]George M. Marsden, "Everyone One's Own Interpreter? The Bible, Science, and Authority in Mid-Nineteenth-Century America," in *The Bible in America: Essays in Cultural History* (New York: Oxford University Press, 1982), p. 80. Also see Herbert Hovenkamp, *Science and Religion in America 1800-1860* (Philadelphia: University of Pennsylvania Press, 1978); and Theodore Dwight Bozeman, *Protestants in an Age of Science: The Baconian Ideal and Antebellum American Religious Thought* (Chapel Hill: University of North Carolina Press, 1977).

[124]See Sidney E. Mead, *The Lively Experiment: The Shaping of Christianity in America* (New York: Harper & Row, 1963) pp. 1-15, 103-33; and Nathan O. Hatch, "*Sola Scriptura* and *Novus Ordo Seclorum*," in *The Bible in America: Essays in Cultural History* (New York: Oxford University Press, 1982), pp. 59-78.

[125]Charles Hodge, *Systematic Theology* (Grand Rapids, Mich.: Eerdmans, 1952), 1:183-84.

[126]Ibid., 1:186-87. Hodge offered this opinion against the nagging threat of the totalitarianism of the Church of Rome. And more recently Otto Weber argued that the first implication of Scripture's perspicuity was "the openness of Scripture for everyone." Accessibility to Scripture is not dependent on the "obligatory interpretation provided by the Church"; it is not "a secret book which can only be decoded by [the] initiated," but perspicuity "makes it possible for 'every Christian to deal with Scripture without tutelage' " (Weber, *Foundations of Dogmatics,* 1:281).

itation in some form to the principle, *No creed but the Bible.*" Sounding much like Catholic critics during the Reformation, Nevin lamented the disarray autonomous appeals to perspicuity brought upon Protestantism. But for Nevin this was not the prophetic warning of Tridentine Catholicism but historical contemplation. He wrote, "If the Bible be at once so clear and full as a formulary of Christian doctrine and practice, how does it come to pass that where men are left most free to use it in this way . . . they are flung asunder so perpetually in their religious faith, instead of being brought together?"[127] The feigned ecumenism of a variety of sects was merely a way of affirming their particular form of sectarianism, each justified by an appeal to the clarity of the Bible.

Nevin's corrective was to discard the autonomy of private judgment and restore a Catholic-Protestant hermeneutic in which perspicuity was governed by the living tradition of the church embodied in its historic creeds. The controlling force of Protestant tradition itself, as many have argued, always existed alongside the confession of Scripture's accessibility and clarity. The need to restrain perspicuity arose from the desire to mitigate the atomistic tendencies of separating Scripture's clarity from an eclectic appeal to a Protestant theological rule and thereby salvage perspicuity within the larger framework of the Protestant hermeneutical tradition.[128]

Conclusion

The subject of Scripture's clarity and obscurity neither begins nor ends with the Protestant Reformation. Nonetheless, what Protestantism does with perspicuity is somewhat unique in that the subject becomes more prominent in its own right inasmuch as the appeal to Scripture's clarity becomes more apologetic. The significance of perspicuity within Protestant hermeneutics is routinely coupled with the focal issue of rejecting certain, perceived, forms of totalitarianism; it is, as Popkin put the matter, a question of differing authorities.[129] Among the list of themes commonly put forward to describe what happened to biblical interpretation in late

---

[127]John W. Nevin, "The Sect System," *Mercersburg Review* 1 (September 1849): 491-93.

[128]The desire to restrain the application of perspicuity received a different reading from dissenting and primitivist Protestantism, as it did from latitudinarians generally. For example, Frederick Farrar complained that although the Reformation was an immense step forward in interpretation, it did not escape the error of dogmatism: "The whole Bible from Genesis downwards was forced to speak the language of the accepted formulae, and the 'perspicuity of Scripture' was identified with the facility with which it could be forced into semblable accordance with dogmatic systems." He complained that seventeenth-century divines spout their assertions of Scripture's perspicuity [namely Hollaz and Quenstedt], but such assertions "furnish no assistance and solve no difficulty, and which can only be maintained in detail by an accumulation of special pleas" (Farrar, *History of Interpretation,* pp. 26-27).

[129]Richard H. Popkin, *The History of Skepticism from Erasmus to Descartes* (New York: Harper & Row, 1964).

medieval and Protestant circles, we find the theme of authority—really, contention over authorities, authoritative interpretation and its justification—often surfacing in a manner that encompasses the more discrete themes of medieval interest.[130] And within Protestant theology the topic of authority is routinely associated with the message that Scripture bears, the evangelical force and direct address of Scripture to the believing reader. This emphasis, in turn, serves as a justification for the Protestant message itself. From the reassertion of its normative-literal sense, in contrast to an ecclesial-literal sense, Protestants insisted that when read properly (i.e., *protestantly*), it yielded a sufficient (i.e., salvific) awareness of the gospel.

The topic of clarity itself in the various developments of Protestantism is hermeneutically ambiguous. It embodies a larger struggle over biblical interpretation inherited from the Middle Ages (and the tensions of multiple senses, literal sense, and authoritative interpreters and interpretation). But it is confessionally unambiguous; it invites the reader to approach the text with the confidence that Scripture is meant to be understood (and it also supplies a ready answer concerning what is to be understood—the gospel of God). The affirmation that Scripture is clear at first associated with how that is the case (for Zwingli, Luther and Calvin), but post-Reformation Protestants tended to disassociate the affirmation of Scripture's clarity from a demonstration of how that is the case (as is the tendency in scholastic circles and the rising setting of early modernity). This split between Scripture (its message perceived to be theological in nature) and how Scripture is to be understood (methodological premises understood to unlock or justify any credible assertions) is the burden we inherit in the present era, to which we now turn.

---

[130]Thus G. R. Evans, *The Language and Logic of the Bible: The Earlier Middle Ages* (New York: Cambridge University Press, 1984); *The Language and Logic of the Bible: The Road to Reformation* (New York: Cambridge University Press, 1985); *Problems of Authority in the Reformation Debates* (New York: Cambridge University Press, 1992); Guy Fitch Lytle, ed., *Reform and Authority in the Medieval and Reformation Church* (Washington, D.C.: Catholic University Press, 1981).

PART II

LITERARY & THEOLOGICAL INTEREST IN SCRIPTURE'S CLARITY

THERE IS A CONSENSUAL MANNER OF READING CHRISTIAN SCRIPTURE—A POSITIVE AND constructive regard for the text that is informed by attending to the text itself as perspicuous. Thus, the clarity of Scripture is intimately related to how we read the text: confessing Scripture as perspicuous entails reading it in a manner that is congruous with Scripture as text (attentive to its textuality, chapters six and seven) as well as its presumptive rendering of its own message and our world (attentive to its intratextuality, chapters eight and nine). The meaning of the biblical text is the text itself, established by the text itself and understood by attending to the Christian reading of Scripture as text. That is, Scripture renders its own clarity, by its own means, in the community of its faithful readers.

The reader's orientation to Scripture may be described as textual inasmuch as what is being understood and the manner in which it is understood are inseparable. This approach is often in contrast with disciplines applied to reading the biblical text that attempt to supply meaning from historical, literary or philosophical domains or reference. And although it is customarily confused with a simplistic or ahistorical acceptance of the text, the Christian reading of Scripture as perspicuous is inherently historical, literary, philosophical and even critical but not primarily so.

This topic is addressed through a conversation with contemporary literary criticism regarding the nature of texts, especially as they challenge Christian assumptions about the nature of Scripture and the issue of clarity and obscurity. The current fascination with treating the Bible *as* literature has produced much that is thoughtful, even the development of a literary doctrine of Scripture, although much of what is offered is paralleled (or preceded) by the Christian tradition itself. By comparing literary attempts to understand texts as texts and in con-text with the orientation to Scripture as text, the case for a Christian reading of Scripture as perspicuous can be better understood.

Pursuing a contemporary statement of Scripture's perspicuity in dialogue with the development of modern literary criticism serves to illustrate the nature of confessing clarity at present. What follows is an attempt to chart a renewed way along an old path; all the while avoiding the inclination to sacrifice the Christian understanding of Scripture to an unequivocal critical domain, and also avoiding the tendency to withdraw Scripture from scrutiny and criticism. It may be that our interest in perspicuity not only indicates the need for a restatement of its historical focus but also a restatement of the Christian doctrine of Scripture, one that treats Scripture itself with a sufficient degree of seriousness.

6

TEXTUAL CLARITY

Learn . . . the meaning of the saying, "Nothing beyond what is written."

1 CORINTHIANS 4:6 (NRSV)

This is George.
He lived with his friend, the man with the yellow hat. He was a good little monkey, but he was always curious.
This morning George was looking at some of his friend's books. They were full of little black marks and dots and lines, and George was curious: what could one do with them?
The man with the yellow hat came just in time.
"You don't tear a book apart to find out what's in it," he said. "You READ it, George. Books are full of stories. Stories are made of words, and words are made of letters. If you want to read a story you first have to know the letters of the alphabet. Let me show you."

H. A. REY, *CURIOUS GEORGE LEARNS THE ALPHABET*

THE PROTESTANT CONFESSION *SOLA SCRIPTURA,* WITH ITS ATTENDING CONVICtions regarding Scripture's sufficiency, inspiration, authority and clarity, provides a specific grammar about how Christians regard the meaning and understanding of Scripture. *Sola Scriptura* is not simply an affirmation about Scripture as an object of interest and inquiry; it is itself a commitment to understand Scripture as principally significant, which means we cannot have what the text is about without the text itself. There is no necessary distinction drawn between word and meaning; the meaning is clear from the "naked words" themselves, as Martin Luther offered.[1] Thus, *sola Scriptura*—as in naked words—is itself a form of *criticism.* And confessing that the text we read is *Scripture* is accompanied by the burden that it is best understood on its own terms. We note David Kelsey's distinction between treating biblical texts as *texts* or as *Scripture* in relation to the object of one's inquiry; the former is primarily historical in orientation (either by historical means or

[1]Cited in James Samuel Preus, *From Shadow to Promise: Old Testament Interpretation from Augustine to the Young Luther* (Cambridge, Mass.: Belknap, 1969), p. 254.

according to what it must have meant in its original setting); the latter is ecclesial in that it is ruled by the theological prejudgments of faithful reading most often associated with the Christian community. Often the goal of treating biblical texts as *texts* precludes theological partiality, while treating biblical texts as *Scripture* may (and should, to Kelsey) include or take up the historical treatments of biblical texts as *texts*.[2]

Credibility and authority are, then, related to Scripture as text, its self-specifying identity, and accompanied by a confession regarding the custom of reading Scripture as perspicuous. This does mean that we desire to isolate Scripture, denying the challenges raised by historical and critical models of interpretation, but neither do we wish to sever the actual shape and character of the Bible as Scripture from the question of how we are to understand it.[3] The contention of this chapter is that in the face of the genuine challenges promoted by historical-critical methodology, with its critical interest with matters extrinsic to the text (the genesis of a text, its author's intent or affective results of a text) a distinctly Christian interest in the text of Scripture is often sacrificed. Instead we might be concerned with a more Christian manner of interacting with Scripture. As Hans Frei observes:

> Historical-critical inquiry has every right to be called a method. It has canons for what is evidence, for analyzing the authenticity of sources. Hermeneutics, by contrast, has no set of agreed-upon principles or procedures except that a text or a discourse is to be understood in some extended context other than merely its original historical setting and is to be seen therefore as a *linguistic* world with an integrity of its own.[4]

By reconstructing our awareness of matters intrinsic to Scripture instead of ripping it apart to find what is in it, and exploring how the persistent affirmation of Scripture's clarity points us in this direction, we hope to refashion a sense of Scripture's textual clarity.

Sola Scriptura as Criticism

A persistent, even if often abused, theme within Protestant biblical interpreta-

---

[2]David H. Kelsey, *The Uses of Scripture in Recent Theology* (Philadelphia: Fortress, 1975), pp. 198-201.

[3]This also means that the assertion *sola Scriptura* is not to be taken in an absolute sense of *solitaria Scriptura;* the deference afforded Scripture, and affirmations of its sufficiency, inspiration, authority and clarity modify the confession of *sola Scriptura* so as to unite Scripture with the means of understanding Scripture. Consult Robert M. Grant with David Tracy, *A Short History of the Interpretation of the Bible* (London: SCM Press, 1984).

[4]Hans W. Frei, *Types of Christian Theology,* ed. George Hunsinger and William C. Placher (New Haven, Conn.: Yale University Press, 1992), p. 144.

tion is the methodological stipulation that "Scripture is its own interpreter" (*Scriptura sui interpres* or *Scripturam ex Scriptura explicandam esse:* Scripture is to be explained from Scripture). And the confession *sola Scriptura* reflects the outlandish assertion that the Bible has its own hermeneutics.[5] It addresses the tension of authoritative theological tradition and a constructive assertion of Scripture's authority and self-authenticating qualities. Its implementation has consistently been associated with the suggestion that clear texts are employed to interpret unclear or obscure texts, which seems to be another outlandish Christian claim. Stated negatively, "Understanding is not achieved by putting Scripture aside."[6] The now routine observation that the Bible once was treated as a "self-glossing book" by the rabbis and Christian interpreters alike is important at present because it is suggested that we should (must) now reconsider how this practice will show us the way forward, toward better understanding of how texts function, even in light of our "critical" circumstances. "One learns to study" the Bible, Gerald Burns observes, "by following the ways in which one portion of the text illumines another."[7] An important effect of this admission is that "the Bible effectively blocks any attempt to understand it by reconstruction of its textual history and a working back to an original, uninterpreted intention."[8] It is precisely the effort to regard authorial or original intent in this "uninterpreted" fashion that motivates advocates of this interpretative strategy. Instead of accepting the intractable necessity of interpretation, the assertion of the author's intent is an attempt to disambiguate the question of textual meaning.

Asserting, once again, the practice of (self-)interpretation is not to retreat into a closed, uncritical, presumption that the Bible is a simplistically unified "book" but rather that our handling of the text must represent what the text appears to be about. For example, "it means that the parts are throwing light

---

[5]Lindbeck's comment: "Each text should be interpreted in its own terms: the Bible has its own hermeneutics" (George Lindbeck, "Scripture, Consensus, and Community," in *Biblical Interpretation in Crisis,* ed. Richard John Neuhaus [Grand Rapids, Mich.: Eerdmans, 1989], p. 82). Also consult Gerhard Ebeling, *Word and Faith* (Philadelphia: Fortress, 1963), pp. 305-32.

[6]G. C. Berkouwer, *Holy Scripture,* trans. Jack Rogers (Grand Rapids, Mich.: Eerdmans, 1975), p. 112 (also pp. 105-38 for larger treatment of this theme); and "From Light to Dark Should Be the Movement," cited in H. D. McDonald, *What the Bible Teaches About the Bible* (Wheaton, Ill.: Tyndale House, 1979), p. 141.

[7]Gerald L. Bruns, "Midrash and Allegory: The Beginnings of Scriptural Interpretation," in *The Literary Guide to the Bible,* ed. Robert Alter and Frank Kermode (Cambridge, Mass.: Harvard University Press, 1987), p. 626.

[8]Ibid., p. 627. Bruns's conclusion: "For what is at issue with respect to the Scriptures is not what lies behind the text in the form of an original meaning but what lies in front of it where the interpreter stands. The Bible always addresses itself to the time of interpretation; one cannot understand it except by appropriating it anew" (pp. 627-28).

on the earlier, even as they themselves always stand in the light of what precedes and follows them."[9] The actual appeal to clear and unclear texts corresponds with this premise of textuality, justified both theologically (Scripture has God as its ultimate author) and textually (Scripture refers to itself); thus we desire to speak of a theological textuality and the confession *sola Scriptura* as akin to a form of criticism as feasible as historical, critical and literary models, just more explicitly Christian.

In actual practice the characterizations of clear and unclear texts, with the former norming the latter, expresses as much about the prejudices of the interpreter and particular interpretative community as it does about whether a text can be considered actually clear or unclear.[10] Within Protestant hermeneutics the principle that Scripture is *sui ipsius interpres* is as much polemical as it is interpretative; it represents the prejudgment of an interpreter and community and does not solve the tension between the interpretative tradition of a text and the actual history of that text.[11] In this setting perspicuity serves the ends of Protestant theological hermeneutics rather than its own purpose as a general hermeneutical concern. As G. C. Berkouwer pointed out, the confession that Scripture is its own interpreter is directed against both authoritative tradition and subjectivism (that which is beyond and independent of Scripture or not derived intrinsically from the unity of Scripture and faith). And as we have already seen, the confession that Scripture is clear does not carry with it the notion of a simplistic, objective clarity, but it is the condition within which a Christian reading of Scripture is best described. It is not simply the case that any particular pericope, sentence or verse is clear or unclear, but that the whole (Scripture) is the home or milieu of any particular pericope, sentence or verse, and Scripture is taken to be clear as to its goal. How Protestants reinforced the determinative nature of Scripture was not to abandon text in favor of historical or spiritual witness but to assert text as its own witness: "Scripture is clear and interprets itself with clarity."[12] This can and should yield a genuinely self-critical approach to Scripture as text.

---

[9]Ibid., p. 627. The effect, Bruns notes, is that "the Bible effectively blocks any attempt to understand it by reconstruction of its textual history and a working back to an original, uninterpreted intention. This self-interpreting text is also self-effacing with respect to its origins. The whole orientation of Scripture is toward its future, not toward its past." The most significant result for contemporary historical-critical interests is the consistent deemphasis of the (human) author of biblical texts in both precritical and postcritical interpretative circles.

[10]For example, the observations of James D. G. Dunn, *Baptism in the Holy Spirit* (London: SCM Press, 1970), pp. 103-8.

[11]Or so it is argued by Dilthey and observed by Gadamer in Hans-Georg Gadamer, *Truth and Method,* trans. Joel Weinsheimer and Donald G. Marshall (New York: Crossroad, 1989), pp. 174-84.

[12]Berkouwer, *Holy Scripture,* pp. 192, 268.

Self-critically justifying Christian convictions about Scripture as text by moving from (supposedly) clear texts to (assumedly) unclear texts is not unlike arguments for justifying claims among ethicists and philosophers,[13] and it is especially akin to how literary critics treat the concern for what a given text means. Basil Mitchell's description is especially helpful:

> Scholar A takes a certain passage to be the clue to the author's overall meaning. The sense of this passage seems to him quite obvious and also its importance in the work as a whole. However, he recognizes that some other passages are on first reading difficult to reconcile with this one, as he has chosen to interpret it. So he has to bring these apparent recalcitrant passages into line by finding an interpretation of them which will fit; or, failing that, by conceding that they are discrepant, but dismissing the discrepancy as comparatively unimportant. . . . Scholar B, on the other hand, starts with a hunch that the key lies elsewhere, in a different passage from the one A relies upon. This passage he interprets different from A and his overall exegesis based on it requires him also to interpret differently from A, A's own original passage.[14]

Such justifications indicate a critical concern for intrinsic readings—critical in that the exercise of interpretation is spoken of as tempered and directed by an effort to explain one's own readings in comparison to another's, intrinsic in that justifications appeal to the form of the texts themselves. When we turn to the subject of understanding Scripture, we note that instead of vitiating the theological tradition that Scripture is its own best interpreter (in principle) and that texts regarded as clear are employed to understand texts regarded as unclear (in practice), the justification of one's assertions regarding a text's meaning(s) displays a discriminating sensitivity toward particular texts. How does one address this discrepancy? Mitchell offers:

> It might be thought that they should first try to reach agreement on which passage to start from; then try to agree on its meaning; and then consider what implications this has for the interpretation of the rest. It is obvious, I think, that this strategy will not work. B does not want to start from where A wants to start from. If he concedes this point, he has probably lost the argument already. So he tries to explain why he does not want to start from there: because, let us suppose, (a) the passage does not mean what A thinks it does, (b) to interpret the passage the way A proposes and to give it the importance he claims for it distorts the overall interpretation. [But] B can hope to persuade A of (b) only by going through all the

[13]Jeffrey Stout, *Ethics After Babel* (Boston: Beacon, 1988), pp. 24-28. This suggestion is from William C. Placher, *Unapologetic Theology: A Christian Voice in a Pluralistic Conversation* (Louisville: Westminster John Knox, 1989), pp. 123-37.

[14]Basil Mitchell, *The Justification of Religious Belief* (New York: Oxford University Press, 1981), p. 46.

> other relevant passages and comparing how they look on A's interpretation with how they look on his own. And this is, ultimately, the only way also in which he can hope to persuade A of (a). For part of his argument about the meaning of this original passage will be that, if interpreted in A's manner, it will make nonsense or less good sense of some or all of the rest. In the end, A and B will need to take one another right through the text, and the argument will consist in each trying to conceive the other of the need to give each passage the weight and significance that, in terms of his own interpretation, it ought to bear.[15]

Justifying one's reading of any particular sentence or subject is guided by the investment in justifying an inferentially unabridged understanding of the text. There is no simple or objective or abstract starting point, nor must there necessarily be. However, the effort of understanding does move along a resolute pathway, "right through the text," and is bound up with an invitation to read along with. In this way the critical concern that Scripture be regarded as intertextually norming involves a detailed explanation of the experience of interpretation. And the effort to understand the obscure by means of the clear is the beginning of interpretation, not its conclusion.[16]

That Scripture is to be understood by its own means—or as Luther said, it is "better to read Scripture according to what is inside"[17]—is also built upon the self-identifying nature of its purpose (a subject we will turn to in chapter seven). While there are many ways in which the text Christians refer to as Scripture can be understood and employed, and many are profitable in their own right, there also is a Christian manner of appropriating Scripture as text that is literary, critical, historical and theological.[18] This Christian manner is derived from attention to the text itself.

Extrinsic and Intrinsic Clarity

By contrast, credibility and authority within contemporary critical scholarship are founded in the authority of historical and critical disciplines to provide

---

[15]Ibid., pp. 46-47.

[16]Note the agreement with the argument of Bruce Marshall, "Meaning and Truth in Narrative Interpretation: A Reply to George Schner," *Modern Theology* 8 (1992): 173-79.

[17]Martin Luther, *Luther's Works,* ed. Jaroslav Pelikan, 56 vols. (St. Louis: Concordia, 1955-1976), 8:142, referring to the rabbinical method of reading according to the upper and lower vowel points (or what is above or below).

[18]By attending to the text as the formal object of faith we concede that Scripture is also formally subject to critical examination. Conclusions drawn from or assertions of a text's meaning are subject to scrutiny, confirmation and correction. Rather than making Christian concentration upon Scripture immune from critical review by rejecting historical, biographical and scientific methods, reading with primary attention to the text subjects assertions of meaning and truth to the domain of the text itself.

meaning for texts and is characteristically an exercise in perceiving Scripture's meaning, not as significant in itself but only within the larger context of critical studies or knowledge grounded in historical reference. For example, if something is historical, it is allowably true. Among the alternatives to this type of historical reference is the reunion of critical and theological interests in so-called postcritical approaches to Scripture.

Censures of extrinsic concerns such as historical and critical methodologies are intimately involved with a postcritical assertion of Scripture's textuality. For example, we note the most promising suggestions of Northrop Frye:

> The general principle . . . is that if anything historically true is in the Bible, it is there not because it is historically true but for different reasons. The reasons have presumably something to do with spiritual profundity or significance. And historical truth has no correlation with spiritual profundity, unless the relation is inverse. . . . Nothing said here will be new to Biblical scholars, who are well aware that the Bible will only confuse and exasperate a historian who tries to treat it as a history. One wonders why in that case their obsession with the Bible's historicity does not relax, so that other and more promising hypotheses could be examined. . . . If the historical element in the Bible were a conscientious, inaccurate, imperfect history . . . we could under-stand how important it would be to make a fuller reconstruction of that history. But when it shows such an exuberant repudiation of everything we are accustomed to think of as historical evidence, perhaps we should be looking for different categories and criteria altogether.[19]

Unfortunately, the routine disassociation of critical and theological interests among many interpretative models is supported by a passing intellectual setting, which is applied so as to preclude theological interests in Scripture as text. Robert Alter notes:

> The historical criticism of the Bible is rooted in a view of truth associated with the nineteenth-century positivism that does not sit well with any sense of the moral or spiritual authority of Scripture. In this view, what counts is what really happened once in the coordinates of earthly time and space, what can be uncovered with the archaeologist's spade, measured by carbon dating, or at least inferentially determined as the actual material cause behind the elaborate layers of verbal mediation that constitute the biblical text.[20]

The irony of such historical method—by which we mean the assumedly universal and scientific reference that evaluates all instances of language, text

---

[19]Northrop Frye, *The Great Code: The Bible and Literature* (New York: Harcourt Brace Jovanovich, 1982), pp. 40, 42.

[20]Robert Alter, *The World of Biblical Literature* (New York: BasicBooks, 1992), p. 203.

and consideration of truth—is that it effectively undercuts any sense of historical reflection and responsibility—by which we mean assessing the usefulness, function and morality of knowing and knowledge. The supposedly historical science of critical method, according to critic Allen Tate in 1940, "is in the long run the unhistorical method."[21]

For example, reading the Bible as one would read any other book has been a dominant (and roughly profitable) tool in contemporary critical studies, but this has been accomplished by situating the text in the larger and defining field of literature, history, critical or human knowledge, and experience, and is premised on consciously protecting the text from both real and potential distortion by reading. This is routinely expressed as an anxiety, a strict, mutually exclusive, either-or choice between what the text originally meant to the author (the only true meaning of significance) and how any other way of reading the text leads to distortion and error.

Benjamin Jowett's 1860 essay "On the Interpretation of Scripture" provided us with the now-routine suggestion that the Bible should be read "like any other book." The premise was the exercise of "a critical spirit," which would exorcise the demons of dogmas and denominational conflicts that have come to possess the text (thus obscuring the original author's intent and thus the texts only genuine meaning). To Jowett, *critical interpretation* is not governed by *theological prejudice,* therefore we *either* preclude multiple interpretations *or* we renounce any hope of certainty. As Jowett maintained, "If words have more than one meaning, they may have any meaning."[22] This univocal notion of meaning is historical: "Scripture has one meaning—the meaning which it had to the mind of the prophet or evangelist who first uttered or wrote, to the hearers or readers who first received it."[23] This model drives an interpreter to *the* initial setting to look for meaning in a reference external to the text under consideration, and its method presumes that Scripture is clear or obscure according to the degree that the reader understands this reference and rejects other influences: "to combat the obscuring of the true meaning of the biblical texts through traditional interpretations being forced upon them."[24]

---

[21] Allen Tate, "Miss Emily and the Bibliographer," in *Collected Essays* (Denver: Swallow, 1959), reprinted in *The New Criticism and Contemporary Literary Theory: Connections and Continuities,* ed. William J. Spurlin and Michael Fischer (New York: Garland, 1995), p. 15.

[22] Benjamin Jowett, "On the Interpretation of Scripture," in *The Interpretation of Scripture and Other Essays* (London: George Routledge, n.d.), p. 31.

[23] Jowett, "On the Interpretation of Scripture," in *Essays and Reviews,* 7th ed. (London: Longman, Green, Longman, and Roberts, 1861), pp. 330-43; reprinted in *Religious Thought in the Nineteenth Century,* ed. B. M. G. Reardon (London: Cambridge University Press, 1966), p. 315.

[24] Paul R. Noble, "The *Sensus Literalis:* Jowett, Childs, and Barr," *Journal of Theological Studies* 44, no. 1 (1993): 3.

It would appear to be ridiculous to protest this, and the only choice seems to be between accepting critical knowledge as the field of study in which Scripture is to be understood, or retreat into anti-intellectual, naive and precritical shell that argues the Bible is immune from criticism. An attempt to conceive of Scripture as text (theological textuality) has no genuine home in this setting. And with regard to Scripture's clarity the dichotomy of historical or textual understanding has created a split between what anyone might make of the text and what only the rightly informed can understand. Meaning is captive within historical reference, to be unlocked through an understanding of the situatedness of the text. The alternative to the either-or dichotomy of critical (historical, authorial) versus anticritical (as in naive, precritical) is not to say that understanding the Bible is above history, culture or other literature but that its understanding or meaning is not to be found in context but in Scripture *as text.*

Within contemporary literary criticism the textual orientation alluded to is concerned with understanding the meaning of a text by means of what is *intrinsic* to a text, rather than, primarily, *extrinsic* to the text. Sometimes the orientations of extrinsic criticism are referred to as "heresies" (hardly a kind characterization); these matters include the genetic, intentional and aesthetic or affective fallacies. They share a feigned appreciation for the text but only as a matter of exploiting a text regarded as authoritative by means of ulterior purposes.[25] The genetic fallacy concerns the romantic orientation to explain a text's meaning by extratextual circumstances, by supposedly causal antecedents in social, economic or political spheres; the meaning of a text was transferred to its genetic context. This genetic interest is also carried over into literary relationships between proximate texts, the hypothetical development of the text itself (that is, the diachronic interest in meaning of texts through its apparent development).[26] The intentional fallacy seeks to understand a text by

---

[25]For arguments regarding these approaches as "heresies" see René Wellek and Austin Warren, *Theory of Literature* (New York: Harvest, 1942) pp. 61-127; William K. Wimsatt Jr. and Cleanth Brooks, *Literary Criticism: A Short History* (New York: Vintage, 1957), pp. 454-75, 522-49; William K. Wimsatt Jr. and Monroe C. Beardsley, *The Verbal Icon: Studies in the Meaning of Poetry* (Lexington: University of Kentucky Press, 1954), pp. 3-39.

[26]The distinction of diachronic (studying meaning through the development of a text, by comparing and contrasting the process through which a text was probably constructed) and synchronic (understanding the meaning of a text by means of the instance being considered, often by comparing and contrasting how the text differs from other texts) arises from the work of Ferdinand de Saussure, *Course in General Linguistics* (New York: Philosophical Library, 1959). And the tendency to emphasize diachronic matters as determinative of a text's meaning is characteristic of a genetic fallacy. The "history of a word (a *diachronic* study of its use) may explain *how* a word came to be used with some particular sense at a specified time, but in order to find out *what* a lexeme means at that particular time we have only to look at the contemporary *usage*" (Peter Cotterell and Max Turner, *Linguistics and Biblical Interpretation* [Downers Grove, Ill.: InterVarsity Press, 1989], p. 132).

means of comprehending the creative intellect of the author; the meaning of a text is determined by the individuated author's design for the text and understanding the text is through the union of author and reader. And the aesthetic or affective fallacy confuses a text's meaning with the effects of a text (confusing what a text is with what a text does); the meaning of a text, for example, is (solely) the reader's response. Thus, approaches that not only evaluate but also regard what is significant about a text in terms of the perspicuity of contextual or nontextual inquiry (such as psychology, biography and personality) are characteristically extrinsic in orientation.

Intrinsic criticism is built on the premise of restraining interest to the relationship of meaning and the text, but not so as to restrict the potential of a text to influence our understanding of that text or other texts. This interest is closely allied with the tendency to stress a *synchronic* study of texts (while admitting that texts do have authors, histories, settings, and effects, the meaning of a text is still proper to the text itself, understood by means of the text). *Extrinsic* criticism regards perspicuity as a matter of the context illuminating the text or translating the ideas of the text to make them clear to contemporary readers; intrinsic criticism employs the descriptive figure of text as both reticent *and* sociable but ultimately determinative of its own meaning and averse to paraphrase or translation.[27] In one sense, the difference between intrinsic and extrinsic critical approaches is a matter of bearing and orientation, the former moving from the text to the world, the latter moving from the world to the text.

If advocates of intrinsic models of criticism have rejected an exclusive dependence upon history and the limitations of relying upon extrinsic interests in order to understand specific texts, they are merely saying that one cannot live by bread alone, not that one can live without bread. Scripture gives us history without footnotes, without introduction, without preface (omissions that contemporary biblical critics have taken as their vocation to correct). We offer no theories about what history must supply to text, what is determinative of a text's meaning other than the text, but neither does it preclude historical situat-

---

[27]We may add an additional fallacy, the "heresy of paraphrase," on the advice of Cleanth Brooks. A text's meaning and significance is not to be found in the shared values, ideas or politics of a text and its readers, the meaning of a text cannot be reduced by paraphrase or translation; instead the meaning of a text belongs to its structure. As Brooks argued, one cannot simply discover what the true content is within the form, as one would open an envelope to discover its content. Brooks argues against paraphrase in connection with the criticism of poems; it is not that one could not paraphrase in general terms what a poem is about but that the tensions and irony of a poem's structure resist extracting any single statement of a poem by referring it to something outside the poem itself. See Cleanth Brooks, *The Well Wrought Urn* (New York: Reynal & Hitchcock, 1947), pp. 176-96.

edness (although it obviously denies historicism).[28] Properly speaking, the proponents of reading texts remind us that we cannot have what the text is about without having the text itself. We cannot lose sight of the plot of the text; we must not concentrate exclusively upon the author's study on the one hand, nor exclusively on the protagonist's character on the other hand. One must corroborate text and context—compare, contrast, but not correct text by context. One must not loose sight of the goal—which is to understand the text.

Intrinsic Clarity Illustrated

A perennial problem for biblical critics is the relationship, both thematic and literary, between "Scripture" and other, proximate themes and texts, especially when biblical texts appear to quote or rely upon "other" texts. Regarding the Gospel of John, what are we to make of the similarities between the Gospel of John and Gnostic, Hellenistic or Neo-Platonic "themes"? Will the meaning of the text only be found if we seek to discover the "author" of this anonymous text (wherein authorial intent is the only guarantor of a text's meaning)? The once-popular suggestion that the prologue was influenced by Gnosticism was founded upon the significance of the prologue for Gnostic readers; their response became the prologue's historical background (illustrative of the influence of the affective fallacy).[29] There is also the matter of similarities between the Gospel and Platonic themes, although the Gospel seems to outstrip Platonism.[30] Attention has now turned to the influence of Hellenized Judaism, especially the significance of Philo of Alexandria, for understanding the Gospel of John.[31] It seems that the Gospel "shared" Philo's vocabulary and subject matter concerning "logos," "beginning" and the source of creation (God) and the instrumentality of creation (the logos). So how does one evaluate the relationship of historically proximate sources and the Gospel of John (a question raised by genetic interests)?

The effort to emphasize Scripture as text presumes to reject the theory, in principle, that all instances of similarity necessarily denote a deterministic form of dependence. This formal premise seeks to open up the text under scrutiny

---

[28]As T. S. Eliot reminds us, "The Bible has had a literary influence . . . not because it has been considered literature, but because it has been considered the report of the Word of God" ("Religion and Literature," in *Selected Prose*, ed. John Hayward (Harmondsworth, U.K.: Penguin, 1953), p. 33.

[29]Elaine H. Pagels, *The Johannine Gospel in Gnostic Exegesis: Heracleon's Commentary on John* (Nashville: Abingdon, 1973).

[30]David Lyle Jeffrey, *People of the Book: Christian Identity and Literary Culture* (Grand Rapids, Mich.: Eerdmans, 1996), p. 56.

[31]Craig A. Evans, *Word and Glory: On the Exegetical and Theological Background of John's Prologue* (Sheffield: Sheffield Academic, 1994).

to a differing manner of reading by eschewing strictly historical determinatives. Frank Kermode offers, "For example, Chrysostom, sixteen centuries ago, remarked at the outset of his commentary on John that when we read this Gospel, we are not after all conversing with a particular person, so there is no point in asking where he lived or what sort of education he had. Chrysostom gives his attention to other matters; not for him those arduous modern inquiries into sources Jewish and Greek and into the beliefs and needs of some hypothetical community."[32] This opens up the real possibility that the Gospel of John did not necessarily "borrow" themes or sources in a naive sense, as if the religion of such sources was "on loan" to them, as if the Gospel would be best or primarily understood in light of their sources. But neither does the Gospel arrive at its similarities with other themes and texts by means of divine revelation or even ecstatically (as some have asserted in an effort to protect the uniqueness of biblical texts). Quite possibly, the relationship between the texts in question would be best described as follows: authors of Scripture appropriated, exploited and tyrannized their various "sources" in order to realize their purpose(s).[33]

Following Bakhtin, Stephen Prickett suggests that the Bible both translates and is itself a translated text; this is also both a historicized and historical argument. The examples are significant: Scripture utilizes languages, contexts and texts in its very construct (Mesopotamian, Egyptian, Canaanite); it is subject to translation in its communication and use (the Septuagint and the explanation of the law in Targums or Aramaic paraphrases); though the speech of Jesus was probably Aramaic, the Gospels present us with a Greek "translation" (in

[32]Kermode adds regarding his primary interest in matters intrinsic instead of extrinsic: "There is a case to be made for the label 'postcritical.' In deciding not to be hindered by this immensely powerful tradition of largely disintegrative commentary, one hopes, without forgetting its importance, to regain some of the advantages of the precritical commentators who knew nothing about the Higher Criticism" (Frank Kermode, "John," in *The Literary Guide to the Bible,* ed. Robert Alter and Frank Kermode (Cambridge, Mass.: Harvard University Press, 1987), p. 441.

[33]Although some might object to the seditious and deceptive character of words such as appropriate, exploit and tyranny, it seems necessary to refer to biblical texts' use of other texts in such terms, primarily because, as this chapter contends, biblical texts are not best represented as an instance of a general category of religious literature but function as a particular domain in which "meaning" is sought *in* rather than simply *with*, *near* or *around* the text under consideration. Secondarily, and anecdotally, it appears that biblical texts are explicitly exploitive, celebrating the tyranny of their message in relationship to competing messages and celebrating their creativity (and not merely borrowing and concealing research sources hoping not to get caught by a historically informed scribe). As Frank Kermode noted, "The notion that nobody ever thought anything that had not been thought before is curiously strong in biblical studies; it is an illegitimate inference from a much more defensible position, that there are linguistic and cultural constraints on what can be intended" (ibid., p. 444).

the popular form of the language of classical culture); the early Christian attitude toward the literary dimensions of the text were governed by the text received or delivered rather than an interest in its origins (the transmission and understanding of the "new testament" was immediately subject to translation in the Christian mission).[34] The Bible, as a collection of varying texts in tension with external texts and a collected text with internal tensions, as well as a text still subject to the tensions of clear texts interpreting unclear texts, serves as an adequate invitation to doubt simplistic ideas of reading. And reading Scripture is not a naive or objectivist exercise; instead it is concerned with discerning Scripture's own custom.[35]

When the Gospel of John employs the trope of descending and ascending to depict Jesus Christ, the text not only displays a thorough awareness of similar Hellenistic patters, but it also sought to dismantle their ability to depict divine identity: "No one has ascended into heaven except the one who descended from heaven, the Son of Man" (Jn 3:13 NRSV).[36] This assertion serves

---

[34]Stephen Prickett, *Words and the Word: Language, Poetics and Biblical Interpretation* (Cambridge: Cambridge University Press, 1986), pp. 213-14. Prickett concludes his summary of the nature of the Bible as a translation with the assertion that "the Bible not only illustrates Bakhtin's thesis, but actually provides one of the supreme examples of the way in which discourse arises and takes its meanings from the intersecting of contextual and linguistic boundaries."

[35]Compare this with Wesley Kort's arguments regarding Scripture's intertextuality and polyphonic voice: "Biblical texts reveal the phenomenon of intertextuality. This is the case not only between biblical texts and other ancient Near Eastern and otherwise non-canonical material but also between biblical texts themselves. Furthermore, biblical literature is polyphonic in its juxtaposition of literary strands within it, in its refusal to conceal or to repress varying accounts: the two Creation stories, the two versions of the rise of the monarchy or the introduction of David to the court of Saul, and dissonance among the Gospels in the New Testament, for example. In addition, biblical texts are polyphonic in their literary forms. Indeed, there seems to be a certain formal inventiveness represented, a kind of formal explosion and diversification: proverb and narrative, lyric and law, parable and apocalypse, legend, saga, riddle, autobiography, oracle. There seems to be an insufficient generic vocabulary to cover all of the types. Finally, the historical, cultural diversity is significant. Babylonian, Egyptian, and Canaanite influences are felt, as well as the consequences of Persian, Hellenistic, and Roman cultures" (Wesley A. Kort, *Story, Text, and Scripture: Literary Interests in Biblical Narrative* [University Park: Pennsylvania State University Press, 1988], pp. 131-32).

[36]For emphasis, note the numerous explicit references to descending-ascending: John 1:9, 18, 51; 3:12-14, 16-17, 19, 31; 5:18-24, 30, 36-38, 43-44; 6:29, 32-33, 38, 41-42, 50-51, 58, 62; 7:27-29, 33-36; 8:14-15, 18-19, 21, 23, 26-29, 38, 40-42; 9:4-5, 39; 10:17-18, 32-38; 11:23-27; 12:23-26, 27-28, 30-36, 44-50; 13:1, 3, 20; 14:9-11; 15:15, 21-24; 16:5, 27-28, 30; 17:1-5, 7-8, 11-14, 16, 18, 21, 23-24, 25-26; 20:17 (and implicit references double the number). The contention is that although ascending-descending is a theme within the Gospel's religious setting, the Gospel rejects the pattern of human ascending to acquire divine knowledge in order to descend to make it known. Thus, no one ascends/descends to become aware of divine knowledge; and only Jesus descends and ascends revealing God's identity ("the one who comes from above is above all" [Jn 3:31]; and not even the angels descend in order to ascend but are said to ascend and descend on the Son of Man [Jn 1:51]).

as a significant theme in the Gospel, and it certainly plays upon (or exploits) the currency of ascending-descending models, but its "meaning" and the development of the theme are rendered within the Gospel itself. The Gospel of John rejects any possibility of human or angelic descending-ascending (note how the sequence is important to the argument), positing a strict prohibition of this patter: "No one has ever seen God. It is God the only Son, who is close to the Father's heart, who has made him known" (Jn 1:18 NRSV). In addition, structural observations of the Gospel confirm this prohibition, especially in the unconventional theological assertions made by means of the conventional use of being and becoming in the Gospel's prologue. The philosophical troubles of being and becoming are not necessarily "John's" problems even though the Gospel adopts the irreducible tension in order to celebrate the uniqueness of the Word. For the Gospel of John, as Frank Kermode observes:

> That which *was* crossed over into *becoming*. . . . It stands for the condition of the eternal at the threshold of that which is not eternal but *becomes*—the eternal on the point of an unheard-of participation in that which cannot be eternal because it is created, because it has or will become. It is in contrast with this becoming on the other side of the threshold that the uniqueness of this *was* is affirmed.[37]

This type of "bridge" is employed in the Gospel not to indicate the universal features of religious consciousness the Gospel is tapping into but is best understood as a thorough rejection of the conventional relationship of the antithetical categories of religious-philosophical depictions of light and dark, being and becoming, ascending and descending, life and death, physical and spiritual (or earth and heaven), and time and eternity, just for starters.[38] The Gospel of John

---

[37]Kermode, "John," p. 445. Kermode continues: "The whole narrative, its past and its future, must fall under the rule of the great antithesis of being and becoming, be governed by the presence of the *was* in the *become*, the light in the darkness" (p. 447).

[38]An additional and more familiar example is from the book of Acts. When Paul, in his address at the Areopagus in Acts 17, quotes Greek poets, he does so not to reinforce their common religious awareness but to exploit their vulnerability (their religiosity *and* ignorance), and he does so by exploiting their poets. He reinforces their ignorance of God and introduces the "God who made the world and everything in it is the Lord of heaven and earth and does not live in temples made by hands" (Acts 17:24). Paul's religion was "the gospel of Jesus and the resurrection" (Acts 17:18, 31). Far from being simply a borrower of the poetry of Aratus and Epimenides, or referring the listener to Zeus or stoicism to understand the meaning of his message, we are struck with the tyranny of Paul's assertions that the true God is revealed in the resurrection and understood by means of repentance (Acts 17:30-31). The same could be said of Paul's denunciation of "the wisdom of words," "philosophy" and human taught messages (1 Cor 1—2; Col; Gal, respectively) in which Paul adopts the rhetorical forms of his antagonists in order to argue that he does not depend upon their rhetorical forms to present and defend the gospel!

did not just borrow the literary forms; it transformed in the union of form and content significant historical and religious texts and themes. This historical argument does not minimize, dismiss or contradict the historicity of the Gospel text; it is because the Gospel of John is so close to speaking in prevailing idiom that the uniqueness of the Gospel is evident. In this manner authors of Scripture were not simply dependent upon their culture(s), religious contexts and educational benefices; they were genuinely *authors* of *texts*, the meaning of which is intrinsic to an actual reading of those texts.

This comment on the Gospel of John is to demonstrate that there is more to the practice of intrinsic criticism than its associations with the older form of the so-called New Criticism.[39] Practitioners of intrinsic criticism do share an affinity for textuality as a matter of emphasis and significance but not necessarily an absolute textuality.[40] Intrinsic critical interests represent a long-standing and widely practiced effort to give some sense of priority to interpretation as a "set of technical and ad hoc rules for reading," and this is most often set in contrast to the contemporary tendency to seek a critical, "unitary and systematic theory

---

[39]The textual orientation being discussed in chapters six and seven is reminiscent of the Anglo-American (so-called) New Criticism associated with the likes of Cleanth Brooks, William K. Wimsatt Jr., René Wellek and John Crowe Ransom, among others. For a balanced and realistic evaluation of New Criticism see Mark Royden Winchell, *Cleanth Brooks and the Rise of Modern Criticism* (Charlottesville: University of Virginia Press, 1996). With the qualifications of the caricature of New Criticism offered by Winchell (and those acknowledgments concerning Brooks mentioned in this chapter) the textual orientation offered herein merely serves to illustrate how perspicuity can be understood within the contemporary climate of literary criticism. What is illustrated in this discussion might be termed "contextualized" New Criticism. See Richard E. Palmer, *Hermeneutics* (Evanston, Ill.: Northwestern University Press, 1969), pp. 70, 174-75, 221-26.

[40]The antecedents of contemporary intrinsic criticism are legion, including, but not limited to: Anglo-American New Criticism, biblical realism in nineteenth-century Germany especially through the influence of Karl Barth, Pietistic admonitions about Bible reading, and certain sixteenth-century Reformers and Anabaptists. The contemporary legacy of New Criticism (the most popular form of intrinsic criticism in the middle of the twentieth century) extends to the regions of structuralism, poststructuralism and deconstruction. See Paul de Man, *Blindness and Insight: Essays in the Rhetoric of Contemporary Criticism,* 2nd ed. (Minneapolis: University of Minnesota Press, 1983); Paul A. Bové, "Variations on Authority: Some Deconstructive Transformations of the New Criticism," in *The Yale Critics: Deconstruction in America,* ed. Jonathan Arac (Minneapolis: University of Minnesota Press, 1983), reprinted in *The New Criticism and Contemporary Literary Theory: Connections and Continuities,* ed. William J. Spurlin and Michael Fischer (New York: Garland, 1995), pp. 161-82; William E. Cain, *The Crisis in Criticism: Theory, Literature, and Reform in English Studies* (Baltimore, Md.: Johns Hopkins University Press, 1984); Robert Detweiler, "After the New Criticism: Contemporary Methods of Literary Interpretation," in *Orientation by Disorientation: Studies in Literary Criticism and Biblical Literary Criticism,* ed. Richard A. Spencer (Pittsburgh: Pickwick, 1980), pp. 3-23; and Robert Detweiler and Vernon Robbins, "The Eclipse of Realism: Twentieth Century Hermeneutics," in *Reading the Text: Biblical Criticism and Literary Theory,* ed. Stephen Prickett (Oxford: Basil Blackwell, 1991) pp. 225-80.

of understanding," wherein texts are understood according to their meaning and meaning is a partner of understanding, indeed a partner to enlightenment itself wherein the means of enlightening is inherent in the goal of understanding.[41] In the contemporary setting, clarity and obscurity have been at the heart of critical interest in the nature of interpretation, with the emphasis that forces interpreters to understand clarity and obscurity as matters of language itself, texts in general, and understanding and meaning as hidden or revealed by matters extrinsic to what is written (sacred or otherwise). One may observe that the shift has been toward universal models with prejudice shown toward regional, textually specific and heuristic understanding of interpretation (the type of interest represented in our discussion of the Gospel of John above).

What intrinsic interests represent is akin to the effort within Christian theology to unite the characterization of the text as Scripture with its best manner of being understood. This is the advice of Zwingli: "the Word of God brought with it its own enlightenment."[42] Thus, retreating to, or better, reaffirming the association of Scripture's clarity with attention to the text itself carries with it the burden of treating the text as Scripture. Preference for the working premise that we regard the text as Scripture is significantly linked with the assertion of Scripture's clarity within the Christian tradition. Instead of coming to mean a general hermeneutical theory of how all literature should be understood or an assertion independent of the Christian concern for Scripture as text, perspicuity is intimately bound to the constructive and realistic orientation to how Scripture should be treated. Clarity orients the concern for Scripture as text between the two extremes of textual aestheticism (the a-critical treatment of Scripture as a "linguistic sacrament" or the sentimental theory that Scripture is like a poem: it should "not mean but be")[43] and textual indeterminacy (the hypercritical association of meaning or its lack to the sovereignty of the reader or the dismissal of the mutuality of textuality and reader). As a descriptive assertion it functions as a regard for Scripture as text wherein the success or failure of that undertaking can only be measured within the practice of a Christian reading of

[41]Hans W. Frei, *Theology and Narrative: Selected Essays*, ed. George Hunsinger and William C. Placher (New York: Oxford University Press, 1993), p. 124.

[42]Ulrich Zwingli, "The Clarity and Certainty of the Word of God," in *Zwingli and Bullinger*, ed. and trans. G. W. Bromiley (Philadelphia: Westminster Press, 1953), p. 76. Zwingli argued: "When Noah was commanded to build the ark he believed God, that he would indeed destroy the whole earth with the flood. That he did so was not due to any human enlightenment, otherwise the many who paid no heed but built houses and married and lived according to their own desires would easily have sowed doubt in his mind, saying Ah, but that which was told you is simply a delusion presented to your mind no doubt by an apparition. It may be seen, then, that the Word of God brought with it its own enlightenment, by which Noah knew that it was from God and not from any other (Gen 6)."

[43]Frei, *Theology and Narrative*, pp. 140-41.

Scripture, precisely because a Christian reading presumes the informing of Scripture, and it is ruled by the premise that without knowing precisely how this is the case the affirmation of Scripture's clarity is the means employed to account for this circumstance.

There are affinities between these suggestions regarding the reading of Scripture as text and various critical approaches to understanding literature (formalist, intrinsic, structuralists, etc.), and readings from various critical approaches may appear to be supportive of a Christian reading of Scripture, but such affinities are casual rather than evidence of a general theory of how texts are best understood to be clear or obscure.[44] There are few limitations or rules involved in a Christian reading of Scripture as text (and such matters are primarily theological); one such rule being that we have sufficient confidence to proceed on the basis of Scripture: to act and interact, respond obediently or disobediently, believe or distrust accordingly. That is, the relationship of the Christian community and Scripture is described in terms of *sufficient* clarity, and this is our working assumption within the Christian community. Interestingly, if not surprisingly, a persistent motif in the vast and unmanageable contemporary hermeneutical landscape is the matter of textual clarity and obscurity, with the working assumption that texts are obscure until enlightened because texts obscure (inherently) what is most important, or that the obscure in a text is best clarified by a critical means extrinsic to a text, that texts are distant until rendered contemporary by the clarity of proximity, or obtuse until decoded.

Theological Textuality

In the contemporary climate of textual sensitivity, literary-critical interests and theological particularity, a commitment to Scripture's clarity invites a critically aware defense of how this confession of faith functions as a condition of Christian identity; precisely because the assertion of Scripture's clarity appears to be countercritical or a censure of criticism.[45] The justification offered is oriented

---

[44]The argument being offered is addressed by Frei: "It is at least possible that in regard to realistic narrative literature, the function of general hermeneutics should be formal rather than material; it should be confined to identifying a piece of literature as belonging to that particular genre rather than some other, rather than claiming to interpret its meaning or subject matter. . . . As for the latter task, there may be no single interpretive device to satisfy it (nor is there necessarily any need for such a weighty interpretive device!), due to the nature of this type of literature. And it does not matter whether it is found in the Bible or elsewhere. In a sense, every narrative of the sort in which story and meaning are closely related may have its own special hermeneutics" (Hans W. Frei, *The Eclipse of Biblical Narrative: A Study in Eighteenth and Nineteenth Century Hermeneutics* [New Haven, Conn.: Yale University Press, 1974], p. 273).

[45]See David Tracy, "Literary Theory and Return of the Forms for Naming and Thinking God in Theology," *Journal of Religion* 74 (July 1994): 302-16.

toward a theological assessment of Scripture's textuality; and it is built upon three observations proposed by the work of Hans Frei regarding Scripture's literal or plain sense and ostensive reference.

First, the contention over textual clarity or obscurity is not uniquely Christian, although the Christian confession of Scripture's clarity is materially different from interest in clarity and obscurity which preoccupies current literary and biblical criticism. While postcritical literary theorists and Christian theologians tend to view Scripture as imminent and familiar, critical literary and historical-biblical practitioners regard the text as distant and cryptic "so that, for example, 'present' is the antonym of 'past' rather than either the synonym of 'near' or the antonym of 'far.'"[46] Finding a place for clarity in the contemporary setting focuses upon the transparency of relationships occasioned by a certain regard for the text (postcritical and theological models tend to stress accessibility, which is textually oriented or justified, and for critical models there is an orientation to the translucent quality of communion of the author's and reader's minds, shared notion of reality or being in the world, or to the other extreme an objectified realization of possible intent historically and distantly construed).

Second, the contemporary quandary concerning a relationship of theology and literary criticism provides an indication of the minimal components of a commitment to Scripture as text. Our "informal rules under which [Scripture] has customarily been read in the community, in the midst of much disagreement about its contents, [have] been fairly flexible and usually not too constrictive."[47] Frei names three such commitments: a "Christian reading of Scripture must not deny the literal ascription to Jesus" of New Testament literature; "no Christian reading may deny either the unity of Old and New Testaments or the congruence . . . of that unity with the ascriptive literalism of the Gospel narratives"; and "any reading not in principle in contradiction with these two rules is/are permissible," for example, a low-powered employment of historical-critical and literary readings that would integrally link textual and theological concerns.[48]

---

[46]Frei, *Theology and Narrative,* p. 131. Frei directed these characterizations specifically at those who propose synchronic links to address the contemporary disclosure between text and reader, but employ diachronic language in order to justify overcoming the distance between text and reader and thus orient their hermeneutical agenda. In other words, in order to overcome *distance* and *distanciation* (diachronic characterizations) and the widely recognized problem that there is no proper understanding of texts from the past, the *present* coincidence or "fusion of horizons" (H. G. Gadamer) by which we make our own or appropriate the distant or the foreign.

[47]Ibid., p. 144.

[48]Ibid., pp. 144-45. Frei's paragraph reads, "The *minimal* agreement about reading the Scriptures (as distinct from their status or scope) has been as follows: First, Christian reading of Christian Scriptures must not deny the literal ascription to Jesus, and not to any other

Third, we observe that regard for what is plain and established is not a simplistic commitment to textuality or formalism but warranted by the community's "rules for reading its sacred text."[49] There is no simple choice between text and community, especially concerning what we mean by Scripture's clarity. As Frei suggests, the assertion of Scripture's clarity is not invoked to further "an obscurantist anticritical reading of the text" but a manner of reading in context that is self-critically situated in "the customary use to which a text has been put in the context of the community's belief and life."[50]

Frei's own development of these themes is depicted in his work on christology and the Gospels.[51] Probably the most significant preoccupation of contemporary biblical scholarship has been the quest for the historical (Jesus of history) in contrast to or comparable with the theological (Christ of faith). Frei's response was to maintain that the Gospels "present Jesus' identity as that of a singular, unsubstitutable person," but that the manner of this presentation was in a novel- or history-like character. The result: "We cannot, for instance, inquire into the 'actual' life and character of Jesus inferred from the records," and "With regard to the Gospels, we are actually in a fortunate position that so much of what we know about Jesus . . . is more nearly fictional than historical in narration."[52] According to Frei the perspicuous nature of the narrative character of the Gospels (textually) joined with the interpretive finality associated with the Gospels in the Christian interpretative tradition forms an insoluble union. That is, the Gospels are regarded as clear inasmuch as Jesus' identity is only available to us through the description of his actions, specifically through

---

person, event, time or idea, of those occurrences, teachings, personal qualities and religious attributes associated with him in the stories in which he plays a part, as well as in the other New Testament writings in which his name is invoked. This ascription has usually also included the indirect referral to him of that 'Kingdom of god,' the parabolic proclamation of which is attributed to him in the texts, and of which he himself was taken to be (in the phrase of Austin Farrer's) the 'self-enacted parable' both in word and deed. Second, no Christian reading may deny either the unity of Old and New Testaments or the congruence (which is not by any means the same as literal identity) of that unity with the ascriptive literalism of the Gospel narratives. Third, any readings not in principle in contradiction with these two rules are permissible, and two of the obvious candidates would be the various sorts of historical-critical and literary readings."

[49]Ibid., p. 144.

[50]Ibid., p. 108.

[51]Hans W. Frei, *The Identity of Jesus Christ: The Hermeneutical Bases of Dogmatic Theology* (Philadelphia: Fortress, 1975). Frei originally published this material as a series of articles, "The Mystery of the Presence of Jesus Christ," *Crossroads* 17, nos. 1-2 (1967): 69-96. Also note Frei's "Theological Reflections on the Accounts of Jesus' Death and Resurrection," *Christian Scholar's Review* 49, no. 4 (1966): 263-306.

[52]Frei, *Identity of Jesus Christ*, pp. 87, 144.

the display of his obedience in reference to God the Father, and not "by grasping certain of his inherent personal characteristics"—not by seeking the actual man apart from the story as a storied figure.

In response to the search to clarify the actual identity of Jesus, routinely thought to be distorted or aggrandized as the Christ of faith according to biblical scholarship, Frei offers, "But do we actually know that much about Jesus? Certainly not, if we are asking about the 'actual' man apart from the story."[53]

> We cannot have what they are about (the "subject matter") without the stories themselves. They are history-like precisely because like history-writing and the traditional novel and unlike myths and allegories they literally mean what they say. There is no gap between the representation and what is represented by it.[54]

This inextricable connection between the narrative and the narrated character leads Frei to affirm that the Gospels' ostensive reference is to the text rendered identity of Jesus Christ (meaning and reference are not conjoined in matters extrinsic to the text). He believed this link between the Gospels and christology helped to explain why the various "quests" after a historical Jesus (he mentioned James M. Robinson as an example) and the hermeneutical projects of demythologization (from the likes of Bultmann) are ultimately frustrating, distort the uniqueness of Jesus Christ and function to subvert Scripture's sufficiency by "adding a kind of depth dimension to the story's surface, which is actually a speculative *inference* from what is given in the story, rather than a part of it."[55] Quests after the actual (historical) Jesus posit an illegitimate dichotomy of history and text resulting in the critical assumption that the text does not necessarily render the identity of Jesus Christ but characteristically obscures that identity.

The categories employed by Frei as his reading of the Gospels unfolds—confidence in their ostensive reference and perspicuity, history-like observations of the texts, unitive regard for Jesus' identity and actions—are not interpretively previous to actual observations of the texts.[56] Frei maintained that "the theoretical devices we use to make our readings more alert, appropriate, and intelligent ought to be designed to leave the story as unencumbered as

[53]Ibid., pp. 102-3, 106.

[54]Ibid., p. xiv.

[55]Ibid., p. 90.

[56]Regarding Frei's methodological program, Jeffrey Stout argued that "the theological metalanguage he has worked out is intended to display how the stories work, thus aiding in their understanding, without in any way presuming to take their place" ("Hans Frei and Anselmian Theology," unpublished paper, p. 10).

possible."[57] In the case of the Gospels—because of their character as realistic narratives and the historical attestation of their literal reading—it is necessary to pursue a "case-specific reading" without regard for the broader hermeneutical issues of a universally applicable literary theory that would, in effect, make Scripture a member of a larger and more dominant literary class.[58]

Frei's insistence upon the Gospels' ostensive reference is closely allied with the Christian regard for the text as Scripture. His point: to say what we do about Jesus Christ is inextricably united with Christian regard for the Gospels. And in turn, this regard for the Gospels is a condition of Christian identity. To read the text in this manner, rather than another, is to regard Scripture as text *theologically*. Thus, "the story as story . . . should be taken in its own right and . . . if it is read for its own sake, it suggests that Jesus' identity is self-focused and unsubstitutably his own."[59] And Frei regards the customary use to which Scripture has been put within the Christian community—its binding normativity—as attestation of the sufficiency and clarity of Scripture. Frei offers: "The truth to which we refer we cannot state apart from the biblical language which we employ to do so. And belief in the divine authority of Scripture is for me simply that we do not need more. The narrative description there is adequate."[60] The sufficiency of the biblical language to depict the unique identity of Jesus Christ entails the (negative) restraint on supplanting Scripture's authority—its "privileged status [as a] source of intelligibility and truth"—by appeals to another conceptual system, be it predominantly philosophical or linguistic or theological.[61] "The identity of the Christian savior is revealed completely by the story of Jesus in the Gospels and by none other."[62] As a restatement of a Protestant confession of *sola Scriptura*, Frei's invocation of the notions of clar-

---

[57]Frei, *Identity of Jesus Christ*, p. xv. Frei added that the appropriate method of interpretation is simply "to observe the story itself—its structure, the shape of its movement, and its crucial transitions" (p. 87). As Mark Ellingsen suggested, Frei's presuppositions regarding the interpreter's role "aim to be 'formal,' not 'material' presuppositions. That is, they purport not to affect the content of the biblical text" (*The Evangelical Movement: Growth, Impact, Controversy, Dialog* [Minneapolis: Fortress, 1988], p. 371).

[58]Hans W. Frei, "The 'Literal Reading' of Biblical Narrative in the Christian Tradition: Does It Stretch or Will It Break?" in *The Bible and the Narrative Tradition*, ed., Frank McConnell (Oxford: Oxford University Press, 1986), pp. 66-67. In addition, Frei's intent in pursuing the description of christology in this manner was to display that "no matter whether one is a believing Christian or not, one can make sense of the Gospel story in its own right, and that making sense of it that way entails important consequences for a theology based on this narrative" (Frei, *Identity of Jesus Christ*, p. xvii).

[59]Frei, *Identity of Jesus Christ*, pp. 102-3.

[60]Hans W. Frei, "Response to 'Narrative Theology: An Evangelical Appraisal,'" *Trinity Journal* 8, no. 1 (1987): 23.

[61]Stout, "Hans Frei and Anselmian Theology," p. 6.

[62]Frei, *Identity of Jesus Christ*, p. 88.

ity and sufficiency served to ground christological claims by restricting adventures beyond or behind the narration.[63] But this leaves us with the implication that contemporary concerns with extrinsic or universal models of interpretation have actually concealed a coherent understanding of Scripture's theological textuality. In essence, matters extrinsic to the text have come to eclipse the Christian conventions associated with theological textuality, obscuring both the means of discerning Scripture's ostensive reference and a substantive understanding of Scripture as text.

Textuality and Scripture as Text

It seems absurd to argue that contemporary Protestantism lacks a substantial doctrine of Scripture (have we done anything but argue about the nature of Scripture and its interpretation?), but this is precisely the case made by several significant observers. Wesley Kort argues that we have failed to appreciate the textuality of Scripture, thus an insubstantial doctrine of Scripture does not arise from our lack of attention to Scripture but a misdirected appreciation of Scripture. Kort contends that the functional status of Scripture in present culture tends to demean an appropriate understanding of Scripture as text:

> In our culture, the Bible, like any text, will readily be assigned a functional role because of how we tend to view textuality. Texts, we tend to think, have a derivative status granted by the functions they perform. Texts are considered helpful but dispensable, and they derive their importance from something else: the ideas or the events that can be extracted or reconstructed from them.[64]

Kort directs our attention to David Kelsey's influential work, *The Uses of Scripture in Recent Theology*. Kelsey argues that theologians as diverse as Karl Barth, Paul Tillich, Rudolf Bultmann and B. B. Warfield share a tendency that actually discounts Scripture, in differing degrees. The theological function of Scripture is most significant for these theologians—what makes Scripture of

---

[63]Frei comments, "The nature of the narrative therefore imposes a limit on theological comment. It is not likely that we shall be able to get beyond the descriptive accounts presented to us in the Gospels concerning the resurrection and the relation of God's and Jesus' actions. And if we do go beyond them in explanatory endeavors, we are clearly on our own and in speculative territory, just as we have suggested that we are in speculative realms when we look beyond the narrative for the writers' and Jesus' own inner intentions. In that instance, our speculation would be historical; in the present, metaphysical. But it is never easy and usually not desirable to transform a literary description, such as a narrative sequence, into an *explanatory* scheme using abstract concepts and categories. What is perfectly fitting in a narrative may be banal or absurd in an explanatory scheme drawn from our general experience of occurrences in the world" (*Identity of Jesus Christ,* p. 125).

[64]Kort, *Story, Text, and Scripture,* p. 138.

interest is that it is a means to something more important. The text itself can and often does obscure what is truly important: divine intervention for Barth, religious symbols for Tillich, instances of authentic existence for Bultmann or doctrine for Warfield. What is important among these theologians is not found in attention to Scripture itself, but is "determined by decisions that are literally pre-text, i.e. logically prior to any attention to any particular text taken as authority for any theological proposal."[65] The degree to which Scripture is regarded as clear or obscure differs greatly, especially between Barth and Bultmann, but this difference is governed by the degree to which one is alert to the clarity or obscurity of Scripture as text. This is not surprising, and it does not deter our interest in whether the interaction of text and reader can in some way be characterized as Christian and perspicuous. It does aid our understanding of the focus on hermeneutics as an attempt to struggle over the nature of Scripture as clear or obscure, but it leaves to be addressed the nature of such matters.

In this light Kort points us to Hans Frei's argument about the *eclipse* of biblical narrative. Current attention has turned away from the possibility that the Bible represents a viable world toward the interpretive premise that the biblical story must be fit into the contemporary world and contemporary story.[66] The suspicion of hermeneutics is based in a fundamental rejection of the clarity of the Bible to represent reality. In the place of clarity we face the split of the text and its meaning. Frei argues, "To close the gap between the words of narrative and the 'real' meaning, one had to appeal to one or more of the following: historical occurrences; the mind of the author as distinct from his words; ideas independent of both, as well as of the words of the text. In all three cases, the meaning is the subject matter as distinct from the words."[67] In the shift away from what the text says to its reference, its source, its composition, indicates that the text itself is regarded as inherently obscure.

Kort's own argument concerning Scripture focuses on its textuality, by which he means more than Scripture is circumstantially or casually a text. A literary doctrine of Scripture in terms of its narrativity and textuality shares with reality in that we cannot encounter reality, according to Kort, "apart from the textuality of memory and expectation."[68] He plots the course of Scripture's tex-

---

[65]Kelsey, *Uses of Scripture in Recent Theology,* p. 170.

[66]Frei, *Eclipse of Biblical Narrative,* p. 130: "It is no exaggeration to say that all across the theological spectrum the great reversal had taken place; interpretation was a matter of fitting the biblical story into another world with another story rather than incorporating that world into the biblical story."

[67]Ibid., p. 268.

[68]Kort, *Story, Text, and Scripture,* p. 117.

tuality between the more prevalent and extreme categories of *writing* and *canon*. By *writing* Kort points to the disruptive, obscuring and evasive split between what is written and what is written about (it does not refer to the actual act of writing). The negative connotations associated with writing stem from the general prejudice that places a text within the larger field of writing, thus prohibiting a text from exerting authority in itself. Writing places us in the indeterminate existence between identity and difference. A given text, as an instance of writing, lacks sufficient clarity to direct us to an adequate goal; its intelligibility depends upon the larger field of similar and dissimilar texts.[69] By *canon*, Kort refers to the privileging of text(s) as central in the textual field; the debate centers on whether such actions are arbitrary and if attributing authority artificially shelters a text from its legitimate textual domain. In Jewish and Christian history the subject of canon is a mixture of textual, theological and social forces: "Canon-making is intentionally a limited and limiting act."[70] The positive effect is that there is an exertion of identity in the canon, the negative effect is that the text loses its identity among texts.

Instead of pluralizing Scripture by means of writing, and isolating Scripture by means of canon, Kort suggests a literary doctrine that seeks to "purpose" Scripture as textual "center." Pure and uninfluenced textuality is an illusion—we must privilege a text in order to function (speak out of) at any given moment. No text, not even Scripture, "has autonomy or complete originality."[71] Kort's effort is to understand how we must situate a notion of Scripture within the larger and presumably more intelligible field of narrativity and textuality. While attentive to the Christian effort to hold together the text of Scripture and what Scripture is about, this approach is at odds with a descriptive or circumstantial commitment to Scripture as text. For Kort narrativity and textuality are unavoidable, thus Scripture is unavoidably best understood in these terms. But the effort to understand Scripture in terms of *sola Scriptura* involves a commit-

---

[69]Kort properly links this orientation to writing to the work of Derrida and Barthes, and their influence in Mark Taylor's trying *Erring: A Postmodern A/theology* (Chicago: University of Chicago Press, 1984).

[70]Kort, *Story, Text, and Scripture,* p. 123. On the *forces* of canon-making, see James Barr, *Holy Scripture: Canon, Authority, Criticism* (Philadelphia: Fortress, 1983); Hans von Campenhausen, *The Formation of the Christian Bible* (Philadelphia: Fortress, 1972); Brevard Childs, *The New Testament as Canon* (Philadelphia: Fortress, 1985); and James A. Sanders, *Canon and Community* (Philadelphia: Fortress, 1984).

[71]Kort's entire statement reads, "We end, then, with the recognition that, while no text has autonomy or complete originality but shares with other texts a common field, one marked by differences and similarities, we cannot project ourselves on this field as though on some unmarked expanse, dislocated wanderers with no beginning place, no goals, and no guiding way. This is because we cannot divest ourselves completely of continuity, coherence, or identity as individuals, groups, or a culture" (Kort, *Story, Text, and Scripture,* p. 128).

ment to textuality because there is no other means (i.e., it is unavoidably by this means) to realize God's word to us that saves through the gospel of Jesus Christ.

The importance of Scripture's clarity again returns to the means whereby Scripture is regarded as clear—the affinity of *sola Scriptura* and *Scriptura sui interpres*. It is the relationship of Scripture and the conditioned reader that is addressed by the confession of *Scripture's* clarity. What Kort provides is an invaluable description of the contemporary bent to look exclusively behind or beyond Scripture itself (the form) for something truly significant (the meaning) in authorial intentions, original events or historical circumstances to discern clarity. Because we routinely separate texts from what texts are about, Kort observes:

> We posit a temporal lag between events and the texts that record them: Events occur, followed by the texts that analyze, describe, or interpret them. Furthermore, this temporal lag coincides with a loss, for events are compromised in accounts. Texts are no substitute for "being there." Interpretation of texts, then, becomes not only freeing the incarcerated thoughts that they contain but also reconstructing the events they record or entities they describe as those events and entities can be thought of as actually having happened or existed.[72]

Instead, our orientation must be textual in that what we confess to be Scripture is text, thus for "the Christian interpretative tradition truth is what is written, not something separable and translinguistic that is written 'about.' "[73] What we are encouraged to seek and what we seek from God is united (unavoidably) textually, and what we regard as clear is what is made known textually. That is, clarity is not a problem to be solved by being made aware of something other than what the text is about.

The Form and Substance of Scripture

A Christian interest in Scripture as text is to be distinguished from interest in literary history, biography or religion in general of which Christianity might be just one instance. Scripture, Christian theology reminds us, is the principle of knowing *(principium cognoscendi)* and the formal object of faith. In addition, understanding Scripture is not accomplished by regarding it as a means toward something else. The study of Scripture is, in a manner of speaking, an end in itself, but not by being simply an aesthetic desire. The suggestion offered here is that we regard reading Scripture as text as an effort to understand the text,

---

[72]Ibid., pp. 112, 119-33.
[73]Frei, *Theology and Narrative,* p. 108.

not reading with understanding as something supplied outside the act of reading, not reading for understanding as the quest to read to find out something else rather than what one read, not even reading instead of understanding as the acceptance of alternatives to meaning.

This means to correct the error of segregating the *forma* (form as to the words, teaching and subject of Scripture, which is also historical) and the *substantia* (the substance or essence of Scripture's doctrine). The form varies; the substance is constant; yet there is a unity in both form and substance, as well in the relationship of form and substance. So Calvin: "The covenant made with all the fathers is so far from differing from ours in substance and reality that it is altogether one and the same."[74] In Calvin's work these themes are employed to address the progress or historicity of revelation, the relationship of law to gospel, Old to New Testament, and Israel and the church. The eschatological unity of antitype and type, and of history and inscripturated narration, lead us away from segregating historical texts and the theological propose of such texts to Christian readers. "It assists our faith not a little, to compare the reality with the type, so that we may seek in the former what the latter contains."[75] The revelation of God in Christ is richer, fuller and *clearer*: the gospel of Christ differs from the Law "only in respect of *clearness* of manifestation."[76] What was "formerly concealed" is now made known in the gospel, the ancient fathers having "nothing more than little sparks of the true light, the full brightness of which daily shines around us."[77] The historicalness of Scripture is both fixed and affixing in that the latter must be understood in relationship with the former. Our understanding of what a text means (its affixing quality, the greater or clearer significance) is not dissimilar from how a text itself is fashioned.

Within Protestant biblical interpretation the unity of historical form and theological substance has been addressed by utilizing the categories of historical and normative authority. Historical authority is confirmed by and operates on the level of Scripture's formal sense, its historical and narrative features, which are unavoidable. Normative authority alludes to the capacity of the text to address what God offered us by means of the text. This nuance should lead us to affirm the unity of Scripture's authority: what is

---

[74]John Calvin, *Institutes of the Christian Religion,* ed. John T. McNeill (Philadelphia: Westminster Press, 1960), pp. 429-30.

[75]John Calvin, *The Epistles of Paul the Apostle to the Hebrews and the First and Second Epistles of St. Peter* (Grand Rapids, Mich.: Eerdmans, 1963), pp. 339-40.

[76]Calvin, *Institutes,* p. 427, emphasis mine.

[77]John Calvin, *The Gospel According to St John* (Grand Rapids, Mich.: Eerdmans, 1961), pp. 25-26.

normatively authoritative is only available by means of what is historically authoritative, but not all that is historically authoritative is normatively authoritative. What we have by means of Scripture as text is, arguably, a historical and organic whole (at least this appears to be the nature of the text itself as well as its Christian readers). Thus the relationship of historical and normative authority is not dualistic but one of gradation.[78] As Donald Bloesch offers:

> Scripture is not simply the Word of God or human words but the Word of God *in* human words. Instead of speaking of Scripture as having a divine ground and human form, it is theologically more appropriate to contend that Scripture has a human content as well as a human form; at the same time, it also has a divine content and a divinely inspired form. The human form and content serve the divine meaning.[79]

And we cannot have what the text is about (its point, its meaning) without the text itself (its historical form). Or, we may argue, the story is the meaning of the doctrine, not the other way around.[80]

A common weakness within recent Christianity is to regard Scripture as the husk in which the kernel of truth is found. Even a pious claim to have gleaned a principle or truth from the text—ideas that are freed from the circumstance of the text and somehow thereby better suited to address a host of present issues but no longer require the text in its actual form—transgress the nature of Scripture as text. Within a commitment to Scripture as authoritative and perspicuous, "truths" in Christian faith, moral or other, are not captured and released by interpretative discernment (wherein the value of Scripture is the truth of its message without regard for the form of that message). But the tradition of interpretation as discerning significance instead of discerning form has dominated the history of modern hermeneutics, at least since Schleiermacher.[81]

The rather routine assumption of a general hermeneutic effectively enables interpreters to dismiss the form and actual subject matter the Bible speaks of in favor of a union of author and reader. Schleiermacher argued:

> Neither its language nor its genre requires that there be a special hermeneutics for

---

[78]Berkouwer, *Holy Scripture,* pp. 191-92.

[79]Donald G. Bloesch, *Holy Scripture* (Downers Grove, Ill.: InterVarsity Press, 1994), p. 88.

[80]This theme is taken from the work of Hans Frei, as noted by William Placher in Frei, *Theology and Narrative,* p. 17.

[81]Schleiermacher sought a "general" hermeneutics on the premise that the process of human understanding is universal: "We could manage quite well with the general alone" (Friedrich Schleiermacher, *Hermeneutics: The Handwritten Manuscripts,* AAR Texts and Translations 1 [Missoula, Mont.: Scholars Press, 1977], pp. 215-16).

> the Bible, nor does its double layers of meaning. Does the fact that it is inspired justify a special hermeneutics? Inspiration, as an infusion into the mind, should not influence the work of interpretation. If in the case of the Bible, as in every other case, the goal of hermeneutics is to understand the texts as their original hearers understood them, the fact that they are inspired does not affect the interpretation at all.[82]

Instead of guaranteeing a Christian interpretation of the Bible, Schleiermacher's general hermeneutic authorizes a dismissal of a claim to the actual form itself. Gadamer summarizes the effect of Schleiermacher's thrust: "Undoubtedly it is an important step in the development of historical consciousness that understanding and interpretation—of both the Bible and the literature of classical antiquity—was not completely detached from all dogmatic interest. Neither the saving truth of Scripture nor the exemplariness of the classics was to influence a procedure that was able to grasp every text as an expression of life and ignore the truth of what was said."[83]

The split between form and content is a beguiling, seductive temptation. It is presumed in modern hermeneutics, in its more modest form of historical positivism as well as the metaphysical instances of idealational hermeneutics.[84] Beginning with the premise of historical distance and dissimilarity between text and reader, we are advised to seek a unity in the dialogue of reader and spirit of the author. This model is just as easily translated into a search for what is doctrinally significant, experientially pietistic or empirically factual according to the various readers' tastes. In substance these perspectives obscure the confession of the text as perspicuous because they dismiss the text itself in their efforts to understand the text as representative of something clearer, more accessible. The supposed clarity of the biblical text is regarded in terms of its transparent representation of particular historical incidents or universal religious perception. Our goal, as Christian readers, is to understand what has been provided *as* text, and *in* the text, and to *see by means of* the text, not *through* the text. This involves, as Karl Barth noted, "a radical re-orientation concerning the goal to be pursued, on the basis of the recognition that the biblical texts must be investigated for their own sake to the extent that the revelation which they attest does not

---

[82]Ibid., p. 216.

[83]Gadamer, *Truth and Method,* p. 197.

[84]Frei, *Theology and Narrative,* pp. 126-28. An example of idealational hermeneutics is found in C. H. Dodd's preference for the genius of the biblical authors: "Their words convey a personal experience of reality, and our aim is to participate in it, rather than merely to assess the logic of their arguments" (*The Authority of the Bible* [New York: Harper & Brothers, 1929], p. 31). The form of the biblical text may be the most difficult obstruction to the author's religious brilliance, according to Dodd.

stand or occur, and is not to be sought, behind or above them but in them."[85]

Thus, we can better understand why it is that commitments to Scripture as perspicuous, authoritative or without error—affirmations common in contemporary conservative as well as historic Christianity—share one obvious element: it is *Scripture itself* that is our concern. We speak of Scripture as inspired, Scripture as authoritative and Scripture as perspicuous. But we do not necessarily speak of the text's author's intention or historical circumstances as perspicuous, nor of the clarity of the readers' horizon or influences in reading. We might be in a position to, once again, "learn . . . the meaning of the saying, 'Nothing beyond what is written' " (1 Cor 4:6 NRSV). Our conventional concern is with the form (Scripture) and its relationship with how the content (its message) is best understood, not simply a concern regarding the message behind, before or beneath the form. This commitment is disciplinary in that our focus is with the text, not simply the events that stand behind the text or are latent within the text.[86] While the pre-

---

[85]Karl Barth, *Church Dogmatics* I/2, ed. G. W. Bromiley and T. F. Torrance, trans. G. W. Bromiley (Edinburgh: T & T Clark, 1936-1969), p. 494. The quote from Karl Barth reads in full: "As I see it, this does not mean an annulling of the results of biblical scholarship in the last centuries, nor does it mean a breaking off and neglect of efforts in this direction. What it does mean is a radical re-orientation concerning the goal to be pursued, on the basis of the recognition that the biblical texts must be investigated for their own sake to the extent that the revelation which they attest does not stand or occur, and is not to be sought, behind or above them but in them." Barth's emphasis on the singular revelation of God in the Word (Christ) means that neither Scripture or preaching can properly be named the Word of God (p. 530), yet he does get to the argument over the unity of form and content by means of appealing to Scripture as a (indispensable) "witness" to the revelation of God in Christ: Scripture singularly "recollects the incarnation of the eternal Word. . . . Thus Scripture imposes itself in virtue of this its content" (Barth, *Church Dogmatics* I/1, p. 108).

[86]Wesley Kort comments: "The tendency to take narrative as a product of originally separate ingredients, facts and ideas or beliefs, seems to affect biblical scholarship as well. Two dominant interests are to be found: the reconstruction of the factual history of ancient Israel, early Judaism, Jesus, or the Church, on the one hand; and developmental or systematic treatments of the beliefs or theologies of the communities from which the narratives came, on the other. While this division of labor or interest is in itself not objectionable, the assumption from which it may come or to which it may lead—namely, that we have to do first of all with two originally separated ingredients, facts and beliefs, and that narratives are products of those ingredients—must be questioned. . . . Biblical scholarship has as one of its objects the reconstruction of a coherent history behind the biblical text. When augmented by theological interests, this history becomes a series of God's mighty acts, a *Heilsgeschichte*. The validating theological ground of biblical narrative is a sequence of events behind the texts that, in occurring, created particular responses. . . . Liberal and conservative biblical scholarship, although motivated theologically in different ways, agree that biblical narratives derive their religious meaning from something behind them, from a series of events, from a history it is the task of the biblical scholar to reconstruct." Kort, *Story, Text, and Scripture*, pp. 11-12, 139-40. For discussions of the themes of text or event see John H. Sailhammer, *Introduction to Old Testament Theology: A Canonical Approach* (Grand Rapids, Mich.:

sumption of a distinction between text and event is a rather routine critical contrast, in terms of Scripture's clarity its resolution may not be desirable (perspicuity actually presumes the contrast between the accessible and inaccessible, and only functions appropriately in this light).

A commitment to Scripture as perspicuous embodies an awareness of the tension of text or event, rather than simply ignoring such an anxious relationship. But the resolution of the tension is not found in confusing one with the other (e.g., that text is as good as history), nor implicitly justifying history by means of text (that text is best understood as history). That Scripture is clear in its own ways is founded on the premise of distinguishing the accessible and the inaccessible, but always with the purpose of conserving our attention to the text itself. That is, just because "all things in Scripture are not alike plain in themselves, nor alike clear unto all," as the Westminster Confession reads, does not indicate that the resolution of tensions is found in a commitment to the simplicity of either text or event, or their relationship. Instead, clarity functions as a critical convention that rules how we affirm the union of the text, what the text is about, and how one reads the text. Yet these are no small matters.

There is no simple and absolute choice between author, text or reader; there is also no necessary choice of author, text or readers for Christians interested in understanding Scripture's clarity. That is, supposing we understood the historical conditions, the authorial psychology or intentions in writing one thing rather than others, the reader's circumstances, and then the relationship of the three, possibly in some hierarchy, we still do not have the ability to say that the biblical text is clear in its own respect. Instead, in the Christian manner of reading Scripture its clarity is intrinsic in relation to its proper reading. The affirmation of Scripture's clarity is itself an affirmation of how Scripture is best understood on its own terms, rather than by means of historical or aesthetic attention to how a text is understood. It is not simply that Scripture is clear, and all other texts are obscure. The clarity of Scripture is not a unique claim in itself. But neither is the Christian confession that all texts are necessarily clear and thus Scripture as a text must be granted this characterization of clarity.

This can be illustrated by observing the interest in and contention over texts in the contemporary history of literary criticism. In 1941 John Crowe Ransom wrote a corrective to the extremes of textual formalism (from its proponents) and the suspicions about textuality (from its opponents). He argued that the preference for texts involved the working assumption that a text supplied its own meaning and that the meaning of a text cannot properly be said to be

---

Zondervan, 1995), pp. 36-85; *The Pentateuch as Narrative* (Grand Rapids, Mich.: Zondervan, 1992), pp. 7-22.

supplied (determined) from biography or intentionality, nor from historical, archaeological or philological knowledge, nor from reader's prejudices or psychology, nor from how various people made use of it or understood it to mean something rather than another, nor from genre comparisons across the field of literature. Meaning, Ransom argued, is what the text itself is about.[87]

Within a Christian reading of Scripture Ransom's argument can aid us in discerning the effects of asserting that Scripture can be regarded as an instance of the teaching that it asserts; it is both the assertion and the realization of the assertion. Generalizations from history, philology or an author's biography can be inferred from the texts but should not be imposed upon texts. To be concerned primarily with the biography of the author or primarily with the circumstances of the reader is to be distracted from the task of understanding the text itself. In principle, Ransom encouraged readers to view meaning as equivalent to a text's organization of its own content, but meaning is not something beyond the text's own content.[88] The legacy of Ransom's argument has been primarily directed against the seemingly conservative effort to define a text's meaning by linking meaning to the text's author.

What Is Fallacious About Intentionality?

The notion of an author's intention implies the belief that there exists something against which the text can be measured, can be clarified by knowing or discerning.[89] But this notion begs the question of the meaning of a text itself. For example, there is a genuine discord between the possibility of ascertaining and possessing God's intent through the traditional and institutional community (and thus tradition forming the constitutive literal sense of Scripture), and the dangerous possibility that Scripture's literal sense is ascertained within the community but cannot properly be possessed by anything other than the text (and thus the

---

[87]John Crowe Ransom, *The New Criticism* (New York: New Directions, 1941). A central essay of this work was entitled "Wanted: An Ontological Critic." On the criticism of New Criticism in general, see Wayne C. Booth, "What Is Not Old About the New Critics," *Humanities* 6 (April 1985): 7-8; Edgar Lohner, "The Intrinsic Method: Some Reconsiderations," in *The Disciplines of Criticism: Essays in Literary Theory, Interpretation, and History*, ed. Peter Demetz, Thomas Greene, and Lowry Nelson Jr. (New Haven, Conn.: Yale University Press, 1968), pp. 170-83; and Lynn M. Poland, *Literary Criticism and Biblical Hermeneutics: A Critique of Formalist Approaches* (Chico, Calif.: Scholars Press, 1985).

[88]Art Berman, *From the New Criticism to Deconstruction: The Reception of Structuralism and Post-Structuralism* (Urbana: University of Illinois Press, 1988), pp. 26-59.

[89]On the advice of E. D. Hirsch, historically oriented interpreters have denied the autonomy of the text by championing the author; see Hirsch's *The Aims of Interpretation* (Chicago: University of Chicago Press, 1976); and *Validity in Interpretation* (New Haven, Conn.: Yale University Press, 1967). For a helpful critique, criticism and reaffirmation of Hirsch's work see P. D. Juhl, *Interpretation: An Essay in the Philosophy of Literary Criticism* (Princeton, N.J.: Princeton University Press, 1980).

dual possibility that Scripture and community coinhere as well as Scripture reforming the church). Against this backdrop the effort to pursue the human author's intention for a text illustrates the effective displacement of the text itself.

Intentionality appears to take three general forms in recent circumstances: religious or psychological, historical and literary (with occasional overlap among methods). While the influences of historical and literary interests have somewhat overshadowed the famed religious intentional fallacy associated with Schleiermacher, they are properly understood as an effort to sustain intentionality. The germ of intentionality was a meeting of the minds of author and reader via the medium of the text. Schleiermacher placed religious (as in psychological) interpretation alongside grammatical interpretation wherein psychological interest is a reconstruction of the original creative act of writing. Authors can be fully understood directly from their texts. This is founded upon a perspicuous, as in congenial, union of author and reader that is guaranteed by the individual's participation in universal life. So Schleiermacher offered, "The interpreter must then establish the same relationship between himself and the author as existed between the author and his original audience."[90] Even better, it is distinctly possible for readers to understand authors better than authors understood themselves because of the explicit, conscious efforts of readers to understand (whereas authors simply wrote in their times and language for whom these matters were just normal).[91]

This form of intentionality met several efforts of correction in the last two centuries, especially in terms of historical- and literary-critical models. Reading the Bible (and other significant texts) in modern culture has been profoundly influenced by the "need for an informing authorial presence with which we can contend."[92] Eschewing the quest to realize the meeting of the author's and interpreter's minds in the act of interpretation (a religious or psychological intentional fallacy), historical and literary proponents of the author's intention contend that we are to seek to become aware of the objective, conscious act of the author in writing (and maybe what was to be realized in the act of writing),

---

[90]Schleiermacher, *Hermeneutics,* p. 216.

[91]For a helpful explanation of this in Schleiermacher, see Gadamer, *Truth and Method,* pp. 184-99. Gadamer notes, "The better understanding that distinguishes the interpreter from the writer does not refer to the understanding of the text's subject matter but simply to the understanding of the text—i.e., of what the author meant and expressed. This understanding can be called 'better' insofar as the explicit, thematized understanding of an opinion as opposed to actualizing its contents implies an increased knowledge. Thus the sentence says something almost self-evident. A person who learns to understand a text in a foreign language will make explicitly conscious the grammatical rules and literary forms which the author followed without noticing, because he lived in the language and its means of artistic expression. The same is true of all production by artistic genius and its reception by others" (pp. 192-93).

[92]Alter, *World of Biblical Literature,* p. 153.

not the subjective states of an author's mind or personal psychology.[93]

For example, E. D. Hirsch offers that unless one is seeking after the willful intent of a text's author, one is not seeking the meaning of the text. Unless one is seeking the cognitive union of author and reader via the text, one is not seeking meaning. Thus, "all valid interpretation, of every sort, is founded on the re-cognition of what an author meant."[94] The author's meaning is not inferred from the text, the meaning of the text is the author's intent. This appeal is for objectivity inasmuch as the goal of interpretation is the "shareable content of the speaker's intentional object."[95] While the meaning of a text is objective in the text itself (one meaning—the author's), the text's significance to the reader may vary (significance is always meaning—to readers).[96] Early in his career Hirsch offered that this may be the last gasp for an increasingly challenged location of (objective) meaning in texts in any real sense.[97]

This was an influential position championed by Hirsch for a time but a position that he later admitted was too narrow and limiting. He still maintains that authorial intention is the foundation of meaning—the fixed objects that the author refers to in their original writing. However, instead of restricting meaning to what an author could have possibly maintained at the time of original writing, Hirsch's alteration allows for an extension of meaning fulfillment that is still subsumed by the concept originally written. He still resists ideas of change and alteration that would violate the original enunciation, but he conceives of authorial intention as a concept, one linked with meaning. So Hirsch: "The identity of meaning in different applications is preserved only when the application is an instance subsumed by the original-intention concept."[98] This, Hirsch explains, is the nature of writing and meaning linked by the concept of

---

[93]Hirsch, *Validity in Interpretation,* p. 4.

[94]Ibid., p. 126.

[95]Ibid., p. 219.

[96]Ibid., p. 63.

[97]So what Hirsch offers is work "to give encouragement to those who are still willing to entertain the belief that knowledge is possible even in textual interpretation" (*Aims in Interpretation,* p. 12). It is hardly difficult to see why conservative evangelicals would find this "encouragement" encouraging to their work of historical-authorial appeals.

[98]E. D. Hirsch, "Meaning and Significance Reinterpreted," *Critical Inquiry* 11 (December 1984): 214. Hirsch adds, "We cannot limit meaning to what was within an original event any more than we can limit a concept to its original enunciation. A concept is by its nature both an 'internal' generality and an 'external' array of things embraced by the generality; it is both an 'intention' and an 'extension.' To think of several different items belonging to the extension of a concept is certainly not to think in each case of a different concept! When I think of my Schwinn instead of my son's Blue Streak, I do not thereby change my concept of a bicycle. When I apply Shakespeare's sonnet to my own lover rather than to his, I do not change his meaning-intention but rather instantiate and fulfill it. It is the nature of textual meaning to embrace many different fulfillments without thereby being changes" (p. 210).

intention. Hirsch maintains these transformations are significant; yet they are minor in terms of the control and objectivity of authorial intent. They allow for a literary notion of intentionity as a corrective to the subjectivist factors of religious intentionality, on the one hand, and the objectivist factors of historical intentionality, on the other hand. Yet Hirsch's solution remains bound to authorial intentionality as the basis of meaning (an insistence not lost on evangelicals interested in Hirsch's defense of fixing meaning with original intention).[99] And the result is the same: the clarity of Scripture is still bound to discovering the intention of the author (i.e., that intention clarifies).

In contrast to Hirsch's affirmation of intentionality, we may observe an alternative literary interest, one cast as a criticism of intentionalism itself. The orientation of intentionalism was rigorously questioned a generation earlier in Wimsatt and Beardsley's essay "The Intentional Fallacy,"[100] which opened the floodgates of demurral in literary criticism (biblical criticism remained relatively unaffected for interesting reasons, most having to do with Hirsch's type of argument in favor of authorial determinacy and objective interpretation). The meaning of a text is what the community of its readers takes it to mean. For the Wimsatt and Beardsley formula the error remains the same for historical, literary-authorial, and religious or psychological intentionalism: to equate the meaning of a text with the author's intent is to confuse what was actually written with what might have been intended and so much more.[101]

The fallacy of intentionality represents a not-so-naive appeal to an objective, unmediated historical fact against which competing readings must be adjudi-

---

[99]For a rather straightforward (and sometimes uncritical) use of Hirsch within evangelical hermeneutics see Elliott E. Johnson, *Expository Hermeneutics: An Introduction* (Grand Rapids, Mich.: Zondervan, 1990); Walter C. Kaiser, *Toward an Exegetical Theology* (Grand Rapids, Mich.: Baker, 1981); *The Uses of the Old Testament in the New* (Chicago: Moody Press, 1985). For an appreciation of Hirsch's stress on authorial intent with some adjustments based on theological differences, see David S. Dockery, *Christian Scripture: An Evangelical Perspective on Inspiration, Authority and Interpretation* (Nashville: Broadman & Holman, 1995); and Kevin J. Vanhoozer, *Is There a Meaning in This Text? The Bible, the Reader, and the Morality of Literary Knowledge* (Grand Rapids, Mich.: Zondervan, 1998). And for a more significant adjustment to Hirsch but a general appreciation for the historicalness of authorial intent, see Millard J. Erickson, *Evangelical Interpretation* (Grand Rapids, Mich.: Baker, 1993). The emphasis on obscurity and clarifying by means of distinguishing meaning and significance is represented in Grant Osborne, *The Hermeneutical Spiral: A Comprehensive Introduction to Biblical Interpretation* (Downers Grove, Ill.: InterVarsity Press, 1991). A critique and minor complaint regarding Hirsch's influence in evangelical circles is offered by W. Edward Glenny, "The Divine Meaning of Scripture: Explanations and Limitations," *Journal of the Evangelical Theological Society* 38, no. 4 (1995): 481-500.

[100]William K. Wimsatt Jr. and Monroe C. Beardsley, "The Intention Fallacy," *Sewanee Review* 54 (1946), reprinted in Wimsatt and Beardsley, *Verbal Icon,* pp. 3-18.

[101]William K. Wimsatt Jr., "Genesis: A Fallacy Revisited," in *On Literary Intention: Critical Essays,* ed. David Newton-de Molina (Edinburgh: Edinburgh University Press, 1976).

cated, especially applicable in measuring the special pleading from Christian readers about Scripture. And of particular interest to our topic is the association of a text's meaning—what is the obvious, singular and perspicuous intent of a text—with the author's design for a text. For instance, critical suspicions of allegorical interpretations of Jesus' parables contest that such extravagant meanings were inappropriate and unacceptable because they could not have possibly been intended by the original author, not simply that such interpretations were historically unlikely.[102] For Wimsatt and Beardsley texts are authored, but this is significantly different from determining meaning by appeal to the author of the text (as it is for intentionalism). The shift from an authored text to the author of the text may seem subtle and insignificant, but in Christian theology this shift corresponds to the rise of modern critical interest in origins, sources and factual causes for textual effects.[103] Associating clarity with original expression (historically or circumstantially) or the actual author's intentions (psychologically or personally) presumes a feigned association of objectivity and clarity.

But meaning in author's intent, strictly speaking, is an artificial reconstruction of a conversation between author, the author's world, text (and possibly audience) in which the text succumbs to a larger situation. An illustration of this is found in Richard Friedman's *Who Wrote the Bible?* which attempts to reconstruct the social, political, geographical and literary worlds of individual biblical authors in order to "shed light" on the text.[104] Of this attempt Robert

---

[102]G. B. Caird, *The Language and Imagery of the Bible* (Philadelphia: Westminster Press, 1980), p. 165.

[103]This is also David Dawson's argument about the misrepresentation of allegory in the ancient church. He noted, "Modern commentary on allegory . . . has tended to follow the misleading self-interpretations of the ancient writers by focusing on the text being read: allegorical reading is then said either to violate the integrity of that text, to unveil its deeper meaning, or to demonstrate that it has no meaning at all. But these approaches overlook the revisionary function performed by allegorical reading in its historical, social, and cultural contexts. Allegory is not so much about the meaning or lack of meaning in texts as it is a way of using texts and their meanings to situate oneself and one's community with respect to society and culture" (*Allegorical Readers and Cultural Revision in Ancient Alexandria* [Berkeley: University of California Press, 1992], pp. 235-36).

[104]Robert Elliott Friedman, *Who Wrote the Bible?* (New York: Summit, 1987). Friedman outlined his effort as follows: "When a book is studied in a high school or university class, one usually learns something of the author's life, and generally this contributes to the understanding of the book. Apart from fairly advanced theoretical literary considerations, most readers seem to find it significant to be able to see connections between the author's life and the world that the author depicts in his or her work. . . . The more obvious this seems, the more striking is the fact that this information has been largely lacking in the case of the Bible. Often the text cannot be understood without it. . . . I mean to be more specific about who the writers of the Bible were: not only when they lived, but where they resided, the groups to which they belonged, their relationships to major persons and events of their historical moment, whom they liked, whom they opposed, and their political and religious purposes in writing their works. I mean to shed more light on the relationship among the various authors. . . . I

Alter observed that it exemplifies the intractable problem of "unscrambling the omelette," and it goes this effort one better: "Unscrambling the omelette is actually less insuperable a difficulty than figuring out when the original eggs were laid, and by which hens."[105] For most "old" texts—Scripture especially—there is simply no significant (direct) evidence to reconstruct the author's intentions (about the specific work under consideration or the author's immediate world), except the finished work itself, kept and read in specific communities.

The credibility of assertions founded in authorial intent (the fallible or infallible nature of conclusions about authors and their texts) are not necessarily related to the nature of a text as text, nor how a text is best understood, nor the possibility of finding meaning in text as opposed to discovering meaning in the author's world. And this is precisely what is so troubling about authorial intentionalism—that in the name of objectivity we lose sight of the text itself. And this intentionalism is misdirected attention; as Wimsatt and Brooks observe, "Even where we know a great deal about the author's personality and ideas, we rarely know as much as the [text] itself can tell us about itself; for the [text] is no mere effusion of a personality."[106] It is an appropriate exercise (for certain purposes of summary or historical reference) to move from the text back to the author, but not from the author to the work, nor to realize the text's meaning by a reference extrinsic to the text.[107]

To question the determinism of authorial intent is not to deny that authors have intentions for texts, nor to insist that authors were in an ecstatic frenzy. While a text is not merely an extension of its author's mind and personality, neither would we wish to deny that every text is the product of language, of history, of a particular culture. The conviction that texts have autonomy is not to be taken as absolute.[108] A particular emphasis on the text as distinguished

---

mean to shed more light on the chain of events that brought all of the documents together into one work" (pp. 16, 31-32).

[105]Alter, *World of Biblical Literature,* p. 163. The expression "unscrambling the omelette" comes from Sir Edmund Leach. Alter wrote that Friedman's work "seeks to pinpoint the temporal, geographical, and social location of each of the major biblical writers. One can admire the intellectual detective work of such undertakings, but given the paucity of reliable historical data we have, especially when anonymous authors who have been edited and combined with each other are involved, historical scholarship is bound to be more than halfway to historical fiction" (pp. 161-62).

[106]Wimsatt and Brooks, *Literary Criticism,* p. 114.

[107]The effect of Wimsatt and Beardsley's argument about intentional fallacy was to make the author a function of the text (*Verbal Icon,* p. 4).

[108]Roland Barthes's assertions about the "death of the author" represent the ultimate consequences of the preoccupation with authorial intent; externally imposed meaning(s) are futile once the author is removed. Barthes taught a generation of literary critics to converse about a text doing or saying things rather than the author by arguing for the strictly literal sense of a text ("The Death of the Author," in *Image-Music-Text* [New York: Hill & Wang,

from an emphasis on the author or the reader is not necessarily the same as denying historicity of texts or the influence of readers in understanding.[109] An emphasized concern for the text as text stresses that the form of the text is the test of its significance and meaning among its readers.

Sympathy to the concerns and the premises of authorial intention are understandable, especially among those fond of the critical optimism of early modernity—fixed and unequivocal meaning, certainty of a more significant and mathematical sort, indubitable rather than socially or religiously grounded accounts of significance. In its most positive light authorial intent argues that correspondence between text and author leads to greatest clarity, with imprecision as the necessary consequence of a text hopelessly severed from its author. Yet, the concentration on Scripture as text does not rely upon the theory of how texts and authors relate. This is in contrast to how Scripture as text might be understood as one instance of how authorial intent determines, establishes or fixes meaning.

An illustration:

> Bear in mind that our Lord's patience means salvation, just as our dear brother Paul also wrote you with the wisdom that God gave him. He writes the same way in all his letters, speaking in them of these matters. His letters contain some things that are hard to understand, which ignorant and unstable people distort, as they do the other Scriptures, to their own destruction. (2 Pet 3:15-16)

It is routinely presumed that better historical information would eliminate obscurity, and an interview with a text's author would conclusively determine what a given text should be taken to mean. And this text is routinely taken to justify such a condition for meaning. (Scripture twisting is taken as a popular idiom for distorting an author's true intention and meaning.)

But notice what is not found in this text. Distorting Paul's routine message about the Lord's patience (supposedly not hard to follow if one simply reads his

---

1977], pp. 146-47). If, in Barthes' sense, textual autonomy necessitates the death of the author, the other extreme would be to assert that textual autonomy necessitates the death of the reader; neither will suffice except as a display of textual indeterminacy or determinacy, respectively.

[109]The caricature of Anglo-American New Criticism, or textual formalism, is that the focus on a text or poem as autonomous, historically or even from the reader or in the relationship of text and reader, is absolute. But this is rarely the case among its proponents, although such simplistic dogmatism is often found among its followers. René Wellek argued that the emphasis on a literary work as a work of art among New Critics did not and should not be conceived to mean "a denial of the relevance of historical information for the business of poetic interpretation" (*Concepts of Criticism,* ed. Stephen G. Nichols Jr. [New Haven, Conn.: Yale University Press, 1963], p. 7). See also René Wellek, *The Attack on Literature, and Other Essays* (Chapel Hill: University of North Carolina Press, 1982).

letters, e.g., Rom 2:4) is a practice or habit of the ignorant (morally unlearned, not historically distant or darkened) and unstable (cp. 1:12; 2:14; 3:17; and it probably alludes to Peter's legacy of Lk 22:32). Paul, it seems, does say some things that are difficult to understand and, because of this lack of clarity in his letters, they are particularly susceptible to torturous readings. Not only the obscure matters of Paul's writings but also "other" Scripture are similarly distorted. Our interest in distorted readings is focused precisely on the abused texts (Paul's and other Scriptures), not on authorial or nontextual matters. Paul's obscure texts are seized upon to be distorted presumably because one could not as readily distort the things he writes the same way of in all his letters; obscurity and distortion are two differing descriptions, and the latter does not necessarily follow from the former.[110]

Where does this distortion lead? To the destruction of the ignorant and unstable—hardly a blameworthy consequence for misreading obscure Pauline phrases! But the fault is a moral one, and it is thought to rest with the readers and not with the distorted obscure texts (not an uncommon accusation regarding the supposed misuse of biblical texts; cp. Gal 1:6-9; 2 Thess 2:15; 1 Tim 1:3-7; Tit 1:9-11; 2 Jn 4-10). Also, it is not the confession or opinion that certain texts are obscure that disqualifies one's Christian identity or standing in the community of interpreters. Then what made Paul's "hard to understand things" hard to understand in the first place? From one side of the spectrum some argue that, in essence, God and Paul did a poor job of communicating or accommodating the profundity of divine revelation (it was God's wisdom, after all); while others simply doubt that clarity in understanding (as in lacking ambiguity) is possible because of the nature of human language. But this is precisely to miss the point: the obscurity of some things in Paul's letters is one thing; the distorted readings of such matters is another. *That* there are hard to understand readings in Paul's writings is hardly debatable, but how we should regard this reference in 2 Peter to obscurity is important because it exposes us to the prospect that it is not resolved through harmonization (obscure matters made clear by submitting them to other proximate texts, themes, ideas). God's wisdom in Paul's message is a familiar theme, though the matter of obscurity is

[110]Calvin's remarks follow this characterization, a comment on 2 Peter 3:16: "Whence is this obscurity, for the Scripture shines to us like a lamp, and guides our steps? To this I reply, that there is nothing to be wondered at, if Peter ascribed obscurity to the mysteries of Christ's kingdom, and especially if we consider how hidden they are to the perception of the flesh. However, the mode of teaching which God has adopted, has been so regulated, that all who refuse not to follow the Holy Spirit as their guide, find in the Scripture a clear light. At the same time, many are blind who stumble at mid-day; others are proud, who, wandering through devious paths, and flying over the roughest places, rush headlong into ruin" (*Epistles of St Peter,* pp. 367-68).

not settled by employing common rhetorical evaluations but through the pneumatic existence of those with the mind of Christ, exhibiting in this contrary way the power of God (1 Cor 1:17—2:16). Whether in the 2 Peter text or 1 Corinthians, resolving obscurity is not portrayed as naturally accomplished (it is not simply textually, linguistically or historically accomplished either).

What would prevent the twisting or distorting of Paul's letters asserted in 2 Peter? We find no cause to believe that better historical information or an interview of the author should be our recourse. In fact, we do not find an encouragement to "correct" obviously obscure matters in Paul's letters in this text (the supposed pseudepigraphal notions about dating 2 Peter would certainly prevent that possibility; are we to infer a tradition concerning obscurity?). What made certain things hard to understand in Paul's letters may not be of concern in the 2 Peter text, but it may be addressed from within that text itself, albeit by an alternative not commonly found in modern hermeneutical circles, namely that such matters are not problems to be solved or that necessarily must be solved because of the sufficiency or competency of the community's knowledge of the truth in Christ (2 Pet 1:3-4; 1:12, 19; 3:2).[111]

We have certainly come a long way from the Christian tradition of the Middle Ages that asserted that authorial intent *does* determine the sense of Scripture but that by *author* Christians meant God. Accounting for this conviction in the current literary milieu should not simply lead us backward to obscurantism (to ignore the human author and assert divine authorship in order to avoid or suspend critical estimates of Scripture as text is itself contrary to Christian confessions regarding the nature of Scripture as text).

It is this discrimination that encourages Protestants to qualify assertions of Scripture's authority; for example, the Bible is without error *in what it affirms* or *properly understood.*[112] This provision has even been employed to explain the

[111]But we have ignored an obvious option, that the author of 2 Peter might be intentionally misrepresenting Paul's letters as obscure to bolster his own authority in rebutting false teachers (2 Pet 2:1; 3:2) and that 2 Peter's faint praise of Paul is actually damnation. After all, the "dating" of this text is dubious to many, precisely because it is reminiscent of the historical and authorial associations of authority in postapostolic Christianity. This assertion of Paul's obscurity may allude to the quarrelsome past of Paul and Peter (cf. Paul's reference to confrontation in Gal 2:11-14) and may exhibit the continuing tension between Christian factions (1 Cor 1:12-13) that were still struggling with personal animosities as well as Christian concerns. These suspicions will not be quelled by assertions that disregard the supposed authority of authors to determine meaning from the contexts of texts.

[112]See John Goldingay, *Models for Scripture* (Grand Rapids, Mich.: Eerdmans, 1994). The second article of the Lausanne Covenant (1974) reads, "We affirm the divine inspiration, truthfulness and authority of both Old and New Testament Scriptures in their entirety as the only written Word of God, without error in all that it affirms, and the only infallible rule of faith and practice."

possibility that the author's beliefs might in fact differ significantly from what we can understand the text to assert (regarding cosmology, historicity or prophetic subjects). We observe this distinction in Charles Hodge's account of the infallibility of what the Bible *teaches*. The Bible was without error in that it *taught* without error but not concerning the author's own convictions or perspective.[113] As one historian noted, for Hodge, "the writers might have been in error in what they themselves thought and said, but they did not teach any such errors."[114] This is more than an assertion that the authors were human; it concerned the representation of the world within Scripture itself. For Hodge, inspiration was plenary—it extended to the words of the Bible and not just the ideas. This argument is well founded, sound and appropriate. It is strongly supported by a thorough consideration of Christians' regard for the biblical text as well as the text's depiction of itself.[115] The problem, methodologically, is that Hodge proceeded to vitiate this argument by suggesting that the theologian looks for what the Bible taught by moving beyond or behind the form to "God's system."

The confession regarding the nature of Scripture focuses our attention to the manner in which Scripture exists as text, and the way(s) in which it teaches or recommends its own use, even to the extent that we distinguish between author and text giving priority to the text. Knowing what an author believed as an individual, either through the text or the world of the author, or even what the author intended to say, does not tell us what a text actually says. For that we must go to the text itself.

Conclusion

We may wish to ask, Where does this text-oriented approach fit in the spectrum of options regarding interpreting texts? It may not fit as we suppose it

---

[113]Hodge wrote concerning plenary inspiration, "It asserts that they were fully inspired as to all that they teach, whether of doctrine or fact. This of course does not imply that the sacred writers were infallible except for the special purposes for which they were employed. They were not imbued with plenary knowledge. As to all matters of science, philosophy, and history, they stood on the same level with their contemporaries. There were infallible only as teachers, and when acting as the spokesmen of God. Their inspiration no more made them astronomers than it made them agriculturists. Isaiah was infallible in his predictions, although he shared with his countrymen the views then prevalent as to the mechanism of the universe. . . . The sacred writers also, doubtless, differed as to insight into the truths which they taught" (Charles Hodge, *Systematic Theology* [reprint, Grand Rapids, Mich.: Eerdmans, 1981], 1:165).

[114]Claude Welch, *Protestant Thought in the Nineteenth Century* (New Haven, Conn.: Yale University Press, 1972), 1:203.

[115]For this justification of plenary inspiration, both in its appreciable influence and renown among Christians as well as its textual demonstration, the arguments of Warfield remain thorough and convincing; see B. B. Warfield, "The Biblical Idea of Inspiration," and " 'God Inspired Scripture,' " in *The Inspiration and Authority of the Bible,* ed. Samuel G. Craig (Phillipsburg, N.J.: Presbyterian & Reformed, 1948), pp. 131-68, 245-98.

should. Are we really left with the idea of middle ground, mediating extremes or combining themes?

> On one side of the spectrum, some say that the only correct meaning of a text is that single meaning the original author intended it to have. On the other side stand those who argue that meaning is a function of readers, not authors, and that any text's meaning depends upon the readers' perception of it. Between the two stand other options. Perhaps meaning resides independently in the texts themselves, regardless of what the author meant or of what later readers understand from them. These issues are crucial because our definition of the task of hermeneutics will depend on our answer to where meaning resides—in a text, in the mind of the reader, or in some combination of the two?[116]

Attention to the text itself, in contradistinction to attending to author's intent or primarily to reader's interests may not be a combination of the choices—it may be another kind of choice, one that eschews strict ideas of exegesis or eisegesis in favor of a fluid notion of intergesis (the subject addressed in chapter seven).[117] What seems to be the closest thing we have to a Christian tradition about understanding, meaning and Scripture is the assertion that Christians admit to a privileged text, a privileged community and a privileged mode of reading. Reading with attention to the text behaves, within the Christian tradition, as a reminder of what a faithful manner of reading looks like.

With regard to Scripture's clarity we may avoid the notion that perspicuity is itself a methodology or a hermeneutic, in the modern sense, although it certainly presumes the far-reaching faith structure of Christian theology. Reading Scripture as text raises an interesting series of confrontations with assumptions about meaning and texts, and it may provide us with responses to those who concentrate upon matters extrinsic to the text to understand the text. But we have yet to consider the tremendous shift in our world toward the significance of the reader (a shift only in strictly modern terms but always native to the Christian use of Scripture). There is a revived interest in the inseparable relationship of texts and readers that both challenges as well as elucidates the confession of Scripture's perspicuity.

---

[116]William W. Klein, Craig L. Blomberg, and Robert L. Hubbard Jr., *Introduction to Biblical Interpretation* (Dallas: Word, 1993), p. 6.

[117]See George Aichele and Gary A. Phillips, "Exegesis, Eisegesis, Intergesis," *Semeia* 69-70 (1995): 7-18.

7

INTERTEXTUALITY & SCRIPTURE'S CLARITY

These things happened to them as examples and were written down as warnings for us, on whom the fulfillment of the ages has come.

1 CORINTHIANS 10:11

In order to be proclaimed and heard again and again both in the Church and the world, Holy Scripture requires to be explained. As the Word of God it needs no explanation, of course, since as such it is clear in itself. The Holy Ghost knows very well what He has said to the prophets and apostles and what through them He wills also to say to us. This clarity which Scripture has in itself as God's Word, this objective perspicuitas which it possesses, is subject to no human responsibility or care. On the contrary, it is the presupposition of all human responsibility in this matter. All the explanation of Scripture for which we are responsible can only be undertaken on the presupposition that Scripture is clear in itself as God's Word; otherwise it will at once disintegrate. And all scriptural exegesis for which we are responsible can lead only to the threshold beyond which Scripture is clear in itself as God's Word.

KARL BARTH, *CHURCH DOGMATICS*

THE MUCH-ACCLAIMED COLLAPSE OF THE CULTURAL CHRISTIAN INFLUENCE IN the West is accompanied by a vigorous discussion about the so-called canon of Western literature and the very notion of a classic. To put the matter much too simply, the literary canon is comprised of classics that not only should be read but are read, for whatever reasons. It exemplifies a discrimination between texts and in turn raises serious questions of historical justification for privileging one text above another (what makes a classic a classic seems to many an arbitrary privileging of one text over another to reinforce ideological prejudices). In particular, how are we to address the analytical recognition that the Bible has been treated as a classic (something many Christians are interested in defending)? Or is a classic, in particular the Bible, simply acknowledged by readers for what it is, namely, valuable, worthy of being read and able to be read with clarity?

When considering how privileged texts are best treated (recognizing that when such texts, especially Scripture, are read we are actually rereading such texts), literary and theological interests are turned to the subject of intertextuality (which includes how the text treats itself and how the text involves readers). The appeal to intertextuality involves the reader in both the textual nature of Scripture as and the social nature of reading.

Clarity and Classics

In an effort to understand the role of Scripture in Western religious traditions, a theological effort has been mustered to suggest that the role of the Bible is akin to that of the classic.[1] Bound up with such efforts is the admission that classics, and this may be the case especially with the Bible, have an apparent transparent influence—they are regarded as integral and thus readily readable, intelligible and thus perspicuous. As Frank Kermode observes, the recognition of the literary "canon" or "classic" accounts for how a text is "more or less immediately relevant and available."[2]

George Lindbeck noted, "Masterpieces such as *Oedipus Rex* and *War and Peace,* for example, evoke their own domains of meaning."[3] We take this as analogous to a most basic characterization of how we might understand the transparency of classic texts.

> They do so by what they themselves say about the events and personages of which they tell. In order to understand them in their own terms, there is no need for extraneous references to, for example, Freud's theories or historical treatments of the Napoleonic wars. Further, such works shape the imagination and perceptions of the attentive reader so that he or she forever views the world to some extent through the lenses they supply.[4]

To say as much about a culture's relationship with classics invites, even necessitates, saying even more rigorously how this is applicable to communities of faith. That is, in an elemental way, the very notion of a literary "classic," even the religious classic in traditions of the book such as Judaism, Christianity and Islam, concerns how a text is transparent upon its readers (in these cases,

---

[1]Frank Kermode, "The Argument About Canons," in *An Appetite for Poetry* (Cambridge, Mass.: Harvard University Press, 1989), pp. 189-207; Krister Stendahl, "The Bible as a Classic and the Bible as Holy Scripture," *Journal of Biblical Literature* 103, no. 1 (1984): 3-10.

[2]Frank Kermode, *The Classic: Literary Images of Permanence and Change* (New York: Oxford University Press, 1985), pp. 15-16.

[3]George Lindbeck, *The Nature of Doctrine: Religion and Theology in a Postliberal Age* (Philadelphia: Westminster Press, 1984), p. 116.

[4]Ibid., pp. 116-17.

Jews, Christians and Muslims, and how transparency would elude other readers or inhibit the acceptance of hybrid readings). We are faced with several ways of accounting for significance of the Bible as a classic. In a general and practical sense the Bible is a classic because of its significance as a culturally established text (whether it should be so is another question).

The suggestion that the Bible can be understood as a classic, in contemporary theological circles, is often associated with the work of David Tracy. He offers, "We all find ourselves compelled both to recognize and on occasion to articulate our reasons for recognition that certain expressions of the human spirit so disclose a compelling truth about our lives that we cannot deny them some kind of normative status." Classics, then, "disclose" our common way of being in the world, "a normative element in our cultural experience, experienced as a realized truth."[5] Tracy's reference to Scripture's function is founded upon attention to how it discloses in new experiences—that is, opens rather than closes—the same event (Jesus Christ) in "ever different situations."[6] The Scriptures are the foundational and thus normative means of witness to this event that happens now, where "we may see, dimly but really, the real Jesus in this Christ."

> Yet we can only hope to see the reality of that event with clarity by also turning from the present experience of the event to the classic, paradigmatic and normative witnesses to the event in the New Testament. . . . Those memories function as both confirmatory and dangerous as they provoke, elicit, challenge, confront, disclose and transform all later, including present, experiences of the Christ event for the Christian.[7]

According to Tracy, Scripture is to be regarded as the classic normative expression, clarity is perceived by means of the disclosure between reader and Christ event, and Scriptures are thus only a series of relatively adequate witnesses and memories.

What Scripture, like a classic, discloses or perspicuously points to indicates what one perceives to be the material object of faith; this may or may not correspond with one's conception of Scripture's formal purpose, but it usually

---

[5]David Tracy, *The Analogical Imagination: Christian Theology and the Culture of Pluralism* (New York: Crossroad, 1987), p. 108. Tracy continues: "My thesis is that what we mean in naming certain texts, events, images, rituals, symbols, and persons 'classics' is that here we recognize nothing less than the disclosure of a reality we cannot but name truth. With Whitehead, here we find something valuable, something 'important'; some disclosure of reality in a moment that must be called one of 'recognition' which surprises, provokes, challenges, shocks and eventually transforms us; an experience that upsets conventional opinions and expands the sense of the possible; indeed a realized experience of that which is essential, that which endures."

[6]Ibid., pp. 248-49.

[7]Ibid., p. 259.

does. For example, if Scripture discloses the gospel whereby one may experience salvation (as proposed by the Westminster Confession), or the existential encounter of Christ in the present (as in Tracy), or the assuring potential of faith in Christ and reform of the church by means of Scripture (as in Luther), then we might be tempted to say that one finds clearly in Scripture what is most congenial to the reader. But the confession of perspicuity is more dangerous than this: it does not simply reassure, Scripture illumines and may speak against us as easily as it speaks for us. Scripture is clear by an exertion of its own clarity and not simply the power of words, symbols or modes of being in the world, and after its own formal pattern, and not simply the social constructs of contemporary readers. "There are the two first possibilities of interpretation, as a result of which the Word of God, quite apart from the clarity which it has in itself, may even as a human word, so to speak, go its own way on its own feet."[8] While one may understand the classic, pervasive influence of Scripture as read in our circumstances, the clarity of Scripture calls attention to the persuasive influence of Scripture in our reading circumstances, so self-evident to Christians that it constitutes our identity in that we subordinate ourselves to Scripture.[9]

How the text is transparent upon consideration by Christians—as Scripture or seen as a whole—is best expressed by observing the self-involved patterns *in* the text. This subject is addressed by looking at how the concept of intertextuality is used in literary and theological studies. That is, how Scripture behaves when its readers display attention to its assertive qualities (its authority as descriptive as well as ascriptive, the matter of Scripture's own domain of meaning, its constitution so to speak) belongs to the discussion of its clarity because Scripture's clarity, so it is contended, is not a different matter than how one attends to the text as Scripture.

[8]Karl Barth, *Church Dogmatics,* I/2, ed. G. W. Bromiley and T. F. Torrance, trans. G. W. Bromiley (Edinburgh: T & T Clark, 1936-1969), p. 714.

[9]Barth noted, "The necessary and fundamental form of all scriptural exegesis that is responsibly undertaken and practiced in this sense must consist in all circumstances in the freely performed act of subordinating all human concepts, ideas and convictions to the witness of revelation supplied to us in Scripture. Subordination is not opposed to freedom. Freedom means spontaneous activity in relation to an object, such as is characteristic of human conduct and decision, as opposed to merely passive conduct determined from without and subject to necessary development. But freedom does not necessarily mean the divine sovereignty over the object, nor as human freedom does it necessarily mean a relation of reciprocal influence between the object and the freely acting self over against the object. If there is an object in regard to which any other appropriate reaction is excluded, why should not human spontaneity in face of it consist in man's putting himself under it without at the same time putting himself over it? . . . In that God's Word is given to us is Holy Scripture, an object is given to us which requires our spontaneous activity, but this activity of subordination" (ibid., p. 715).

Intertextuality and Interpretation

An important literary, philosophical and theological term, *intertextuality* represents a unique focal point in contemporary hermeneutical discussions; it also represents the shift from primarily historically critical interests to textually literary models.[10] Intertextual models of reading denote the multifaceted efforts to understand texts in relation to proximate texts—the literary or philosophical attempts to delineate the actual experience of working with a text by attending to the text itself—how this might be justified in the current critical milieu, and how these matters impinge upon the commonplace concern over intelligibility and clarity for textually oriented religions. Intertextuality also addresses the *social* space of understanding texts, and it thereby challenges simplistic notions of textual autonomy (the text that is alone, independent of other texts and the reader[s]). Not only are biblical texts readings of other texts, select sources, various and sometimes competing traditions, but they are also read in terms of other texts, preferred sources and in light of various and sometimes competing traditions. As was the case in our concern for classics, intertextuality involves us in the compromising questions associated with the social space of texts—texts that have already been read and are possibly being reread or read otherwise.

Our concern: how it is that what is clear and self-evident *within* one textual range, canon or setting, is more likely than not obscure and imperceptible *outside* that setting. And correspondingly, as an extension of the Christian concern to understand the Bible as "internally glossed," what does intertextuality contribute to our characterization of Scripture as clear?[11]

Julia Kristeva introduced the current literary use of the term *intertextuality* in the 1960s, and it is used philosophically not simply of written texts but the self, experience and any instance of signification.[12] As it is employed by philos-

---

[10]Prominent examples of this convergence include Daniel Boyarin, *Intertextuality and the Reading of Midrash* (Bloomington: Indiana University Press, 1990); Jay Clayton and Eric Rothstein, eds. *Influence and Intertextuality in Literary History* (Madison: University of Wisconsin Press, 1992); Sipke Drasima, ed. *Intertextuality in Biblical Writings: Essays in Honour of Bas van Iersel* (Kampden, Netherlands: J. H. Kok, 1989); Heinrich Plett, ed. *Intertextuality* (Berlin: Walter de Gruyter, 1991); Michael Worton and Judith Still, eds., *Intertextuality: Theories and Practices* (Manchester, U.K.: Manchester University Press, 1990).

[11]George Lindbeck, "Scripture, Consensus, and Community," in *Biblical Interpretation in Crisis* ed. Richard John Neuhaus (Grand Rapids, Mich.: Eerdmans, 1989), p. 75.

[12]Julia Kristeva, *Desire in Language: A Semiotic Approach to Literature and Art,* ed. Leon S. Roudiez, trans. Thomas Gora, Alice Jardine and Leon S. Roudiez (New York: Columbia University Press, 1980); for the philosophical implementation of intertextuality see Roland Barthes, *A Lover's Discourse: Fragments,* trans. Richard Howard (New York: Hill & Wang, 1978); Roland Barthes, "Theory of the Text," in *Untying the Text: A Post-Structuralist Reader,* ed. Robert Young (Boston: Routledge, 1981), pp. 31-47.

ophers and linguists, intertextuality denotes networks of signs within larger sign systems; thus oriented within this framework the inquirer seeks to understand how one instance of textuality has meaning—the network of signs generate meanings in relation to other texts. In this way it involves much more than simply a study of sources. Intertextuality represents an awareness that no text is free or unencumbered but constrained by the boundaries of textuality itself. This semiotic theory forms the basis for structuralist criticism and the possible extension and postponement of meaning according to poststructuralism.[13] In these forms intertextuality concerns the connections between texts made by readers and may exist between any texts (the social space of the textual), and it removes the strict separation or delineation of reader, writer and text.[14] Simply put, we both read and are read by texts in ways that question *and* affirm our relationship with texts. "Part of what is at stake in determining the text is ascertaining *how* it can be read, by whom, and in what context."[15]

In forms more focused on literary textuality there is a stress upon the inner framework that can be considered its own field of study. Such uses in narratology or poetics as a form of biblical criticism stress the "self-referring or intralinguistic relations between texts."[16] Especially in the reading of Old Testament texts the emphasis on intertextuality also involves an awareness of the "self-glossing character of the Bible."[17] For rhetorical criticism of biblical texts, intertextuality represents the readers' comprehension of the interplay among texts and the issues of authority and persuasion in the actual use of texts while noting the inclusion, translation and allusion to certain texts, and the exclusion, rebuttal and dismissal of other texts.[18] In practice this interest has tended to be more akin to source critical interest in *influences;* the concern then becomes whether one text utilized by, was dependent upon or should be understood in

---

[13]Jonathan Culler, *The Pursuit of Signs: Semiotics, Literature, Deconstruction* (Ithaca, N.Y.: Cornell University Press, 1981); *Framing the Sign: Criticism and Its Institutions* (Norman: University of Oklahoma Press, 1988).

[14]On the theme of social space see Roland Barthes, *Image Music Text,* trans. and ed. Stephen Heath (New York: Hill & Wang, 1977); and his "Theory of the Text."

[15]Gary A. Phillips, " 'What Is Written? How Are You Reading?' Gospel, Intertextuality and Doing Lukewise: Reading Lk 10:25-42 Otherwise," *Semeia* 69-70 (1995): 136.

[16]Anthony C. Thiselton, *New Horizons in Hermeneutics* (Grand Rapids, Mich.: Zondervan, 1992), pp. 38, 471-514; also Edgar V. McKnight, *Meaning in Texts: The Historical Shape of a Narrative Hermeneutic* (Philadelphia: Fortress, 1978); Meir Sternberg, *The Poetics of Biblical Narrative: Ideological Literature and the Drama of Reading* (Bloomington: Indiana University Press, 1985).

[17]Robert Alter and Frank Kermode, eds., *The Literary Guide to the Bible* (Cambridge, Mass.: Harvard University Press, 1987), pp. 626-27.

[18]Wayne C. Booth, *The Rhetoric of Fiction,* 2d ed. (Chicago: University of Chicago Press, 1985); Stanley C. Fish, "Rhetoric," in *Critical Terms for Literary Study,* ed. Frank Lentricchia and Thomas McLaughlin (Chicago: University of Chicago Press, 1990), pp. 203-22.

light of another text (i.e., be thought of as clear or clarified by identifying the influence of another text). Intertextuality stresses that source critical interests, allusions to other texts, and the reading, rereading(s) and rewriting of texts, including biblical texts, not only involves the use of sources, but it addresses how we should understand the selectivity itself and what that depicts about how we might read the text.

The Gospel of Luke offers us numerous opportunities to address these features of intertextuality. The Gospel begins with the author's reference to other, "many" accounts of what had been brought to pass "among us," places these accounts in the social relationship of those "who from the beginning were eyewitnesses and servants of the word," which then leads us to consider this "orderly account" in some unspecified contrast to the "many . . . orderly accounts" investigated by the author, and lastly introduces us to the goal of confirming what Theophilus has been taught (1:1-4). The text is itself a reading and rewriting of what the writer, sources and reader(s) share in common. The Gospel of Luke is itself a rereading and rewriting of the Christian faith.

The experience of reading the Gospel is itself an exploration of transposing texts (the Lukan, i.e., Greek, stylistic, adaptation of Septuagint texts that is not unrelated to the type of readers the Gospel desires); then there is the matter of the relationship of the Gospel with political, cultural, social and economic complexities (providing a critique and transformation of such circumstances for the readers). There are persistent challenges to appropriate or received readings of common texts. Taking Luke 4 as an example: Jesus' temptation and dialogue with the devil (4:1-13), Jesus' self-assuming association of messianic fulfillment in his presence (Is 61:1-2 as employed in 4:16-21), and Jesus' subsequent provocation of the synagogue crowd concerning the prophets Elijah and Elisha (and himself) and the relationship of Jews and Gentiles (4:25-29). These texts are not simply about sources or dependence upon sources; they display a rewriting and demand a rereading in their own terms. As Gary Phillips observed, "I read Luke's text, then, intertextually situated within a messy literary critical tradition and cultural setting that strives to make sense of the complexities of Luke's text as a reading about writing and a writing about reading."[19]

In addition, the text creates a social setting positioned in terms of discipleship. It includes and excludes, encourages and chides, both characters and readers with its narration of narrative, characterizations that transcend ques-

[19]Phillips continued, "A reading/writing in which the two activities are conceived together as a semiotic act in which I am implicated. Reading intertextually means, by this definition, focusing upon the writing of Luke as a web of discourses and upon my reading likewise as an intersection of critical pressures" (" 'What Is Written?' " p. 124).

tions of historical reference and confront the willingness or resistance of readers to what is clear and obvious in one light—in light of Jesus as the revealer and reinterpreter of Scripture. This is demonstrated in Jesus' confrontation with the lawyer's self-justifying effort to interpret the law in his favor and again open up the question of Gentiles, Jews and neighbors (10:25-37). This scene plays upon the shared understanding of two spliced texts (Deut 6:5 and Lev 19:18), the apparently clear and received perception for both the lawyer and Jesus (10:28) in response to Jesus' apparently open ended questions: "What is written in the Law? How do you read it?" (10:26).[20] Jesus turns the lawyer's question, "Who is my neighbor?" (10:29), around and asks, "Which of these three do you think was a neighbor to the man who fell into the hands of the robbers?" (10:36). This turn is also contrary to the lawyer's self-justifying question, a move that displays Jesus interpreting the Law to say genuinely to those interested in inheriting eternal life (10:25-28, 37), "Go and do likewise" (10:37). The disciple of Jesus reads the Law as clearly depicting this conclusion and thus takes the position of a learner who is sitting "at the Lord's feet and listening to what he said," even as Mary did (10:39).

The Gospel draws to a conclusion with a forceful rereading and rewriting of "Moses and all the Prophets" in the likeness of Jesus (Lk 24:27), and experience of Jesus who "opened the Scriptures" (24:32) to those who were "foolish" and "slow of heart to believe" what the prophets had said (24:25). And with this confrontation we are told "everything . . . written about me in the Law of Moses, the Prophets, and the Psalms must be fulfilled," which includes the proclamation of the forgiveness of sins "in his name to all nations" (24:44-47). What is necessary to be fulfilled includes the continued preaching and witnessing which stands in continuity with those witnesses and what they have handed down to explain "the things that have been fulfilled among us" (1:1-2). Having the text "opened" to us, like those along the road to Emmaus, involves being confronted by the obvious in light of our resistance to the obvious, but takes place within the social space of the disciple with minds opened to "understand the Scriptures" (24:45), where the knowing disciple is a receiver before the unveiling of Jesus as the (re-)interpreter of Scripture.

---

[20]Ibid., pp. 111-47. Phillips comments regarding Jesus' conversations with a lawyer and Martha: "Two characters engage in conversation with Jesus: both want answers to their questions; both maneuver rhetorically in their conversation to get Jesus to respond the way they want; both are trumped by Jesus who reads and rewrites his interlocutors' words; both yield without further contest to the more able Jesus; both are effectively silenced and disappear from the narrative. . . . [T]hese dialogues disclose something about Jesus' role as a dominating reader of texts and people, and Luke's narrative as an imposing intent on making its readers see, hear, and act (10:24) in a very directed way" (p. 113).

Theological Intertextuality

Literary ideas of intertextuality as influence pursue interpretation that is sensitive to linguistic texture, including repetition, allusion, word play and metaphor. In each instance, in the variety of ways intertextuality can be conceived, there is a common concern to discern the relationship of readers and texts—how texts lure readers by various levels of linguistic interplay, and how readers attempt to catch texts' meaning, even in the more modest or naive appeal to influences.[21] And for our interests it is important to notice how intertextuality is routinely employed to address the struggle to discern a textually oriented concern for Scripture's clarity.

Conventionally intertextuality addresses the manner in which one text utilizes another text in its composition or how the use of one text by another displays both the independence and interdependence of texts and readers. Materially it is used to portray a self-enclosed and shared linguistic structure or cultural idiom that makes possible the description of the Christian writings as canon and Scripture. This includes both the simple lexical core and corresponding interpretive warrant for authoritative texts; how the text and its vocabulary extend to a grammar that is not only an instance of the vocabulary but also a ruled use of how that vocabulary is best understood.[22] This leads us to think seriously about Scripture's treatment of itself in terms of intertextuality, indicating the way in which Scripture serves "as an interpretative medium for its component texts . . . not simply [as] a historical phenomenon—something that happens to texts when they are assembled into collections under certain conditions—but also a hermeneutical principle."[23]

While Christian interpreters readily refer to something analogous to intertextuality in order to address the particularly Christian interest in how New Testament literature utilizes Old Testament literature, including what renders that Testament *Old,* attention to intertextuality also addresses the extension of the text's own discernable treatment of itself—its self-reflexive traits—to the expli-

---

[21]On the image of *lure* see David M. Gunn and Danna Nolan Fewell, "The Lure of Language," in *Narrative in the Hebrew Bible* (New York: Oxford University Press, 1993), pp. 147-73.

[22]"Some doctrines, such as those delimiting the canon and specifying the relation of Scripture and tradition, help determine the vocabulary; while others (or sometimes the same ones) instantiate syntactical rules that guide the use of this material in construing the world, community, and self, and still others provide semantic reference. The doctrine that Jesus is the Messiah, for example, functions lexically as the warrant for adding the New Testament literature to the canon, syntactically as a hermeneutical rule that Jesus Christ be interpreted as the fulfillment of the Old Testament promises (and the Old Testament as pointing toward him), and semantically as the rule regarding the referring use of such titles as 'Messiah' " (Lindbeck, *Nature of Doctrine,* p. 81).

[23]Charles M. Wood, *An Invitation to Theological Study* (Valley Forge, Penn.: Trinity Press International, 1994), p. 67.

cation of a text's immanent meanings—how the text is used by those supposedly yielding to the text's influence. Instead of appealing to a sort of lexical or biblicist hermeneutics (either philologically, historically or literalistically), intertextuality signals the dual desire to self-critically acknowledge both what Scripture says and how it says it. Rather than striving for a singular, transcendent methodology that will unlock Scripture's otherwise obscure meaning, "inner-biblical" attention to textuality recognizes the multiformity of biblical texts and the regional interests of how texts "re-use," "re-contextualize," "reformulate" or "re-interpret" other texts.[24]

Not only concerned with the variety and diversity of textual self-reflection, intertextuality is also employed to understand how various texts render similar subjects within their textual or canonical domain. The perspective whereby we read Scripture as a whole and texts "are known and read in terms of this collection" involves more than a historical commitment to inherited tradition or an arbitrary canon. Because attention to Scripture's intertextuality is theologically oriented to its sufficiency and employment as the divine oracle, Harry Gamble observes, "Since the canon has such results, it cannot be regarded only as an anthology; in its actual effects, the canon is a hermeneutical medium which by its very nature influences the understanding of its contents."[25]

Building upon the work of David Yeago we may speak of theological intertextuality as a form of attention to "the pattern of judgments present *in* the texts" instead of imposing *on* or deducing *from* the texts something that they are about.[26] The *textual* emphasis of intertextuality directs our attention to the judgments of Scripture, instead of a search for the previous or extrinsic significance of a text. One understands the teaching of a text by attending to what it says and implies, not by speculating about its conceptual and terminological background. Yeago's description of such themes attempts to diagnosis the displacement or confusion of textual *judgments* (a text's point, uncovered by paying close attention to what is said and the contingent manner in which conceptual resources are deployed) with *conceptual terms* (some particular,

---

[24]Michael Fishbane, *Biblical Interpretation in Ancient Israel* (Oxford: Clarendon, 1985); George B. Caird, *The Language and Imagery of the Bible* (London: Duckworth, 1980); and H. G. M. Williamson, "History," in *It Is Written: Scripture Citing Scripture: Essays in Honour of Barnabas Lindars* (Cambridge: Cambridge University Press, 1988), pp. 25-38.

[25]The larger quote from Gamble reads, "Canonization entails a recontextualization of the documents incorporated into the canon. They are abstracted both from their generative and traditional settings and redeployed as parts of a new literary whole; henceforth, they are known and read in terms of this collection" (Harry Y. Gamble, *The New Testament Canon: Its Making and Meaning* [Philadelphia: Fortress, 1985], p. 75).

[26]David S. Yeago, "The New Testament and the Nicene Dogma: A Contribution to the Recovery of Theological Exegesis," in *The Theological Interpretation of Scripture: Classic and Contemporary Readings,* ed. Stephen E. Fowl (Cambridge: Blackwell, 1997), pp. 87-88.

contingent verbal and conceptual resource); in turn this is applicable to a Christian interest in doctrine (a teaching that urges certain judgments) by evaluating what the judgments imply (i.e., this is or is the same as that).[27]

When interest in conceptual backgrounds dominates our interpretive practices, a model of conceptual clarity is employed whereby one text is determinative of (i.e., vitiates) the significance and judgments of other texts. A result is the critical and simplistic exclusion of conceptually divergent instances of teaching, often in terms of one text negatively interpreting other texts. To cite Yeago's example, when a concept of incarnation is preeminently associated with one text such as the Gospel of John's prologue, then another text that contains the concept of incarnation is acceptable (understood clearly) "if and only if its conceptual idiom is identical with that of the first 14 verses of John." This leads to the critical practice of minimizing non-Johannine christological traditions (or pointing to the divergent concepts of incarnation that make a unitive christology an impossibility).[28] Methodologically, according to this premise, one ascertains a doctrinal concept standing *behind* one text, and that doctrinal concept is regarded as determinative and clarifying of its actual use, even in its textual instantiation; other texts that display apparently divergent uses of similar doctrinal concepts are regarded as obscure and interpreted (clarified) by the abstractly principal conception. Because texts *contain* doctrinal concepts but are not themselves the meaning of the concepts, a model of conceptual clarity also entails the premise of textual obscurity. This unfortunate tendency should not be equated with the practice of interpreting clear texts by means of unclear texts. Finding (unitive) ways by which Christians live with our regard for Scripture as one book tests both the limits we tend to impose on what constitutes Scripture's clear message as well as our confidence that Christians can be formed by the actual understanding of the text. Scripture's message is not understood by means other than Scripture.

Premodern Christian efforts to understand how Scripture interprets Scripture charitably attended to the potentially unitive and consensual reading of Scripture's teaching, all the while presuming that the essential clarity of Scripture would not prohibit but encourage one's awareness of Scripture's judgments. Modern criticism endeavors to suppose conceptual clarity (usually historical in preference) that in turn determines (i.e., vitiates) the significance and judgment of other texts (what they can possibly mean is specified by means of the abstractly clear interpreting the textually unclear). Theologically unitive readings of divergent texts (divergent in conceptual apparatus) are methodologi-

[27]Ibid., pp. 93-97.

[28]Yeago's example is James D. G. Dunn, *Christology in the Making: A New Testament Inquiry into the Origins of the Doctrine of the Incarnation* (Philadelphia: Westminster Press, 1980).

cally precluded. A postcritical retrieval of premodern practices offers, according to Yeago, the opportunity "to inquire attentively into what the texts say and how they say it, in search of unifying common judgments which may be rendered in very diverse ways."[29]

Attending to the *circumstantia litterarum* (the way the words go) involves attention to the coherence of assertions in biblical texts; it also entails the highlight that presumably what is of interest to be understood is illumined in this manner rather than another. As Bruce Marshall offered, the plain sense of Scripture is congruous with what is most appropriate according to the whole: "No interpretation can count as an identification of the plain sense, no matter how well supported by external argument, which fails to agree with the way the words go—not simply in this or that passage, but in the scriptural canon as a whole."[30] Thus the justification of Christian claims about the text's plain sense should not maintained on strictly external grounds, nor should the plain sense be regarded as fixed or final as if it inhibits the continual assimilation of alien (externally grounded) convictions or thought.[31] The plain sense is text-bound inasmuch as it is particularly Christian, and as a theological account Scripture's plain sense delineates the patterns within which intertextuality behaves as a doctrinal convention.

Discerning Allusions

Intertextuality, in this more comprehensive sense, leads us to consider the interplay of texts seeking to exert authority and readers finding themselves at play with the texts. This is specifically accomplished through the employment of allusion: the choice of similar or identical vocabulary, similar grammatical composition or similarly formed narratives. But allusion is as much a social convention as well as it is an exhibition of textual methods and preference, as David Gunn and Danna Nolan Fewell have noted: "Allusions reflect the larger text or context of literary expression and give the reader a sense of both the commonality and the uniqueness of the work in question." In this manner, attention to allusion explores issues of immanent or textual authority:

> Stories . . . attempt to control. Allusions can provide support for social, theologi-

---

[29]Ibid., p. 96.

[30]Bruce Marshall, "Absorbing the World: Christianity and the Universe of Truths," in *Theology and Dialogue: Essays in Conversation with George Lindbeck,* ed. Bruce D. Marshall (Notre Dame, Ind.: University of Notre Dame Press, 1990), p. 94.

[31]Ibid., pp. 95-97. Marshall concludes, "If Christians find that they must consistently reject beliefs they have good reasons for holding true because they cannot successfully revise their identification of the plain sense in order to 'adapt' plausible external beliefs to the biblical text, then this would show that Christianity, and particularly the biblical text, lacks assimilative power" (p. 97).

> cal, or political claims; allusions can also be parodied or disclaimed in a story's attempt to promote a different message. In the larger corpus of biblical narrative, some connections are more apparent than others. Recognition of associations depends upon the degree to which the reader is familiar with the whole of the biblical text, the extent to which the parallels are thought to be explicit, and the willingness of the reader to consider certain narratives in conjunction with others."[32]

Intertextuality serves multiple purposes, but most prominent in the current setting, it serves as a revision in the search for Scripture's meaning, away from a strictly authorial and historical model to a literary and readerly model.

> Historical critics have been unwilling to view narratives in conjunction unless they were considered to be by the same author, in the same literary trajectory (that is, chronologically placed in the history of tradition), or obviously alluding to a literary precedent. Recent theorists have realized that many texts compete, whether or not they have had historical contact. It is this competing of texts that makes intertextual reading an enlivening, if unsettling, process.[33]

In this light, attention to historical interests by Christian interpreters, usually considered in the form of authorial intent, is a commendable overreaction to the fragmented regard for how meaning and reading Scripture are to be regarded. It is commendable because genuine texts are circumstantially and historically authored, but it is an overreaction because it tends to undermine the very premise that gives it significance, namely the *text* that is of concern to understand. Ultimately, competent historical critics seek "in the text something that is not the text, something the text of itself, is not seeking to provide."[34] Gadamer's characterizations of historical critics are widely regarded as accurate: "He will always go back behind [the texts] and the meaning they express to enquire into the reality they express involuntarily." The effect is important: interpretation "is necessary where the meaning of a text cannot be immediately understood. It is necessary wherever one is not prepared to trust what a phenomenon immediately presents to us."[35] Consequently, while we are routinely confronted with general proposals or an assumption regarding textuality, real-

---

[32] Gunn and Fewell, *Narrative in the Hebrew Bible,* p. 163.

[33] Ibid., p. 165.

[34] Frank Kermode, "The Canon," in *The Literary Guide to the Bible,* ed. Robert Alter and Frank Kermode (Cambridge, Mass.: Harvard University Press, 1987), p. 607.

[35] Hans-Georg Gadamer, *Truth and Method,* trans. Joel Weinsheimer and Donald G. Marshall, 2nd ed. (New York: Crossroad, 1989), p. 336. Gadamer continued, "The psychologist interprets in this way by not accepting the expressions of life in their intended sense but delving back into what was taking place in the unconscious. Similarly, the historian interprets the data of tradition in order to discover the true meaning that is expressed and, at the same time, hidden in them."

ism and clarity, the particular Christian concern over Scripture's clarity, although incidentally sharing these common assumptions, disavows that these matters are being simply religiously employed. They seem analogous (as we learned in chapter four regarding the matter of translations), but the clarity of Scripture and the clarity of texts generally differ in that the specific claims of texts, including Scripture, are not incidental to their meaning.

Gadamer, commenting on Rudolf Bultmann, has put the matter this way: understanding texts involves a living relationship between the reader and the text, and relates to the previous connection with the matters the text deals with (what Bultmann referred to as fore-understanding, or that which does not simply result from understanding but is already presupposed).[36] Understanding Scripture "presupposes a relationship with the content of the Bible."[37] This presupposition derives from our relation to the text itself; "thus, the hermeneutical significance of fore-understandings in theology seems itself theological."[38]

What this discussion provides is a way to understand the analogous relationship of clarity and texts in diverse fields such as philosophy, literature and theology. Clarity may be a very common presumption in these fields, just as obscurity is the presumption of some forms of historically critical models, but what one actually declares is rendered clearly by a text is not a different matter than what the text is about and a manner of expressing one's relationship with the text. And the confession of Scripture's clarity is not simply a matter of superficial textuality, precisely because what Scripture provides is transformative rather than simply informative (e.g., the assertions of Jn 5:38-39; Rom 1:16; 1 Cor 1:18).

As an example, in this setting intertextuality serves to discipline the manner in which we might regard authors and characters in Scripture. Biblical personalities and authors are constituted more so by their storied character than by an existence independent of the text (e.g., the way David is treated in Acts 2 and Abraham in James 2). It is in this manner that the importance of the author is recognized: storied character (i.e., on occasion an author explicitly but usually

---

[36]Ibid., p. 331.

[37]Ibid., pp. 331-32. Gadamer offers, "Hence the presupposition that one is moved by the question of God already involves a claim to knowledge concerning the true God and his revelation. Even unbelief is defined in terms of the faith that is demanded of one. The existential fore-understanding from which Bultmann starts can only be a Christian one."

[38]Ibid., p. 332. Gadamer also noted that since Christian theologians maintain "Scripture is the word of God . . . that means it has an absolute priority over the doctrine of those who interpret it. . . . Interpretation should never overlook this. Even as the scholarly interpretation of the theologian, it must never forget that Scripture is the divine proclamation of salvation. Understanding it, therefore, cannot simply be a scientific or scholarly exploration of its meaning" (p. 331).

anonymously or implicitly) is persuasive in that we are taught by the text to care who is speaking and about whom.[39] Instead of exhibiting the modern preoccupation with individuals, biblical texts (especially narrative texts) may actually display a tendency to resist this understanding. So Robert Alter offers:

> Biblical tradition itself went to great lengths to hide the tracks of the individual author. There is no proclamation of authorship, no notion of literary contests as among the Greeks, no hint of any individual writer aspiring to eternal fame through literary achievement (a recurrent topos and governing idea of Western literature). Instead, the writer disappears into the tradition, makes its voice his, or vice versa.[40]

Observations of a biblical text's own use of sources and interaction with characters, stories and recurrent themes presume an intertextual construct, often leading to the neglect of factors that presumably characterize a perspicuous text.

One obvious demonstration will suffice at this point (it is so obvious it almost seems self-serving): the person known as Melchizedek. Scant remarks, thin descriptions and oblique references hardly make for a reliable biography or characterization. How much should one infer from silence after all? When Abram returned from the defeat of kings with his nephew Lot, his path crossed that of a priest-king named Melchizedek, received a blessing from this king of Salem bearing bread and wine, and proceeded to give Melchizedek a tenth of his spoils (Gen 14:18-20). Later we read a cryptic notation from a Davidic psalm:

> The LORD has sworn and will not change his mind: "You are a priest forever, in the order of Melchizedek." (Ps 110:4)

Who was Melchizedek? (A better form of the question would be: Who *is* Melchizedek?)[41] When we cross the path of Melchizedek again, the letter

---

[39]So "to be sure, the self, as speaker or writer, is not the transcendent, self-sufficient entity that the devotees of nineteenth-century romantic hermeneutics had hypothesized. To this extent, the decentering of the self offers an important correction. However, this does not justify the assumption that audiences do not care who is speaking, nor that all arguments are simply manifestations of societal and structural power. While admitting the force of the postmodern critique of the autonomous self, we can still attempt to construct a notion of personhood that can account for the personal and directed nature of discourse. The speaker is certainly not the purely autonomous entity that many Enlightenment thinkers (both rationalists and romantics) imagined. Nevertheless, the speaker still remains a concrete locus to whom character is attributed" (David S. Cunningham, *Faithful Persuasion: In Aid of a Rhetoric of Christian Theology* [Notre Dame, Ind.: University of Notre Dame Press, 1990], p. 109).

[40]Robert Alter, *World of Biblical Literature* (New York: BasicBooks, 1992), pp. 2-3. Also consult D. N. Fewell, ed., *Reading Between Texts: Intertextuality and the Hebrew Bible* (Louisville: Westminster John Knox, 1992).

[41]Alter reminds us that there is no simple either-or between storied characters and real historical people in biblical narratives: "The real point, I think, is that they are both at once, and that double identity is the source of their special authority, even for the reader who is not prepared to refer them to the category of revelation" (*World of Biblical Literature*, p. 209).

"to the Hebrews" reintroduces him:

> This Melchizedek was king of Salem and priest of God Most High. He met Abraham returning from the defeat of the kings and blessed him, and Abraham gave him a tenth of everything. First, his name means "king of righteousness"; then also, "king of Salem" means "king of peace." (Heb 7:1-2)

All is well and good to this point (except that Abram is now regarded as Abraham by the Hebrews text, a consistent matter in Hebrews). The account of Melchizedek's identity from Genesis is fairly represented, even with some interpretative comments on the etymology of his name. Similarities with Philo's treatment of Melchizedek concern the etymological sense of his name and title, although the similarities in the allegorical treatment in Philo and Hebrews does not go much further.[42] However, Hebrews takes up where few of us could have possibly imagined:

> Without father or mother, without genealogy, without beginning of days or end of life, like the Son of God he remains a priest forever. . . . This man, however, did not trace his descent from Levi, yet he collected a tenth from Abraham and blessed him who had the promises. . . . He of whom these things are said belonged to a different tribe, and no one from that tribe has ever served at the altar. For it is clear that our Lord descended from Judah, and in regard to that tribe Moses said nothing about priests. And what we have said is even more clear if another priest like Melchizedek appears, one who has become a priest not on the basis of a regulation as to his ancestry but on the basis of the power of an indestructible life. (Heb 7:3, 6, 13-16)

Do we really doubt that Melchizedek had a physical mother and father or that they had a genealogy? (Or was he, as some have supposed, a theophany?) How does what Moses wrote as well as did not write, even about birth and death—two certain matters in ordinary understanding—regulate what is to be known about this figure? What we learn is that the typical employment of Melchizedek is not dependent upon historically determined matters or information available other than in the authoritative text, and the authorial authority of Moses is confined to the text itself, even to the extent that what the text describes and does not describe is what Moses said or did not say. The christological arguments of Hebrews aside (i.e., Heb 5:6, 10; 7:23-28; 9:11-14), the employment of a textual or typical life seems to transcend even matters of life and death. And as a type of Jesus Christ the significance of Melchizedek is manifold; the latter is made like the former. But in this respect even "our Lord"

---

[42]F. F. Bruce, *The Epistle to the Hebrews* (Grand Rapids, Mich.: Eerdmans, 1964), pp. 133-60; Harold W. Attridge, *The Epistle to the Hebrews: A Commentary on the Epistle to the Hebrews* (Philadelphia: Fortress, 1989), pp. 186-95.

has a genealogy, though Melchizedek does not, according to the biblical chronicle.

Is this a fair example? It seems so extreme. The power of this sample is not that it is so provocative (which it is) but that it is so explicit whereas what is assumed in the preponderance of biblical allusions and explicit quotations is subtle but nonetheless provocative. Theologically, the obvious self-interest displayed in quotation and allusion is taken as sufficient display of the text's demeanor—its self-attesting clarity. In his confrontation with Erasmus, Luther chides, "What are the apostles doing when they prove what they preach by the Scriptures? Is it that they want to hide their own darkness under greater darkness?" He concludes: "Does not all this prove that the apostles, like Christ himself, appealed to Scripture as the clearest witness to the truth of what they were saying? With what conscience, then, do we make them to be obscure?"[43]

Literary critics attentive to the nature of the Bible as literature have pointed out the routine formation and reformation of the literary tradition of the Hebrew Bible. Robert Alter remarked that the Hebrew Bible, "because it so frequently articulates its meanings by recasting texts within its own corpus, is already moving toward being an integrated work, for all its anthological diversity."[44] Alter's work on allusion in the Bible refers to three basic categories: "local allusion for the definition of theme, allusion dictated by actual continuity and narrative reenactment, allusion to models as part of an ideological argument." But there are no fixed or rigid formulas that biblical allusions appear to follow. The life of the text, so to speak, is rather founded in what Alter refers to as "ideological models" or the recurring employment of the formative authority of certain texts, certain characters and certain circumstances governed by the transparency of allusions that is only possible when the "overarching unity" of the materials is presumed.[45] Even explicit recollections or quotations, not so much allusions as the formal aspects of literary technique, only work when this unity is presumed (e.g., 2 Chron 36:20-21; Acts 2:16; and Heb 2:6; 4:4).[46]

Its Own Light

It is in this vein—the suspicious and mysterious recasting of authored texts—

---

[43]Martin Luther, "On the Bondage of the Will," in *Luther and Erasmus: Free Will and Salvation,* ed. Gordon Rupp and Philip Watson (Philadelphia: Westminster Press, 1969), pp. 161-62.

[44]Alter, *World of Biblical Literature,* p. 51. This theme is also the focus of Northrop Frye, *The Great Code: The Bible and Literature* (New York: Harcort Brace Javanovich, 1982).

[45]Alter, *World of Biblical Literature,* pp. 117, 128.

[46]"Whereas . . . patterns of repetition, tension, contradiction or omission were when within the historical paradigm as evidence of sources and perhaps clumsy or unfinished editing, within the literary paradigm these very same features acquired an entirely positive significance" (Anthony Thiselton, *New Horizons of Hermeneutics* [Grand Rapids, Mich.: Zondervan, 1992], pp. 49-50).

that the Christian assertion concerning a relationship between the human author and the divine Author is so important, especially in reference to the prophetic office or utterance. So Karl Barth offered, "All the explanations of Scripture for which we are responsible can only be undertaken on the presupposition that Scripture is clear in itself as God's Word. . . . And all scriptural exegesis for which we are responsible can only lead to the threshold beyond which Scripture is clear in itself as God's Word."[47] But the path forward in our explanation of these assertions traverses the theological conception of the relationship between God and prophet (or spokesperson); and that relationship is simply not equal, and our confession is that such a relationship is not coterminous (e.g., Is 40:6-8; 55:8-11). When asserting that God is Scripture's Author, we do not mean that God is simply another author; we may speak of "double agency" or "double speaking" instead of a double author.[48] Indeed, we should distinguish the relationship of God's and humans' discourse in the "voice" of Scripture but not so as to have one without the other.[49] An example of this might be addressed by 2 Peter 1:19-21:

> And we have the word of the prophets made more certain, and you will do well to pay attention to it, as to a light shining in a dark place, until the day dawns and the morning star rises in your hearts. Above all, you must understand that no prophecy of Scripture came about by the prophet's own interpretation. For prophecy never had its origin in the will of man, but men spoke from God as

---

[47]Barth, *Church Dogmatics*, I/2, p. 712.

[48]For a provocative, even if overstated, account of the relationship of God as author and authority of Scripture and the biblical text's reference to authority, see Sternberg, *Poetics of Biblical Narrative*, pp. 58-83. For a critique of Sternberg's views, see Nicholas Wolterstorff, *Divine Discourse: Philosophical Reflections on the Claim That God Speaks* (Cambridge: Cambridge University Press, 1995), pp. 240-60.

[49]Wolterstorff comments, "Biblical prophecy, as recorded for us in the prophetic books of the Old Testament, regularly moves back and forth in just this way between the prophet speaking in the name of God by virtue of having been deputized to do so, the prophet speaking in his own voice but delivering a message from God, and the prophet speaking in his own voice and not delivering a message from God." He notes that prophets can be said to be "commissioned" to communicate by God, and "deputized" so that what as communicated "God is then and there once again saying that very same thing." And commenting on Deuteronomy 18 he notes, "The prophet is one who speaks *in the name of* God. As a consequence, those who hear the prophet speaking, when he is speaking in his prophetic capacity, are confronted with that which counts as God speaking; the utterances of the prophet are the medium of God's discourse." And "the biblical notion of the prophet blends the concept of one who is commissioned to communicate a message from someone, with the concept of one who is deputized to speak in the name of someone. The prophet, speaking in the name of God, communicates a message from God. Hence it's true for a double reason that hearers are confronted with 'the word which the Lord has spoken.' It's true for a double reason that obedience to the message of the prophet is not a matter of obeying the prophet but a matter of obeying God" (*Divine Discourse*, pp. 45-48).

they were carried along by the Holy Spirit.

When the prophets spoke, God was speaking, and the present community actually has a better viewpoint of a certain word being even more certain (interestingly, even if separated from the apostolic witness, 2 Pet 1:15).[50]

Instead of confusing God's speaking with human speaking, the Protestant tradition focuses upon the theological orientation "that it is God's Word in human form." So Karl Barth offered, "What makes the Word of God, in the form in which we encounter it, obscure and in need of interpretation are the ideas, thoughts and convictions which man always and everywhere brings to this Word from his own resources." The trouble rests, then, with the ordinary human circumstance of understanding: "We are laden with the images, ideas and certainties which we ourselves have formed about God, the world and ourselves."[51] The word is clear in itself—it is objectively perspicuous because it is God's word to us—but it is mediated by human words and obscured by human understanding, though not in its form as human words. The testimony of the apostles and prophets—the mediating form of God's word—has become "capable of explanation."[52]

We do find in Barth, as in Calvin, an admission that the characteristic human experience is one of "darkness" to which the prophetic word is likened to a "light shining in a dark place." Calvin remarked, "I therefore extend this darkness, mentioned by Peter, to the whole course of life" and the resolution of the contrast of darkness and light to the eschatological realization of the "morning star." The figure of "light shining" is contrasted to the perpetual darkness and obscuring experience of the human moral (or to put the matter Christianly, spiritual) condition in death:

---

[50]Calvin noted, "The meaning is, that the beginning of right knowledge is to give that credit to the holy prophets which is due to God. He calls them the *holy men of god,* because they faithfully executed the office committed to them, having sustained the person of God in their ministrations. He says that they were *moved*—not that they were bereaved of mind, (as the Gentiles imagined their prophets to have been,) but because they dared not to announce anything of their own, and obediently followed the Spirit as their guide, who ruled in their mouth as in his own sanctuary. Understand by *prophecy of Scripture* that which is contained in the holy Scriptures" (John Calvin, *The Epistles of Paul the Apostle to the Hebrews and the First and Second Epistles of St. Peter* [Grand Rapids, Mich.: Eerdmans, 1963], pp.343-44; from his comments on 2 Pet 1:21).

[51]Karl Barth, *Church Dogmatics*, I/2, p. 716. Barth continued, "In the fog of this intellectual life of ours the Word of God, which is clear in itself, always becomes obscure."

[52]Ibid., p. 717. While not wholly satisfying according to our discussion of textuality in chapter six, Barth's characterization of the witness of the Word to the words of scripture and its clarity displays the integral link of his revelational objectivism (God's identity in relation to us) and soteriological objectivism (our identity in relation to God), as noted by George Hunsinger, *How to Read Karl Barth: The Shape of His Theology* (New York: Oxford University Press, 1991), pp. 76-151.

> Peter . . . intimates that all are immersed in darkness who do not attend to the light of the word. Therefore, except you are resolved willfully to cast yourself into a labyrinth, especially beware of departing even in the least thing from the rule and direction of the word. Nay, the Church cannot follow God as its guide, except it observes what the word prescribes.[53]

There is no remedy to this obscuring darkness by leaving the text—its rule and direction—in favor of an explanation that does not agree with the nature of Scripture as the text of the Spirit of God.[54] And contrary to suspicions regarding the readers' condition (which Calvin admits as universal precisely because of the universality of human sin as the hindrance of understanding), the Christian reader stands in a unique position of certainty, being able to see prophecy self-fulfilled or fulfilling itself because it is its historical and spiritual fulfillment that renders the prophetic word clear to the Christian reader.

To Calvin, the struggle with certainty, understanding and obscure or illumined readings are moral and spiritual in nature. The contrast is between the profanity of "whatever men bring of their own" and what arises from the Spirit-awareness of the text itself. The denial of "private" interpretation in 2 Peter is a contrast, not between individual ideas and the church as a whole but between understanding that arises from a differing source than the Spirit in the text: "because the Spirit, who spoke by the prophets, is the only true interpreter of himself."

> This explanation contains a true, godly, and useful doctrine,—that then only are the prophecies read profitably, when we renounce the mind and feelings of the flesh, and submit to the teaching of the Spirit, but that it is an impious profanation of it, when we arrogantly rely on our own acumen, deeming that sufficient to enable us to understand it, though the mysteries contain things hidden to our flesh, and sublime treasures of life far surpassing our capacities. And this is what we have said, that the light which shines in it, comes to the humble alone.[55]

There is an admission in Calvin's comments that the negation "no prophecy of Scripture came about by the prophet's own interpretation" can just as easily

---

[53]Calvin, *Epistles of St Peter,* p. 342 (from his comments on 2 Pet 1:19).

[54]Luther concurs with this characterization: "With these words all the fathers who interpret Scripture in their own way are refuted, and their interpretation is invalidated. It is forbidden to rely on such interpretation. If Jerome or Augustine or anyone of the fathers has given his own interpretation, we want none of it. . . . The Holy Spirit Himself must expound Scripture. Otherwise it must remain unexpounded. Now if anyone of the saintly fathers can show that his interpretation is based on Scripture, and if Scripture proves that this is the way it should be interpreted, then the interpretation is right. If this is not the case, I must not believe him" (Martin Luther, *Luther's Works,* ed. Jaroslav Pelikan, 56 vols. [St Louis: Concordia, 1955-1976], 30:166).

[55]Calvin, *Epistles of St Peter,* p. 343, from his comments on 2 Pet 1:20.

be taken to refer to the source of Scripture as a text itself as it can to refer to evaluating our understanding of Scripture. But these are not two different choices for Calvin because understanding the nature of Scripture as text is not different from the exercise of understanding the text itself:

> The faithful, inwardly illuminated by the Holy Spirit, acknowledge nothing but what God says in his word. However, another sense seems to me more simple, that Peter says that Scripture came not from man, or through the suggestions of man. For you will never come well prepared to read it, except you bring reverence, obedience, and docility; but a just reverence then only exists, when we are convinced that God speaks to us, and not mortal men. Then Peter especially bids us to believe the prophecies as the indubitable oracles of God, because they have not emanated from men's own private suggestions.[56]

Christian theology regards the unity of God and the prophetic voice in text to be essential. From texts such as 2 Peter 1:19-21 Luther advised that understanding Scripture was not at the disposal of the human reader without God's explanation as well as aid: "If God does not open and explain holy writ, no one can understand it; it will remain a closed book, enveloped in darkness."[57] Luther mused, "Scripture is its own light. It is a fine thing when Scripture explains itself."[58] It is Luther's understanding that "God gives His Word and the interpretation too."[59] The reader is not passive, but the reader endures a moral struggle concerning being ductile toward the text properly understood.[60]

Clarity is closely related to a matter of perspective in relation to the text; it has far more to do with the reader than one would casually assume. Seeing something clearly concerning Scripture is, simply put, a matter of perspective, spiritual or moral—that is, not simply circumstantial (Acts 26:17-18; 2 Cor 3:1—4:7; Eph 3:3-10; 1 Pet 1:10-12). Through the employment of a model of progress of revelation or the genuinely historical unfolding of revelatory understanding in texts, a Christian reading of Scripture is understood to become more direct, explicit and clear according to this suggestion. In this relationship of natural or

---

[56]Ibid., p. 343, from his comments on 2 Pet 1:21.

[57] Luther, *Luther's Works,* 13:17. The quote, commenting on Psalm 68:14, reads, "These bishop-kings do not only step forward freely and courageously and expose themselves to danger on behalf of the sheep of Christ, instead of running for cover, as the herdsmen, the greedy, and the hirelings (John 10:12) usually do. But they also have a clear view and understanding of their teaching and are able to expound and explain the obscure verses of Scripture. Christ refers to this in John 10:3, where He says that the gatekeeper, the Holy Spirit, will open the door to those that enter. For if God does not open and explain Holy Writ, no one can understand it; it will remain a closed book, enveloped in darkness" (13:16-17).

[58]Quoted in A. Skevington Wood, *Captive to the Word: Martin Luther, Doctor of Sacred Scripture* (Grand Rapids, Mich.: Eerdmans, 1969), p. 162.

[59]Luther, *Luther's Works,* 7:151, from his comments on Gen 41:25.

[60]Ibid., 3:168.

common knowledge of God and special knowledge in Scripture, the latter is always regarded as clearer than the former.[61]

As for the conceptual relationship of divine revelation in the Christian texts, this relationship is addressed by referring to God's accommodation in expression to human capacity with regard for our circumstances, aptitude and temperament. As Calvin said, "For who even of slight intelligence does not understand that, as nurses commonly do with infants, God is wont in a measure to 'lisp' in speaking to us?" Thus we must not confuse understanding by means of God's accommodation with understanding God's real existence, nor can we transcend God's accommodation to arrive at a greater or loftier manner of understanding. We are, simply put, responsible for what is known and knowable by means of God's accommodation to our circumstance. With Calvin this is not simply a theory of how language functions, although Calvin envisions the insufficiency of language as such to traverse the inestimable distinction between God and human beings. Instead he likened the realization of accommodation to the entirety of the Christian understanding of the world, and God's accommodating "forms of speaking do not so much express clearly what God is like."[62] Calvin saw Scripture as just one instance of God's accommodating to the human circumstance—a circumstance most evident in our sluggishness in moral capacity and our blurredness in vision.[63]

---

[61]"Just as the old bleary-eyed men and those with weak vision, if you thrust before them a most beautiful volume, even if they recognize it to be some sort of writing, yet can scarcely construe two words, but with the aid of spectacles will begin to read distinctly; so Scripture, gathering up the otherwise confused knowledge of God in our minds, having dispersed our dullness, clearly shows us the true God. . . . He has from the beginning maintained this plan for his church, so that besides these common proofs he also put forth his Word, which is a more direct and more certain mark whereby he is to be recognized" (John Calvin, *The Institutes of the Christian Religion,* ed. John T. McNeill, trans. Ford Lewis Battles [Philadelphia: Westminster Press, 1960], p. 70).

[62]Calvin's argument, in full, is directed against those who fail to recognize the language of accommodation when speaking of God and thus "imagined a corporeal God from the fact that Scripture often ascribes to him a mouth, ears, eyes, hands, and feet. . . . Thus such forms of speaking do not so much express clearly what God is like as accommodate the knowledge of him to our slight capacity. To do this he must descend far beneath his loftiness" (ibid., p. 121).

[63]Ford Lewis Battles, *Interpreting John Calvin,* ed. Robert Benedetto (Grand Rapids, Mich.: Baker, 1996), p. 130. He noted, "We are here, cautioned by Calvin's own self-warning, to seek after a definition of divine accommodation that neither repudiates the anthropomorphisms of Scripture in our quest of pure Spirit, nor so clings to the anthropomorphic mode of thought and worship as ourselves, veiled by flesh, to lose sight of our God. In the divine rhetoric accommodation as practiced by the Holy Spirit so empowers the physical, verbal vehicle that it leads us to, not away from, the very truth. Thus accommodating language and the truth to which it points are really a unity. One cannot say this of the tempered speech of human rhetoric" (p. 136).

Conclusion

Thus far it is obvious that the contemporary concern for reading the Bible as literature, as one book, as a work, as a literary and classical text, raises important questions about the subject of Scripture's clarity. As John Barton notes, "One very salutary effect of this fresh enthusiasm for the Bible as text, despite the difficulties already hinted at, is that it sets a high premium on what used to be called the perspicuity of Scripture."[64] (What "*used* to be called"? How, then, should we refer to this today?) Both in terms of its self-glossing character, and in the actual use readers make of it, Scripture is regarded as perspicuous. We must then begin with Scripture's clarity, not arrive at a conclusion of its clarity in order to proceed.

---

[64]John Barton, *People of the Book? The Authority of the Bible in Christianity* (Louisville: Westminster John Knox, 1988), p. 61.

8

READING WITH CLARITY

The secret things belong to the Lord our God, but the things revealed belong to us and to our children forever, to observe all the words of this law.

DEUTERONOMY 29:29

But here you will say, "All this is nothing to me; I do not say that the Scriptures are obscure in all parts (for who would be so crazy?), but only in this and similar parts." I reply: neither do I say these things in opposition to you only, but in opposition to all who think as you do; moreover, in opposition to you I say with respect to the whole Scripture, I will not have any part of it called obscure. What we have cited from Peter holds good here, that the Word of God is for us "a lamp shining in a dark place" (2 Peter 1:19). But if part of this lamp does not shine, it will be a part of the dark place rather than of the lamp itself. Christ has not so enlightened us as deliberately to leave some part of his Word obscure while commanding us to give heed to it, for he commands us in vain to give heed if it does not give light.

MARTIN LUTHER, "ON THE BONDAGE OF THE WILL"

WHEN WE SPEAK OF SCRIPTURE'S CLARITY, WE REFER TO THE RELATIONship of the text and the readers. We confess that the text's relationship with Christian readers and Christian readers' relationship with the text is described in terms of the light of the text and the enlightenment of the readers. We seek to occupy the landscape of the text's vision—to live as those whose way in the world is created by the text itself. In this respect Christians have been interested in the ethics of the interpreter, not just the ethics of interpretation.[1] The confession of clarity has as much to do with the reader but always with an affinity to the text. So, Luther contended, "If Scripture is obscure or equivocal, why need it have been brought down to us by act of God? Surely we have enough obscurity and uncertainty within ourselves, without our obscurity and

[1]Exemplary of this historical and literary orientation to the reader is Jeffrey's work; see his chapter "Literary Theory and the Broken-Hearted Reader," in *People of the Book: Christian Identity and Literary Culture,* ed. David Lyle Jeffrey (Grand Rapids, Mich.: Eerdmans, 1996), pp. 353-73.

uncertainty and darkness being augmented from heaven!"[2]

Often, and unfortunately, the kind of orientation to the textuality of Scripture that I am developing in these chapters is accused of isolating the text in an uncritical manner as if the text were a repository of self-sufficient meaning. This approach is accused of objectifying and thereby removing the text from historical constraints (like the authors' intent) or from the readers' frames of reference (the readers' perception or textual affectionalism). But as we have noted, texts (especially Scripture for Christian theology) involve and seek to create their own social space. Scripture is to us "a light shining in a dark place" (2 Pet 1:19). In addition, Christian interpretation has always addressed the readers' contribution to, setting in relation to, or meaning or creating reception of Scripture. It is our commitment that "the revealed things belong to us and to our children forever, to observe all the words of this law" (Deut 29:29).

In light of the unfortunate polarization of text and reader, literary critic and theorist William Spurlin has drawn a useful distinction between strict textual autonomy and strict authority of the readers' response. Instead of following a text-reader polarization more characteristic of reader-response theories (advocated by Stanley Fish), Spurlin suggests we draw our attention to the *relation* of reader to text and concentrate on reader *reception*. Instead of the "radical displacement of the locus of interpretive authority from the text to the reader and by extension the reader's interpretive community," he directs our attention to the role of the text in reading.[3] The text-reader relation is not so much a problem to be solved (like a whodunit detective story or murder mystery) as it is a necessary condition of addressing understanding and meaning in relation to texts.[4] By following Spurlin's

---

[2]Martin Luther, "On the Bondage of the Will," in *Luther and Erasmus: Free Will and Salvation*, ed. Gordon Rupp and P. Watson (Philadelphia: Westminster Press, 1969), p. 163.

[3]William J. Spurlin, "New Critical and Reader-Oriented Theories of Reading: Shared Views on the Role of the Reader," in *The New Criticism and Contemporary Literary Theory: Connections and Continuities*, ed. William J. Spurlin and Michael Fischer (New York: Garland, 1995), pp. 234-35; also see William J. Spurlin, "Theorizing Signifyin(g) and the Role of the Reader: Possible Directions for African-American Criticism," *College English* 52 (November 1990): 732-42.

[4]Interestingly, Spurlin suggests that the polarization between objective paradigms in criticism occur most prominently in reactions to New Criticism and the type of textual orientation addressed in these chapters, especially in the (extremes) of authorial intentionalism from the likes of E. D. Hirsch and P. D. Juhl. Likewise, suspicions of objectivism prompted the development of subjective forms of criticism (like Stanley Fish's reader-response discussions) to lessen the perceived hegeonomy of text oriented emphases. That is, the characterizations offered by literary theorists often succumb to a simplistic, and political charged, either-or adversarial critique. Spurlin noted, "I am proposing that this all-or-nothing logic is problematic and that any responsible discussion of reading must discern, at least, a reader *and* a text, which is not only the project of work on reader reception, but of the New Criticism as well" (Spurlin, "New Critical and Reader-Oriented Theories," p. 234); he appeals, in support of this observation, to a provocative work by Tzvetan Todorov, *Literature and Its Theorists: A*

suggestions we will consider how the Christian interpretive interest in the perspicuous appreciation, reception and response to Scripture can be better understood. To put the matter in the setting of Christian theology, it is not accidental that the subject of Scripture's clarity was such a disputed and essential subject in Luther's encounter with Erasmus concerning the nature of the human will.

Looking for a Response

The interest in the relationship of text and reader—the functional and (for Christians) salvific interest in Scripture—directs our attention toward a doctrine of Scripture that does not consider the nature of Scripture in isolation from its readers. (Books are made for human readers, after all, not human readers for books.) When we speak of readers, we do not merely mean Scripture's audience, as in the historical setting of a text's first readers, but those who can and should read it profitably. But we must also face the suspicion that this turn to the text and the perspicuous nature of the relationship of the reader and the text is a rejection of the *possibility* of arguing for a fixed and stabilizing manner of discerning how we understand texts, including Scripture.

Reversing the hermeneutical interest from authorial, historical backgrounds to the reception of texts among readers seems to render the character of the text itself inconsequential and its influence insignificant or tenuous. Adopting a stress on reading, the competency of the reader, and the interaction between the reader and text involves a shift away from a privileged role for formal (maybe even positivistic ideas concerning) "understanding."[5] Thus so-called reader response models of criticism are viewed with great suspicion. What Christians do with the relationship of Scripture as text and the hermeneutics of understanding (a theory of how we know and therefore understand) is illustrative of this dilemma. Contemporary biblical and literary criticism wrestles with the relationship of texts and readers, often with exaggerated denials of text in favor of reader. When addressed from a theological perspective, the relationship of texts and readers challenges the traditional affirmation that Scripture is a means of God's address to Christians (does God speak by means of Scripture? or, is the reading of Scripture simply a reflection of the readers' sensibilities?). Even the rather mild use of reader response criticism by biblical scholars,

---

Personal View of Twentieth-Century Criticism, trans. Catherine Porter (Ithaca, N.Y.: Cornell University Press, 1987).

[5]"The literary paradigm of 'reading' has an advantage over more traditional hermeneutical theory in focusing attention on semiotic reading-competencies and the inter-active dimensions of reading between the reader and the text. But in exchanging it for 'understanding' the privileged status of its function at certain times and in given cases as an epistemological medium or disclosure-medium is in danger of being lost from view" (Anthony Thiselton, *New Horizons in Hermeneutics* [Grand Rapids, Mich.: Zondervan, 1992], pp. 501-2).

which is most often simply oriented to a reaffirmation of historical criticism by finding the original readers, is still generally thought to threaten the notion that God speaks by means of the text of Scripture to the Christian reader.[6] We are still faced with the need to discern the theological relationship between Scripture and Christian readers, without losing our focus on Scripture as text. "Reading the Bible to discern what God said or is saying by way of the text is obviously different both from reading it to discern the literary qualities of the text and from reading it to discern the theology of the biblical writers. . . . Nonetheless, these interpretative practices share in common their focus on the text itself—the text we have."[7]

In order to understand what Christians mean when we claim that God speaks by means of the text of Scripture, Nicholas Wolterstorff builds upon a distinction between locutionary and illocutionary actions from the speech-action theory of J. L. Austin. A locutionary act is simply uttering or inscribing words, but an illocutionary act is performed by way of a locutionary act: "Illocutionary acts are related to locutionary acts by way of the *counting as* relation." Illocution is a functional concept. It is regarded as authorization for response. The possibility that Christians understand God to speak by illocutionary acts, "leaving it open how God performs those actions," offers Wolterstorff an opportunity to argue that God communicates by speaking, commanding and promising: God appropriates Scripture as an instrument of discourse.[8] Wolterstorff's argument leads us away from confusing the agency of text/textualism, author/Author and interpreter/interpretation, and opens a way to address the unity or relationship of what *Scripture says* and what *we do with* what it says.[9]

Anthony Thiselton seized upon the notion of illocutionary acts to portray how Protestants, especially Luther, employed the clarity of Scripture to encour-

---

[6]George Aichele, ed., *The Postmodern Bible: The Bible and Culture Collective* (New Haven, Conn.: Yale University Press, 1995).

[7]Nicholas Wolterstorff, *Divine Discourse: Philosophical Reflections on the Claim That God Speaks* (Cambridge: Cambridge University Press, 1995), p. 17.

[8]Ibid., pp. 33-36, 75.

[9]Ibid., p. 20. Wolterstorff's argument is as follows: "It is sometimes said that the Bible—be it now the Hebrew Bible or the Christian Bible—that the Bible is God's book. By which is not meant that the Bible is *a collection* of books by God, God's *opera omnia*. . . . What is meant is that . . . the Bible is *one* book of God. I suggest that the most natural way of understanding this claim is to understand it in terms of divinely appropriated human discourse. . . . It's not very plausible to understand it as God just taking some text, however produced, and doing something so as to bring it about that those words serve as the medium of divine discourse. For what the writers *said* matters, that is, it matters what illocutionary acts they performed: what they were referring to, where they were speaking literally and where metaphorically, what cosmological picture served as background to their discourse, and so forth" (ibid., pp. 53-54).

age readers that there is sufficient authorization to act on the text's plain or natural meaning. It is this emphasis on clarity as functional and efficacious. We must then naturally ask, sufficient or efficacious for what? "The answer in the context of epistemology would be: Scripture provides a ground on which we may confidently *proceed*. The context in theology would be: Scripture provides a witness to Christ to which we may confidently *respond*."[10] Perspicuous is how we characterize the affinity of Scripture and Christian readers.[11]

The relationship of illocutionary actions and Scripture's clarity is amply demonstrated in the famous, yet very odd text of Psalm 119—famous because it is the longest of the Psalms as well as one of the most elaborate, odd because it describes a loving and effervescent vulnerability to statutes, commandments and law! Its basis is the unity of God's desires and laws, and the responsiveness of God's faithful: "You are good, and what you do is good; teach me your decrees" (v. 68). The psalm is a meticulous work of devotion, assurance and hopeful prayers for enlightenment:

> Open my eyes that I may see
> wonderful things in your law.
> I am a stranger on earth;
> do not hide your commands from me. (vv. 18-19)
> Let me understand the teaching of your precepts;
> then I will meditate on your wonders. (v. 27)
> Teach me, O LORD, to follow your decrees;
> then I will keep them to the end.
> Give me understanding, and I will keep your law
> and obey it will all my heart. (vv. 33-34)

---

[10]Thiselton, *New Horizons,* pp. 184-85, emphasis his.

[11]Perspicuity, as a principle on which Christians act confidently (that is, in faith) on God's word, is a significant and yet ancillary matter to the experience of the text as God's word. So Luther noted of the somewhat strange language of Psalm 119:105. "A wonderful statement! Why not a lamp to my eyes and a light for seeing? Can feet be lighted or the paths see? But the nature of faith for this life is expressed. For eyes must be taken captive to the obedience of Christ and be led by the Word alone, which is perceived by the ears and is not seen with the eyes. For we believe the invisible but not the inaudible. . . . Therefore the Word of God, which gives light to the feet and the paths, is wonderful. Not so the word of the letter and of human wisdom, which empties faith, because it makes faith understanding what it says and because it shows itself to be a lamp to the eyes. Then it is not free not to say, 'a lamp for the paths and a light to the feet.' For the Word encloses the light as the lamp does the candle, and this for the feet. But for the paths the light is not thus enclosed. Why this? . . . [W]hen you have begun to walk and to do what you believe, then the way is recognized more clearly than your feet recognize it, so that you have the light more brightly as a result of believing with the heart alone. . . . The doers are much more enlightened in faith than the speculative, as even the philosopher [Aristotle] says in his *Metaphysics* [I.1], than an experienced person acts more surely" (Martin Luther, *Luther's Works,* ed. Jaroslav Pelikan, 56 vols. [St Louis: Concordia, 1955-1976], 11:485-86).

Your hands made me and formed me;
give me understanding to learn your commandments. (v. 73)
I am your servant; give me discernment;
that I may understand your statutes. (v. 125)

It appears that the psalmist has every intention of following, acting on and obeying as well as loving, rejoicing and hoping in God's ways, commands and laws. The one so devoted comes close to fusing or merging love of God with love of God's law but so as to express devotion, never confusing God with God's law: "In the night I remember your name, O LORD, and I will keep your law" (v. 55), "Your are my portion, O LORD; I have promised to obey your words" (v. 57), and "Your righteousness is everlasting righteousness and your law is true" (v. 142).

The dilemma, and our question, has to do with this assertions that God's law is true, trustworthy or truth (vv. 86, 138, 142, 151 and 160; as well as righteous, v. 7; good, v. 39; even eternal, v. 89). How can a command be *truth?* C. S. Lewis put it this way:

> A modern logician would say that the Law is a command and that to call a command "true" makes no sense; "The door is shut" may be true or false but "Shut the door" can't. But I think we all see pretty well what the Psalmists mean. They mean that in the Law you will find the "real" or "correct" or stable, well-grounded, directions for living.[12]

One can argue that for God's commands to be both "commands" and "true" has to do with how well such speech acts function for or among the responsive;[13] and this may correspond with what the psalm suggests.[14] Thus love and

---

[12]C. S. Lewis, *Reflections on the Psalms* (London: Geoffrey Bles, 1958), pp. 60-61. He continued: "There are many rival directions for living, as the Pagan cultures all round us show. When the poets call the directions or 'rulings' of Jahweh 'true' they are expressing the assurance that these, and not those others, are the 'real' or 'valid' or unassailable ones; that they are based on the very nature of things and the very nature of God."

[13]So Paul Ricoeur suggests, "In the case of an order, when I tell you to close the door, for example, 'Close the door!' is the act of speaking. But when I tell you this with the force of an order and not of a request, this is the illocutionary act. Finally, I can stir up certain effects like fear by the fact that I give you an order. These effects make my discourse act like a stimulus producing certain results" ("The Model of the Text: Meaningful Action Considered as a Text," in *Interpretive Social Science: A Reader,* ed. Paul Rabinow and William M. Sullivan [Berkeley: University of California Press, 1979], p. 76).

[14]Austin posed a distinction between constative language (which strives to be accountable to objective reference) and performative language (which is circumstantial and depends upon meaning already present and judged appropriate or inappropriate accordingly) and concluded that all language is performative. "It is essential to realize that 'true' and 'false' . . . do not stand for anything simple at all but only for a general dimension of being a right and proper thing to say as opposed to a wrong thing in these circumstances, to this audience, for

obedience toward the law are not simply conformity but transformative in relation to God.[15] It is through the confident postulate of God's perspicuous word that the psalm recounts that therein is "light" found: "Your word is a lamp to my feet and a light for my path" (v. 105), and "The unfolding of your words gives light; it gives understanding to the simple" (v. 130). Asserting the clarity of God's law is not a different matter than asserting the confident means of expressing a love of God's law, attending to God's law is not a different matter than loving God, and reference to God's word as light is not a different matter than the means by which one loves God.[16]

The confession of Scripture's clarity is not equivalent to an assertion about how language in general functions or how Scripture is reliable compared to other writings, but it does assert that Scripture does with certainty accomplish its purpose (cp. Is 55:10-11). Scripture *works* with regard to the readers and hearers of the text; it is clear to those who with due appreciation and expectation attend to its transforming potential. As Anthony Thiselton proposes, we can regard Scripture's focus as "transactional," at least in certain respects.[17] It is essential within the Christian commitment to Scripture to be vulnerable to (and find the ways in which we are made vulnerable to) the text that confronts in order to clarify. For example, it was Bonhoeffer's suggestion that we seek to read Scripture "over against" rather than simply "for" ourselves.[18] This being

---

these purposes and with these intentions" (J. L. Austin, *How to Do Things with Words,* ed. J. O. Urmson and Marina Sbisà, 2d ed. [Cambridge, Mass.: Harvard University Press, 1975], p. 144). Thus illocutionary acts have force not as something it exerts but something it has by its appropriate execution and has to do with the way an utterance is taken; see Stanley Fish, *Is There a Text in This Class? The Authority of Interpretive Communities* (Cambridge, Mass.: Harvard University Press, 1980), pp. 221-22.

[15]This suggestion is from Walter Brueggemann, *Interpretation and Obedience: From Faithful Reading to Faithful Living* (Minneapolis: Fortress, 1991), p. 155.

[16]Kort's examples of "The Appearance of God in Narrative Form," his chap. two, offers a suggestive recommendation to address the unity of the love of God, the love of God's narrative, the love of God's law and the appropriate nature of this relationship (in terms of character, atmosphere and tone); Kort, *Story, Text, and Scripture: Literary Interests in Biblical Narrative* (University Park: Pennsylvania State University Press, 1988), pp. 24-49.

[17]Ibid., p. 32. Or as Nancey Murphy suggests, following J. L. Austin, getting the meaning of a text is " 'orationalized' as a communal (shared, intersubjective) response to the text—a living of its import rather than a mere hearing of it" ("Textual Relativism, Philosophy of Language and the Baptist Vision," in *Theology Without Foundations: Religious Practice and the Future of Theological Truth,* ed. Stanley Hauerwas, Nancey Murphy and Mark Nation [Nashville: Abingdon, 1994], p. 261).

[18]Dietrich Bonhoeffer, "The Presentation of New Testament Texts," in *No Rusty Swords,* trans. E. H. Robertson (London: Collins, 1970), pp. 302-20. Bonhoeffer's suggestion that we expose ourselves to reading Scripture "over against" instead of "for" ourselves is reminiscent of the convention of regarding Scripture as confrontational: "Either I determine the place in which I find God, or I allow God to determine the place where he will be found. If it is I who say

the confessional ambition, actual commitments vary concerning how this might be the case, especially apparent in our observations about the reader and what it means to read in a certain way (i.e., Christianly).

Looking for a Text *and* a Class

A consistent criticism of an emphasis on text[19] rests on the assumption that it neglects the reader and the influence of interpretation, that the reader or interpreter is something to be feared and even avoided! The *cure* for this anxiety is captured by Stanley Fish's essay "Introduction, or How I Stopped Worrying and Learned to Love Interpretation."[20] Instead of fixating on objective and unaffected texts, Fish argued that meaning is an event, something that happens, not on the page, where we are accustomed to look for it, but in an interaction between the flow of print and the actively mediating consciousness of a reader.[21] Form matters because it can aid us in our response to a text, but Fish avoided the biographical and historical fallacy of attributing meaning to the author, passed on the option of attributing meaning to the text and instead located meaning in the mind in the act of reading. The meaning of a text, its value or significance, Fish argued, is not *in* the text, but texts are valued and thus understood in a manner that cannot be simplistically influenced by the text.[22]

This influential community, to Fish, is not a specific group but the assumptions we take to be important and obvious or self-evident (perspicuous?): "It is interpretive communities, rather than either the text or the reader,

where God will be, I will always find there a God who in some way corresponds to me, is agreeable to me, fits in with my nature. But if it is God who says where He will be, then that will truly be a place which at first is not agreeable to me at all, which does not fit so well with me" (Dietrich Bonhoeffer, *Meditating on the Word* [Cambridge: Cowley, 1986], pp. 44-45).

[19]Stanley Fish reported the origin of the title to a prominent work of his as follows: "On the first day of the new semester a colleague at Johns Hopkins University was approached by a student who, as it turned out, had just taken a course from me. She put to him what I think you would agree is a perfectly straightforward question: 'Is there a text in this class?' Responding with a confidence so perfect that he was unaware of it (although in telling the story, he refers to this moment as 'walking into the trap'), my colleague said, 'Yes; it's the *Norton Anthology of Literature*,' whereupon the trap (set not by the student but by the infinite capacity of language for being appropriated) was sprung: 'No, no,' she said, 'I mean in this class do we believe in poems and things, or is it just us?' " (*Is There a Text in This Class?* p. 305).

[20]Ibid., pp. 1-17; Fish details his conversion from thinking in terms of the "fallacies."

[21]Stanley Fish, *Surprised by Sin: The Reader in Paradise Lost* (New York: St. Martin's Press, 1967), p. x.

[22]Fish, *Is There a Text in This Class?* chaps. 15-16. It has been noted of Fish's model: "Even the identification of what might seem the most objective, incontrovertible characteristics of a text is always already an interpretation by a reader" (Aichele, *Postmodern Bible,* p. 30).

that produce meanings."[23] To Fish we are not left with relativism and subjectivity (we are not isolated in interpretation). There is an objectivity in judgment according to Fish, in a manner of speaking, but the correctness of reading must be judged in accordance with the reading community, and illumination is derived from recognizing the implicit beliefs, norms and values all readers necessarily hold.[24] There is "never a moment when one believes nothing, when consciousness is innocent of any and all categories of thought, and whatever categories of thought are operative at a given moment will serve as an undoubted ground."[25]

So Fish tells us that readers are participants in certain communities but formed without historical determinatives (we cannot avoid being influenced; we are often influenced without being aware; such influences are unchangeable). There is neither an autonomous text nor an autonomous reader. The reader does not decode a text; the reader creates a text. By working from assumptions about texts, combined with expectations about what must be found therein, we proceed to find these expectations (met) in the text. We have a reader (which is significant in her social setting) and a text (but one that is not simply significant in itself). Fish undermines textual autonomy and authorial intent by locating meaning in the interpretive community (thus, Fish's model asserts a social model of reading competence that derives from participating in a cultural tradition).[26] And genuine reader-response criticism, to Fish, eschews any premise that the reader is simplistically constrained by textual givens; it is not the case that there is simply text and nothing else.[27] Thus Fish

---

[23]Fish continued, "To put it another way, the claims of objectivity and subjectivity can no longer be debated because the authorizing agency, the center of interpretive authority, is at once both and neither" (*Is There a Text in This Class?* p. 14).

[24]We shouldn't think of Fish's work in isolation from its conversation with Fish's own education and background at Yale, under the tutelage of New Critics such as Cleanth Brooks, as well as Fish's continued interaction with the intellectual underpinnings of New Criticism. David Hirsch noted that Fish practiced new criticism "with a slightly different rhetorical posture. . . . What Fish actually did in his criticism was to seek out image patterns, ironies, and paradoxes, just as the New Critics had instructed him, but instead of attributing 'meanings' to an author or a text, he attributed meanings to the mind in the act of reading" (David H. Hirsch, *The Deconstruction of Literature: Criticism After Auschwitz* [Hanover, N.H.: University Press of New England, 1991], p. 4). Maybe Fish should be regarded as a *new* New Critic.

[25]Fish, *Is There a Text in This Class?* p. 320. Due credit is given to Wesley Kort's treatment of Fish; his insightful treatment of Fish for the purpose of constructing a doctrine of Scripture forms the basis for this evaluation of Fish regarding clarity.

[26]The characterization of Fish's model of reader-response critical theory as social, in relation to psychological or intersubjective models, is derived from Michael Vander Weele, "Reader Response Theories," in *Contemporary Literary Theory: A Christian Appraisal,* ed. Clarence Walhout and Leland Ryken (Grand Rapids, Mich.: Eerdmans, 1991), pp. 125-48.

[27]Fish, *Is There a Text in This Class?* pp. 2-17. The *early* Fish practices a criticism of "affective stylistics," which stressed word-for-word analysis of a text and how a reader's response

offers, "There is no such thing as literal meaning if by literal meaning one means a meaning that is perspicuous no matter what the context and no matter what is in the speaker's or hearer's mind, a meaning that because it is prior to interpretation can act as a constraint on interpretation."[28]

In practice the reading community supplies in the act of reading what a text means in that the reader's social setting performs as a constraint determining a text's understanding. Fish's advice is not relativistic in that he suggests interpretive communities do objectify their assumptions and realize (or for Christians, confess and seek to be regulated by) that norming or centering is the disciplinary goal of the interpretive community.[29] But Fish suspects that any argument that a text has a quality or value, such as the Christian assertion regarding Scripture, is an expression of closed and isolated communities of interpretation.[30] Regardless of the possibilities (or impossibilities), the Christian presumption is that to be Christian we are influenced, vulnerable and somewhat pliable in relation to a text (which forms our understanding of reading as a political exercise, and not a benign event of amusement). The commitment to Scripture as text, in itself, involves the norming premise that *we* seek our identity in the *text.* Or, as Pietist J. A. Bengel suggests, those who have been entrusted with the gift of Scripture "should make a right use of it. Scripture itself teaches what that use is, namely, to *perform* it. In order to perform it, we require knowl-

---

was scripted by the text. See his *Surprised by Sin* and *Self-Consuming Artifacts: The Experience of Seventeenth-Century Literature* (Berkeley: University of California Press, 1972). The *later* Fish rejected even this implicit dominance of the reader by the text to the observation that readers (already) dominate a text.

[28]Stanley Fish, *Doing What Comes Naturally: Change, Rhetoric, and the Practice of Theory in Literary and Legal Studies* (Oxford: Clarendon, 1989), p. 4.

[29]We should not underestimate how much Fish's argument has to do with the issue of how texts are regarded as clear or unclear; this issue of clarity is precisely what is important to Fish. He remarked, "In the view I put forward, determinacy and decidability are always available, not, however, because of the constraints imposed by language or the world—that is, by entities independent of context—but because of the constraints built into the context or contexts in which we find ourselves operating." "What this suggests is that categories like 'the natural' and 'the everyday' are not essential but conventional. They refer not to properties of the world but to properties of the world as it is given to us by our interpretative assumptions." and "That is what the ordinary is, that which appears to be there independently of anything we might say or think about it. It does not require comment . . . because it is obvious, right there on the surface; anyone can see it. But what anyone sees is not independent of his verbal and mental categories but is in fact a product of them; and it is because these categories, rather than being added to perception, are its content that the entities they bring into being seem to be a part of the world in the sense that they were there before there was anyone to perceive them. In other words, while the ordinary and the obvious are always with us because we are always in the grip of some belief or other, they can change. . . . I have lingered over this . . . because it seems to me to bear (however indirectly) on the question most frequently debated in current literary discussions: What is in the text?" (*Is There a Text in This Class?* pp. 268-72).

[30]Ibid., pp. 338-72.

edge, knowledge that is open to all who possess rectitude of heart."[31] Bengel's characterization is both charitable (the text is "open") and arduous (understanding is not detached from reading as a moral act). Attention to the text itself, as the text functions in identifying the reading community, the community's response to and appropriation of the text, forms the essential relationship of text and readers that makes a Christian reading of Scripture as text credible (Scripture is *norma normans,* or the standardizing norm, of faith). When observations about what a reader is, and what a text is, and what their possible relationship looks like actually confront the instance of reading, we still need to account for *both* reader and text.

In our appropriate concern for the ethics of the reader, the significance of the reader in the reading process, and our critical methodologies, we may actually be led to neglect the text being read. As Daniel Patte reminds us:

> Fascinated by our own interpretative prowess, we forgot that the text claims our attention, teaches us, moves us, convinces us, empowers us, or degrades us. We are oblivious to the fact that this particular text with its particular constraints affects us and has power upon us. The more we are confident of being in control of the text (for instance, as an object that we analyze in critical studies) or of the reading process, the more we submit to constraints of the text. Yes, we do initiate the reading process. But in so doing we give life back to the inert text on the page, which now takes charge by claiming our attention and calling for responses to the issues that is raises. We readers cannot but respond and react to what the text proposes to us. Because it is written, fixed on pages, the text constantly remains in control, in a position of power; it keeps the initiative, and it sets the subject matter of our dialogue.[32]

Patte urges us to bear in mind that "the text imposes constraints on the reading process"; for example, the "text demands a response from us even as we read it." Reacting to a text—positively (by adopting its encouragements or seeking to reenact its enacted patterns of behavior), negatively or indifferently (by ignoring it, rejecting it or responding with boredom or weariness)—means "we are transformed by the text." He argues, "After reading, we are no longer the same persons; we are now defined as persons who are indifferent, bored, and left weary by this specific text, its subject-matter, and/or the way it presents this subject-matter."[33]

---

[31]John Albret Bengel, *Gnomon of the New Testament,* ed. Andrew R. Fausset (Edinburgh: T & T Clark, 1866), 1:6.

[32]Daniel Patte, *Ethics of Biblical Interpretation: A Reevaluation* (Louisville: Westminster John Knox, 1995), pp. 98-99. Also consult his *Religious Dimensions of Biblical Texts: Greimas's Structural Semiotics and Biblical Exegesis* (Atlanta: Scholars Press, 1990).

[33]Patte, *Ethics of Biblical Interpretation,* pp. 97-98. He continues, "We male European-American

What Fish alerts us to is the concern for what we do with texts, not simply that we are (passively) addressed by texts.[34] At stake in Fish's challenges is whether the Christian readers' relationship to the text is influenced by the formal nature of Scripture as text: whether Scriptures teaches, promises or encourages in a perspicuous manner.[35] This relationship between text and community is to be expressed in terms of a unitive evaluation:

> The normative or literal meaning must be consistent with the kind of text it is taken to be by the community for which it is important. The meaning must not be esoteric: not something behind, beneath, or in front of the text; not something that the text reveals, discloses, implies, or suggests to those with extraneous metaphysical, historical, or experiential interests. It must rather be what the text says in terms of the communal language of which the text is an instantiation.[36]

Our concern is not with the either-or anxiety over the text *or* the class but with the genuinely critical interaction (self-aware and self-critical) of text *and* reader.

The Clarity of Reading

Be assured that Fish does have his own version of textual clarity and obscurity, not simply found in reader subjectivity but in the actual use of actual texts: "It is important to realize what my argument does *not* mean. It does not mean that a sentence can mean anything at all." He offers, "Any reading that is plain and obvious in the light of some assumed purpose (and it is impossible not to assume one) is a literal reading; but no reading is *the* literal reading in the sense that it is available apart from any purpose whatso-

---

critical exegetes commonly presuppose that we are in control of a reading process in which the text is passive when we strive to be self-conscious about our role in this process, for instance, by using critical methods and justifying their use. Such presuppositions are plausible, based as they are on the strong evidence of the readers' role. Yet they fail to raise seriously the issue of the role and power-authority of the text—especially, the power of a classic such as the Bible. Forgotten, ignored, suppressed, the power-authority of the text can exert itself in complete freedom upon us as critical readers; we confuse the effects of the text upon us with our interpretive abilities."

[34]"The reader's response is not to the meaning, it is the meaning" (Fish, *Is There a Text in This Class?* p. 3).

[35]This notion coincides with Thiselton's characterization of Luther's debate with Erasmus and it offers a strong defense of the epistemological nature of Scripture's clarity: "Luther develops this strategy [about Scripture's clarity] as a polemic against Erasmus in the context of theories of knowledge. Erasmus argued that the biblical texts offer insufficient coherence and clarity to offer a firm *basis for action.* Luther insisted that such a suspension of judgment constituted a self-defeating paralysis. He urged that the way ahead was always clear enough to indicate the next practical step" (Thiselton, *New Horizons,* p. 23).

[36]George Lindbeck, *The Nature of Doctrine: Religion and Theology in a Postliberal Age* (Philadelphia: Westminster Press, 1984), p. 120.

ever."[37] It is not that some uses of language are ambiguous; for that to be the case there would necessarily be "sentences that always and only mean one thing, and I would contend that there are no such sentences." Fish offers his conclusion: "I am as willing to say that all sentences are straightforward as I am to say that all sentences are ambiguous. What I am not willing to do is say that any sentence is by right either one or the other. That is, I wish to deny that ambiguity is a property of some sentences and not of others."[38] What is plain and perspicuous about a text is not simply a matter of subjectivity; the awareness of clarity is actually unawareness—it is so natural that one's reading might not even be construed as an interpretation! Thus, obscurity would be unnatural.

We can very easily perceive the pressure that is exerted upon proponents of one type of reading, a pressure that would exclude any sense of ambiguity because such an admission would implicitly challenge the convictions that make a reading appear clear in the first case. To say that Scripture is obscure is inconsistent with the conviction that Scripture provides any reliable awareness of Christian identity, thus Luther "will not have any part of it called obscure," and he is able to claim (quite naturally and obviously for him) that "Scripture is the clearest book in the world."[39] The same conviction is present in Zwingli as well:

> We should hold the Word of God in the highest possible esteem—meaning by the Word of God only that which comes from the Spirit of God—and we should give to it a trust which we cannot give any other word. For the Word of God is certain and can never fail. It is clear, and will never leave us in darkness. It teaches its own truth. It arises and irradiates the soul of man with full salvation and grace. It gives the soul sure comfort in God. And in God the soul lives, searching diligently after him and despairing of all creaturely consolation. For God is its only confidence and comfort. Without him it has no rest: it rests in him alone (Ps 77): "My soul refused to be comforted; I remembered God, and was refreshed." Blessedness begins indeed in this present time, not essentially, but in the certainty of consoling hope. May God increase it in us more and more, and never suffer us to fall from it. Amen.[40]

---

[37]Stanley Fish, "Normal Circumstances, Literal Language, Direct Speech Acts, the Ordinary, the Everyday, the Obvious, What Goes Without Saying, and Other Special Cases," in *Interpretative Social Sciences,* ed. Paul Rabinow and William M. Sullivan (Berkeley: University of California Press, 1979), pp. 253, 261.

[38]Ibid., p. 254.

[39]Luther, "Bondage of the Will," p. 163; and from James Samuel Preus, *From Shadow to Promise: Old Testament Interpretation from Augustine to the Young Luther* (Cambridge, Mass.: Harvard University Press, 1969), p. 253.

[40]Ulrich Zwingli, "The Clarity and Certainty of the Word of God," in *Zwingli and Bullinger,* ed. and trans. G. W. Bromiley (Philadelphia: Westminster Press, 1953), p. 93.

There is no mistake about this: Scripture's clarity is a particularly religious judgment of how the text and its (proper) readers relate. Perspicuity is not one element of the interpretation of Scripture; it is inherent in the very conviction that we should be attentive to Scripture in a manner that corresponds with what the text purports to represent. But this does not mean that the Christian admission of perspicuity is generally a quality of all writings, nor of all readings, but that at least it is the case that Christian readings of Scripture are inherently oriented to what we confess to be Scripture's clarity. (This may also be in contrast to all other readings; however, it is attributable to God through the Spirit rather than simply our construal of the text, its message [if that is different from the text], or the meaning assigned to the text by an authorizing body.)

So Fish offers his own confession of textual clarity, so obvious to the readerly oriented critical community: "A sentence is never not in a context. We are never not in a situation. . . . A set of interpretative assumptions is always in force. A sentence that seems to need no interpretation is already the product of one."[41] For our purposes we observe that however we conceive of the relationship of text and reader—and there are many such ways within and without the Christian tradition—we are disciplined by the question of readerly concern for clarity and obscurity and the corresponding concern for the influence of the text upon readers. The question is not whether Scripture in isolation from Christian readers means something clearly to anyone in general but whether the relationship of Scripture and Christian readers is understood as a relationship illumined by means of the relationship of text and readers.[42]

---

[41]Fish, "Normal Circumstances, Literal Language," p. 257.

[42]For example, a perennial censure of New Critics (and formalism generally) is the tendency to "exclude interpretive activity altogether." Poland argued that because New Critics and theologians indebted to them, such as Hans Frei, argued that a text's meaning is its realistic or ostensive sense (that of the text itself), this meant that they advocated a naive a-interpretive position. She said of Frei's assertion that if the text literally means what it says, "then all the readers of the Gospels would interpret them the same way." In one sense Poland is correct (as is Frei): the Gospels *are* about Jesus Christ when understood *literally,* and all interpreters do, at least tacitly, agree that literally the Gospels are about Jesus Christ. (What Frei wants us to understand is that *literally* is also *consensually* a Christianly practice.) Lynn M. Poland, *Literary Criticism and Biblical Hermeneutics: A Critique of Formalist Approaches* (Chico, Calif.: Scholars Press, 1985), pp. 135-36; also see David Tracy, "Literary Theory and Return of the Forms for Naming and Thinking God in Theology," *Journal of Religion* 74, no. 3 (1994): "Surely Hans Frei . . . [was] not wrong to insist that God's identity is Christianly established in and through the passion narrative's rendering of the identity of and presence of Jesus as the Christ" (p. 310); and George Lindbeck, "Scripture, Consensus, and Community," in *Biblical Interpretation in Crisis,* ed. Richard John Neuhaus (Grand Rapids, Mich.: Eerdmans, 1989): "The biblical message as classically interpreted is relatively stable: what chiefly changes are the philosophies and other culturally conditioned outlooks which are interpreted within the framework" (p. 88).

To Interpret or Not to Interpret

This raises a more routine topic, one that hits at the heart of conservative biblical scholarship, concerning the necessity of interpretation. Denials of the need to interpret biblical texts are pious to some (biblicists), painfully simplistic to others (the academy) and occasionally still part of how the evangelical community views interpretation.[43] A recent Bible translation's advertisement reads "Now no interpretation needed."[44] F. F. Bruce, hardly a lightweight in evangelical circles, advised us that the interpretation of the Bible is an "explanation of what is not immediately plain in the Bible."[45] Another biblical scholar offered an analogy concerning his own work and the Bible's clarity: "In writing this book I am seeking to make its meaning clear. It should not require interpretation; interpretation is needed only when something is unclear. If scripture is clear in meaning, why does it require interpretation?"[46] This is, in effect, an argument that Scripture is clear and unclear in its outward qualities as language, that clarity has to do with clarity of locution (what is said, understandable, historically or among the readers), rather than clarity of illocutionary significance (addressing the unity of the message expressed and its reading). The question of a need to interpret also reflects a naive view of language functioning as value or culture-neutral symbol system readily transparent to readers (or even to the point of confusing what Luther referred to as the outer and inner clarity of Scripture).

To be fair, there is a tendency within Luther's characterizations of Scripture's clarity that comes close to a naive view concerning the need for interpretation. Luther objected when, in principle, the comparison of a clear text and an obscure text was allowed to continue endlessly. So Luther derided those who had a habit of obscuring sufficiently clear passages:

> The result of this method will be that no passage of Scripture will remain certain and clear, and the comparison of one passage with another will never end. . . . To demand that clear and certain passages be explained by drawing in other passages amounts to an iniquitous deriding of the truth and injection of fog into the light. If one set out to explain all passages by first comparing them with other passages, he would be reducing the whole of Scripture to a vast and uncertain chaos.[47]

---

[43]See James Callahan, "The Bible Says: Evangelical and Postliberal Biblicism," *Theology Today* 53 (January 1997): 449-63.

[44]World published the translation *God's Word* with the cover reading "Today's Bible translation that says what it means." The advertisement noted: "The Bible: the all-time bestseller—but hardly the best understood. *God' s Word:* the revolutionary new translation that allows you to immediately understand exactly what the original writers meant."

[45]F. F. Bruce, "Interpretation of the Bible," in *Evangelical Dictionary of Theology,* ed. Walter A. Elwell (Grand Rapids, Mich.: Baker, 1984), p. 565.

[46]John Goldingay, *Models for Scripture* (Grand Rapids, Mich.: Eerdmans, 1994), p. 346.

[47]Luther cited in A. Skevington Wood, *Captive to the Word: Martin Luther, Doctor of Sacred*

Yet Luther maintained that the other extreme was to ignore the whole of Scripture: "Well known is the stupidity of the ostrich, which thinks it is totally covered when its head is covered with some branch. Thus a godless teacher seizes upon one particular saying of Scripture and thinks his notion is fine, not noticing that he is maintaining his position as one who is bare and unarmed on every side."[48] The tension, Luther noted, was not so much between clear and obscure texts as it was a matter of contrast between "the plainest testimonies of Scripture" and those "intoxicated with their own ideas."[49] On occasion the interpreter must simply leave "the Scriptures uninterpreted," as when Scripture refers to the subjects of the unity of God and the trinity of persons *rather than* pushing the text beyond what it clearly explains.[50] That is, Luther did not so much argue that clarity was simply the opposite of interpreting, but the clarity of the text was evidently that which was consistent with a Christian reading of Scripture.

Even in Luther's more acerbic moments, he did not abandon the thought that the confession established the right understanding of Scripture with Scripture as a "touchstone." If the choice was between church and Scripture, then Luther responded with an either-or alternative, deciding against the institutional church: "When anything contrary to Scripture is decreed in a council, we ought to believe Scripture rather than the council."[51] Scripture, for Luther, was *norma normans non norma normata* (Scripture was an unregulated regulator, by it everything was to be judged but nothing might judge it). And yet, even this was not a simplistic dismissal of interpreter and interpretation, authority and church, but instead much closer to a reliance upon Scripture *in* (the faithful) tradition.[52] Often Luther's polemical tone is taken to be an absolute polarization of Scripture to the exclusion of church, but Luther's distinctions concern priority and authority, and were tempered by his differentiation concerning the institutional church and the fellowship of the Spirit. Councils might clarify con-

---

Scripture (Grand Rapids, Mich.: Eerdmans, 1969), p. 162.

[48]Luther, *Luther's Works,* 9:35, cf. 24:104.

[49]Ibid., 16:242.

[50]Ibid., 34:228.

[51]Ibid., 32:81.

[52]An essentially accurate theological assessment of the relationship of Scripture, the church and tradition is offered by David Tracy's unitive model of *Scripture in tradition.* Instead of an absolute dismissal of theological setting and influence in the simplistic Protestant use of *Scripture alone,* and also instead of the older Roman Catholic *Scripture and tradition,* Tracy observes that the appeal to Scripture's plain sense is best demonstrated by its association with the plain *ecclesial* sense. See David Tracy, "On Reading the Scriptures Theologically," in *Theology and Dialogue: Essays in Conversation with George Lindbeck,* ed. Bruce D. Marshall (Notre Dame, Ind.: University of Notre Dame Press, 1990), p. 38; *The Analogical Imagination: Christian Theology and the Culture of Pluralism* (New York: Crossroad, 1981), pp. 233-339.

troverted matters, but where Scripture was plain, there was no need to wait for councilor confirmation: "I refuse to wait until councils decide whether we are to believe in God the Father, Maker of heaven and earth, in his only Son, Jesus Christ our Lord, in the Holy Ghost, etc. The same applies as well to all other manifest, clear, and certain portions of Scripture which it is needful and profitable for me to believe."[53]

The revolution known as the Reformation is extraordinary because Scripture was employed as the instrument of reform—it is not so much that Luther severed Scripture from the church (or even tradition) but that he believed that Scripture was the source of reform for the church because the church owes its identity to Scripture.[54] Luther merely codified the perennial tension concerning a proper reading of the Bible and the Bible's own authority, suggesting that Scripture's clarity was understood to address this tension.[55]

The contrast between clarity and interpretation also misconstrues the very idea of reading; it assumes that reading is value free or neutral rather than ideological. Russian literary critic Mikhail Bakhtin encouraged us to think of all reading as translation. Discourse, he argued, is marginal in that it "lives, as it were, on the boundary of its own context and another, alien context."[56] Thus, every use of a word is a recontextualization that complicates rather than simplifies our understanding of texts.

The most basic assertion of a Christian reading of Scripture is a caution, warning us not to move beyond the congruity of how we regard the text as clear and Scripture's nature as text. Scripture as its own grammar or rule means we perceive that the meaning of the biblical text is the text itself, established by the text itself and understood by attending to how we read the text as Christians. This type of suggestion is abundantly demonstrated by David Dawson's case concerning how Christian "readers" can be understood by observing the

---

[53]This quote is found within this comment: "In matters where we can plainly see what is God's word and will, we will not wait for the decrees and decisions either of councils or of the church; we will rather fear God, and go right ahead and act accordingly before the question is even raised whether councils should be called or not. . . . Suppose the councils should delay, and I should have to die before they could make up their minds. What would become of my soul, meanwhile, since it is not supposed to know what to believe but to await the decision of councils, when I need faith here on earth?" (Luther, *Luther's Works,* 45:148).

[54]See Jaroslav Pelikan, *The Reformation of the Bible, the Bible of the Reformation* (New Haven, Conn.: Yale University Press, 1996).

[55]"Not until the Protestant Reformation is the literal sense understood as authoritative—because perspicuous—in its own right, without authorization from the interpretative tradition" (Hans W. Frei, *Theology and Narrative: Selected Essays,* ed. George Hunsinger and William C. Placher [New York: Oxford University Press, 1993], p. 123).

[56]Mikhail M. Bakhtin, *The Dialogic Imagination: Four Essays,* ed. Michael Holquist, trans. Caryl Emerson and Michael Holquist (Austin: University of Texas Press, 1981), p. 284.

relationship of literal and allegorical meaning in contrast to Jewish and Gnostic "readers." What makes one a Christian reader is not a hermeneutical theory about how texts function, or even about what Scripture obviously means, but it is about how Christians read differently (i.e., Christianly). Reading itself is a political act, not immune from prejudice and without a soul if it lacks genuine partiality. Dawson's argument is not about whether a text possesses a specific meaning but how the "honorific title" of "literal sense" is "given to a kind of meaning that is culturally expected and automatically recognized by readers. . . . The product of a conventional customary reading."[57]

What "makes" a text clear or obscure has much to do with the reading community itself, how Scripture is made use of as text, and how the politics of reading as a community formed by its common reading informs our understanding of Scripture, which functions as perspicuous. Stanley Hauerwas sets his argument against both extremes, conservative and traditional liberal views of biblical criticism in the modern era: their "most prominent shared assumption is that the interpretation of the biblical texts is not a political process involving questions of power and authority. By privileging the individual interpreter, who is thought capable of discerning the meaning of the text apart from the consideration of the good ends of a community fundamentalists and biblical critics make the Church incidental."[58] To understand the Scripture's "meaning" is simply not the objective practice of the critically qualified; thus Hauerwas rejects the presumption that the Bible should be read like any other book as well as the "sin of the Reformation," which is the assertion of *sola Scriptura* that serves to sever Scripture from "a Church that gives it sense." It is simply absurd to continue the "heresy" that the Bible is interpreted solely "on its own terms."[59] "Meaning," Hauerwas maintains, is discerned within the appropriate reading community: "The Church, through the guidance of the Holy Spirit, tests contemporary readings of Scripture against the tradition."[60]

Dismissing the faithful interpretative community in favor of an objectivity of historical situation, authorial intent or aesthetic textuality is equivalent to Luther's suspicions regarding an institutional church that mediated (controlled and interpreted for the reader) Scripture under its guise. The choice goes beyond whether one interpretative community or another is privileged; it goes to a contrast between a community self-critically informed by Scripture as nor-

---

[57]David Dawson, *Allegorical Readers and Cultural Revision in Ancient Alexandria* (Berkeley: University of California Press, 1992), pp. 7-8, 235-40.

[58]Stanley Hauerwas, *Unleashing the Scripture: Freeing the Bible from Captivity to America* (Nashville: Abingdon, 1993), pp. 25-27.

[59]Ibid., pp. 25, 155.

[60]Ibid., p. 27.

mative and norm in text, or a community authorized by historical or despotic (arbitrary, nontextual) authority.[61]

These are the issues that the likes of Fish and Bakhtin can alert us to. The very nature of telling adopted by biblical texts, but certainly not only by such texts, indicates that we are listening in on another's conversation, and we choose to include ourselves in the company of the readers of biblical texts. Historically these texts are only indirectly ours but still ours as the rightful heirs to their reading.[62] "It is not that believers understand some new propositional content unknown to unbelievers or to enquirers; it is that . . . they perceive themselves as *recipients or addressees*."[63] We are told of others' lives, others' faith and the demands of the gospel on others, and we infer (by faith) how such directions are ours, but within that presumption we are not to add to, nor take away from, what is written but perform and show ourselves to be faithful interpreters (doers) of the text (as in Deut 4:2 and Rev 22:18-19).

Texts as Prepared for the Reader

Without reverting to confusing a text's meaning with the author's meaning, literary criticism concerned with fiction has suggested a manner of regarding how a text entails both the invocation and the evocation of a proper response but without necessarily confusing one for the other (as we saw in Luther and

[61]Note Alter's observations: "The consideration of authority in interpretation, though paramount for both Christian and Jewish tradition, would seem to be no more than vestigially pertinent to modern secular readers, and perhaps to many modern religious readers as well. Apart from religious fundamentalists and certain intellectual sectarians within the academic world, few readers today look to an institution or authoritative figure that will serve as arbiter of interpretation, fixing its rules and procedures and licit range of application. What we share as interpreters in place of such authority are certain tacit or explicit preferences dictated by the spirit of the age—like the fondness for the concrete (which in fact will inform much of my own argument) that can be related to the modern attachment to archaeology as model and metaphor for grasping the past; and like the postmodern avidness for any kind of reading that will destabilize or multiply meanings" (Robert Alter, *The World of Biblical Literature* [New York: BasicBooks, 1992], p. 89).

[62]These themes have been developed in critical efforts to understand fiction, the novel and similar genre; see Seymour Chatman, *Story and Discourse: Narrative Structure in Fiction* (Ithaca, N.Y.: Cornell University Press, 1978); R. Alan Culpepper, *Anatomy of the Fourth Gospel: A Study in Literary Design* (Philadelphia: Fortress, 1983).

[63]Thiselton, *New Horizons*, p. 598. He is referring to the work of Wolterstorff, who argued that narrative texts do not simply function (work, causally) as propositions offered for reflection but as illocution (proposition conveyed with a certain force, as noted earlier in this chapter). Wolterstorff characterized the "world" generated by a text as an assertive, coherent narrative world that involves propositions: historical narrative is, unlike fiction, not simply a description to be considered, but involves assertive truth claims. We do not have what the text is about without the narrative world of the text See Nicholas Wolterstorff, *Art in Action: Towards a Christian Aesthetic* (Grand Rapids, Mich.: Eerdmans, 1980); *Works and Worlds of Art* (Oxford: Clarendon, 1980).

Calvin, their commitments to the unity of Scripture and the Holy Spirit addressed this question of invocation and evocation).[64] This issue is also evident in the concept of indirection; narratives, historical narratives (possibly even fiction)[65] have a manner of addressing reality and truth, but within a conversation, by means of its own structure, and as fiction, story and verse.

With the works of Wayne Booth and Wolfgang Iser, for example, we have been introduced to the notions of "implied author" and "implied reader." Booth has articulated the desire to discern by means of the author what is embedded in the text, the rhetorical strategies woven into the text, leading (hopefully) to a meeting of the minds of author and reader (but between the page and the reader, in the notion of rhetoric or fiction).[66] His is an effort to understand how a reader must play along with the text, which entails "the author's means of controlling his reader."[67] Iser, playing on Booth's term, turned to the reader implied in the text: "the predispositions laid down . . . by the text itself," which embodies "all those predispositions necessary for a literary work to exercise its effect." For Iser the implied reader "as a concept has his roots firmly planted in the structure of the text; he is a construct and in no way intended to be identified with any real reader."[68]

Iser's effort to objectify the reader as a textual artifact seeks to overcome the subjectivity that is suspiciously lurking around the interest in readers. And while a profitable indicator of the ways in which readers read texts, Iser's view of meaning transcends these seemingly modest observations about reading. Meaning is understood in terms of reference and event for Iser, that something other

---

[64]Wolterstorff helps us in this regard (invoking J. L. Austin's model of locutionary acts): "Acts of asserting, commanding, promising, and asking (when brought about by locutionary acts) are all *il*locutionary acts; by contrast, acts of communicating knowledge, when brought about by illocutionary acts, are all *per*locutionary acts." The acts of asserting can be justified by being regarded as, but not necessarily causing, a response: "Asserting, commanding, promising, and asking do not *consist in* the transmission of knowledge" (Wolterstorff, *Divine Discourse,* p. 33).

[65]Wolterstorff dislikes the supposition that fiction tells the reader to and how to respond, suggesting instead that fiction suggests actions, but historical narrative commands a proper response by its force: "Rather than asserting, the teller of fiction *invites us to imagine.* The designative content of a piece of fiction might be exactly the same as the designative content of a piece of history; what makes one fiction and the other history is simply, to say it again, the illocutionary stance taken toward that content" (ibid., p. 243). In this regard Wolterstorff praises Meir Sternberg, *The Poetics of Biblical Narrative, Ideological Literature and the Drama of Reading* (Bloomington: Indiana University Press, 1985).

[66]Aichele, *Postmodern Bible,* p. 2.

[67]Wayne C. Booth, *The Rhetoric of Fiction,* 2nd ed. (Chicago: University of Chicago Press, 1983), p. xiii.

[68]Wolfgang Iser, *The Act of Reading: A Theory of Aesthetic Response* (Baltimore: Johns Hopkins University Press, 1978), p. 34.

than the text itself is actualized when that advanced by the text is experienced by the real reader.[69] There is a critical (and historical) objectivity to discerning the implied reader and, thus, the appropriate reference and response to the text, as well as a corresponding commission of professional authority for judging any particular reading. But one cannot realize the text appropriately without this aide (thus, when this model is adopted by those advocating reader-response criticism it is nonthreatening to the contemporary academic community).[70] Iser's model is appealing to historically minded interpreters because it seeks to overcome the gap between the text and the reader who, after all, is central in this task (the text is functionally about the reader, who is its reference, implied and contemporary).[71] When employed as a theological-critical technique, interest in the implied reader recommends that what we do with a text should be regarded as an effort of faithful reflection (*nachdenken*—thinking through in correspondence with what is given), but when severed from this (theological) mooring, we are left to wonder how Scripture as text realizes its end (in a literary-critical model).[72] Implied authors and implied readers are *interpretative* constructs and as such reflect the hermeneutical conventions of the reader(s) and not simply the object of the text. As such, implied readers are a reflection of interpreters who find what is obvious, plain and clear to them in a text.[73]

The defense of our position—that regard for Scripture as text coupled with the confession that the relationship of text and reader is addressed by perspicu-

---

[69]Iser wrote, "Meaning is the referential totality which is implied in the aspects contained in the text and which must be assembled in the course of reading. Significance is the reader's absorption of the meaning into his own existence. Only the two together can guarantee the effectiveness of an experience which entails the reader constituting himself by constituting a reality hitherto unfamiliar to himself" (ibid., p. 151).

[70]The influence of reader-response criticism in biblical criticism, to date, has been exaggerated or overblown. While *concern* for the reader has been given prominence, it is still a concern for the reader implied in the text that forms the basis of the encounter of reading. See Wolfgang Iser, *Act of Reading;* and Stephen D. Moore, *Literary Criticism and the Gospels: The Theoretical Challenge* (New Haven, Conn.: Yale University Press, 1989).

[71]Aichele, *Postmodern Bible,* pp. 46-47. Also see Bernard C. Lategan and Willem S. Forster, *Text and Reality: Aspects of Reference in Biblical Texts* (Philadelphia: Fortress, 1985).

[72]For example, Powell posits that the quest for the (historical and original) implied reader leads to the pursuit of the ideal reader (the reader "described and defined entirely by the text"); while Keegan must suppose that the implied reader is the faith community, united by the Spirit in the real and inspired (implied) author and also the inspired (implied) reader. See Terrence J. Keegan, *Interpreting the Bible: A Popular Introduction to Biblical Hermeneutics* (New York: Paulist, 1985), pp. 146-55.

[73]Robert Fowler, *Let the Reader Understand: Reader-Response Criticism and the Gospel of Mark* (Minneapolis: Augsburg/Fortress, 1991), pp. 26-31; Wolfgang Iser, *Prospecting: From Reader Response to Literary Anthropology* (Baltimore: Johns Hopkins University Press, 1989); Susan R. Suleiman and Inge Crosman, eds., *The Reader in the Text: Essays on Audience and Interpretation* (Princeton, N.J.: Princeton University Press, 1980).

ity, with the attending methodological assumption that the text is the meaning of the doctrine and not the other way around—would be tenuous against a strictly historical- or literary-critical setting. Yet this manner of addressing what we observe in Scripture does not provide a causal interpretative procedure whereby we finally arrive at *the real meaning* of a text, as if by a better manner of understanding the relationship of text and reader. Objectifying the manner of understanding texts—a central, if not the central, contemporary hermeneutical task—can be easily substituted for what a text itself supposedly means. That is, the perspicuity of hermeneutics is often a substitute for the perspicuity of Scripture.

While the privilege of interpretation is founded in faith, it also entails the attending burdens, including the obligation to regard the text as prepared for the reader. Privilege, obligation and devotion are at the heart of a Christian reading of Scripture. Christian strategies of reading the Bible have, at times, and should return to, emphasized interpretation as a matter of testimony and conviction, rather than simply the decoding of a text's information in relationship with the author's world.[74] We are not innocent nor are we ideal readers: it takes a willful reading of faith to read the Bible as *Scripture.* We are not faced with a choice between text and reader, but our concern is with how *Christian readers* regard and makes use of Scripture as *text.* How, constructively, the text-reader relationship is realized within Christian theology is the subject of the next chapter.

Conclusion

The relationship between our understanding of Scripture and the orientation to Scripture as text is a matter of the discerning what Scripture is *about.* What it is about, to many, is its meaning, but caution should be exercised at this juncture. What Scripture is about is, simply put, what it is about (and not its meaning as if meaning were something separable from Scripture itself). That is, Scripture's meaning is not a different matter than what we have by means of the text. Or, one could say: Scripture is not about meaning, but its meaning is what Scripture is about. But this does not presume to neglect what is involved in reading Scripture inasmuch as the purposeful reading of Scripture is nothing less than a *reading.* And reading Scripture *as* a unified, intertextual, self-referring and perspicuous whole is our manner of affirming that Scripture *is* the Word of God. To this topic—reading Scripture as God's word—we turn in the next chapter.

---

[74]The works of Brueggemann, Kermode, and Ricoeur are, for different reasons, suggestive of how we might construe reading biblical texts in relationship to the will. See Brueggemann, *Interpretation and Obedience;* Frank Kermode, *The Sense of an Ending: Studies in the Theory of Fiction* (New York: Oxford University Press, 1967); Paul Ricoeur, *Fallible Man* (New York: Fordham University Press, 1986); *Oneself as Another* (Chicago: University of Chicago Press, 1992).

9

SCRIPTURE'S INTRATEXTUALITY

The unfolding of your words gives light; it gives understanding to the simple.

PSALM 119:130

The text speaks of a possible world and of a possible way of orienting oneself within it. The dimensions of this world are properly opened up by, disclosed by, the text.

PAUL RICOEUR, "THE MODEL OF THE TEXT"

THE THEOLOGICAL APPRECIATION FOR THE TYPE OF PRECRITICAL INTERPRETAtive interests we have been pursuing—the clarity of Scripture understood by means of Scripture's texture—may be able to find a home within a postcritical hermeneutical landscape (with a shared admission of critical self-interest and the ethical recognition of plain or ordinary readings). Instead of seeking *the* comprehensive hermeneutical model, which is just as positivistic, objectivistic and biased in liberal as well as conservative circles, postcritical biblical interpretation seeks to recognize the consequence of critical self-interest (and recognizing my particularity as well as others'), rather than renouncing the prejudice of advocacy interpretations. While we may never feel *at home* in this setting, our comfort is not of concern but is rather an indication that we are at present living in the circumstances of having to find our own way once again (having faltered in our attempts to provide political cohesion, certitude and foundations in the cultural project of modernity and Western Christendom). It is precisely in the shifting landscape of current hermeneutical paradigms that specificity is required from those who would espouse a uniquely theological understanding of the interpretation of Scripture. This is especially the case in light of the lingering suspicion in critical circles that uniquely theological interests are insipidly naive, and that there is a genuine difference between informed and enlightened critical interpretations of Scripture and plain and ordinary readings.

Ordinary *and* Critical Readings

In Daniel Patte's revisioned ethical paradigm "plain or ordinary readings" are regarded as routine. For Patte, all readings that appear as routine or ordinary are founded upon preunderstandings, prejudices and interests as conditions for understanding rather than obstacles to understanding. Instead of "critical and uncritical" readers, Patte shifts his concern to the relationship of "critical and ordinary" readers as differing instances of advocacy. We are led to concede that "faith-interpretations" of devotional, idiosyncratic and instinctive types (even extreme fundamentalistic types to Patte) are "legitimate" "ordinary readings" in that they seek to account for an experience of the "power-authority" of the text.[1] The problem with "faith-interpretations" is not that they are generated on the premise of certain faith commitments or that they are justified within a certain view of Scripture's power (authority) but that this experience of the text is "universalized"—it is championed as one-dimensional or *the only* correct experience (understanding) of Scripture.[2]

Essential to Patte's admission of guilt in his own practices of critical interpretation is the admission and examination of our preunderstandings and historicity as essential to the self-critical task. Thus, the phenomenon of interpretation expresses our interests that are only properly understood as "in front of" the text.[3] What makes a reading "ordinary" and "self-evident" has to do with the interpreter's perspective (as we saw in chapter eight concerning Stanley Fish),

---

[1]Daniel Patte, *Ethics of Biblical Interpretation: A Reevaluation* (Louisville: Westminster John Knox, 1995), pp. 73-100. The methodological premises of his nonevangelical fundamentalist approach include: "(1) We would acknowledge the specific contextual character of our own critical interpretations by affirming, rather than denying, their complex (both positive and negative) relationship with evangelical fundamentalist interpretations. . . . (2) We would conceive of the relationship of our critical interpretations with noncritical interpretations—ordinary readings and their theological justifications—in a nonhierarchical way, since we would recognize that critical interpretations make explicit the legitimacy that ordinary readings already have. (3) This kind of critical practice would truly be *critical* (in accordance with our vocation as critical exegetes) precisely because following evangelical fundamentalists, it would affirm the power-authority of the biblical text in the process of interpretation" (p. 92).

[2]Ibid., p. 83. Thus, the "disastrous consequences of fundamentalist interpretations do not result from the experience of the power-authority of the biblical text, but from the subsequent absolutization of this experience."

[3]In the post-Bultmannian setting this involves the admission that the biblical text is historical as well as the historical nature of our own exegetical practices; see Rudolf Bultmann, "Is Exegesis Without Presuppositions Possible?" in *Existence and Faith. Shorter Writings of Rudolf Bultmann* (London: Fontant, 1964), pp. 342-51 (where Bultmann discusses the term *Vorverständnis* as employed by Schleiermacher and Dilthey); also consult Hans-Georg Gadamer, *Truth and Method*, 2nd ed., trans. Joel Weinsheimer and Donald G. Marshall (New York: Crossroad, 1989), pp. 235-305; Anthony C. Thiselton, *The Two Horizons: New Testament Hermeneutics and Philosophical Description with Special Reference to Heidegger, Bultmann, Gadamer, and Wittgenstein* (Grand Rapids, Mich.: Eerdmans, 1980), pp. 51-84, 92-103.

and this admission transforms the critical enterprise.

> If the distinctive task of critical exegetical readings is not to legitimate ordinary readings (which, from this perspective, would be illegitimate on their own), what is it? In this new light, I can only conclude that *the goal of critical exegesis is the bringing to critical understanding of an ordinary reading*. According to this . . . definition, a critical reading should not be envisioned as a negative assessment of ordinary readings, but as the elucidation of the actual features of the text (and its context) that are reflected by ordinary readings.[4]

There is a positive relation between ordinary and critical readings, in that the latter seeks to elucidate the former. What is addressed in Patte's constructive model is how one experience of the text validates a certain way of existing in the world and how its legitimacy may be appreciated by those who do not share this experience.

In similar ways the theologically oriented confession of Scripture's clarity is oriented to accessibility of Scripture, without ignoring the necessity of interpretation, the ethics of the interpreter, as well as the unitive attention to critical and ordinary readers/readings as nonhierarchical. Simply put, Scripture's clarity, as we have seen, is not *the* resolution to interpretative discrepancies, nor *the* corrective to idiosyncrasies, but the most direct account for how Christians regard their relationship with Scripture. Just as interest in Scripture's literal sense was not simply a grammatical but a theological characterization (christological in focus), the justification for ordinary readings is not simply that everyone has one but that the claim of Scripture's accessibility entails the transparency of Scripture's purpose when read in this manner. Perspicuity is not a justification for any reading of Scripture but the plea for a conventional association of Scripture's texture (Scripture as text) with Scripture's point (the gospel of Jesus Christ) addressing the validation of a Christian reading of Scripture and offering a description of its legitimacy.

Structuralism . . .

The postcritical shift to textuality exemplified in Patte's ethical interests leads us to the heart of current interest in structural criticism as an avenue by which to approach the questions about Scripture as text. Its concern for the structure of language is grounded in an attempt to reveal the deep structure that underlies the surface of meanings of any literary construct (any code or social behavior having the characteristics of a language). Modestly, structuralism seeks to explain what we know already from the text and explain why we know this. The linguistic basis for structuralism leads to a commitment that the text is

---

[4]Patte, *Ethics of Biblical Interpretation*, p. 74.

atemporal inasmuch as the author of a text is irrelevant in matters of meaning (according to Ferdinand de Saussure).[5]

In practice, a structuralist concern is to show how texts make sense, the mechanisms through which a text is meaningful. The concern is not to show what words mean but how competence is displayed by the users of language, the rules of language and how this knowledge forms real sentences. The tendency is to do the close, deep structural reading associated with a text-oriented criticism, but there is only a passing reference to meaning related to the text. When Roland Barthes urged us to consider the author dead, the text liberated from the limits of imposing an absolute authority on a text such as an author's intent, he pointed to an absolute literalism whereby the text means nothing but itself.[6] The text only has an inside; it is a closed system of signs.

Structural criticism directs our attention to the actual use or employment of language in the present, in contrast to its history, so a word's meaning is only addressed in the present.[7] Then attending to the structurally implied systems or rules regarding the relationship of a text's units illumines what is latent in the system of language. The problem of clarity is determined by the social system of language that is strictly formal: attentiveness to the system of language forms irradiates the hidden code of language behind all human expression. A structuralist notion of perspicuity is founded upon the conception of a vast ontological intertextuality, and the application of structural strategies tends to avoid not only the subjectivity of the reader but that of hermeneutical prejudice itself by appeal to objectivity.

As Paul Ricoeur notes, structural criticism treats the text as a worldless entity as we are forced to exist in a state of suspension regarding any textually referred-to world. Structuralism "proceeds from the suspension . . . of ostensive reference"—which is always thought of as only the world behind the text mentioned (referred to) by the text. By avoiding the confusion of reference *behind* the text by shifting to reference *in front of* the text, Ricoeur himself seeks to advance a unique paradigm of reading that moves from the status of the text

---

[5]Structuralism seeks to study language synchronically (in its present form), rather than diachronically (historically or developmentally). See Ferdinand de Saussure, *Course in General Linguistics,* ed. Charles Balley and Albert Sechehaye, trans. Wade Raskin (New York: Philosophical Library, 1959); Michael Lane, ed., *Introduction to Structuralism* (New York: BasicBooks, 1970).

[6]The *early* Barthes exemplifies the structuralist approach to text and meaning and the common goal or observation of an utter nonsymbolic sense; see Roland Barthes, *Elements of Semiology,* trans. Annette Lavers and Colin Smith (New York: Hill & Want, 1968).

[7]Saussure distinguishes between *parole* (any particular instance of language, such as a sentence) and *langue* (the system of relationships that constitute language and is the premise for any *parole*); thus the components of language have meaning only in their relationship with other components in *langue* (Saussure, *Course in General Linguistics,* pp. 14-15, 111-20).

itself (what may be considered a kind of "objectivity") inasmuch as its meaning is actualized in a new situation.[8] Ricoeur's desire is to embrace a hermeneutic of "disclosure and appropriation" that is founded on a "depth-semantics . . . which requires a specific affinity between the reader and the kind of things the text is *about.*" And what it is about is "the non-ostensive reference of the text." Disclosure, it seems, fulfills the necessity of accounting for a type of transparency or clarity, not between the mind of the text's author and the mind of the reader but the disclosure that is possible in front of the text, in the reference of the text as it "speaks of a possible world and of a possible way of orienting oneself within it."[9]

When Ricoeur speaks of "the reference of the text" as "its power of disclosing a world," we are confronted with a new twist on the split between what a text *meant* and what it *means.* There is the (lost) notion of what it meant (the "behind the text" or diachronic interest in the text's origins and formation as determinative of its reference and meaning) and a present "literary meaning of the text" (the "in front of the text" or synchronic interest in how the text refers to possible worlds). The "power-authority of the text," according to Ricoeur, is not simply the world of the text into which we are absorbed but the world created in the fusion of horizons between the timeless world of the text and the present reader who is not only in the world but also transcends it.[10] And in

---

[8]Ricoeur addresses the tension by advancing a hermeneutic in which "we may actualize the potential non-ostensive references of the text in a new situation, that of the reader. . . . [W]e create a new ostensive reference through the kind of 'execution' which the act of reading implies. . . . Therefore what we want to understand is not something hidden behind the text, but something disclosed in front of it. What has to be understood is not the initial situation of discourse, but what points toward a possible world. . . . It wants to grasp the world-propositions opened up by the references of the text" (Paul Ricoeur, "The Model of the Text: Meaningful Action Considered as a Text," in *Interpretive Social Science: A Reader,* ed. Paul Rabinow and William M. Sullivan [Berkeley: University of California Press, 1979], pp. 94, 97-98).

[9]Ibid., pp. 97-98. To Ricoeur, structural analysis plays the mediatorial role objectifying what a text says and disciplining the subjectivity of readerly pursuit of an intuitive grasp of the original author's intentions (that is, by rejecting the notion of an intuitive union that we share with the author and by means of which achieve understanding). We begin with the text and move from explanation *(Erklären)* and validation to understanding *(Verstehen)* and guess; thus new dimensions of our being in the world. Ricoeur's conclusion: "Disclosure is the equivalent for written language of ostensive reference for spoken language."

[10]This general approach is shared by diverse hermeneutical projects, including Werner H. Kelber, *The Oral and the Written Gospel, The Hermeneutics of Speaking and Writing in the Synoptic Tradition, Mark, Paul and Q* (Philadelphia: Fortress, 1983); Paul Ricoeur, *Interpretation Theory: Discourse and the Surplus of Meaning* (Fort Worth: Texas Christian University Press, 1976); Norman R. Peterson, *Rediscovering Paul: Philemon and the Sociology of Paul's Narrative World* (Philadelphia: Fortress, 1985); Anthony C. Thiselton, *New Horizons in Hermeneutics* (Grand Rapids, Mich.: Zondervan, 1992).

turn, understanding the meaning of Scripture as text is not textually oriented (as if Scripture's meaning is its point) but referentially oriented (Scripture's meaning is made possible by its power/authority). While troubling to some, these commitments do indicate a way forward once we have escaped the attempt to orient critical interpretation to matters behind the text (and with that, we are in general agreement). Consider, as an explanation, Hans Frei's comments regarding Ricoeur's suggestions: "The 'referent' 'in front of the text' is precisely that restorative 'sense' of the reading of second naïveté, for which text and reader come to share a common referential world . . . which they cannot share in critical reading of the 'meaning behind the text.' Meaning 'in front of the text' is a centered world of meaning made accessible and viable to an equally centered self."[11] The question that remains, it seems, still concerns our interest in Scripture itself and whether this interest requires the sense of referentiality Ricoeur insists upon.

. . . and Poststructuralism

By extending the question of meaning "in front of the text," poststructuralism does structuralism one better: it deconstructs that structure or code, revealing its lack of any relation beyond itself. Deconstruction, the most obvious and popular application of poststructuralism, seeks to dismantle the structures of meaning (philosophical, cultural, political, theological and textual) in order to discern how they were formed, usually pointing to the incompetencies of the structure that give the illusion of completeness and distrusting systems (constructs) in general. For example, language is, to Derrida, an arbitrary and conventional system of signs that bears no necessary relationship to an external reality, and poststructuralists routinely deny the referentiality of all language. As a reaction to the critical effort to seek truth in the primitive origins, poststructuralism presumes that such origins are inherently inaccessible (a sobering critique at least, subverting the supposed certainty of reconstructed traditions).[12]

Poststructuralism is truly a strategy of reading oriented toward the function or performance of texts and language in social practice, not so much focused upon skepticism but drawing our attention to what we (can or can't) do with texts.[13] Among literary critics one sometimes finds the admission that a text

---

[11]Hans W. Frei, *Theology and Narrative*, ed. George Hunsinger and William C. Placher (New York: Oxford University Press, 1993), p. 134.

[12]Consult Jacques Derrida, *Of Grammatology*, trans. Gayatri Chakravorty Spivak (Baltimore: Johns Hopkins University Press, 1976); *Margins of Philosophy*, trans. Alan Bass (Chicago: University of Chicago Press, 1982).

[13]An observation offered by Gerald Graff, *Professing Literature: An Institutional History* (Chicago: University of Chicago Press, 1987).

sometimes transcends authorial intention(s), and theologians occasionally suggest that somehow the intention of the ultimate Author of Scripture (i.e., God) usually transcends the historical author's intention and knowledge, but poststructuralists maintain that it is always the case that text transcends authorial intent and other artificial boundaries.[14] While an author might intend to communicate a message, language always speaks a tongue of its own; so the reader must decipher that tongue (of language itself, not author or text as the source of meaning). All language is context for poststructuralists, and alternatively the context is not to be sought in historical horizons or historical situatedness. Whereas readers attending to structural characteristics might view the text as verbal icon, poststructuralists are iconoclasts—rather than viewing text as metaphysic, poststructuralists view reading as antimetaphysic. Whereas our project of reading Scripture as text is realistic in strategy (but must not succumb to the temptation of naive realism), poststructuralists hold that any belief in reality is necessarily naive.[15]

Because within poststructuralism there is no neutral position from which to decide or assert a text's meaning in a manner consonant with arbitrary interpretative controls, there is little hope of valuing the text as an independent entity somehow immune from questions of privilege and ideology. Deconstruction legitimizes questions once thought to be excluded from the interpretation of texts by encouraging readers to cross borders and boundaries imposed on texts. Rather than questioning meaning altogether (usually associated with a dualistic form of determinacy versus indeterminacy), deconstruction challenges the restrictive means by which meaning has been construed as fixed by appealing to an obvious reading of a text (the undecidibility of reading). It simultaneously affirms textual meaning (from one position or setting) and disaffirms the simplicity of singular meanings (from any position or setting). Reading any text, and it seems especially the case when considering how we read Scripture, is about more than texts; it involves us in thinking about ourselves as readers of texts, our responsibility to acknowledge "the otherness" of all texts; this is what draws intertextuality (discussed in chapter seven) and deconstruction together. As Gary Phillips notes, "What deconstruction and intertextuality share is an attention to the excessiveness of text and subject that traverses the . . . text and therefore makes the reading and re-reading of Scripture inherently risky and demanding."[16]

---

[14]Harold Bloom, ed., *Deconstruction and Criticism* (New York: Seabury, 1980).

[15]George Aichele, ed., *The Postmodern Bible: The Bible and Culture Collective* (New Haven, Conn.: Yale University Press, 1995), pp. 70-148.

[16]"Deconstructive reading and intertextuality combine then to give us a way to think about how readers as subjects are constructed in relation to texts and about the responsibility we have

With regard to the Christian effort to read with attention to the text, deconstructionism questions the coherence of general, theoretical, uncritical assertions like the perspicuity of Scripture, and it does so by raising the tension of clarity and obscurity itself. Thus: "As a practice of reading, deconstruction makes explicit what is hidden, repressed, or denied in any ordinary reading. Every reading is blinded by a set of presuppositions about the nature of texts and of reality, and yet without some such assumptions no reading would be possible."[17] If Protestant characterizations of Scripture's clarity have merely been another way of claiming a foundational and therefore determinative meaning to Scripture's interpretation—an either-or, objectivity-subjectivity tension—then deconstruction offers a piercing attack upon this theoretical substructure. But if perspicuity is employed to depict the Christian justification for its reading of Scripture, which is itself continually open and potentially more dangerous than simply reassuring (rather than operating as a premise by which certain readings are enabled), then the confession of perspicuity persists as a Christian characterization of its textual orientation. It is not that Christians have overcome the lack of a textual center according to deconstructionism, it is not that Christians have been relieved of the burden of interpreting its intertextuality, and it is not that perspicuity is an uncritical mask for the genuine struggle over stability and equilibrium in the postmodern intellectual and cultural climate.

Early Protestant commitments to textuality, contrary to poststructuralist characterizations of the entire Western tradition, are only tangentially rather than systematically "logocentric" (the primary error of textualism according to deconstruction).[18] Like poststructuralist suspicion of theories of textuality, Christian

---

to become critical readers and writers of a certain . . . sort, to become aware, to beware. [It is] an invitation to reflect, therefore, on *my* reading strategy, *my* network and production of texts, *my* social context, *my* obligation. Reading deconstructively . . . is an acknowledgement that reading and writing, especially as it concerns the Bible, is always about 'more than' texts; it is ever about reading subjects, cultural positions, ideologies, ethical responsibility, and a 'more than,' an 'otherness,' that escapes critical assessment" (Gary A. Phillips, "'What Is Written? How Are You Reading?' Gospel, Intertextuality and Doing Lukewise: Reading Lk 10:25-42 Otherwise," *Semeia* 69-70 (1995): 116.

[17]Aichele, *Postmodern Bible,* pp. 130-31. Aichele et al. continue, "No neutral or objective reading is ever possible; reading is always interested. Deconstruction rejects all 'container' theories of meaning. Meaning is not in the text but is brought to it and imposed upon it. The understanding of the author or of the original audience is not decisive; it is merely one reading among many. Texts may lend themselves more to some readings than to others, but the results of any reading have more to do with the readers' interests than with the text itself. Interpretation is an expression of power, the result of violence exercised upon the text in the act of reading, which is always an act of appropriation, a taking possession."

[18]Derrida discerned that in Western thought, speech has always been the paradigm for presence and any notion of truth, and all attempts to establish fully coherent systems of thought have stressed "the metaphysics of presence." *Logocentrism* is Derrida's term to denote

commitments to the perspicuity of the text have been at times indifferent to general theories of meaning or hermeneutically all-encompassing claims. This is especially evident in the Reformation's denial of institutional and traditional hermeneutical regulation, its representation of Scripture as a relatively autonomous text, the reading of its literal sense as intrinsic and intertextual, the unsettling subservience to Scripture as the standardizing rule that is not ruled, and its correspondingly overwhelming stance over against extratextual construals of reality, which were seen as ominous conditions of apparent ambiguity and relativism to the Reformation's detractors. Such precritical commitments are also shared in certain postcritical circles, with certain qualifications.

For example, Christian commitments to perspicuity may seem to move in a direction opposite that of poststructuralism: *away from* an indefinite intertextuality (ontological grammar from which we cannot escape in order to understand) *to* a self-transparent intratextuality (Scripture's grammar into which we are absorbed in order to understand). We still speak of textuality, but of a different sort (theologically textual, not merely philological or historically grammatical).[19]

Poststructuralism questions the miracle of the Word meeting us in the word (or it makes that miracle even more of a miracle). In contrast, there is a congruence in this encounter of God and the Christian reader in Christian thought, usually associated with the so-called "literal [plain or obvious] sense" of the text. Hans Frei offered this characterization:

> I wish to propose that the meaning of the "literal sense" in biblical reading . . . says that among other uses or capacities to use a text Christianly which go into a Christian understanding of a text, there is a *descriptive* use—more appropriate to some texts than to others. And *if* one speaks in terms of "reference" to a subject matter described—a complex, perhaps confused, perhaps indispensable way of speaking—then there is not a *split* reference to the described subject matter. The text means what it says, and so the reader's redescription is just that, a redescription and not the discovery of the text as symbolic representation of something else more profound. But in the *process* of redescription we can—and indeed can-

---

the invariable presence of the logos (speech, reason, Word of God) for Western metaphysics. See Derrida, *Of Grammatology*.

[19]For example, Luther argued, "There are two sorts of knowledge: first, that of names; and second, that of the subject matter itself. To one who has no knowledge of the subject matter, the knowledge of the names will be of no help. . . . Grammar alone does not give us this meaning; . . . this comes from our knowledge of sacred things. . . . Take care above all that you have a firm knowledge of the subject matter; after that it will be easy to learn the grammar. To err in matters of grammar is to commit a venial sin, but to sin in the subject matter is a mortal sin" (Martin Luther, *Luther's Works*, ed. Jaroslav Pelikan, 56 vols. [St Louis: Concordia, 1955-1976], 3:67, 72-73). And, "grammar is indeed necessary and what it says is true; it should not, however, rule the subject matter but ought itself to serve it" (3:70-71).

> not do other than—employ our own thought structures, experiences, conceptual schemes; there is neither an explicit mode for showing how to *correlate* these things with the job of redescription, nor is there a fundamental conflict between them. Without knowing success or lack of it in any given case beforehand, it is an article of faith that it *can* be done; it *is* done.[20]

Without committing ourselves to a naive form of linguistic realism, or a universal epistemic notion of the perspicuity of truth, a Christian reading of Scripture proceeds (even in this postmodern setting) to describe its basis in the premise that God addresses us by means of Scripture, read piously and read trustingly. Scripture *means* what it *says*—the text can be taken literally; whatever else it means, it means at least what it says. The prospect of determining or understanding the nature of interpretation in general, or even the particular capabilities of Christians as interpreters of Christian texts within the hermeneutical field, is subordinated to the description concerned with how Christians practice their optimistic fidelity to reading Scripture. The instance (not capacity, necessarily) of delight in "Your word is a lamp to my feet and a light for my path" (Ps 119:105) means to challenge both casual and causal (faithless?) assumptions about the Word and words. How one understands this event—"The unfolding of your words gives light; it gives understanding to the simple" (Ps 119:130)—is oriented toward faith in divine efficacy (living is the word):

> Indeed, the word of God is living and active, sharper than any two-edged sword, piercing until it divides soul from spirit, joints from marrow; it is able to judge the thoughts and intentions of the heart. And before him no creature is hidden, but all are naked and laid bare to the eyes of the one to whom we must render an account. (Heb 4:12-13 NRSV)

There is an ambiguity in this relationship (indeed in this text just cited, as the expression "account" struggles to render the "word," that is, *logos*), but the ambiguity is in part the basis of our confession regarding Scripture's clarity. Efforts to characterize our reading of texts in terms of an inherent ambiguity (as deconstructionists do) may be unsettling, sobering, but probably accurate in affirming a tension similar to the Christian concern for the obscurity *and* clarity of Scripture. The necessity of the assertion "living is the word" is not philosophically, linguistically or ideologically necessary (nor is the Christian confession necessarily dependent upon a demonstration that words can or do in fact live).

The Christian confession is not about the futility or meaningfulness of words as such but about the efficacy of God's word in human words, and it is a confes-

---

[20]Hans W. Frei, *Types of Christian Theology,* ed. George Hunsinger and William C. Placher (New Haven, Conn.: Yale University Press, 1992), p. 44.

sion that only necessarily applies to this instance only. As is the case with a text like Isaiah 40:1, 6-8; God asks the prophet to announce comfort to the people, and the prophet realizes the futility of human words to provide God's comfort; yet God's word stands and does not whither or fade. And similarly we can employ the images of rain and snow from heaven that descend to the earth, watering and causing growth, seed to the sower and bread to the eater (Is 55:10-11). God's word does not return to God empty but accomplishes God's purpose, usually in conflict with human words (cp. Is 55:9; 59:21; 2 Sam 23:2; Jer 1:7, 9). God's words are God's means of accomplishing God's purposes—the God whose thoughts and ways are higher than our thoughts and ways.

Poststructuralism challenges historical, authorial, textual and reader-oriented strategies regarding meaning by subverting the possibility of meaning in relation to any one dimension of reading. Meaning, for deconstructionism, is not denied but neither is it inherently fixed in the relationship of form and content or in the author's intent or historical mind or in the reader's mind. Meaning is simply not fixed by these relationships.[21] This is not to dismiss deconstructionism, but it is to suggest that our choices for where we might find meaning are not as simple or obvious as one might at first think, nor are the choices between ideology and objectivity (or truth, or reality).

The Genesis of Obscurity

We may willingly admit that Scripture's clarity is not, as has been said, a naive and anticritical preclusion of interpretation, nor a simplistic confusion of one's own opinions and the influence of the text itself (or vice versa). But then we are faced with the recognition, especially apparent in contemporary literary criticism concerning narratives (and Scripture in particular), that such texts do not simply conceal their latent, true sense in the story; instead, narratives "make interpretation necessary and virtually impossible." Rather than asserting that Scripture is in some sense genuinely perspicuous to the reader, we are faced with the assertion that Scripture is not simply prone to misunderstanding by the simple but inherently obscure even to those critically skilled.[22] More

---

[21]Frei observed: "For Deconstructionists . . . the discovery of the illusory character of linguistic meaning as truth is liberating, and with that liberation comes a way of reading a text which reverses the prior belief that texts opens to us a world, into the conviction that the world (or a world) must be seen as an indefinitely extended and open-ended, loosely interconnected, 'intertextual' network, a kind of rhetorical *cosa nostra*" (Frei, *Theology and Narrative,* p. 124).

[22]Frank Kermode, *The Genesis of Secrecy: On the Interpretation of Narrative* (Cambridge, Mass.: Harvard University Press, 1979), p. 125. He added regarding the Gospel of Mark's employment of parables: "We are most unwilling to accept mystery, what cannot be reduced to other and more intelligible forms. Yet that is what we find here: something irreducible, therefore perpetually to be interpreted; not secrets to be found out one by one, but Secrecy" (p. 143).

interpreters mean more interpretations, not simply better interpretations; and the greater the authority a text is accorded, the more intensely it is studied and the more mystery and secrecy it acquires. Thus, we may surmise, Scripture's supposed clarity is little more than a comforting, but ultimately utopian, vision of our sovereignty as readers.[23]

These observations are from the provocative work *The Genesis of Secrecy* by Frank Kermode, a literary scholar who has done for critical interest in narrative what poststructuralists have done for textuality: he has forced the questions of ambiguity, obscurity and disappointment to the forefront of our interest in interpretation. Kermode argues that we interpret, in part, because we seek to "satisfy ourselves with explanations of the unfollowable world"; this is premised on the notion that "all narratives are essentially dark" and that our relation to them is ultimately as "outsiders"—"we stand alone before them, aware of their arbitrariness and impenetrability, knowing that they may be narratives only because of our impudent intervention, and susceptible of interpretation only by our hermetic tricks."[24] His argument concerning clarity and obscurity is itself rather straightforward: what we find clear about a text depends

> in some measure on the fashion of the period—what it seems natural or reasonable to expect a text to say. This is another way of affirming that all narratives possess "hermeneutical potential," which is another way of saying that they must be obscure. The apparently perspicuous narrative yields up latent senses to interpretation; we are never inside it, and from the outside may never experience anything more than some radiant intimation of the source of all these senses.[25]

Kermode, it seems, has narratives function as both clear and obscure, or to

---

[23]Ibid. pp. 144-45. Kermode concluded, "What is the interpreter to make of secrecy considered as a property of all narrative, provided it is suitably attended to? Outsiders see but do not perceive. Insiders read and perceive, but always in a different sense. We glimpse the secrecy through the meshes of a text; this is divination, but what is divined is what is visible from our angle. It is a momentary radiance, delusive or not. . . . When we come to relate that part to the whole, the divined glimmer to the fire we suppose to be its source, we see why . . . there has to be trickery. And we interpret always as transients . . . both in the book and in the world which resembles the book. . . . We may not see it, as Dante did, in perfect order, gathered by love into one volume; but we do, living as reading, like to think of it as a place where we can travel back and forth at will, divining congruences, conjunctions, opposites; extracting secrets from its secrecy, making understood relations, an appropriate algebra. This is why we satisfy ourselves with explanations of the unfollowable world—as if it were a structured narrative, of which more might always be said by trained readers of it, by insiders."

[24]Ibid., p. 145.

[25]Ibid. Also note the work of Kelber on the relationship of orality, anteriority and Gospel narratives, and clarity; his concern is with the relationship of the canonical gospels with their oral and literary precursors, and how this reveals and obscures the non-textual substratum. See Werner H. Kelber, "Narrative and Disclosure: Mechanisms of Concealing, Revealing, and Revealing," *Semeia* 43 (1988): 1-20.

use his phrases, they display an "uninterpretable radiance," a "simultaneous proclamation and concealment," a "radiant obscurity."[26] And this, he tells us, is to correct the "myth of transparency" that permeates modern scholarship—a myth founded on the rejection of what is written in favor of what it is written about (and therefore reversed by returning to what is written).[27]

That Kermode utilized a text so central to the history of Christianity (Mark's Gospel), and a passage so central to the characterization of the gospel as clear and accessible or obscure and private (Mk 4, the parable about parables) to deconstruct assumptions of clarity ironically demonstrates his argument. In the history of the parable (both in its composition in Mark's Gospel and its subsequent utilization within the Christian tradition) we confront a forceful explanation of accessibility and inaccessibility:

> When [Jesus] was alone, those who were around him along with the twelve asked him about the parables. And he said to them, "To you has been given the secret of the kingdom of God, but for those outside, everything comes in parables; in order that 'they may indeed look but not perceive, and may indeed listen, but not understand; so that they may not turn again and be forgiven.' " (Mk 4:10-12 [Is 6:9])

That Kermode sought out this parable about parables is itself employed as a means to cure us from our affection for the obtainable, unimpeded access, the certain. This is not simply because this text may say as much about the illusion of accessibility and certainty, and this is not simply because our interpretations of this text say as much about our failure to find the text accessible and certain. Kermode has also interpreted the illusionary quest as a cultural and social phenomenon: "We are in love with the idea of fulfillment" he suggests, "and our interpretations show it."[28] That we might be prone to seek closure where there is little reason to and presume clarity where there is actually obscurity indicates that Kermode is about more than simply interpreting texts; he is about interpreting interpreters by means of interpreting texts.

Kermode's challenge to simplistic notions of transparency, founded upon his desire to be concerned with what is written rather than what is written about, leads him to conclude that "insiders"—those who have glimpsed the momentary radiance of the text—are also precluded from a totality of understanding; our insiders' secret knowledge is that we are all ultimately outsiders (insiders simply know this, while outsiders struggle with the myth of transparency). This strategy is calculated to violate the coherence of the narrative and

[26]Kermode, *Genesis of Secrecy*, pp. 28, 47.
[27]Ibid., pp. 118-19.
[28]Ibid., p. 65.

to elicit an expectation of latent and ultimately inaccessible meaning (or meaning retention). It leads us away from accessibility and away from simplistic notions of clarity, and the faith concerned with such a text is not led to understanding. To Kermode, Scripture not only does not but should not be employed to render a (supposedly) coherent view of reality, the world. That is, he objects to the constructive effort to work from intertextuality to intratextuality—*from* the text itself interpreted by its own means and self-sensible *to* the world or cultures of the readers being absorbed by the text—a crucial assertion, as we will see below. The vitality of Kermode's argument becomes more apparent when his critics attempt to find a place for or to counter Kermode's emphasis upon textual particularity *and* the text's depiction of an ultimately inaccessible world. His argument is both credible and troubling: credible because it suits the necessary admission that not even the confession of Scripture's clarity is a conclusive justification for having understood completely and troubling because it directly challenges the charitable assumption of (Scripture's) clarity.

The Genesis of Clarity

Meir Sternberg objects to Kermode's employment of secrecy, privacy and obscurity as a paradigm for all interpretative reading. Such is not the Bible's rule as a whole, to Sternberg: "The Bible has many secrets, but no Secret, many levels of interpretation but all equally accessible."[29] Sternberg's own rationale is based in his effort to advise us of a unitary ideology and narrative procedure in the biblical text that strictly mitigates Kermode's paradigm of obscurity: "Nothing is more alien to the spirit of biblical narrative than discourse fashioned or meaning hidden across the sea (Dt 30:11-14), than speaking in riddles, than the distinction between spiritual insiders and carnal outsiders, than the very idea that anyone with the least claim to inclusion (Dt 31:11-12) . . . may suffer exclusion."[30] Because clarity or accessibility is what the narrator persuasively asserts regarding the text itself, we must succumb to this or be judged as rebels, reading "in bad faith" and incompetent.[31]

---

[29]Meir Sternberg, *The Poetics of Biblical Narrative: Ideological Literature and the Drama of Reading* (Bloomington: Indiana University Press, 1985), p. 49.

[30]Ibid. He continued: "On the contrary, since exclusion figures here [Kermode on the parables of Mk 4] not as a sanction against certain readers but as a threat to the writing itself, the need to forestall it comes to regulate the strategy of narration. Where the nation's sense of identity and continuity hangs in the balance, it devolves on the text that forms the national heritage and chapter to make sense. Hence the active steps taken to lower the threshold of intelligibility by a poetics thriving on the oblique and the ambiguous." We should actually regard the instances of parables, Sternberg advises, more charitably than Kermode allows.

[31]Ibid., pp. 4-7, 50.

The relationship of obscurity-clarity and outsider-insider tensions is addressed, not by "the mixed-bag technique," wherein a text appeals to both simple and sophisticated in differing ways (which simply reinforces ideological diversity), but by what Sternberg calls "foolproof composition, whereby the discourse strives to open and bring home its essentials to all readers so as to establish a common ground, a bond instead of a barrier of understanding."[32] As Tamara Cohn Eskenazi notes, foolproof composition is actually a modest term depicting the construction of biblical materials that "lead readers to definitely prescribed conclusions." Competent readers—those who give attention to the narrative's clues—are responsive to what is provided in the text (i.e., the author's intentions conveyed in the narrative providing a new, biblical, historiography) as well as what is deliberately omitted (i.e., the gaps, silences, indeterminacy, ambiguity). But the narrative does not fail to convey the truth of its assertions, even if these assertions of truth are nuanced, ambiguous, conflicted or indeterminate. The narrative conveys this true historiography, but it must be "teased out" because it is not always explicit or simplistically perspicuous.[33] The various facets of the larger truth of the narrative are not mutually exclusive but readings on a continuum.

Sternberg's assertion of "foolproof" model, and the corresponding issue of clarity or obscurity, has more to do with his commitment to the archetypal competence (omnipotence) of biblical narrator who successfully, forcefully persuades. The practical effect of this observation is that the less competent "underreader" does not really get the Bible's message wrong, only less fully (thus his preference for foolproof composition instead of the mixed-bag analogy demonstrates how the message of the Bible is to be understood by the reader).[34]

This commitment—that the Bible "always tells the truth in that its narrator is absolutely straightforwardly reliable"—simply overturns Kermode's paradigm

---

[32]Ibid., p. 50. "By foolproof composition I mean that the Bible is difficult to read, easy to underread and overread and even misread, but virtually impossible to, so to speak, counterread. . . . The essentials are made transparent to all comers: the story line, the world order, the value system. The old and new controversies among exegetes, spreading to every possible topic, must not blind us (as it usually does them) to the measure of agreement in this regard. The bedrock agreement is neither accidental nor self-evident. Not accidental, because it derives from the Bible's overarching principle of composition, its strategy of strategies, namely maneuvering between the truth and the whole truth; nor self-evident, because such a principle does not often govern literature operating at the Bible's level of sophistication and interpretive drama" (pp. 50-51).

[33]Tamara Cohn Eskenazi, "Torah as Narrative and Narrative as Torah," in *Old Testament Interpretation: Past, Present, and Future,* ed. James Luther Mays, David L. Petersen and Kent Harold Richards (Nashville: Abingdon, 1995), pp. 17-18.

[34]Aichele, *Postmodern Bible,* p. 113.

of secrecy. The biblical narrative is not elitist, it does not provide differing messages to "insiders" and "outsiders." Sternberg claims, "The reader cannot go far wrong even if he does little more than follow the statements made and the incidents enacted on the narrative surface."[35] Instead of obscurity subsuming clarity as in Kermode, clarity precludes obscurity for Sternberg. And even if Kermode correctly identified a role for obscurity, Sternberg argues that it is only a theme of the New Testament projected (improperly) upon the (Old) Testament. Speaking of the (Old) Testament Sternberg commented, "Still less can it protect itself against being yoked by violence, in the manner of the christological tradition, with a later text whose very premises of discourse (notably 'insider' versus 'outsider') it would find incomprehensible."[36]

The surface reading is protected by asserting its immunity from genuine criticism by means of obscurity. Emptying the commitment to a surface reading of self-critical reflection involving its readers supposes that clarity is a property of what the text is about (the narrator's omniscience) instead of something that can be said of the text or how the text is best regarded. Such a strategy pushes the struggle over clarity or obscurity into a narratological sanctuary that makes the admission of genuine obscurity impossible.

Wesley Kort's critique of Kermode's work is similar to Sternberg's in that he also sought to defend a notion of narrative that entails an assumption of clarity. Kort seems to object that Kermode has taken "the problem passages and puzzles in the Gospel [of Mark], rather than its clearer, more coherent aspects, as central to an understanding of its author's intentions."[37] Instead of moving from the supposedly clear to the obscure (a traditional practice among Christian interpreters), the move from obscurity to clarity in Kermode's argument does not necessarily lead to inaccessibility; it may simply reflect the reoccurring frustration interpreters experience when they fail to undertake the "pilgrimage" through which the "narrator" may successfully lead us to an understanding of reality. The narrative/narrator, Kort remarks, does not articulate a simplistic unity of discordant realms of reality "but discloses a underlying unity despite the apparent separation between them."[38]

In Hans Frei's response to Kermode's work we meet the historical and theological assertions that whatever is to be made of the tension of clarity and obscurity in certain biblical narratives, it is admittedly the case that, in principle at least, Christians have presumed clarity to be regulative of the admission of

---

[35]Sternberg, *Poetics of Biblical Narrative,* p. 51.

[36]Ibid., p. 50.

[37]Wesley Kort, *Story, Text, and Scripture* (University Park: Pennsylvania State University Press, 1988), p. 94.

[38]Ibid., p. 95.

obscurity. Attention to and regard for the literal sense is accompanied by the "assertion that the text is more nearly perspicuous than not and that, therefore, the dialectic insider/outsider as well as disclosure/concealment must end in the asymptotic subordination of the latter to the former in each pair." Even more than this, Frei maintains that in principle the insider-outsider dialectic is dissolved, just as for Kermode but in the opposite direction, in the Protestant interpretative tradition: "In principle there is no interpretive outsider."[39] But the disclosure-concealment tension remains, in part because the Christian interpretative tradition characteristically treats Scripture as a *realistic* narrative (accessible but not without subtlety), and in part this upholds the role of the Spirit in the disclosure of the text by means of the text; so that our concern is with what is written.[40]

Continuing these theological observations, Ronald Thiemann's response to Kermode defends the manner of obscurity characteristic of narratives: ambiguity, the unexpected, latent meaning and a reluctance to provide premature closure. Yet Thiemann does not yield to the temptation that biblical narratives are therefore, necessarily, hopelessly, secretive. He observes that the current hermeneutical climate suffers under the anxiety of an unyielding either-or dichotomy: either the text "must be totally perspicuous or totally indeterminate." From this burden there is no escape, only the admission that the assertion of clarity does not eradicate the reality of obscurity. Instead of resolving the tension we are led to abandon the former because the latter is so obviously (clearly!) the reality of the modern world. Thus, "Kermode does not really transcend his own dichotomy but finally absorbs one term of his contrasting pair into the other."[41]

Instead of arguing that Scripture is either obstinately clear or clearly obscure, Thiemann suggests a self-critical practice that concedes the "phenomenon of narrative obscurity" but finds (by means of faith as response to the

---

[39]Frei, *Theology and Narrative,* p. 108.

[40]Thus Frei wrote: "We are all insiders. . . . Calvin has it that our hearts and minds may need illumination, the text does not. It is plain for all to read. The odd, philosophically ambiguous status of 'reference' in this tradition, for which literal and historical, word and thing were congruent in a semiotic rather than epistemological or representational way meant that the text did not communicate—as though by way of a channel of absence—the presence of God. The text did not refer to, it *was* the linguistic presence of God, the fit embodiment of one who was himself 'Word,' and thus it was analogous to, though not identical with Incarnation. . . . We are not barred from the truth though we might well be if the relation between text and truth is of the sort Kermode proposes and then says we do not have. But for the Christian interpretative tradition truth is what is written, not something separable and translinguistic that is written 'about' " (Frei, *Theology and Narrative,* p. 108).

[41]Ronald Thiemann, "Radiance and Obscurity in Biblical Narrative," in *Scriptural Authority and Narrative Interpretation,* ed. Garrett Green (Philadelphia: Fortress, 1987), pp. 25-26. Here Thiemann refers to the work of Richard Bernstein, *Beyond Objectivism and Relativism: Science, Hermeneutics, and Praxis* (Philadelphia: University of Pennsylvania Press, 1983).

text) a discernible character in the biblical story. This type of claim, Thiemann observes, is particular in nature: "Consequently the claim that narrative texts can depict and illumine a followable world is one that Christians are concerned to defend not as a general principle but as a proposition true with reference to the Bible."[42] He is looking for "the way illumination emerges from obscurity in biblical narrative," and he contends that a Christian regard for Scripture's narrative focus orients our response (reading) to the text:

> Faith not only accepts narrative obscurity, it presupposes that the meaning of the narratives is latent within their rich and nuanced depictions. But in responding with faith, the reader recognizes a followable world within the texts and accepts an invitation to enter that world. In so responding, the faithful reader becomes a disciple who acknowledges that the chief character in the stories (and the one who issues the invitation to faith and discipleship) is God.[43]

It is precisely as a Christian reading (response) to the text that perspicuity is located. Thiemann's case can be stated negatively: "Illumination is unachievable only if it is construed as a perfect light that dispels all darkness and banishes all shadows"; and positively: "Scripture . . . presents a complicated but finally coherent narrative that invites the reader to consider the world there depicted as the one true reality."[44]

This crucial literary-theological assertion by Thiemann rests upon the union of a perspicuous orientation toward Scripture and the presumption of textual realism, at least regarding Scripture's literary traits. Kermode's serious doubts about the ability to move from Scripture's intertextuality to its supposedly intratextual significance and implications force him to regard the declaration of Scripture's clarity as illusory. Thus the declaration of Scripture's clarity is something of a self-fulfilling prophecy (it appears clear only because we say that it is clear). But instead of leading us away from a commitment to perspicuity in Christian encounters with the text, Kermode proves to be a catalyst to account for the genuine obscurity that does not under-

---

[42]Thiemann, "Radiance and Obscurity," p. 25.

[43]Ibid., pp. 30-31. For Thiemann's fuller account of this argument, see Ronald F. Thiemann, *Revelation and Theology: The Gospel as Narrated Promise* (Notre Dame, Ind.: University of Notre Dame Press, 1985), pp. 112-56. Thiemann tackles Kermode's own challenge by actually risking an explication of two narrative texts (David's accession to the throne in 1 Sam 16—2 Sam 5, and the Gospel of Matthew), each of which point to what Thiemann calls a "pattern of identification through hiddenness" or what is often referred to as indirection (pp. 31-38).

[44]Thiemann, "Radiance and Obscurity," pp. 26, 28. He added, "We do not have to accede either to interpretive relativism or to the political and moral relativism such a position might entail. Nor must we accept the bleak vision that narratives yield only obscure tales and unfollowable worlds. . . . Whether or not the reader chooses to follow, the world depicted in this narrative is surely followable."

mine but define Scripture's clarity.[45] That is, instead of simply discerning the genesis of secrecy, Kermode has forced Christian theologians to consider how and why the assertion of perspicuity is regarded as the genesis of clarity.

Biblical Realism and Intratextuality—Our Conclusion

For Thiemann the clues to how Scripture can be characterized as both "mysterious" and "followable" are found in a commitment to reading biblical narrative in realistic terms (a commitment he learned from Frei, who learned as much from Barth, etc.). This characterization of Scripture as realistic is meant to explain what it is that Christian readers of Scripture apprehend or grasp when they look to Scripture as illuminating a practice of belief and understanding. It refocuses our attention on the relationship of Scripture as text and the reader. Thiemann's argument is that the Gospel "stories are coherent, and that they function to invite the reader into the world of the tale."[46] Frei's observations are similar; the Gospels concentrated as they are on Jesus Christ not only provide "focus for inner-canonical typology" but also "provide the interpretative pattern in terms of which *all* of reality is experienced and read in this religion."[47] And similarly, we have George Lindbeck's celebrated comment: "It is the text, so to speak, which absorbs the world, rather than the world the text."[48] The realistic qualities of Scripture as text are employed to explain how it is that Christian readers interact with the text by means of the convention of perspicuity.

This link between clarity and intratextuality (being absorbed by the text) is specifically addressed in Karl Barth's treatment of Scripture's clarity. Because of its clarity in itself the word of God "needs no explanation," it confronts us, though mediated in concrete form thus involving the risk of being understood and not understood. Correspondingly, the concrete task of one's relationship with Scripture is displayed in our subordination to the written form of Scripture.

Its "intrinsic clarity" is evident as the word "meets us right in the thick fog of our own intellectual life, as having taken the same form as our own ideas,

[45]Ibid., p. 28.
[46]Ibid., p. 38.
[47]Frei, *Theology and Narrative,* p. 148. He added, "Understanding is an ability rather than a process or internal event, a capacity to follow an implicit set of rules unintelligible except in the examples of text or discourse in which they are exhibited. You do not ask how understanding is possible but what rules govern a particular linguistic operation such as the functioning of concepts in a Christian context. Understanding is the competence to follow and the judgment to apply or not to apply them" (pp. 101-2).
[48]Lindbeck, *Nature of Doctrine,* p. 118.

thoughts and convictions," but so as to seemingly overturn by this accommodation.

> It can become clear to us only when this fog breaks and dissolves. This is what is meant by the subordination of our ideas, thoughts and convictions. If the Word of God is to become clear to us, we cannot ascribe to them the same worth as we do to it. We cannot try to appraise the Word of God by reference to them; or to cling to them in face of the Word of God. The movement which we have to make in relation to it—and quite freely, of course—can only be that of yielding, surrender and withdrawal.[49]

The word never ceases to be "clear in itself—clear always by reason of the clarity which it possesses in itself," so as to invite understanding "not only of fundamental self-explanation in virtue of its intrinsic clarity, but also of the interpretation which its human witnesses are at least partially capable of giving."[50] Thus, subordination to the word is the premise of interpretation, and yielding to the word is premised upon its clarity.[51]

Similarly, what Lindbeck's reference to the text absorbing the world has to do with Scripture's perspicuity is primarily to be discovered in the presumed use made of Scripture: that the textually rendered "world" of the canonical narration is both realistic and accessible to Christian readers. Lindbeck also uses the characterization of Scripture as followable to refer to the way in which the Bible supplies "directions for coherent patterns of life in new situations" and is treated "as a perspicuous guide to life and thought."[52] The term *intratextuality* is employed by Lindbeck to describe how Christian readers of Scripture treat the ascriptions of authority, sufficiency and clarity when called to account for their actual use of Scripture, or what Lindbeck termed "faithfulness as intratextuality."[53] Perspicuity is analogous to intratextuality; they each serve as affirmations of hermeneutical conventionality.

When we turn to an assessment of the commitment that makes intratextuality and perspicuity workable characterizations of Scripture as text, we face

---

[49]Karl Barth, *Church Dogmatics,* I/2, ed. G. W. Bromiley and T. F. Torrance, trans. G. W. Bromiley (Edinburgh: T & T Clark, 1936-1969), p. 716.

[50]Ibid., p. 717.

[51]Ibid. Barth added, "To interpret God's Word must and can now mean to interpret Holy Scripture. And because the interpretation of the Word of God can take place only through man's subordination, this subordination now comes concretely to mean that we have to subordinate ourselves to the word of the prophets and apostles; not as one subordinates oneself to God, but rather as one subordinates oneself for the sake of God and in His love and fear to the witnesses and messengers which He Himself has constituted and empowered."

[52]Lindbeck, "Scripture, Consensus, and Community," p. 98.

[53]Lindbeck, *Nature of Doctrine,* p. 113.

what can be referred to as realistic certainty.[54] Not simply realism, not simply certainty, but a sufficient means whereby Scripture is construed: "Between the clarity intrinsic to the subject matter and the ambiguities intrinsic to our fallen and creaturely situation, it [is] considered possible to wrest sufficient certainty . . . for us to hear and repeat the Word of God, that we and others might come to trust and obey it in life and in death."[55]

Such observations are confirmed by the suggestions of literary critic Erich Auerbach concerning realism in Western literature (whose observations weigh heavily in contemporary literary-theological models). Biblical literature is "mysterious and 'fraught with background,' " as well as "tyrannical" in its claim to truth.[56] On the one hand, Auerbach observes the disclosure/concealment tension and the necessity of reading as in an act of interpreting; on the other hand, there is an inseparable link between the authority claimed by Scripture itself and an appropriate reading of the same. He noted that the world portrayed in biblical narrative was characterized by the claim to exclusive authority and claimed to be the "only real world"—not merely a byproduct of its literary character. Auerbach wrote, "The world of the Scripture stories is not satisfied with claiming to be a historically true reality—it insists that it is only the real world, is destined for autocracy. All other scenes, issues, and ordinances have no right to appear independently of it."[57] The text is appreciated because of its ability to draw us into its world, even to the extent that tyranny, although an oppressive term, is still the most appropriate characterization.

---

[54]George Hunsinger, *How to Read Karl Barth: The Shape of His Theology* (New York: Oxford University Press, 1991), pp. 45-46. In the same discussion Hunsinger offered that Barth's "mode of certainty . . . distinguished Barth's realism from the other two views of theological language. Literalism—with its emphasis on univocal reference, propositional revelation, and cognitive address—assumed a mode of certainty which tended to be 'absolute' with a neutrality that was virtually mathematical. Theological truth was thought to be true in much the same sense that numerical calculations were true. Theological propositions were either true or false, and when they were true we could be certain of them. Expressivism, on the other hand—with its emphasis on equivocal reference, emotive revelation, and noncongnitive address—assumed a mode of certainty which tended to be 'relative' with a discretion that was virtually aesthetic. Theological truth was thought to be true in much the same sense that poetry was true. Theological symbols were not so much true or false as functional or dysfunctional with regard to evoking emotive experience; when they were thought to be functional, we could be certain only of their 'truth' for us."

[55]Lindbeck, "Scripture, Consensus, and Community," p. 46, citing Barth, *Church Dogmatics*, II/1, pp. 7, 24, 249, 251, and esp. 439.

[56]Erich Auerbach, *Mimesis: The Representation of Reality in Western Literature,* trans. Willard R. Trask (Princeton, N.J.: Princeton University Press, 1953), pp. 12-23. Also note the employment of Auerbach by Frei, *Eclipse,* pp. 3, 15; and Thiemann, "Radiance and Obscurity," pp. 27-29.

[57]Auerbach continued: "Far from seeking, like Homer, merely to make us forget our own reality for a few hours, it seeks to overcome our reality: we are to fit our own life into its world, feel ourselves to be elements in its structure of universal history" (Auerbach, *Mimesis,* pp. 14-15).

This notion that the Bible somehow invites or draws us into its world transforms the way we employ words such as literature and history and reading and meaning. For example, from Northrop Frye's *The Great Code: The Bible and Literature* we observe this encouragement:

> The general principle involved here is that if anything historically true is in the Bible, it is there not because it is historically true but for different reasons. The reasons have presumably something to do with spiritual profundity or significance. And historical truth has no correlation with spiritual profundity, unless the relation is inverse. . . . Nothing said here will be new to Biblical scholars, who are well aware that the Bible will only confuse and exasperate a historian who tries to treat it as a history. One wonders why in that case their obsession with the Bible's historicity does not relax, so that other and more promising hypotheses could be examined. . . . If the historical element in the Bible were a conscientious, inaccurate, imperfect history . . . we could understand how important it would be to make a fuller reconstruction of that history. But when it shows such an exuberant repudiation of everything we are accustomed to think of as historical evidence, perhaps we should be looking for different categories and criteria altogether.[58]

One of the "different categories" and additional criterion may be our subject of Scripture's clarity, understood to address the union of text, reader and reading. Instead of assuming that clarity is a property of the Bible because it is a literary text or historically accessible or verifiable, current emphases upon clarity focus our attention upon the textuality of the Bible. But not simply that the Bible is a text. Instead we are encouraged to regard the textuality of the Bible in terms specific to its reading among Christian peoples (i.e., those who read it as God's word to them).

It is the suggestion of Frei, Thiemann and Lindbeck, among others, that Scripture's rendering of a world absorbing and accessible textuality is bound up with the *meaning* of Scripture itself. This hermeneutical concern about meaning is complex, but the manner of affirming meaning is rather straightforward: Scripture's point is its meaning. Attention to Scripture as text puts the question of meaning to the text itself and not in a reference outside the text. Meaning is not understood by a direct factual correspondence between the matter of the text and matters otherwise ascertainable. Therefore, the distinction is not historically the difference between what a text meant and what it means but is instead concerned with the gap between our demonstration, performance and discharge of the text and that witnessed to in the text itself. Thus Barth offered that the "universal rule of interpretation is that a text can be read

[58]Northrop Frye, *The Great Code: The Bible and Literature* (New York: Harcourt Brace Jovanovich, 1982), pp. 40, 42.

and understood and expounded only with reference to and in the light of its theme."[59] And George Lindbeck observed:

> The normative or literal meaning must be consistent with the kind of text it is taken to be by the community for which it is important. The meaning must not be esoteric: not something behind, beneath, or in front of the text; not something that the text reveals, discloses, implies, or suggests to those with extraneous metaphysical, historical, or experiential interests. It must rather be what the text says in terms of the communal language of which the text is an instantiation. . . . An intratextual reading tries to derive the interpretative framework that designates the theologically controlling sense from the literary structure of the text itself.[60]

The commitment to read Scripture as realistic and advantageous to Christian understanding, and the theological conviction of reading Christianly in communal context, constitute the framework of the contemporary delineation of the clarity of Scripture. We must also keep in mind, as T. S. Eliot offers, that "the Bible has had a literary influence . . . not because it has been considered literature, but because it has been considered the report of the Word of God."[61] That is, lingering near the desire to pursue the Bible as literature, or in terms of its literary attributes, is the ongoing struggle to account for a seemingly unassuming presumption that Scripture is clear to its readers because it is (also) God's word to us. But it is simply not the case that the confession of Scripture's clarity was ever as unassuming as we might be led to expect; nor was the confession ignorant of the reader with all the attending negative and positive elements that readerly interest entails. The role of the reader and the very notion of reading have invariably been inherent in the Christian use of Scripture. Accounting for that interest in the contemporary climate of literary interest in the Bible not only leads to a reexamination of the very notion of clarity and obscurity, it also helps define what the confession of Scripture's clarity entails in our contemporary setting.

The case for a Christian consensus of reading Scripture in terms of its realistic character and the premise of accessibility may seem suspiciously like an imperialistic claim to authority. In one sense this is what the Christian contention is concerned with (not imperialism but privilege). Historical (and sociological), literary or philosophical interests do not validate Christian attention to the text; instead the consensus has to do with the relationship of a privileged text and privileged community.

Perspicuity genuinely privileges one interpretative perspective of Scripture, not simply describing how Scripture inherently functions or is to be regarded.

---

[59]Karl Barth, *Church Dogmatics,* I/2, p. 712.

[60]Lindbeck, *Nature of Doctrine,* p. 120.

[61]T. S. Eliot, "Religion and Literature," in *Selected Prose,* ed. John Hayward (Harmondsworth, U.K.: Penguin, 1953), p. 33.

Through examining the Protestant interpretive tradition we are appropriately reminded that perspicuity is equivalent to just that, the privileging of one interpretative perspective or glimpse of radiance; this is correspondingly reinforced with the suggestion that the uptake, the illocutionary force, is God's by means of the text (through accommodation to us, in Scripture and our response being Scripture's sufficiency to render what Christians should and do believe with some conviction of obviousness; thus we *confess* Scripture is clear). Instead of offering us a proud and confident foundation upon which to build a theological tradition after our own likeness, the confession of Scripture's clarity may better serve us as a reminder of our need to be constantly evaluating our understanding of God's word by means of God's word. In this manner, Scripture's clarity is a call to seriousness—before God. In this light, it seems appropriate to conclude with a warning, in the form of a parable, from Søren Kierkegaard:

> Imagine a country. A royal command is issued to all the office-bearers and subjects, in short, to the whole population. A remarkable change comes over them all: they all become interpreters, the office-bearers become authors, every blessed day there comes out an interpretation more learned than the previous, more acute, more elegant, more profound, more ingenious, more wonderful, more charming, and more wonderfully charming. Criticism which ought to survey the whole can hardly attain survey of this prodigious literature, indeed criticism itself has become a literature so prolix that it is impossible to attain a survey of criticism. Everything became interpretation—but no one reads the royal command with a view to acting in accordance with it. And it was not only that everything became interpretation, but at the same time the point of view for determining what seriousness is was altered, and to be busy about interpretation became real seriousness. Suppose that this king was not a human king—for though a human king would understand well enough that they were making a fool of him by giving the affair this turn, yet as a human king he is dependent, especially when he encounters the united front of office-bearers and subjects, and so would be compelled to put the best face on a bad game, to let it seem as if all this were a matter of course, so that the most elegant interpreter would be rewarded by elevation to the peerage, the most acute would be knighted, &c. —Suppose that this king was almighty, one therefore who is not put to embarrassment though all the office-bearers and all the subjects play him false. What do you suppose this almighty king would think about such a thing? Surely he would say, "The fact that they do not comply with the commandment, even that I might forgive; moreover, if they united in a petition that I might have patience with them, or perhaps relieve them entirely of this commandment which seemed to them too hard—that I could forgive them. But this I cannot forgive, that they entirely alter the point of view for determining what seriousness is."[62]

[62]Søren Kierkegaard, *For Self-Examination* . . . , trans. Walter Lowrie (Princeton, N.J.: Princeton University Press, 1944), pp. 58-59.